A Historian's Diary, 1935–1980

A Historian's Diary, 1935–1980

Gordon A. Craig

Edited by
Edward Kehler and Bruce Thompson

The Society for the Promotion of Science and Scholarship
Palo Alto, California

The Stanford Historical Society
Stanford, California

The Society for the Promotion of Science and Scholarship
Palo Alto, California

The Stanford Historical Society
Stanford, California

The Society for the Promotion of Science and Scholarship is a nonprofit organization established for the purposes of scholarly publishing, to benefit both academics and the general public. It has special interests in European and British studies.

Published with the assistance of the Stanford Historical Society

Printed in the United States of America

ISBN cloth: 978-0-930664-35-0
ISBN paper: 978-0-930664-36-7

Contents

Editorial Acknowledgments

For permission to publish this volume, the editors are deeply grateful to Deborah Preston, Gordon A. Craig's daughter and literary executor; and to the repository of the diaries, the Department of Special Collections and University Archives, Stanford University Libraries.

James J. Sheehan, Gordon Craig's friend and colleague at Stanford University, kindly agreed to read through the penultimate draft of the manuscript and generously offered to prepare the index. He also referred us to Daniela Blei, his one-time doctoral student, who provided professional proofreading services and editorial advice. Special thanks also go to University Archivists Daniel Hartwig and Josh Schneider, and to Timothy Noakes and Polly Armstrong of the Department of Special Collections, Stanford University Libraries.

Maya Gonzalez, our former student, now a graduate student in the Department of History at the University of Massachusetts, Amherst, also read through the manuscript, typed large sections of it, and contributed many helpful editorial suggestions. Dorothea Kehler and Sara-Rozet Norwick both read through early drafts of the manuscript, proofread, and offered significant advice and consistent encouragement.

Gary Miles, Professor Emeritus of History at the University of California, Santa Cruz, polished our translations of Gordon Craig's Latin quotations.

Norris Pope kindly contributed his publishing expertise from many years at Stanford University Press, and he volunteered to design and typeset this volume for SPOSS—as he has done for a number of other SPOSS books over the years.

Janet Gardiner, recently retired after three decades as Executive Officer of SPOSS, oversaw the publication of three previous volumes of Gordon Craig's essays and long supported the publication of this edition of Gordon Craig's diary. The editors of this volume are also very grateful to the Trustees of SPOSS for their unstinting support, and especially to Peter Stansky, the President of SPOSS and Gordon Craig's successor as Chair of the Stanford History Department, for his continuing encouragement of this project throughout the many years of its gestation.

Edward Kehler and Bruce Thompson
August 2023

A Note About the Transcription

Gordon A. Craig's near-daily record of his life, from June 1935 until November 2000, encompasses 49 separate bound volumes of varying length that average approximately 200 pages each. Each volume contains Craig's handwritten records of his daily activities, encounters, observations, and views, along with numerous newspaper clippings, concert and event programs, travel postcards, personal photographs, and other miscellanea that he pasted into the journals. This publication, limited to the period from 1935 to 1980, along with the record of the 1990 Chequers meeting, makes use of 36 of Craig's 49 volumes. As editors, we have selected passages from these 36 volumes that we hope will be of greatest interest to a general readership. Therefore, diary entries concerning the quotidian aspects of Craig's life have largely been omitted in favor of those that concern his observations and analysis of world affairs, his reflections on university life and administration, and his processes of teaching and writing. Readers will also find his comments on meetings with notable academic, literary, and governmental figures, as well as his participation in conferences, congresses, and symposia. Aside from the overview of Craig's public life, the excerpts from the diaries reveal much of his character, temperament, and values, while also providing glimpses of his private life and of the people and things that he held dear.

To make the diaries more accessible to a wide readership, we have made minor alterations to the excerpted text. For example, the headings for individual diary entries have been normalized, with dates and locations placed in italic type and with Craig's very occasional variations retained. The headings of many diary entries do not include a full date or geographic location; we have provided these when possible.

Craig was a careful writer, and errors in the diaries are remarkably rare. His penmanship is clear and elegant, which has undoubtedly resulted in few errors of transcription. We have corrected his infrequent misspellings and supplied omitted punctuation. Only references to living individuals have been omitted in accordance with Craig's stipulations for publication. When living persons appear in Craig's manuscript, we have replaced their identities with "name omitted" in brackets.

Some additional clarifications have been provided in this text. We have marked all added content in square brackets. For instance, we have striven to supply the full names of individuals to whom Craig has referred only by their first or last names. Similarly, for the convenience of the reader, we have translated phrases written in foreign languages, such as the German expressions Craig habitually used during his stays in Germany. The reader can find additional information and context for the diary entries in the footnotes.

Ellipses.

Gordon Craig made extensive use of ellipses for rhetorical purposes within his own prose, thereby adding nuanced shades of meaning. To preserve this layer of subtle content, the volume editors have chosen to reproduce Craig's own ellipses with unspaced periods (…), which most closely resembles the manuscript's punctuation. By contrast, we have chosen to use spaced periods (often after terminal punctuation) to indicate places where we have omitted material that seemed superfluous to the scholarly value of the diary (. . . .).

We take responsibility for any errors within the transcription or footnotes.

Introduction

On June 25, 1935, Gordon A. Craig, who had recently completed his junior year as a history major at Princeton University, began keeping a diary as he was about to embark on a summer of study and travel in Germany. It was his first visit to Europe since he and his family had left Scotland for North America in 1925. The diary would include his reflections about German cities and sites of interest—a kind of travel journal. But he would also write notes for a possible senior thesis about the failure of social democracy in Germany, and record conversations with ordinary Germans about the Nazi regime. This would be his first attempt to answer some of the questions that would preoccupy him and his generation of American historians of Germany for the next half-century: why did democracy collapse in Germany in 1933? How did the citizenry of a great European nation fall under the spell of a mountebank dictator? To what extent did ordinary Germans accept the lunatic ideology and the vicious antisemitism of their leader and his henchmen?

After his return to the United States, he discontinued the diary, but he would take it up again as a Rhodes Scholar at Balliol College, Oxford from 1936 to 1938. He resumed it again during the war, in which he served first in the State Department and the Office of Strategic Services in Washington, and then as a Marine in the Pacific theater. Another gap followed as he began the busy life of an assistant professor of history at Princeton after the war. But he would resume the diary again in 1958 and continue it, with few interruptions, until the year 2000. He would also fill in the gap years retrospectively, to make the record of his life as complete as possible. Taken together, the thirty-odd volumes of his diary comprise several million words, written over the course of sixty-five years. Although it is not quite as long as John Quincy Adams's diary, which runs from 1779 to 1848 (sixty-nine years), it is surely among the longest-running diaries of the twentieth century.

Gordon Craig was a connoisseur of the genre. He frequently revisited Samuel Pepys's immortal account of life in Restoration England, and commented in his own diary about his favorite passages in Pepys's masterpiece. In a talk he gave to Stanford undergraduates in 1977 about the practice of keeping a diary, he began by quoting Robert Latham, the editor of the definitive modern edition of Pepys's diary, on its genesis. The diary began, Latham suggested, as a by-product of Pepys's "energetic pursuit of happiness. The process of recording had the effect, as he soon found out, of heightening and extending his enjoyment." Craig endorsed Latham's assessment of Pepys's purpose: "Many other people have made the same discovery, and this capacity of enabling one to re-savor old pleasures is perhaps the most endearing aspect of diaries or journals and the most frequent response that one receives from people who are asked why they keep them."[1]

But Pepys's delightfully post-Puritan sensibility did not obscure for Craig the Puritan origins of the genre. He quoted a letter from John Adams, that great descendant of generations of New England Puritans, to his son John Quincy Adams, dated 14 May 1783: "Have you kept a regular Journal? If you have not, you will be likely to forget most of the Observations you have made. If you have omitted this usefull Exercise, let me advise you to recommence it immediately. Let it be your Amusement to minute every day what ever you may have seen or heard worth Notice. One contracts a Fondness of Writing by Use. We learn to write readily, and what is of more importance, we think, and improve our Judgments, by committing our Thoughts to Paper." John Quincy Adams must have taken his father's advice to heart in this instance, because his diary grew to over 15,000 pages and extended over fifty-one volumes by the time of his death in 1848.

The discipline of keeping a diary, according to the senior Adams, improves one's writing, one's thinking, and one's judgment. But again, Craig instructed his undergraduate audience, that's not all:

> Adams, as you can see, was more interested in the practical benefits that keeping a journal could bring, and so was Boswell, when he suggested in 1778 that a journal was a good way of making a man adjust his character: that he should look into it, in short, the way in which a woman looks into a glass when she is dressing. But such considerations are hardly enough to persuade busy people to save a

[1] Gordon A. Craig, "On Keeping a Diary," Gordon Alexander Craig Papers (SCO467), Series 2, Box 21, Folder 9: "Miscellaneous Speeches, 1960s–70s," Department of Special Collections and University Archives, Stanford University Libraries.

> part of their day or week for writing a record of their lives and thoughts. More of them, I am convinced, do so in order to relieve certain frustrations (to say things that they cannot say to others or the things that other people are too busy to stop and listen to). They write it, as William Safire said not so long ago, as a private letter to themselves, or, more precisely, a private letter to their future selves.

Keeping a diary, then, has multiple purposes: as a record and an extension of one's pursuit of happiness, as a means of refining one's judgments and perhaps also one's character, and as a kind of dialogue with one's self, a private voicing of thoughts that cannot readily find public expression. The diary provides an opportunity not only to record one's daily pleasures and impressions, but also to relieve one's daily vexations.

Having established these several motives for keeping a daily record of one's experiences and reflections, Craig then offered his most elaborate assessment of the evolution of his own diary:

> This, I think is the main reason for my own journal, although it should not be inferred from that that I spend much time in it talking about the state of my mind or psyche. I started my journal as a kind of travel record of things seen and heard when I went to Germany in 1935 and later when I went to Oxford in 1936. After I got married, I faltered but then resumed and broadened [it] into a record of daily occurrences, and professional business, and reading and reflection on reading, and work in progress, and musical and theatrical performances seen, and people met, and the like. It also became a place to put material I thought I might use in my writing, half developed ideas, sketches of articles, and the like, as well as a depository of lists, and of anecdotes and jokes heard or read, and of newspaper articles or cartoons that struck my fancy, and of much else. I discovered that, if I kept a decent index, it was a useful means of facilitating memory about people and events as well as about hotels and restaurants and a lot of other stuff that tends to slip away. (I can generally, if I have to, discover where I met so and so, or the name of that good pub on the Haymarket.) Finally, I discovered as the years passed that when I had a free hour at the end of the day, and needed amusement, I could find it by reading at random about what I was up to fifteen years or five years or forty years ago.

But if Gordon Craig's diary was, by his own account, a series of "letters to his future self," written over the course of the last sixty-five years of the twentieth century, why should readers care about those "letters" now, as we approach the second quarter of the twenty-first century?

The short answer is that Gordon Craig was one of the outstanding scholar-teachers of his time, and therefore his diary offers a rare opportunity to look over the shoulder of a great historian as he conceived his major books, reacted to current events, managed his extraordinarily productive and distinguished career, and continued to expand the range of his intellect and experience over the course of a long lifetime.

He was, moreover, a wonderful writer, whose work is a pleasure to read. As his colleague James Sheehan has observed, there is no discernible difference in his case between the voice of the historian, as writer and teacher, and that of the diarist. Whether he was writing for publication, giving one of his masterly lectures, or composing one of the thousands of entries in his diary, he always used the same distinctive style, with perfectly balanced sentences and cadences that remind one of the great nineteenth-century novelists whom he admired and frequently wrote about.

His diary enables us to follow him as he established himself at a relatively young age as one of the stars of Princeton University's Department of History during the 1950s; his surprising decision to accept an invitation to join the then less prestigious Department of History at Stanford University in 1961; his participation in Stanford's rise to prominence as one of the country's greatest universities over the course of the next two decades; his ringside seat for the student protests that roiled both Stanford and his other academic home, the Free University of Berlin, during the 1960s and 1970s; and his reflections as he approached emeritus status at Stanford in 1979.

The editors have chosen 1980 as an end-date for this selection of entries from the diary, although he still had several major books and dozens of reviews for *The New York Review of Books* ahead of him during the 1980s and the 1990s. One of the stipulations that Gordon Craig made when he consented to publication of selections from his diary was that there should be no mention of living persons. His purpose in making this stipulation, undoubtedly, was to avoid the possibility of causing offense or embarrassment to anyone. To have included selections from recent decades would have required numerous ellipses. The editors have therefore chosen (with one notable exception) to exclude the 1980s and the 1990s from this volume.

The exception is a coda: an account of Gordon Craig's participation in a meeting on the consequences of German unification with Prime Minister Margaret Thatcher and a small group of distinguished historians at Chequers in 1990. For the head of a government to consult a team of veteran historians on the ramifications of a major historical transformation is an event so rare that it would have seemed a shame to exclude Craig's account of it. Although some of the participants are happily still very much alive, we have included Craig's narrative of this remarkable seminar. Several published accounts of the seminar have appeared in recent years, and the easily discoverable names of the participants are therefore in the public domain.

Does the diary as a genre have a future? Will anyone in the twenty-first century follow Gordon Craig's example and keep a diary for more than sixty years? It seems highly unlikely that anyone will do so. Just as the personal letter has been rendered obsolete by the advent of email, and the novel is struggling to hold the attention of readers in the age of Netflix, so the diary seems unlikely to survive in a world dominated by social media. People still write about themselves and their activities every day, but they do so in a variety of public forums that did not even exist during Craig's lifetime. The expectations of privacy and the habits of introspection and self-scrutiny on which the diary depended for centuries in Western culture have eroded, probably irretrievably.

All the more reason then, to savor the pleasures of this extraordinary record of the life of one of the outstanding American historians of his time, a distinguished scholar and beloved teacher, and as keen an observer of the world of the now vanished twentieth century as one could ever hope to encounter.

A Historian's Diary, 1935–1980

1

A Student in Hitler's Germany, 1935

[Gordon Craig's diaries begin on June 25, 1935, when, following his junior year at Princeton, he set out by ship from Hoboken to Rotterdam, and then onward by train for a three-month-long stay in Germany, arriving in Cologne on July 4th. Craig traveled from Cologne to Munich, where he attended a short summer lecture course at the University of Munich.]

Thursday, 4 July 1935. Cologne.
. . . This is my first glimpse of a German city and it's very interesting. The streets are filled with Nazis. I came out of the cathedral to find a whole busload about to start off for somewhere or other. Most of those I've seen are young men and some are not very soldierly, but they're all obviously having a good time and are very enthusiastic. . . .

Saturday, 6 July 1935. On board the Rhein Steamer.
. . . The town [Koblenz] is filled with the holiday spirit. There are dozens of kiosks along the river, where one buys cards, or sailor dolls, or lemonade. While I daresay there are more than a few English and Americans here, most of the visitors are Germans—young boys and girls in hiking costumes—complete with big boots and rucksacks—very brown and very enthusiastic.

Across the river towers the Ehrenbreitstein with its fort. My *Kammermädchen* [chamber maid] tells me that it was used by the French and English "*im Kriege*" [during the First World War]. Now the swastika floats over it and someone has painted another huge swastika on the rock with the words, "*Hitler siegt!*" [Hitler triumphs!]. . . .

Back from the water, Koblenz is a tangle of little streets so narrow that one is in danger of being picked off by a tram as he walks along the sidewalks. Many of the stores have signs pasted in the windows—"*Deutscher Geschäft*" [German Business]—the official stamp of approval. Brown Shirts much in evidence. This morning at breakfast my waitress dashed outside to feed sugar to the horses of two of them. I heard "*Heil Hitler!*" used as a farewell for the first time. . . .

Later, Hotel Schneider—Heidelberg: The Rhein journey is not a bit overrated. I say this instead of scattering more superlatives... Shortly after nine stopped writing. I met a Mr. Graybeal and a woman who is travelling with him. Both came over with me on the [R.M.S.] *Statendam,* though I did not meet them, and I noticed them last evening in Koblenz. They're very charming people and I travelled with them by boat to Bingen and then by train on here. We had an hour's wait at Bingen and then strolled about. It's another of these little towns which are all pushed together and have that delightful Old World flavor.

Graybeal used me as his interpreter, and I was delighted to find that I could manage to serve him as such. I think he was impressed, but not nearly so much as I. I was tremendously pleased with my ability to carry on a conversation with a man in our compartment going from Bingen to Mainz. Graybeal's friend had given him an American cigarette, at which he began to speak with me. He professed a desire to come to America. I said that Germany was much more beautiful. He said that might be true but that there was more money in America. There was nothing unusual about the conversation thus far. Later he returned to his theme, however. Yes, Germany was beautiful; but one must live here to know it. One cannot talk. One must pay too much money to the party. He lived in Mainz, said our friend, and worked at Bingen—*ein Handwerkarbeiter* [a craftsman]. If he earned 150 marks, he had to pay 30 marks *zum Partei* [to the Nazi Party]. He got quite worked up—said he would rather have his arm cut off than raise it in a "*Heil Hitler!*"—and he summed up his remarks by saying, "*Ich bin Demokrat. Lieber würder ich im Afrika leben*" [I'm a democrat. I would rather live in Africa].

We left him in Mainz. I felt now that I was on the right track and that I was going to get a lot out of the summer. If I can continue to meet and talk with people, I shall be able to understand better the spirits of the people among whom I am living. How representative our friends' view is, I have yet no way of telling. Certainly, the younger people seem thoroughly in favor of the existing regime. As for the older people, I do not know yet, but hope I can find out. Strange how those words—"*Ich bin Demokrat!*"—struck home! Back in the States, we hear people scoffing at democracy. Yes—even my friend, Jean Ford.[1] And here—"*Ich bin Demokrat!*"— The word seems

---

[1] Craig had a romantic involvement with Jean Ford, whom he described as "his proletarian sweetheart" and years later as "a nice New York girl of decidedly leftist

to mean something—something of value and not to be cast aside hurriedly. "*Lieber würde ich im Afrika leben!*" . . .

Thursday, 11 July 1935. Munich.

. . . Yesterday was spent largely in room-hunting. I finally landed at the Stollsteimers' where I sleep and have *Frühstück* and *Mittagessen* [breakfast and lunch]. In the evening I hunt up a small restaurant and dine there. There is a rather interesting crowd here—a Rhodes Scholar from Oregon, called [Bob] Hayter[2] who is quite all right—a White Russian called Schmirnoff, who has lived in Paris since he was a child—and a German girl called Schwarz who is studying art here.

Hayter and I went to the opening exercises last night and I met practically all of Princeton—Dr. Priest,[3] Wasso,[4] Symington, Wicks,[5] Oechler,[6] and—sprung from some corner of the earth—Ossie Elbert, '34.[7] The exercises were quite good. Later we adjourned to the Löwenbräu [pub] with a couple of girls and sat about.

The university opened today with no end of speeches and lectures. [Professor Maximilian] Spindler,[8] who is running the show, looks like the wrath of God when he talks of the *Vaterland* [Fatherland] and is quite impressive… I think I'll like this a lot. At present, I find the classes too crowded—and filled with eager young souls who want to make an impression. It's going to be hard work though—and the eagerness will wear off, perhaps. There is an *Ausflug* [excursion] this Saturday to the Kochelsee,

---

views." See Gordon Craig, "Tagebuch Volume I: Part Two: A Memoir on the Period September 1935–December 1936," (October 1976), 3; Gordon Alexander Craig Papers (SC0467). Department of Special Collections and University Archives, Stanford University Libraries, Stanford, Calif.

[2] Robert (Bob) Hayter later convinced Craig to apply for his own Rhodes scholarship.

[3] George Madison Priest (1873–1947) was a professor of German literature at Princeton who spent the summer of 1935 in Germany.

[4] Edward Powell Thomson Watson, one of Craig's closest friends from Princeton, was in Germany during the summer of 1935. Craig refers to him frequently as "Wat" and as "Wasso." He later taught in the Department of Management at Northwestern University's graduate school for forty years.

[5] Alden Wicks was an art student from Princeton.

[6] William F. Oechler later taught German and worked as an investment counselor.

[7] Oswald "Ossie" Elbert was an art student from Princeton, who later became a Lutheran pastor.

[8] Maximilian Spindler (1894–1986) was a German historian and expert on Bavarian national history. He maintained some distance from the Nazi Party and had a distinguished postwar career.

Walchensee, and Herzogstand. I think I'll not go. I'm a little tired of wandering about. I dislike crowds and I want to get settled here.

Bought a *Fahrrad* [bicycle]. Must go out later tonight and learn to ride it. . . .

Tuesday, 16 July 1935. Munich.
. . . I saw [Charles M.] Hathaway, the American consul today. We had a long talk about Social Democracy. He posed a rather interesting question—"Why did the Social Democrats give way so easily, and without a fight when the present regime came to power?" I think I'll be writing my thesis on Social Democracy, so I'll have to track this down.

Hathaway made a rather interesting observation about the German people also. He said that he lived in a small village seven or eight kilo[meter]s away. He knew all the people there and found them a hard-working, courteous, pleasant lot. "But," he said, "if someone in uniform came to them and said, 'March!,' they would march. And if that someone said, 'Go and cut off Hathaway's head. He is a bad man!,' they would say, 'We didn't know that.' But they would cut off my head, nevertheless."[9]

Hathaway has promised to put me in touch with [William E.] Dodd, the American ambassador in Berlin. All this will help my work enormously. Watson, who saw him later, extracted some promises of introduction to the officers in the Brown House.[10] We're really getting down to brass tacks as far as our work is concerned. . . .

Friday, 19 July 1935. Munich.
I have been interested in just how far the *dozents* [lecturers] at the university will go in speaking for or against National Socialism. Today in Prof. Raith's[11] class we received our themes—corrected—and Raith indulged in some criticism. One of the boys had said in his that he objected [to] the people of Nuremberg because they hated the Jews so. Raith was very frank. He said that the people in N. hate the Jews no more than the people of Munich (and I must say that I have seen no evidence of Jew-baiting here)—but that Julius Streicher lived in that city. Streicher is, of course, responsible for such papers as *Der Stürmer* [The Stormer] in which the Jews are verbally

---

[9] A nearly word-for-word account of this meeting can be found in the introduction of Craig's *The Germans* (New York: Putnam, 1982), 9–10.

[10] The Brown House was the national headquarters of the National Socialist Party, where many prominent Nazis maintained offices.

[11] Josef Raith (1903–1991) was a specialist in English philology at the University of Munich.

flayed weekly. At the same time, Streicher must stand fairly high in the party and that Raith is able to speak of him in at least a faintly derogatory manner is one evidence that the government here is more liberal than people at home believe.

Another such indication is [Ernst] Hanfstaengl's book of cartoons showing Hitler in comic situations.[12] Many of these are from American papers. I noticed one from the *St. Louis Dispatch.*

In class today, also, one of the girls spoke of having been guided through the *Dom* at Cologne [Cologne Cathedral] and of having been subjected to a lecture on National Socialism at its conclusion. Raith was quite worked up about this—so much so that I missed much of what he said. But the gist of his speech was that, in the first place, Americans should not expect to dictate what will be done in this country—which is, of course, true, but not wholly applicable here if what the girl said really happened for she chose to see the Dom and not to listen to party propaganda. At the same time, Raith deplored such an incident. He said that he thought National Socialism a good thing and that he greatly admired the government, but that he deplored the use of such tactics. My own impression is that one cannot rely too heavily on this girl's impressions. For one thing, such trips through the Dom are not only for *Ausländer* [foreigners]. There were not many foreigners in Cologne when I was there and I was there at about the same time as this Gretchen Ridder, for she came over on the same ship as I. There is no justification for an American objecting to a talk on National Socialism which is intended for Germans. Another thing that I noticed while in Cologne was that there was some kind of celebration intended there soon in the name of the party, which would explain the presence of a great deal of party propaganda. In short, I think the fair Gretchen was leaping before she looked, which is the fault of a great many of the foreign visitors here. Thus, Dorothy Thompson—though she seemed to take very good care in leaping that she would come a cropper…[13]

I rode out to the outskirts of town today on my bike. Came across a great flying field and a friend here tells me that it is for both the army and

---

[12] See Ernst Hanfstaengl, *Hitler in der Karikatur der Welt: Tat gegen Tinte* (Berlin: Verlag Braune Bücher Carl Rentsch, 1933). This strange book, whose title translates as "Hitler in the Caricature of the World: Fact versus Ink," was a compilation of cartoons critical of Hitler, accompanied by commentaries in which Hanfstaengl explained and refuted the criticisms and "lies" of the cartoonists.

[13] Dorothy Thompson (1893–1961) was an American journalist who was expelled from Germany in 1934 for writing critically about Hitler.

commercial companies. He says also that Germany is losing quite a few of her new flyers through their inexperience, so great has been the increase in the flying squads in the last few months. I can well believe this. Two out of every three officers one passes in the street are from the aviation corps.

The streets here are filled with soldiers of one type or another. I was awakened this morning at about seven o'clock by a band marching by singing at the tops of their lungs. (The singing, by the way, was very good.) I have never, till now, given serious thought to the meaning of the phrase "a military caste." One reads, for instance, that Germany, before the war, "was ruled by a military caste," and one gets the impression that the people—poor devils—were held under the thumbs of a small and autocratic group of generals. The military caste, on the contrary, is above and beyond class. It permeates all classes. All families have a son who is a potential soldier. In most cases he has served his training. Families of the lower middle class in many cases have a son who is a lieutenant or something of the sort. This was as true before the war as it is now. This state of affairs, coupled with the respect of authority—(of which Hathaway spoke)—makes Germany a frightening nation, though her people are as docile as lambs when taken separately. There is very little to the military caste theory—at least not per se. If there were, the Social Democrats certainly could have refused to vote the war credits in 1914.[14] But perhaps that's a larger question. . . .

Wednesday, 24 July 1935. Munich.

For the past two days we've been doing a good deal of talking in Raith's course about the present regime. I have been rather disgusted in seeing several people who, in their zeal for a just view of the government, will entertain no thought of any wrong-doing on the part of Hitler's advisers. If Raith says, "Of course, you must not believe everything you read in your papers!," these eager souls nod enthusiastically as if to say, "We must not believe *anything* we read in our papers!"

We talked of *the Jewish Question* today. Raith tries to be perfectly fair and frank but has a tendency to cover up the essential facts of the case. He says, for instance, that it is only a small group in the party which wishes to attack the Jews and that he sincerely hopes that the Jews will be unmolested as time goes on. He admits that, while in theory, the Jews are allowed to remain here as guests, in practice they are discriminated against—"*Deutscher*

---

14 Although anti-militarist in principle, the German Social Democratic Party voted in favor of granting war credits to fund Germany's war effort in 1914.

Geschäft" signs, etc. His solution is that the Jews must "*bleiben ruhig*" [remain peaceful]—whatever that means. At the same time, as an ardent National Socialist, he does not make any plea for toleration. He admits that many innocent Jews are suffering today. But he excuses attacks on them by summoning up recollections of Jewish profiteers in the days of the inflation. In short, he pardons the German people and admits wrongdoing in the present only by using the words "*Die furchtbare Tragödie von Judenthum*" [the awful tragedy of Jewry]. That is as far as he will go; and he answers American protests by referring to the Negro and English protests by pointing to England. In short, Raith is perhaps a good example of the intelligent National Socialist faced by the problems of the day. As an intelligent man he cannot support the anti-Jewish movement without resorting to argument by analogy—here weak. As an ardent National Socialist he supports even this part of the program by calling to witness the earlier suffering of the German people.

Yet even Hitler, I suppose, is vexed by this great problem. Surely it would be better for the sake of the party and the nation to suppress *Der Stürmer*, to shut Streicher's mouth and to make an end to the whole anti-Jewish movement. Yet Hitler cannot do that and remain true to Streicher, who is largely responsible for the success of the National Socialism in Nuremberg and its environs.

I met Prof. [Harvey W.] Hewitt-Thayer yesterday.[15] He has just come down from Berlin. He says that in all his talks there he came to no conclusions—that different people had entirely different views about the party's future. On the other hand, Dr. Priest has been talking to another friend from Berlin who was astonished by the peaceful atmosphere here. The friend said that there was a wide difference between North and South Germany and that, in Berlin, something in the air seems to prophesy that the government is going to crack. Apparently they are not making as much money out of this summer as I had thought. These registered marks, the vice-consul told Watson, are being used only to pay off bonds and other debts of the German government. If the money derived from the use of these traveler's checks is used to buy goods which must be imported—e.g. rubber goods—Germany loses. The tourist boom, if this is so, would seem largely artificial. Perhaps Germany is feeling the economic pinch. Certainly

[15] Harvey Hewitt-Thayer (1874–1960) was one of the fifty original teachers selected by Woodrow Wilson to initiate the preceptorial system at Princeton in 1905. A specialist in German literature, he became chairman of the University's Department of Modern Languages in 1936 and retired in 1943.

she has little—very little—gold… But if this is true, appearances belie the truth. Certainly everyone seems happy and prosperous here. At any rate, if the government cracks, I hope it does when I'm in Berlin…

I have been thinking of writing my thesis on Social Democracy under the Weimar Republic. This of necessity will run hand in hand with the rise of the National Socialists and I shall have to answer Hathaway's question as to why the Social Democrats gave in so easily when the Nazi Revolution came. In my reading on the subject to date I find myself running down interesting little bypaths, any one of which may lead to another but closely related thesis subject.

For instance I have been thinking about [Oswald] Spengler's prophecy, made in 1934, after he had become disgusted with the so-called Socialist Revolution.[16] Spengler talks of a new group which is already working for a return to the old order. He says: "*Während die National-versammlung…beginnen andere über das letzte Jahr anders zu denken. Sie vergleichen, was da gebaut wird, mit dem, was einmal da war.*" And more important: "*Sie ahnen, dass ein Volk in Wirklichkeit niemals zwischen verschiedenen Staatsformen zu wählen hat.*" [During the National Assembly…other people are beginning to think differently about the last year. They are comparing what is now being constructed with what was there previously. They realize that, in reality, a people can never choose between different types of government.][17] Without saying one thing or the other about this last statement—that is, with regard to its truth—it is yet rather amazing how far back on the road to the old order Germany has gone. It's all the more evident now that the army and navy are being built up again. But the intellectual cycle is also complete. After this period as a party state, Germany has returned to the imperial form in deed and in thought. All the racial and other theories which have lain dormant for years are now being spread abroad again. What [Arthur de] Gobineau and [Houston Stewart] Chamberlain taught is being fed to the German people again in large doses.[18] I have already spoken of the new interest in Wagner's aims and the triumvirate of the great composer and Nietzsche and Hitler. But when one comes upon a handsomely bound set of Chamberlain's *Grundlage des 19ten Jahrhunderts* [*Foundations of the Nineteenth Century*] and when

---

[16] Oswald Spengler (1880–1936) was a historian and philosopher of history best known for his belief that Western civilization was in terminal decline. During the early 1930s, Spengler became increasingly critical of National Socialism.

[17] Oswald Spengler, *Preußentum und Sozialismus* (Munich: Beck, 1920).

[18] Arthur de Gobineau (1816–1882) and Houston Stewart Chamberlain (1855–1927) promoted early pseudoscientific theories of racism.

one sees his name spread in every bookstore and when one sees windows filled with the story of the Blonde Beast,[19] one sees how completely the intellectual leaders of the present regime have turned back the clock. There might be stuff here for a thesis. We must look into it more and do some reading. . . .

Thursday, 25 July 1935. Munich.

Coming again to this literary return to Nietzsche and Chamberlain, it might be interesting to find out what impression it makes on intelligent people. I am taking private lessons with a Dr. Scheel, a very good man. I must ask him to talk with me next week about Chamberlain and Nietzsche. Perhaps I'll get somewhere.

It's astonishing to me that, when I sit still and think about Germany as I see it about me, I find that my thoughts are not only confused, but that they are often contradictory. I have changed my attitude more than once since I came here, and I probably shall do so again. Perhaps it is too soon for me to draw conclusions, but at least I can give my impressions here and change them, if need be, later.

I came to Germany prepared to correct impressions received from American newspapers. I am still prepared to do so—though not to the extent of some of my fellows. I was prepared to find Germany not in the least illiberal. I wonder now whether it is or not. I had a long talk with Frau [Eleanor] Stollsteimer this evening.[20] To one who comes from a land where open criticism of the government is the spice which flavors the dinner, it is rather disconcerting to hear critics here lower their voices and to see them close the door carefully behind them before they speak. Perhaps my friend—(she did all this)—was being over cautious; perhaps she was being a little dramatic; perhaps on the other hand she knows from experience that precautions are best. If the last is true, free speech is unknown here. Dr. Priest says that he has had open conversations with Germans who were highly critical of the *Regierung* [government]. I found quite the opposite tonight.

My friend spoke of Streicher and the discrimination against the Jews. She says that the Jews have now been forbidden the use of the public

---

[19] In *The Genealogy of Morals*, Friedrich Nietzsche (1844–1900) referred to the noble class of people as "blond beasts," in what was meant to be a reference to lions, but was misconstrued by the Nazis as a reference to blond Aryans and their innate superiority to people of darker complexions.

[20] Frau Stollsteimer was the proprietress of the lodgings where Craig stayed in Munich during the summer of 1935.

bathing places here in Munich. The Jewish question is still open and tomorrow Streicher speaks in the University on the race question.

Then she spoke of the interesting case in Berlin where two shop-keepers were arrested for selling meat at exorbitant prices. She railed against this as merely another instance of the government's misplaced care for the well-being of the people. She says that the lower working classes are well taken care of—and the moneyed classes—but that the middle class (the white collar classes) are paying for it all. (The taxes are exorbitant; trade has fallen off, etc.) She is scornful of the ruling class. Her typical reaction—(typical of her class, that is)—is directed against, not their character, but their class. She speaks of their wives being *Dienstmädchen* [housemaids], etc. She herself, interestingly enough, is a woman who suffered much in the post-war inflation. Yet she looks back to men like [Friedrich] Ebert, [Heinrich] Brüning, and [Gustav] Stresemann with respect and looks with feelings closely akin to horror upon what is happening today.[21] She said over and over: "*Es geht zu weit, Herr Craig. Es geht zu weit.*" [It's going too far, Mr. Craig. It's going too far.]

These are interesting times. I read Max Buchner all afternoon—a *Münchener* who rails against the "foreign elements" which led in the Revolution of 1919, who sneers at the *Parteistaat* [Party State] and who has only the worst of abuse to give to Ebert and Scheidemann.[22] Tonight I speak with a woman who says her feelings are shared by all intelligent German people. I can hardly be blamed for distrusting my own feelings and not daring to draw conclusions yet…

The Abyssinian Question drags on.[23] I wonder what England's going to do? One can get nothing from the papers here. . . .

By the way, I must not speak about politics at the dinner table, I am told. Herr Wirfel is an ardent National Socialist and Fraulein Schwarz's

---

[21] Friedrich Ebert (1871–1925), Heinrich Brüning (1885–1970), and Gustav Stresemann (1878–1929) were three of the leading politicians of the Weimar Republic.

[22] Max Buchner (1881–1941) was a German historian and editor of the *Gelben Hefte*, a Catholic right-wing national journal. Friedrich Ebert (1871–1925) and Philipp Scheidemann (1865–1939) were leaders of the Social Democratic Party (SPD) who played key roles in the founding of the Weimar Republic after the collapse of the German Empire at the end of World War I.

[23] The Abyssinian Question refers to the ongoing international crisis related to a border dispute between Italy and Ethiopia (then known commonly as Abyssinia) over the boundary between Italian Somaliland and Ethiopia.

father has just received an appointment. Apparently it is feared that I would hurt their feelings.

Saturday, 27 July 1935. Dinkelsbühl.
Yesterday Wasso and I went to a meeting in the university and listened to Streicher talk. I have never been so disgusted with a group of people in my life. Streicher, of course, spoke about the Race Question. I thought then as I think now that it is dreadful to see hundreds of people sitting together and applauding an attack on fellow human beings simply because these human beings have Jewish blood. Streicher spoke for four hours and during that time he heaped the grossest abuse upon the Jewish people. I have other notes on this meeting in the back of this book—notes which I took while he spoke. As I said before, my feelings have not changed with regard to the man and his thoughts. But think of what could have happened if he had been made head of the government police. His name, I am told, was considered seriously and was opposed successfully only by the urgent pleas of Schacht and others. . . .[24]

[The following day Craig set out on a short trip with three colleagues and Dr. Priest, visiting Augsburg, Nördlingen, and Dinkelsbühl.]

Our chauffeur is a Franz __________, a *Münchener* who was born in Orange, N.J. but came here before he learned the language. He fought during the whole war and was wounded only once. As is often the case among people in the common callings here, he is remarkably well educated and remarkably intelligent. I sat with him for a while and talked politics. I mentioned the Streicher meeting and that and some of the "*Juden sind hier unerwünscht*" [Jews not wanted here] signs along the road brought us to the *Rassenfrage* [race question]. Franz says that a good 80% of the people here are opposed to the Jewish policy of the Hitler regime. He went on to say that the present tactics of the government must in time bring its own overthrow. He could not tell when, but he was certain that things could not remain as they are now. For himself, he held to the *Parteistaat*; he believes that three parties are best for a country... He then spoke of war. His experience in the last has taught him to fear it. He says that Germany's great weakness is the fact that the majority of the Natl. Soc. Party are young men who have no memory of the last war. He apparently feels the tension here

---

24 Hjalmar Schacht (1877–1970) was the president of the *Reichsbank* and German Minister of Economics from 1934 to 1937. He was opposed to the more radical aspects of Nazi ideology and gave a speech in August 1935 in which he criticized the excesses of Streicher's *Der Stürmer*.

in Europe. He spoke of the Abyssinian Question and said that there was danger that Mussolini would lose his head and his position over it… Later, Dr. Priest told me that Franz had said that three shopkeepers in Berlin have been imprisoned for selling meat two cents dearer than the government price and that the head of their guild dares not speak for them. What would our opponents to the NRA think of this?[25]

After a short drive through this beautiful countryside, we came to Dinkelsbühl, the second of the walled cities. This is a beautiful old place. We walked out around the wall and through the narrow streets late in the afternoon. In the shadow of these 16th- and 17th-century buildings one feels rather insignificant. We four boys climbed the tower of the church here and looked out over the country. *Herrliches Aussicht!* [Wonderful view!]. Then back to *Die goldene Rose* [The Golden Rose restaurant] for dinner. This we had in the open and over an excellent wine and still better cigars, we sat till eleven o'clock. And—oh!—the talk. We covered everything from the Abyssinian question to Mrs. Roosevelt. But mostly we talked of Germany—Social Democracy—why it fell—the chance of revolution here soon—Hitler's work and its results. Every story that Dr. Priest tells echoes Franz' statement: "*Das Volk ist sehr verbittert.*" [The people are deeply embittered.] We talked again of war. The Herr Professor says that he talked with a child in the *Hitler Jugend*[26] [Hitler Youth] in Munich—and found that the children actually are taught to throw toy grenades at a target! We talked of education, and the Dr. said that he has found in the youth organizations that the tendency is away from education. The children in the schools are being taught to desire to become *Führers!* All this, of course, paints not Germany, but the *Regierung* [government], in very bad colors… How we talked! It's been a glorious day. Now Wasso's asleep and I am going to follow his example.

[Craig subsequently completed his excursion trip. His diary entries for July 28–31 focused primarily on sightseeing and evenings out enjoying theatrical and musical performances.]

Friday, 2 August 1935. Munich.
. . . Raith has been holding forth in great style during these last few days. He has been trying to vindicate Germany's attack on the Jews—which no

---

[25] The NRA was the National Recovery Administration, an agency that set wages and prices during the New Deal.

[26] The Hitler Youth was the Nazi Party's youth organization for boys, known for its ideological indoctrination and activities that strongly resembled military training.

one could do for me after my hearing Streicher's speech. The mental gymnastics of the man are interesting if nothing more. At one time he lays the *Juden-Programm* to the inherent race instinct of the German people. Granted that the instinct is there, certainly the majority of the people here are not in favor of the outrages which have been committed. A man named Becker said to Raith: "If your son fell in love with a Jewess, would his race instinct be strong enough to make him turn away from her?" Raith's answer was typical: "It would be impossible for a son of mine to fall in love with a Jewess." Another man said, "If the race instinct is as strong in the people as you say it is, there is no need for this governmental program against the Jews!" And that is perfectly true. After my conversations with Franz and others, I am convinced that no instinct in the German people would make them attack the Jews as they have done. And that is where the analogy between the Jewish Question here and the Negro Question in America breaks down. In America, the attacks on the Negro are made by groups of people in the South with no governmental backing; here the perfect opposite is true. Raith speaks of the "*grosse Tragödie der Judenthum in Deutschland*" as the fact that innocent Jews are suffering because the people remember the crimes committed by their Galician brothers before the war. The real tragedy is that the German people are being led by this small governmental group into an attack upon a minority group. And the fact remains that 13,000 Jews did fall for Germany in the war.

"But then," says Raith, "you have no right to criticize us for attacking the Jews as long as the Versailles Treaty stands"—thus cleverly but illogically shifting his position to ground of which he is sure. We talked at great length this morning about the question of War Guilt. Despite the fact that the majority of educated people no longer believe that Germany was guilty of bringing on the war, Raith is not satisfied. He says: "One cannot plunge the honor of Germany into the dust in 1919 and then say in 1935—'Oh, that was in 1919.'" Well—if Raith or Germany expects a formal repudiation of the Versailles Treaty and Article 231—(which he says many Germans know by heart)—he is going to be disappointed. Germany, with the aid of Great Britain, has knocked a great hole in the Treaty by means of their recent naval agreement, and she'll have to be satisfied with that.[27]

I brought up the famous "blank check" and was interested in having Raith seem to believe that Germany deserves praise for standing by her

[27] On June 18, 1935, Britain and Germany signed an agreement that allowed Germany to expand its navy, while maintaining limits on the size of the German fleet in relation to Britain's navy.

ally.[28] The "blank check" was certainly a foolish gesture of comradeship! Raith summed up the arguments by throwing most of the guilt on Austria and by blaming the Habsburg regime. Certainly, in that, he's not far wrong. . . .

Friday, 9 August 1935. Munich.

. . . I saw Dr. Priest today and he pointed out an article in the *Neuste Nachrichten* [newspaper], which told that a telegram from Dallas, Texas, had given the story of a female strikebreaker there who had been flogged and driven through the streets.[29] Underneath an editorial comment said that it was typical of the American newspapers which had been most strongly against Germany that they mentioned not even a word about this "break of civilization." The Doc was much disgusted at the rottenness of this attack, even granting that many of our papers have been unjust. For it is quite plain that the *Neueste Nachrichte* has no way of knowing what our papers said.

The stupidness of this parallels that of the picture in Monday's *Völkischer Beobachter*[30] [*People's Observer*] showing "The Jewish mayor of New York and his 'race comrades' applauding a speech by 'Judge Bernard Deutsch(!)'" There may be some truth in the story that Fiorello Laguardia has some Jewish blood but if the "race comrade" sitting on his right isn't Al Smith, I'll eat my hat.[31]

I mentioned these things at dinner today and goaded friend Wirfel, a staunch party man, to the fray. Unfortunately, after a few choice remarks, I had to leave. But [Bob] Hayter tells me the man went mad and quoted at length from *Mein Kampf* to prove conclusively that all is well in Germany. That, as Bob says, is like trying to convince a geologist by reading him

---

[28] The "blank check" refers to Germany's unconditional support of Austria-Hungary in taking punitive measures against Serbia after the assassination of the Austrian heir to the throne, Archduke Franz Ferdinand, in 1914. Emboldened by the guarantee of German support, the Austro-Hungarian government took steps that eventually brought about the outbreak of World War I.

[29] This diary entry apparently refers to a violent altercation and riot that involved ten female strikebreakers being forcibly disrobed and driven through the streets of Dallas. See Michelle Haberland, *Striking Beauties: Women Apparel Workers in the U.S. South, 1930–2000* (Athens, GA: University of Georgia Press, 2015), 40.

[30] The *Völkischer Beobachter* was a national newspaper of the Nazi Party.

[31] Bernard Deutsch (1884–1935) was the President of the Board of Aldermen and a leading figure in the American Jewish community. Al Smith (1873–1944) was a former New York state governor and unsuccessful presidential candidate of Irish-Catholic heritage.

Genesis. . . .

Friday, 16 August 1935. Munich.
. . . I've finished my tutoring with Scheel and Von Reylingen, and am a little sorry. Scheel gave me some tips yesterday on books, etc. and started a new train of thought. If I am to write a good thesis on post-war Social Democracy, I'll have to make a very careful study of the Prussian theory of the state and test the validity of Spengler's thesis—that democracy and parliamentarianism cannot be successful in Germany. Spengler's idea is that a country can have but one form of government—(no choice!)—and that form only which has been evolved from its historical development. . . .

Tuesday, 20 August 1935. Munich.
. . . Yesterday morning, Dr. Priest, Shad Roe,[32] Watson, and I went to the offices of the *Propaganda Ministerium* and had an interview with Herr [Ernst] Leichtenstern, one of the officials.[33] We questioned him closely and he was fairly sincere in his answers. With regard to the Jewish question his standpoint was not unusual. He justified the attacks on the Jews by historical arguments, exactly as Raith did. He said also, as Raith did, that the Jews would be left alone if they caused no trouble, which is nonsense of course.

The Propaganda Office apparently controls all written matters and such avenues of communication as the press, the theater, and the radio. No play can be produced without its sanction. As for plays written by foreigners opposed to National Socialism, they are not produced. Herr Leichtenstern said gently: "There is no point in arousing the people." All books which even mention the existing regime must be approved by the Office or they are in danger of suppression. Writers who cannot find publishers can take their manuscripts to the Office and through it find a publisher. Perhaps that explains why so much nonsense is printed these days. I can't imagine a publisher turning down a manuscript sent to him by the Propaganda Office.

Herr Leichtenstern spoke of the government program of enforced vacations, which is aided by "*Kraft durch Freude.*"[34] I notice in the papers that

---

32 Albert Sutherland "Shad" Roe (1914–1988) was another Princeton student in Craig's class and a frequent companion on his adventures in Germany in the summer of 1935. Roe later became a professor of art history at Cornell University.
33 Ernst Leichtenstern (1895–1945) was at this time *Gaupropagandaleiter* (Regional Propaganda Leader) in Munich and Upper-Bavaria.
34 The *Kraft durch Freude* [Strength through Joy] was a national leisure organization created by the Nazis under the auspices of the *Deutsche Arbeitsfront* [German Labor Front].

a thousand workers have left on a Rhine journey... He said naively that he was astonished at the loyalty of the workers. I imagine that in his official capacity he *would* hear only good of the government when he interrogates them. I can't quite see the portly gentleman prowling the streets like Harun-al-Rashid in search of the workers' real reactions... Watson asked some questions about the Party Program and how far it was being put into practice. The most significant answer was the admission that the government is trying to drive out the middleman and promote state ownership of small industries or at least a stringent regulation of prices. This fits in with Frau Stollsteimer's accounts of the difficulties experienced by the small butchers here. Their prices are fixed and they are allowed only much smaller quantities of meat than usual. The program then will help some people—the lower classes especially. But the small man is being hurt... We forgot to ask about taxes, but we know that in this regard also the little man is suffering. Raith, for instance, had to pay 30% of his 600 RM summer salary to the government. Eleanor S. gets 110 RM a month as a typist and pays 20 RM taxes—(though that may include insurance).[35] The good Frau pays a great deal of taxes, and in addition, must contribute to various party charities—e.g. Winter Help, Mother and Child Fund, etc. My impression is that the white collar classes are suffering extremely here for the benefit of the lower groups; that they feel the tax burden more than the upper classes; and that those upper classes are much better off than other classes. Certainly there is no talk of socialization of the great industries here. Herr Hitler must keep on good terms with the moneyed groups and, at the same time, must continue his great (and expensive) army program so as to keep the *Reichswehr* [military] on his side. *The London Times*, in a recent editorial, mentioned the fact that even the lower salaried workers aren't benefiting from the new order, because prices have risen and their wages have, if anything, decreased. The miners especially are suffering, and Hitler has been forced to organize a special program for their relief.

I asked about colonies. Herr Leichtenstern said that Germany had nothing against acquiring them, but that her internal problems were too pressing at present...

I asked also about Social Democracy in the Saar and was interested in learning that Otto Braun had been active there.[36] I must follow this up. The

---

[35] In 1935, the exchange rate was 2.4 Reichsmarks (RM) to the U.S. dollar.

[36] Otto Braun (1872–1955) was a Social Democratic politician who served as Prime Minister of Prussia from 1920 to 1932, until he was deposed by a right-wing

Saar story should give an interesting chapter to my thesis. Herr Leichtenstern was of the opinion that Braun is still working for the cause in whatever land he now resides—France or Switzerland. . . .

Sunday, 25 August 1935. Vienna.
. . . We . . . found a hotel—the *Kontinental*—on the Donau [Danube] Canal. Then we sallied forth to see the town. Knowing very little about directions, we found ourselves in the Prater, the great amusement park. Before long we tired of that and began to look for a restaurant. As I said, we knew nothing of the city and were quite confused in our first impressions. We were in a rather dirty section of the town. The streets were filled with Jews. The cafés were for the most part empty. I, for one, was quite depressed and thought that Vienna was a very dreary place indeed. Since that time, I have been able to change my opinions. Yesterday I found the city was beautiful—one of the most beautiful cities I've yet visited. I still think that it is easy to become depressed here. Wien today has the outer aspect of a city trying hard to keep up appearances. But one finds parks with grass uncut and weeds flourishing—handsome buildings with dirty windows—and other signs that the fight to keep up appearances is a losing one. And then the cafés, unlike those in Munich, are almost empty. The economic situation here is so bad that people do not have much money to spend. The German love of dinners in restaurants where one can see the world passing by is here, but the Austrians have to pinch to satisfy it. Consequently, in the restaurant in Grinzing last evening, many people came with the dinners in paper bags and bought only wine. There are many beggars. As I sat in the Schweden Café late on Friday evening, I watched four lounging outside waiting for customers to leave. . . .

[The following evening, after a day of sightseeing and strolling on the Cobenzl hill on the outskirts of Vienna]

We found a garden restaurant strung with lanterns and loud with the music of a three-man-band. There we had our first taste of Vienna night life. The people began to stream in, coming down from Cobenzl or up from the city. We were soon joined by a very quiet young man and a middle-aged, rather good-looking Jew. Up to that time, Wat and I were contemplating leaving, but the good Wat struck up a conversation with the Jew and we ordered more wine and stayed. Then a young, rather good-looking girl sat

---

German government shortly before the Nazis took power. Braun went into exile in Switzerland in April 1933; the rumor that he was active in the Saar was false.

down, showed amusement at our questions and was soon talking also. For a while we thought the other man was a stick but, when we pressed him to take a cigarette, we discovered that his reticence came from the fact that he was an *Ausländer* [foreigner]—a Russian engineer from Moscow. Our other friend had fought in Czechoslovakia and Russia during the war; the Russian had fought against the White Russians in the Revolution; Wat and I—thanks to Maurice Hindus and Vincent Sheean[37]—knew a little about Russia; we were all interested in European politics; so we were soon a very congenial group. Only the girl was left out. She had obviously come to solicit business. Indeed, when Wat and our Jewish friend were engrossed in conversation, I found her nudging the Russian and inviting him to go off with her. He refused quietly, because he couldn't leave his friends, and she left just as quietly, but without drinking the wine we had bought her.

We others sat for hours, talking at great length. The Austrian said that the people here do not want *Anschluss* [union with Germany] because it would not help business but would mean ruin for Austrian factories. He said that Austria does not need another port—that she can use that at Trieste. [These views were contradicted by a young Austrian we met on the street-car today. He said that economic conditions are very bad here and that the majority of the people—(excluding the government and the *Vaterländische Front* which it supports[38]) desire *Anschluss* with Germany because they think that it would help business.] Perhaps his views (those of our Austrian friend) were affected by his race; perhaps not. We talked about many other things—Mussolini, of course, and the Abyssinian Question which is now at its most dangerous point. Then we left for home. . . .

Tuesday, 27 August 1935. Nuremberg.
. . . I made my last good-byes to Hayter and the good Frau and had my last meal in Pschorr's, tasting Munich beer for the last time perhaps for years. Then we came on to Nuremberg and are now at the *Roter Hahn* [Hotel]. Nuremberg is another town about which I could go into ecstasies. It is much like Rothenburg and Dinkelsbühl, but on a larger scale. We had sausages and sauerkraut at the Bratwürstherzl [restaurant] on Herzgasse.

---

[37] Maurice Hindus (1891–1969) was a Russian-American writer who specialized in Soviet affairs. Vincent Sheean (1899–1975) was a journalist and writer on world affairs. His National Book Award-winning *Personal History* (New York: Doubleday, 1935) became the basis for Alfred Hitchcock's 1940 film *Foreign Correspondent.*

[38] The *Vaterländische Front* [Fatherland Front] was a Catholic fascist organization that opposed union with Germany on the grounds that it would entail Austria's rule by a predominantly Protestant state.

There we got into a long conversation with a fat and freckled little man from Berlin. He, for one, was all for the Jewish program and we again heard Raith's arguments but without Raith's reservations. Our friend also spoke of the Abyssinian question and opined that there would be no war, despite the fact that Il Duce has 200,000 men in Africa at the present time. Our Berliner believed that Mussolini is looking only for further concessions from England... The evening has been splendid...

Wednesday, 28 August 1935. Nuremberg.
. . . This has been a delightful old town, though, despite the Wintergarten [cabaret, which Craig found disappointing]. It is not as beautiful as Rothenburg or Dinkelsbühl but, in growing into the position of the leading *Handelsstadt* [trading city] in Bavaria, it has lost nothing of its "*Meistersinger*" air and one can still feel the breath of the Middle Ages while he dodges a Mercedes on these crooked old streets. . . .[39]

Saturday, 31 August 1935. Dresden.
We left Jena this morning and came straight through to Dresden, running through the Thuringen Wald—a very beautiful ride—and into Saxony. On the way we had a talk with an electrical engineer in our compartment. He had lived six months in London in 1907, and was very proud of his English which was as limited as that of most Germans. We didn't give him much opportunity to practice it, for the conversation became political and we talked the tongue we came here to learn. Our friend aired views we have heard very often while here—that all Americans are wealthy; that America entered the war for the sake of the money she could get out of it; that she'd go into others for the same reason; that the Abyssinian conflict would turn into a great war between the black and white races; that all newspapers which speak against Germany lie and they lie because they are controlled by Jews. Watson drifted into talking about the Jewish question with him. I was loth to do so, for I fancied that the other man in our compartment looked very Jewish, though he had a *Schwarz-weiss-rot* ribbon in his button-hole.[40] My suspicions were partly confirmed (much to Watson's horror) when we changed trains at Neumark and our engineer said that, in his opinion, the other man *was* a Jew, though a German war veteran. It was an

---

[39] The city of Nuremberg was seriously damaged during bombing raids and fighting during World War II and lost much of the medieval character described by Craig in these passages.

[40] *Schwarz-weiss-rot* [Black, white, and red] were the colors of the Imperial German flag, associated with the Hohenzollern dynasty.

interesting experience, but a very unpleasant one. . . .

Saturday, 1 September 1935. Dresden.

We like this town so much that we've decided to stay over till Tuesday. . . .

[After a morning visiting the city's art collections] we had lunch at the *Italienisches Dörfchen* [restaurant] on the Elbe [River] and spent the afternoon in our room. This evening we had an excellent dinner in the *Rotweinkeller* [restaurant] and had a long conversation with a German stocking manufacturer and his wife. We talked largely of travel and music at first, but after a while we got around to politics. Our friend was a very well educated man but was strongly against the Jews and, indeed, said that one could not understand the problem unless he had lived here. We spoke of trade, and he remarked that the boycott of German goods in America had been felt greatly here and was still being felt.[41] He obviously spoke from experience. In regard to the Abyssinian Question he was very scornful of Italian soldiers (as most ex-service men here are) but was equally scornful of the League [of Nations]. He was sure that war will come—even went so far as to say that France might lend money to Italy and to hint that England would come even nearer to Germany. That would be a real return to the Balance of Power. The only new development in the Abyssinian Question is talk in the papers of a contract between Abyssinia and an Anglo-American firm, giving the firm a concession to oil and mines. If this is true, it may affect the situation somewhat. The latest *Paris Herald* is quiet and is mostly filled with the story of the tragic death of Queen Astrid of Belgium in Switzerland.[42] . . .

[In the interval, Craig traveled through Leipzig on his way to Berlin, sightseeing and visiting a number of art museums.]

Thursday, 5 September 1935. Berlin.

. . . This afternoon we went to the American Embassy for our interview with Ambassador Dodd. We were unable to see him today but we did have a rather interesting talk with his secretary, who turned out to be Herbert Bayard Swope's aunt.[43] With many warnings to us "to be good," "to be discreet," she said that one couldn't be too careful of one's mouth here in

---

41 An international boycott of German goods began in March 1933 in protest against anti-Semitic violence and state policies.

42 Astrid was killed in a car accident while vacationing incognito in Switzerland with her husband, King Leopold.

43 Herbert Bayard Swope (1882–1958) was a well-known American editor, journalist (at *The New York World*) and member of the Algonquin Round Table circle.

Berlin. But she did go on speaking against the government and asking us of the feeling in Bavaria. She feels that the move making Munich the "*Hauptstadt der Bewegung*" [Capital of the Nazi Movement] is calculated to stop opposition in the south. She was very strong in her condemnation of Goebbels and the radicals and full of praise for Schacht's courageous speech warning the government that the movements of the radical group were hurting the economic development of the country. . . .

Saturday, 7 September 1935. Berlin.
. . . This morning we had our interview with Ambassador Dodd, who was very pleasant but who looked more like a tired businessman than a diplomat. He talked very frankly, more so than we had expected. He told us that the boycott against Germany had been stronger than ever since the Jewish Program had resumed its radical character in June. He agreed with us that this program was being used to divert the people's attention from internal ills. At the same time, he spoke very highly of Schacht and said that he had accomplished much good by his economic program. He spoke especially of the agrarian program of keeping the Germans on the land and seeing that the people were fed. At the same time, this agrarian program is causing difficulties, and, as we saw in Munich, small tradesmen are being driven to the wall. Perhaps government warehouses, of which Herr Leichtenstern spoke, will become a reality… The Ambassador said that, in his mind, Schacht was the strongest man in the government… I was disappointed that he had no advice to give me for my thesis on Social Democracy. He said that I might be able to find some modern material in French or in the Geneva Reports, but said that in German there was nothing being printed at present. I was in a bookstore yesterday and could get not a thing… The Ambassador spoke of the Abyssinian Question which is now lying before the League Council. He said that while the controlling section of the government here hopes that the League will be smashed by this controversy, the more moderate group, led by Schacht, are not so sure that a strong League, including Germany, would not be the best thing for the country's future economic development. Leaving the embassy I felt very grateful to Mr. Dodd; indeed I felt, paraphrasing Goethe, that:

> *Es ist gar hübsch von einem grossen Herrn*
> *So menschlich with us Princetons selbst zu sprechen.*[44]

[44] The prologue in Goethe's *Faust* reads: "*Es ist gar hübsch von einem großen Herrn, so menschlich mit dem Teufel selbst zu sprechen.*" [Tis courteous in so great a lord as he, to speak so kindly even to the devil.]

We walked down *Unter den Linden* and bumped into Professor Priest in the Kranzler Café. We had a long talk, telling him everything that has happened to us on the way up from Vienna. Then we invited him to supper before the opera tonight…

Sunday, 8 September 1935. Berlin.
. . . The papers are very indignant because the Communists on trial for the Bremen Affair in New York Harbor have been released by Judge Brodsky. The article in the *Völkischer Beobachter* begins: "*Richter Brodsky ist ein Jude…* "[45]
. . .

Wednesday, 11 September 1935. Berlin.
. . . Yesterday morning I called on Herr [Emil] de Haas at the Carl Schurz House.[46] He was very pleasant and fairly loaded me down with pamphlets telling the economic tale of modern Germany. He says that unemployment has very appreciably decreased here, due in part to the agricultural program—shipping the unemployed out to the land. The farmers are well off here because they are being pressed to raise much more than usual in a market which has no uncertainty because the prices are fixed. The consumer is suffering for that, but of course the other parts of the program are supposed to benefit the consumer. (There are many parallels between this system and our own I have found by reading one of the pamphlets de Haas gave me.) He said, however, that Germany would eventually have to get back her foreign market—that the army couldn't make up for that deficiency forever—and expressed the view that Germany is being hurt more by the unfavorable currency situation—(the mark on foreign exchanges is too dear)—than by the boycott… He said also that the building trades are very well off here. I can understand that. In Munich there was great building activity and it is even more feverish here. The new

---

[45] The Bremen Affair was an incident on July 26, 1935, in which a group of communist demonstrators stormed the German ocean liner S.S. *Bremen* in New York harbor, and tore down its swastika flag in a protest against the German government's anti-communist and anti-Semitic policies. Magistrate Louis Brodsky (1883–1970) dismissed charges against five of the six men on the grounds that the swastika flag was not Germany's official flag. German ships at this time flew both the old Imperial German flag and the swastika flag, so Brodsky argued that no national symbol of Germany had been harmed. The *Völkischer Beobachter*'s coverage focused on Brodsky's Jewish background.

[46] The *Carl Schurz Vereinigung* [Association] was founded by German liberals in 1926 to promote German-American friendship. Emil de Haas was managing director of the CSV at this time.

subway is being laid; down on Göringstrasse, men are working night and day on a huge building; and De Haas says that people all over are repairing and re-building homes and shops. We'd be much better off at home if our building trades were as prosperous. . . .

Thursday, 12 September 1935. Bentheim.
. . . This morning we left Berlin early and arrived in Hannover at about noon. We walked about the *Neu Rathaus* [New Town Hall] in a remarkably beautiful park. The lake is filled with tremendous carp and covered with very fat and contented ducks. We walked a while with a vendor of *Eis* who was shocked because we were stopping only a few hours... Leaving Hannover we took the westbound train. I parted with Wat at Löhne and came on to Bentheim. I will cross the border early in the morning. After a late supper I wandered up the country road. It is a beautiful evening and my last in Germany. The moon was at full and the trees cast dark shadows against the bright sky. The fields were perfectly quiet except for one dog which insisted on making a hell of a racket and a bird which chirped twice and then was still. Off in the distance an old tower stood dark and silent over the furrowed land. The dog continued to bark. I came back. . . .

[Craig subsequently left Berlin, crossed the border into the Netherlands, and sailed back to the United States on the R.M.S. *Statendam*, arriving in New York on September 22nd.]

2

Oxford and Princeton, 1936–1938

[In October 1976, Craig decided to write a memoir of his experiences between September 1935 and December 1936, when he studied at Oxford University as a Rhodes Scholar, in order to fill a gap in his diary. His intention was to describe his stay at Oxford and the beginning of a number of his life-long friendships with Walt Rostow, Philip Kaiser, Arthur Pyper, and Dan Davin, among others.[1]]

. . . They were, I guess, the happiest two years of my life. I loved Oxford from the first and perhaps Oxford loved me, for she gave me much—a chance to read without worrying about grades and to acquire the miscellaneous mind that a historian should have; fine models of scholarship at its best in B. H. Sumner and E. L. Woodward,[2] with whom I had the privilege to work; many friendships which have, unlike the Princeton ones, survived the ravages of time; and my wife, for it was while I was at Oxford that I fell in love with Phyllis and asked her to marry me.[3] I think Oxford

---

[1] Walt Rostow (1916–2003) was a Rhodes scholar at Oxford who became an American economist and theorist of economic development, and served as a National Security advisor in the Kennedy and Johnson administrations. Philip Kaiser (1913–2007) was another Rhodes Scholar and later an American diplomat who served as ambassador to Mauritania, Senegal, Hungary, and Austria. Arthur Pyper (1916–1994) later became master of a series of English prep schools. Born in New Zealand, Dan Davin (1913–1990) was a well-regarded writer of fiction and worked at the Clarendon and Oxford University Presses.

[2] Benedict Humphrey Sumner (1893–1951), a fellow of Balliol College, Oxford from 1925 to 1944, and warden of All Souls College, Oxford from 1945 to 1951, was a renowned historian of Russia, and of diplomacy and international relations. Sir Ernest Llewellyn Woodward (1890–1971) was a historian of British foreign policy and World War I, and the author of *The Age of Reform, 1815–1870* (Oxford: Clarendon Press, 1938), a classic contribution to the *Oxford History of England*.

[3] Phyllis Halcomb Craig (1918–2006) was married to Gordon Craig for sixty-six years. She specialized in early childhood education and worked to establish and run

made me a better human being than I had been at Princeton by teaching me the truth of the Preacher's words, "To everything there is a season," so that I learned, without being troubled by my Presbyterian conscience, that, if work had its place, so did what Kipling, in his poem "To the Companions," called the

> Glorious, unforgotten
>   innocent enormities
> Of frontless days before the beard,
> Where, instant on the casual jest,
> The God Himself of Mirth appeared
> And snatched us to His heaving breast.[4]

It was a wonderful time, in which all of my senses were on the *qui vive* from morn till midnight, lest I miss any of the exciting things that were happening. I can't remember a day or an hour in which I ever felt a bit under the weather, or had a cold or a tooth-ache. I have always been an energetic type, but I blazed with energy at Oxford, and, if properly wired, could probably have lit up all the streets of Jersey City. Nor was I alone. In general, our pace was hectic, and our mood was gay. The fact that, as the months passed, it became increasingly clear that Europe was headed for a major bust-up had a good deal to do with this, of course. We all knew, or thought we knew, what that would mean for us, and we wanted to make the most of life while we had the chance. This added to the tempo and gaiety of our life, and also, I think, made us all more generous, more tolerant, more forbearing. At bottom, we were convinced, everyone at Oxford was a good chap, and Oxford, after all, was what the world was capable of becoming if we could, as we would, get rid of the Hitlers and the Mussolinis.

. . . Tutors were reasonably generous with suggestions about what one should do, but there were few whip-crackers among them. My first tutor was B. H. Sumner, a handsome gaunt man who looked like a Roman

---

child care centers at both Princeton and Stanford. At Stanford, Phyllis Craig worked in close partnership with Dorothea Almond to found and administer the Children's Center of the Stanford Community (CCSC), the Escondido Village Nursery School, the Childcare Resource Center, and the Pepper Tree Afterschool Program. For Phyllis Craig's reminiscences, see "SOHP Interview with Phyllis Craig (November 18, 1986)," *Stanford Oral History Project Interviews* (SC1017), Dept. of Special Collections and University Archives, Stanford University Libraries, Stanford, Calif.

[4] See Rudyard Kipling, *To the Companions* (Garden City, NY: Doubleday, 1933).

Emperor in the last days of imperial decline. My acquaintance with him started when he examined my competence in foreign languages. My exiguous knowledge of French he tested by sending me off to Blackwell's, telling me exactly on what shelf in what room I would find a copy of Langlois et Seignobos, *Introduction aux sciences historiques* and instructing me to read the whole of it over the weekend and come in and talk to him about it. He followed the same procedure with respect to German, sending me to another room and another shelf where I would find a good edition of Meinecke, *Weltbürgertum und Nationalstaat.* After I had satisfied his standards in German and shown a passable understanding of French (he did not like my "exact" translations from Daniel Halévy, *La République des ducs*), he set me a few papers while we sought to determine what should become of me. I wanted to work for a D.Phil.; Sumner thought I should take a B.A.; we compromised on a candidacy for a B.Litt. This had one disadvantage: it ended our tutor-student relationship, for he advised me, because of my interests, to work with E. L. Woodward at All Souls. This turned out well, but, despite all that Woodward was to give me, it was a pity that my apprenticeship under Sumner ended so soon. I had acquired a deep admiration for him, which increased when I heard him give the lectures that were the basis for that wonderful book *Russia and the Balkans* (1937). I dropped in to see him now and then, and once took Phyllis with me (there are Sumners in her family). He gave us strawberries then and later, when we announced our engagement and I was going down, he gave me good editions of *Le Rouge et le Noir* and *La Chartreuse de Parme*, saying that they were good books for a historian. I saw him for the last time in 1948 when he visited Princeton for some weeks. I gave him lunch at the Nass[au Inn], he huddled in a black overcoat looking frail and ill, and we had a very good talk. He died three years later. . . .

[The Craig diaries resume in December 1936, as the author continued his studies at Oxford. The diaries largely concern Craig's social life, his work on his thesis, and his courtship of his future wife, Phyllis Halcomb, with little comment on world affairs. The abdication of Edward VIII, the annexation of Austria by Nazi Germany, and the Munich Crisis of September 1938 were notable exceptions.]

Tuesday, 15 December 1936. Glasgow.

. . . The King has abdicated and George VI is now on the throne. I heard the proclamation at George Square on Monday morning. It was read by a nice old man in a wig—the Lord Provost, I believe. Then the band played

"God Save the King" and three cheers were given for "our sovereign liege lord." That section of the crowd in which I stood was not very deeply moved by the proceedings; but I did note a tense and oppressive silence after the opening words of the proclamation: "Whereas by act of abdication dated etc." Newspapermen spoke of this after the London proclamation also.

It is hard to judge the ex-King's radio speech (11 Dec. 1936). It was not the speech of a strong man; yet it might have been the speech of a very *clever* man. Certainly it was very effective, and thousands of people here must have sighed in unison when he mentioned the lady he loved. I see now that Lady Houston is writing articles on the Power of Love in the *Saturday Review*. Certainly there is an opportunity for "that malignant form of romanticism" of which Croce speaks to break like a wave over the world ... [Prime Minister Stanley] Baldwin's speech in the House was magnificent. I think his foreign policy stupid, but certainly he has borne himself well here. On the other hand, the radio speech of His Grace, the Archbishop of Canterbury, got under my skin. I hardly thought the mention that James II fled and Edward VIII abdicated on the eleventh of December justified by any close similarity. And the remarks about the violation of the spirit of true Christian marriage showed how close together are the C. of E. and the Curia.

England has come through this business well, and is returning to normalcy, although the newspapers are still printing pictures of centenarians who can now boast from their wheelchairs that they have lived under five sovereigns. The most hopeful sign of the whole show is that both communism and fascism were helpless and neither was able to profit from the crisis. Fascism will never bloom in this fog-bound land. . . .

[1938]

Friday, 11 March 1938. Oxford.
The Nazis have entered Austria! Hitler has made the *Anschluss* [Annexation]! All hell will be to pay and very shortly. Phil Kaiser is in the depths of his worst fit of *Weltschmerz* [world-weariness], and with good reason. . . .[5]

Saturday, 12 March 1938. London.

[5] Philip Kaiser was the son of Ukrainian Jewish immigrants from Imperial Russia and had a Jewish upbringing and education.

. . . We reached Paddington at 11:10, using the journey to read all about the *Anschluss*. The *Times* and the *Telegraph* condemned vigorously, but had little to say about what England should do. I don't think she will do anything. Hitler's next move is to walk into Czechoslovakia. When he does that we'll all be in uniform. . . .

Friday, 25 March 1938. London.
. . . Paul [Ward] told a story which he got from Joe Kennedy, the American ambassador.[6] [British Prime Minister Neville] Chamberlain said to Kennedy: "Why should we fight? We'd gain nothing by it and we'd simply prepare the country for the Bolshevists."...Kennedy is worried about the business situation at home and says that the U.S. is going to hell in a hack. He called the press boys in yesterday and asked them to tell America that there isn't going to be a war, so that Wall Street can take heart. . . .

Friday, 20 May 1938. Oxford.
. . . In the evening to the Rhodes House to meet Kennedy, the new American ambassador. His speech was poor. I think Paul Ward is right in saying that he still has the typical Wall Street mind. He gave me the impression of not knowing what's to be done to prevent war—although he shares that fault with many. A strict non-interventionist, I think. . . .

Saturday, 3 September 1938. Jersey City.
. . . The European mess becomes more disturbing. Hitler's speeches at the Nuremberg Conference this week will be important and may decide the issue. . . .

Monday, 12 September 1938. Malvern, Pennsylvania.
. . . The European crisis gets worse, but Hitler's last speech at Nuremberg tonight was not as bellicose as might have been expected.

Wednesday, 14 September 1938. Malvern.
. . . War seems imminent in Europe, and England, I think, will decide the issue.

Thursday, 15 September 1938. Malvern.

---

[6] Paul Ward (1911–2005) was a historian who worked with the Office of Strategic Services (OSS) during World War II. Joseph P. Kennedy, Sr. (1888–1969), father of President John F. Kennedy, served as U.S. ambassador to Britain from 1938 to 1940. He was a notorious pessimist regarding Britain's prospects of surviving a war with Germany.

Phyl sewed most of the day and I worked on Van Wyck Brooks's *The Flowering of New England* and listened to dispatches from Europe. Chamberlain flew to Berchtesgaden today, to consult Hitler. . . .

Sunday, 18 September 1938. Jersey City.
. . . News comes that Britain and France are selling out Czechoslovakia and recommending cession of the Sudeten provinces to Germany in return for neutralization of the rest of the state under a military guarantee…

Thursday, 22 September 1938. Jersey City.
. . . Chamberlain is off to Godesberg today, for his second interview with Hitler. More *Danegeld*? [Money to buy off an aggressor]... Augur opines, in today's *N.Y. Times*, that the weakness of France's air-forces has been the determining factor in the Anglo-French position.[7]

Friday, 23 September 1938. Jersey City.
Again the European crisis. Chamberlain balked at Hitler's demands today, and it looks as though we're pretty close to war. The Czechs, the Poles, the Rumanians, and the Hungarians are mobilizing. The French order for mobilization is ready; and Russia says she'll fight if France observes her treaty obligations. The Prime Minister is still trying to save the peace and is apparently submitting a new plan to Czechoslovakia. But England can't give way too much, and Hitler seems to be risking his great diplomatic victory by asking too much. If war comes, God knows what America will do. It makes my future plans seem very doubtful and most unreal... Some Macaulay and Dos Passos before bed. . . .

Monday, 26 September 1938. Jersey City.
. . . Ann McCormack in today's *Times* opines that Hitler's eight-day waiting period is his biggest mistake to date. He is allowing opinion in other countries to form, and is strengthening the democratic front. For the past hour and a half, I have been listening to Hitler, speaking from Berlin. The usual rant and misrepresentation of fact; and a shady, vicious attack on [Czechoslovak President Edvard] Beneš. Hitler says that the patience of the German people is at an end and that he is ready to take Sudetenland. And yet he said nothing of the Polish or Magyar claims; and—oh, irony!—he thanked Chamberlain for his peace proposals.

---

[7] "Augur Sees Only an Armistice, With Britain Facing Conscription," *New York Times* (22 September 1938): 4. Augur was a penname for British journalist Vladimir Poliakov (1864–1956), author of *Germany in Europe* (London: Selwyn & Blount Limited, 1927).

Roosevelt today sent a cautious appeal to both Hitler and Beneš. The latter has answered already.

Tuesday, 27 September 1938. Princeton.
. . . Europe is even nearer war, if that is possible. Roosevelt's second plea for peace—a tactful, well-worded note—was sent to Hitler tonight. There is still some hope of peace, but only if Hitler backs down. . . .

Thursday. 29 September 1938. Princeton.
. . . War seems to have been averted by the mobilization of the British fleet and by Mussolini's intervention, said to be caused by the Italian King's threat of abdication. The Four Power Conference now meeting in Munich may clear things up. We all hope so. . . .

[Discussion of world affairs peters out after September 1938, as Craig was increasingly absorbed with the preparations for his qualifying exams and his impending wedding. His near daily record ceases for an extended period after Craig's marriage in July 1939. Years after the fact, Craig elaborated on his lack of a written record during the first years of the war in Europe, in a postscript written on November 5, 1974: "Here follows a gap in my *Tagebuch* that extends until 21 May 1941. Given the fact that I was learning to be a college teacher and was also trying to write my doctoral dissertation, my failure to keep a daily record is understandable, but it is regrettable that I did not at least put things down in a pocket diary, as I was always careful to do after 1941."]

3

War and Postwar, 1941–1946

[The diaries resume in the spring of 1941 as Craig welcomed the birth of his first child, Susan, while teaching at Yale and completing his doctorate. This was a busy time and Craig did not comment much on world affairs.]

[1941]

Saturday, 24 May 1941. New Haven.
Last evening as I sat down to a bottle of beer and my conclusion Phyl was—to use the vernacular—taken bad. Telephone—doctor—taxi to hospital, getting there at 10:45 p.m. just as pains really began to come. Mrs. H. on hand to hold my hand.

Phyl took it the hard way, since the Doctor doesn't believe in opiates—probably for biblical reasons. The labor was short but hard; and at approximately 2:45 a.m., Saturday the 24th, a girl, Susan, weighing 8 lbs. 6 ½ oz. was born. Phyl came out of it very quickly and very well.

Home at 4:15 after coffee. Had a double scotch and tried to work. No go. Bed at 7 for three hours. Then to university to pass out cigars. Coffee with Mommsen in Toasty. Then in to see Holborn to talk over last chapter. Gave me Sir Herbert Richmond's *English Strategy* to read and use.

In afternoon to see Phyl and baby. Both well. Then to typist. Then to cocktail party at Gabriels where I was belle of the ball. . . .

Sunday, 22 June 1941. New Haven.
Russia and Germany at war! Everyone delighted, but I'm a bit wary. If Hitler pulls this off, school is out. Meanwhile, we will all sit back and forget the urgency of our own efforts. . . .

Monday, 23 June 1941. New Haven.
. . . No reliable news from Russia.

Saturday, 12 July 1941. New Haven.
. . . I have kept at my Italian and can now read simple prose. [Carlo] Collodi's *Pinocchio* is my limit at present, but I shall improve. I have been rather slack with history of late, but I've gone on a tremendous reading spree outside of that field. Innumerable detective stories, of course, among which only [Georges] Simenon's *La Tête d'un homme* is worth mentioning ... Among other things I've knocked off Stendhal's *Chartreuse de Parme* and *Le Rouge et le Noir*, both of which were worth doing. The first gets a bit tedious after the first volume but the latter is a great book, and Julien Sorel gives me some uncomfortable moments since I recognize in him traits which I possess myself... No English novels worth a damn are being produced, no doubt because of the war. Eric Knight's *This Above All* was a sorry book... The English, for that matter, haven't produced a first-rate novelist since the *last* war. Huxley wrote a great book, and that about completes the picture. I was interested, although depressed, in reading Robert Graves's and Alan Hodges's *The Long Weekend*, a social history of England in the years 1920–1939. A distressing picture of a great country going to pieces under the leadership of a lot of footling old men. The book is something of a hodge-podge but I know of no better account of the period... As an anecdote I have just read Quentin Reynolds's *London Diary, 1940*, an account of London under the Blitz. A brave and encouraging picture, but too desperate. If only the old bastards like Chamberlain and [Defense Minister Thomas] Inskip had done something![1]

These are depressing days, and days which remind us too often of lost opportunities. Alan showed me a collection of Luis Quintanilla's sketches done during the Spanish war. They are as dispiriting as Hemingway's book or that great book by Gustav Regler,[2] *The Great Crusade*, which no one reads. We have frittered away every opportunity which we had to stop Hitler and now, in a much weaker position, we'll have to fight him anyway.

I sometimes feel, however, that we'll let England down just as she let

---

[1] In the anti-appeasement polemic *Guilty Men*, published by Victor Gollancz's Left Book Club in July 1940, "Cato the Younger" describes the selection of "the bum–faced evangelical" Sir Thomas Inskip as Minister for Coordination of Defence as the worst political appointment since Caligula made his horse a consul.

[2] Gustav Regler (1898–1963) was a German journalist and, during the Spanish Civil War, a political commissar of the XII International Brigade. Hemingway wrote the preface to the English translation of his novel, *Das große Beispiel* [The great example], translated by Whittaker Chambers as *The Great Crusade* (New York: Longmans, Green & Co., 1940).

Czechoslovakia down. The President is trying to shove us ahead. He sent forces to Iceland this week. But we're by no means a united nation yet, and the Russian war has muddled our thinking considerably. Many of our diviners and some of the cartoonists for the *Herald Tribune*, to say nothing of the editorial board of the Luce publications, seem to fear Communism as much as they do Hitler.

Well—Russia is still holding out after three weeks. Meanwhile I am reading [Fyodor Dostoevsky's] *Crime and Punishment*, [William] McGovern's *From Luther to Hitler*, and Ernest Bramah's *The Wallet of Kai Lung*. And more detective stories…

Later: Long letter to Winnie Davin—(Dan, if still alive, is somewhere in the east)—complaining about American policy and hoping that Iceland will be followed up… Depression deepened by Berlin report that Germans have taken Vitebsk, rail center on only n-s route west of Moscow… Reading myself to sleep with W. M. Shirer's *Berlin Diary, 1934–41*. Very good and a tremendous attack on the *je-m'en-foutisme* [I don't care-ism] of the democracies.

Sunday, 13 July 1941. New Haven.

News from the Russian front still confused. The Germans claim to have broken through the Stalin line in all strategic points and to be marching on Leningrad, Moscow, and Kiev… Moscow denies this and claims to have won complete mastery in the air on the eastern front and to have downed 133 German planes today… Whatever the truth may be, the Russians are doing a better job with their propaganda than any one of Hitler's opponents to date. They are not only broadcasting stories of European revolt against German domination, but they report tonight that Hitler has broken with Goering! According to the Russians, Hermann opposed the eastern campaign and may even now, because of this stand, be languishing in one of Himmler's rest homes. Wonderful, if true…[3] Anglo-Russian Pact signed today…

Finished Shirer today. A very fair and reasonable account of why the German people will in all probability go on fighting to the bitter end. Shirer certainly kicks our foolish optimists around… Reading McGovern's *From Luther to Hitler*. Good section on T. H. Green.[4]

[Following the July 1941 diary entries, Craig wrote a summary of the

---

[3] This was indeed a false report.

[4] T. H. Green (1836–1882) was a nineteenth-century British philosopher, political radical, and temperance reformer.

following half-year, which he titled "Some Notes on the Princeton Period *August 1941–March 1942.*" This section of the diary is excerpted below. Craig was forced to leave Yale when it dismissed most of its non-tenured faculty after war broke out following the Japanese attack on Pearl Harbor, fearing that student enrollments would decline precipitously.[5]]

We left New Haven at the end of July 1941 and drove down to Princeton. . . . The rest of the summer was lovely. Susan grew in wisdom and power daily; Phyl was wild about the house and puttered all day long; I wandered around the Princeton Library getting used to it again, and hunting down books I remembered. In the evenings we saw friends, for the town was full of them. . . .

As the town filled up with college people again I began to plan my work. There was a confused week when Sherman Kent phoned from Washington to ask me to take a job with him under Colonel Donovan.[6] I went to Washington and looked the business over and finally, after much hesitation, turned the job down.

College started late in September. My first term was a good one but one very crowded with work. . . . The lectures made outside activities almost impossible but I did take an active part in resuscitating the Princeton Federation of Teachers, and in doing so got to know Dave Bowers, who is a fine guy. . . .[7]

The war caused a great dislocation of the customary Princeton way of life. Before the new term began we had a two week period into which we crammed a whole history course for students who wished to "accelerate."

My second term teaching schedule was a very pleasant one. I had my graduate course, plus four precepts in [Elmer] Beller's[8] "17th and 18th Centuries" and four in [Robert] Palmer's[9] "Revolutionary Europe"—all upper-class and graduate work. By this time, however, the war was getting on our nerves. It seemed a pretty soft touch for us to be living in a

---

[5] See William Palmer, *Engagement with the Past: The Lives and Works of the World War II Generation of Historians* (Lexington: The University Press of Kentucky, 2001), 79.

[6] William J. Donovan (1883–1959) was head of the Office of Strategic Services.

[7] David F. Bowers (1906–1945) was a professor of philosophy at Princeton. He was killed in a railway accident.

[8] Elmer A. Beller (1894–1980), author of *Propaganda in Germany During the Thirty Years War* (Princeton: Princeton University Press, 1940), was a member of Princeton's history department from 1924 to 1976.

[9] Robert R. Palmer (1909–2002), an eminent historian of eighteenth-century Europe, taught at Princeton for nearly three decades, from 1936 to 1963.

comfortable house, eating well, teaching a few classes, spending the afternoons playing gin-rummy over heavy teas. So I wrote to Sherman Kent saying that, if the job in Washington were offered to me again, I would accept it. At the end of February I was appointed Associate Social Science Analyst in the Mediterranean Section of the Office of the Coordination of Information. . . . We then spent two weeks putting our affairs in order and pushed off to Washington on 11 March 1942. . . .

I started work on 13 March and discovered to my horror that I was an expert on river transport in Africa. A more pleasant discovery was that Joel Carmichael is working at the Annex of the Library of Congress in the Near Eastern Section.[10] We have lunch together daily between my frantic hours of searching for depth figures and calculations of current on the Benue and Ubangui. . . .

[1942]

Saturday, 28 March 1942. Washington.
Working on the Congo and Ubangui—the idea being to find the possible water routes for carrying oil and gasoline up towards Forts Lamy and Archambault. Having worn my dogs out in the tunnel between the main library and the annex, trying to find material, I felt weary and discouraged today. Worked till four and then came along home to play with Susan, picking up some flowers for Phyl on the way. . . .

Tuesday, 31 March 1942. Washington.
To the Munitions Building where Section G2 of the Military Intelligence is quartered. Went through the five volumes of the so-called McKenzie Report No. 19—a British report on Transport and Communications in the Belgian Congo. Found a lot of good stuff… So back to 25th and E to go through *L'Illustration Congolaise*, marking stuff to be photostated.

Sunday, 5 April 1942. Washington.
Up early. Found in the *Times* that U.S. has recognized Free French Africa (A.E.F.) [*Afrique Équatoriale Française*] and intends to send a consul general to Brazzaville. Meanwhile Lawrence Taylor, whose confidential reports on the situation I read only yesterday, is being sent to B. to act as Johnny-on-the-spot. All this gives both significance and urgency to the job I'm doing. . . .

Friday, 10 April 1942. Washington.

[10] Joel Carmichael (1915–2006) was a historian, editor, and translator.

Worked all week, feeling lost at times but gradually getting the hang of things. The routine is a new one but satisfactory. The bus in the morning is choked to suffocation, but, when I get to work, I manage to get into the smoking room and read the *Times* until I've recovered. Then I work till 1:15 and have lunch with Joel. Since Joel has become enamored of a girl named Isota Tucker in the British Empire section, this is an amusing hour, for he describes his failures to complete a liaison and lays extensive plans for the future throughout the meal. So back to the library and work till 5:30. Home on another wretched bus, arriving at 6:30. Play with Susan for an hour and spend the evening reading and playing the guitar.

Thursday, 30 April 1942. Washington.
Worked till 10 finishing up river section of strategic survey of Belgian Congo.

[The diary continues with an extended summary entry covering the remainder of 1942.]

4 May–20 December 1942. Washington.
From May to August worked at Coordinator's Office, principally on a tremendous survey of trans-African routes, the river section and part of the port and city sections of which I wrote. This work which was onerous but rewarding almost ruined my stomach but aside from that did me no harm. In mid-June I began work on a strategic survey of the Belgian Congo.

It was at this point that Hajo Holborn[11] on one of his trips to town told me that there was a job open at the State Department. He told me about it one night as Phyl, he, and I sat on the Washington roof sipping Tom Collinses. The job, he said, was in the Division of Research & Publication and, while not much in itself, it might become a stepping stone to a career in the Department. If nothing came of it, I would of course go back to teaching.

I was at once filled with all sorts of fantastic dreams in which Mr. Hull[12]

---

[11] Hajo Holborn (1902–1969), one of the major German émigré historians in the United States, was from 1934 until his death in 1969 a professor of German history at Yale University. He worked for the OSS during the war as special assistant to the chief of the Research and Analysis branch, William L. Langer. See Otto P. Pflanze, "The Americanization of Hajo Holborn," in *An Interrupted Past: German–Speaking Refugee Historians in the United States After 1933*, ed. Hartmut Lehmann and James J. Sheehan (Cambridge: Cambridge University Press, 1991), 170–79.

[12] Cordell Hull (1871–1975) was the longest-serving secretary of state, holding the position for eleven years (1933–1944) during the Roosevelt administration.

and I jointly formulated policies which won the war. I said I was interested—indeed, that I would take the job—all this sight unseen.

A few days later I was interviewed by E. Wilder Spaulding of Research and Publication and was practically offered the job on the spot. And at the same time I accepted. A definite offer came a few days later.

The last two weeks at the COI (now the Office of Strategic Services) were good ones. I was fired with the prospect of a new job and consequently did a good job in finishing up the Congo Survey. I finished my appendices on roads, railroads, rivers and telegraphs on July 31 and moved to State on the following day, just as the rest of the boys began a survey of Morocco in which all hands participated and which, they later claimed, made the invasion of North Africa, which was to come in November, a success.

Meanwhile I went to State and the let-down was sudden and shattering. I found that Research and Publication (RP) was a division filled with old gaffers who had neither ambition nor conspicuous talent. I say conspicuous advisedly. I am informed that the editing of the *Foreign Relations* is excellent, but I know that I never heard an interesting or provocative remark uttered in RP in my 3½ months of service there. . . .

My main job was to compile the materials for a wartime record of the administration of the State Department. This I did by going to the different divisions, getting permission to search their files, selecting papers and having them copied. It was a job for an archivist. For a while I hoped that I would have an opportunity to write something on the basis of the stuff I collected. I soon found, however, that no plan had been made to do any such thing.

The job had some good points. I was on my own—I had considerable leisure and could take mid-morning coffee at ease, while reading Drew Pearson's column in the *Post*—I met a lot of people—and I picked up a lot of interesting stuff on the relations of State with other governmental agencies. I was able to collect almost a complete documentary history, for example, of the relations between State and the Board of Economic Warfare. But I was bored and felt useless and decided to try to shift.

The man who saved me was Gene Rostow[13] who, on hearing of my predicament, got me an introduction to Jack Ross, head of the Division of

[13] Eugene Rostow (1913–2002), brother of Walt Rostow, had a storied career in academe and government, most notably serving as Dean of the Yale Law School and director of the U.S. Arms Control and Disarmament Agency (ACDA).

Personnel. I put my problem to Ross, told him I had to change and asked him to find me another job in State if possible. Meanwhile, my researches for RP had brought me into contact with Mr. E. A. Platt of the Special Division who seemed to like my work. I needled him into applying for my services.

Even then, however, I found that my transfer to SD would have to wait upon RP's finding a substitute for me—and that this might last forever. I spent two more horrible weeks—but then Sherman Kent offered me my old job back—Lon Frechtley got me an offer from BEW [the Board of Economic Warfare]—and, armed with these, I went to Ross and said I had to be transferred at once or I would accept one of the other jobs.

Since the African campaign was underway I was more than willing to go back to African work either in BEW or OSS. But Ross wangled my transfer—I spent a week putting my records in order (despite my boredom I had collected an impressive file)—and in mid-November I moved to a desk in the Winder Building, as a drafting officer in the Representation Section of the Special Division [of the State Department].[14]

The new job is satisfactory in every way. The work is concerned with problems rising out of the representation by the Swiss of American interests in occupied territories and the representation of German, Italian and Japanese interest in this country by the Swiss etc. There are always new and interesting problems and there are always lots of them. I'm kept busy all day and don't have time to think of myself or get bored. My immediate boss, James Henderson,[15] is a Foreign Service Officer and a good guy. As a matter of fact most of the officers in the Special Division are Foreign Service Officers and I'm getting the old urge to go into the service. It shouldn't be hard from this vantage point.

Much of my work is concerned with improper action by the enemy in answer to which I write spirited protests. My first was to the Italians because they had spirited away our Consul of Monaco. It was a pretty protest.

Despite the writings of my official life, my private one has been happy since May. Phyl as always is the perfect mate and Susan is trying to become the perfect daughter. I have, at Phyl's urging, done a lot of work around the

---

[14] The Representation Section of the Special Division was established in 1940 and concerned the representation of the interests of belligerent countries.

[15] James E. Henderson (1902–1987) served in U.S. consulates in Canada, Greece, Estonia, Mexico, the Philippines, and Italy over the course of a career in the Foreign Service that began in 1931 and continued into the 1960s.

house—putting up fences to keep out the neighbors—fixing up what we fondly call our rumple room in the cellar—etc. . . .

Monday, 28 December 1942. Washington.
Began work on a lengthy protest to the Germans, who, it appears, in occupying the embassy at Vichy before the Swiss could get there, lifted everything in sight—files, pouch seals, visa stamps, gasoline, cigarettes, a bottle of Vermouth, a case full of jewelry, etc. We're calling it outright "theft" and hoping the Legal Division will pass the wording.

After work trudged all the way in the rain to 8th and K Sts. to join the Public Library so that I could get a copy of *Finnegan's Wake*. My absorption in this after I got home quite disgusted Phyl who went to bed in a dudgeon.

Tuesday, 29 December 1942. Washington.
Finished the protest to Germany. Another on tap re the Monaco affair—the Italians claiming that they are holding our consul to safeguard the Italian members of the Armistice Commission who were captured in Africa.

More *Finnegan* which is very perplexing.

[1943]

Monday, 4 January 1943. Washington.
Slaved all day over a silly question of finding a source of funds to take care of some British seamen who were torpedoed off Martinique and are now interned there.

Henderson has drawn up a list of my duties which I am glad to see, even so generally, defined. They are: "Protests (American interests); United States policy on enemy alien property in the United States and the policy of enemy governments on American property in enemy territory; commendatory letters and instructions; relinquishment of representation of French interests; special problems arising in conjunction with financial assistance to American nationals in occupied China; relinquishment of representation of British interests in French African territories; funds of American official personnel in Thailand." . . .

Tuesday, 26 January 1943. Washington.
Tonight at ten the announcement that the President and Mr. Churchill have met at Casablanca. We had been trying to discover how to take square root for a friend of the Hulls. The announcement stopped all such shenanigans and left us all rather breathless and very exhilarated. Perhaps this will put an end to the bungling in Africa.

Tuesday, 2 February 1943. Washington.

The horrible French in Africa are putting all the Greek refugees from the Dodecanese into pokey because they are technically Italian subjects. We're trying to get them out. Wrote an instruction to Murphy[16] on subject. . . .

Wednesday, 3 February 1943. Washington.

A Hungarian in Casablanca has a device designed to allow airplanes to take off without a runway. Told him to send it on…

Joe Strayer[17] wants me to go back to Princeton as an assistant professor if Princeton gets a contract to give courses to Army men designed to go into re-conquered territory. Don't like to leave Department, but can't turn down such an offer at this stage in my life. It might be years before the chance of advancement comes again. Besides, Phyl is pretty fed up with Virginia and wants to go back. . . .

Thursday, 4 February 1943. Washington.

Wrote Strayer saying I was very interested in offer and would accept if possible to leave. Simultaneously War Manpower Commission begins to talk of freezing men in essential jobs. Would I be more essential here or there? Present job certainly doesn't require much deep thought. Ticklish getting out of it though. . . .

Saturday, 6 February 1943. Washington.

The Japs in their eastern Kiangsi [Jiangxi] campaign have, along with their usual looting and rapine, beheaded an Italian priest. Communicated details to Swiss and suggested they tell the Italian Foreign Office. An innocent gesture designed to further good will among our enemies. . . .

Monday, 8 February 1943. Washington.

[Assistant Secretary of State] Mr. [Breckinridge] Long called for a comprehensive report on situation in North Africa with respect to prisoners and internees still held by French. Worried by attacks on Department in *PM* and *Nation.*[18] Henderson and I worked steadily till 3:30 at which hour I had lunch. Got out a report which reflects a great lack of accurate information on number of former Spanish Republicans and Soviet nationals still interned. [Free French General Henri] Giraud has plenty,

---

[16] Robert Murphy (1894–1978) was an American diplomat in French North Africa during the Second World War.

[17] Joseph R. Strayer (1904–1987) was a prominent medieval historian at Princeton University and chairman of its Department of History from 1941 to 1961. Craig dedicated his masterwork, *Germany 1866–1945* (New York: Oxford University Press, 1978) to "J.R.S."

[18] *PM* was a New York-based daily newspaper of the 1940s.

however, and won't release them till arrangements have been completed to get them the hell out of Africa. The old boy doesn't appear to like the leaders of the masses—but then neither do most of the people in the Department. . . .

April 1943–August 1944

In March 1943 called back to Princeton to run history sections of Army Specialized Training Program. Regretted leaving, for promotion was going through, but offer of asst. professorship and veiled either/or made return unavoidable. On whole State Dept. experience tremendously valuable and included two personal triumphs: (1) the authorship of a telegram that made Ribbentrop angry . . . (2) the authorship of a note of protest to the Germans on deprivation of food ration tickets of Am. citizens of Jewish faith interned in Germany and the successful fight to get same note sent out. After being opposed by Long, [Assistant Secretary of State Adolf A.] Berle, and several others, it went out under [Undersecretary of State Sumner] Welles's signature and got results.

When I left the Dept., Joe Green had a letter inserted in my personnel record, praising my services and suggesting that I be re-employed by Dept. if ever an opportunity presented itself.

I taught in Princeton and was, quite frankly, the best lecturer and teacher the Army boys got. (Since the others were stuffed shirts . . . this does not mean much. But the boys—largely smart Jewish kids from N.Y.—liked me as much as I did them, which means something.)

My civilian teaching went well also. . . .

Best work of this period was in field of research:

(1) *Makers of Modern Strategy*, ed. by Edward M. Earle[19] with collaboration of G.A. Craig and Felix Gilbert.[20]

(2) *The Second Chance: America and the Peace* by John Whitton, Frank Graham, Corwin, Niemeyer, Brumer, Thomas, and myself.

(3) "The Technique of Peacemaking" read as a paper before the

---

[19] Edward Mead Earle (1894–1954) was a historian who specialized in the role of the military in foreign affairs and for twenty years a professor in the School of Economics and Politics at the Institute for Advanced Study in Princeton. During the Second World War, he worked with the OSS, helping to create its Department of Research and Analysis. Earle served as a mentor and friend during the first decade of Craig's career.

[20] Felix Gilbert (1905–1991), one of the great émigré historians who mentored generations of American scholars during the twentieth century, was a close friend and collaborator of Gordon Craig for nearly fifty years.

AHA in December 1943 and published in revised form in the *Yale Review*, Autumn 1944.

(4) Reviews in *N.Y. Herald Tribune*, *Social Research*, *Political Science Quarterly*.

(5) An article on the Belgian Railways Question, accepted by the *American Historical Review* for publication in 1945.

The most satisfying production of this period, however, was that of 8 January 1944—namely the birth of my second daughter DEBORAH GORDON CRAIG.

"Awake, awake, Deborah:
Awake, awake, utter a song."[21]

From May to August 1944 worked one day a week as instructor in psychological warfare for the Office of War Information. This necessitated my going to New York and giving a three-hour lecture on French politics since 1789 to men and women slated to go to France. Good fun.

17 August–8 November 1944.

—Despite the separation from my family which was necessitated by my receiving my commission as second lieutenant United States Marine Corps Reserve, the period opening on 17 August 1944 was one of the most satisfying of my life. The twelve weeks of scrambling through Virginia jungles showed me that I still had muscles and could use them; they brought me a lot of new and good friends; and they were crowded with a hilarious excitement that reminded me of Oxford. Food tasted better and liquor tasted better than they had for years and when I was able to get home I discovered my wife all over again and cursed myself for having neglected her so shamefully. Such things as the compass march, the night infiltration problem, my experiences with the LCVP and O'Neal on the use of shadows need only be mentioned to be remembered.[22]

At the end of 12 weeks I was second in my class, adjutant in the AGOS—Air-Ground Operations School Battalion Parade and commissioned captain as of 8 November. W. T. Deason was first in the class and Mac Taylor and a chap named Oliver third and fourth respectively. They also made captain. Trow Harper of the radio, should have but didn't.

---

[21] From Judges 5:12.

[22] The LCVP, or Landing Craft, Vehicle, Personnel was used for amphibious landings during World War II.

[In November 1977, Craig commented on this entry: "A pity that I didn't find more time to write something about life on the base, my trip to Northwestern University to learn something about the technique of public speaking, the curriculum of the school which I later used in part at Princeton and Stanford, and about the ways we tried to amuse ourselves in this odd in-between period of enforced frustration."]

8 November 1944–9 April 1945.
I was assigned to Marine Corps Schools as of 8 Nov. 1944 to help set up an Instructors Orientation course for all Marine Corps instructors. Original staff: Arthur Sherwood, Major, OIC, and expert on training aids; myself, psychology and public speaking; First Lt. Dave Bell, principles of instruction. The school was (and is) an excellent one, but I wanted to get out in field if possible and worked steadily for a release.

In March 1945, Sherwood was relieved and sent to Command and Staff. Major John Chaisson took over.[23]

In same month, Bell was relieved by 2nd Lt. Bill Mudler and went off to Camp Pendleton.

On 9 April, I was relieved by Capt. D. L. Faw and given leave until 25 April when I am to report at Quonset Point, R.I. for intelligence training. Col. M. B. Twining tells me that I can come back to MCS whenever I want to, either during or after the war.

So home to my family.

[1945]

Monday, 12 April 1945. Princeton.
Home and very happy until Beatrice Earle called at about 5:30 to say that President Roosevelt was dead. A dreadful tragedy and perhaps one which will gum up the works at San Francisco.

Ever since I went to college FDR has been president—always the chief—and I think he always will be for me.

Tonight looked over the collected poetry of W. H. Auden and found his lines on the death of W. B. Yeats, which seem applicable to our present loss:

"... in the importance and noise of tomorrow

---

[23] John R. Chaisson (1916–1972) served with the Marines in World War II, Korea, and Vietnam and rose through the ranks to hold the second-ranking post in the Marine Corps before his death.

When the brokers are roaring like beasts on the floor of the Bourse,
And the poor have the sufferings to which they are fairly accustomed,
And each in the cell of himself is almost convinced of his freedom;
A few thousand will think of this day
As one thinks of a day when one did something slightly unusual"

Auden also says that,

"the words of a dead man
Are modified in the guts of the living."[24]

How modified here?...

Sunday, 29 April 1945. Quonset, RI.
The Naval Air Combat Intelligence School is now in full swing and I am trying hard to keep up with the mass of facts and theory thrown at its students. Recognition of aircraft and shipping will be my big chore, and I have been trying hard to hammer silhouettes of P47's, SB2Cs, and the like into my noggin. In addition, aerial photography, intelligence procedure, communications, and navigation will demand lots of attention...

Two drawbacks to our situation here—the difficulty of getting to work without a car and the difficulty of getting any work done at home, with our neighbors, the Widhelms, holding a continual party...

Germany is close to collapse. Hitler is according to rumor, dying, and the land is being cut to ribbons. A report, now verified, tells us that Mussolini was shot by Milanese patriots yesterday and that his body is dangling in a public square...

Read Conrad's *The Secret Agent.* Excellent!

Tuesday, May Day, 1945. Quonset, RI.
Hitler reported dead.

Wednesday, 2 May 1945. Quonset, RI.
Russians have taken Berlin, and report Hitler and Goebbels suicides. The German forces in Italy have surrendered. Rundstedt is captured; Laval has fled to Spain... Nothing clear from San Francisco...

I'm hard at work on tactics (at present, the part played by the supercharger in planes). Swimming and volleyball in the afternoons.

Saturday, 5 May 1945. Quonset, RI.
The war in Europe just about over. Hitler's armies falling to pieces, and few

---

[24] See W. H. Auden, "In Memory of W. B. Yeats," *Selected Poems* (New York: Vintage Books, 2007), 88–90.

centers of resistance left. The fighting near Munich, where Joe is, is over; I hope he's safe.

A remarkable and important interview with von Rundstedt appeared in the papers today. I include it as a source of future reference...[25]

Took Phyl and thc kids to see the base today...

Monday, 7 May 1945. Quonset, RI.
The Germans are reported to have surrendered but the VE proclamation has gotten all fouled up and is not yet official. This does not prevent the radio from putting on the damnedest amount of nonsense I've heard in a long time. If I hear the Gettysburg Speech quoted again I shall be ill...

A letter to Chaisson and some work on Intelligence Procedure...

Tuesday, 8 May 1945. Quonset, RI.
V-E Day.

Thursday, 31 May 1945. Quonset, RI.
It's been a hard week. We've had exams in Tactics and Navigation and today, Dick Barr, Cliff Beck, Bob Akin, and I briefed a squadron for a simulated strike in Fusan, Korea. We had spent two full nights on our blow ups of the target area, and they were beautiful. Briefing went very well. So for that matter, did the exams.

Wednesday, 6 June 1945. Quonset, RI.
A letter from Ed Earle saying that the OSS has definitely requested my services for a six-month job in Germany. He is vague about the job, although there seems to be some connection with the Control Council. Ed says "I am going to get busy on this and see whether I cannot get Mr. Forrestal's office to give it a shove." The joke is that Ed will do just that... I can't become very enthusiastic about a job about which I know nothing. I still want to be an intelligence officer. But we'll see...

Thursday, 7 June 1945. Quonset, RI.
The Russians seem to be objecting to almost everything—the veto formula, the German control arrangements, and God knows what else. The diplomatic picture is a very pretty mess. . . .

Friday, 8 June 1945. Quonset, RI.
The Russians have accepted the veto formula and given up their insistence on the right to veto discussion. Why they have done so remains to be seen.

---

[25] See "Rundstedt calls Allies too Strong," *New York Times* (5 May 1945), 5.

Harry Hopkins, I dare say, deserves considerable credit.[26] But perhaps it is all a calculated maneuver on the part of the Russians. By blowing hot and cold alternately, they have gradually won complete control over the San Francisco deliberations. On the specific question at issue, as James Reston remarks in the *Times* today, the Russians, by their tactics, have "produced the votes, if not the whole-hearted support, of the small powers for a Big Five veto over virtually every decision in the Security Council."

Having given way here, it is to be expected that Russia will now seek further concessions on other questions—if not at San Francisco then in the control question in Germany. That both Britain and ourselves understand Russia's game is apparent, but there seems to be little we can do about it.

It is, of course, possible that Russia is genuinely wavering between isolationism and whole-hearted world cooperation. [British Secretary of State for Foreign Affairs] Mr. [Anthony] Eden's *Yorkshire Post* is concerned with the possibility of a Russian return to complete isolation with disastrous results.

It seems more likely that Russia is playing both strings at once. She wants an international organization that means something. By being apparently the most reluctant party in the granting of power to that body, she makes *us* more eager to have a really strong international body. At the same time, she strengthens her position in her own zone against the chance of failure.

So far she has played a diplomatic game which is a masterpiece, compared with the fumbling and inconsistent policy followed by us. (The Argentina affair was a horrible mistake!)[27] The dangers of her policy, in view of American public opinion, are obvious…

An exam today on the capabilities of the Jap air force. Did better than I expected…

Monday, 18 June 1945. Quonset, RI.

Letter from Porter King at HQ today. He says that my wish to go to the West Coast will probably be granted. "Orders have been requested," he says, "for you and Lt. Shartel to report to CG, MarFairWest [Marine Fleet Air, West Coast] for sea duty with Air, FMF Pac [Air Fleet Marine Forces,

---

[26] Harry Hopkins (1890–1946) served as a kind of unofficial Chief of Staff and liaison between the American government and its wartime Allies.

[27] The Soviet Union and the United States disagreed about granting Argentina membership in the United Nations because of its apparent sympathies with the Axis countries. The U.S. government remained suspicious of Argentina throughout 1945, even though it finally joined the war against Japan and Germany in March 1945.

Pacific] upon completion of your temporary duty at Quonset." If all goes well, then, I shall be on the coast within the month. . . .

Later: The San Francisco conference will close successfully this week unless the new point used by the Russians causes delay. Russia wishes the conference to reconsider the clause granting broad powers to the General Assembly of the new League.

It is not clear what the Russians are driving at here. But the request has brought a fiery protest from the Australian Foreign Minister, H. V. Evatt,[28] who points out that other clauses in the charter provide for protection against intervention by one state in the internal affairs of another. Evatt says, with a certain amount of justice that "the will of the majority clearly expressed in committees was once again being challenged by one power, with the threat that if the majority did not bow there would be no charter."

More and more as the conference proceeds, Evatt emerges as one of the outstanding delegates; and his role has been that of spokesman for the small powers. A decided improvement over Hughes, the Australian delegate in Paris after the last war. I should like to know more about him, for he'll play a big part in my book on peace conference techniques—when and if written...

Tuesday, 19 June 1945. Quonset, RI.

My orders came in, confirming Porter King's letter. My one hope now is that the OSS deal won't foul them up in some way... Since I may very well be on a CVE in a very short time I have started earnestly to work on my next briefing—a Corsair sweep against Kanoya. . . .

The Russians have announced that the captured Poles have confessed to a kind of E. Phillips Oppenheim plot against the Soviets.[29] That E. Phillips Oppenheim plots have been distressingly real for the last ten years, however, is only too true. The London Poles are a bad lot—and, worse, a stupid lot. The Russian story is by no means beyond credence. . . .

Wednesday, 20 June 1945. Quonset, RI.

Led by [Mexican delegate Luis] Quintanella, the Conference has refused [Francisco] Franco's Spain membership in the new League. It would be

---

[28] H. V. Evatt (1894–1965), an Australian politician and judge, served as President of the United Nations General Assembly from 1948 to 1949, and helped to draft the Universal Declaration of Human Rights.

[29] E. Phillips Oppenheim (1866–1946) was a British writer of pulp novels about international intrigues.

wonderful to be able to believe that they will go further and turf him the hell out of Spain…

Friday, 22 June 1945. Quonset, RI.
Last night I stayed in barracks to finish up a blow-up which I am going to use for my strike against Kanoya. Quite a decent job, the blowup—a chart showing flak positions at Kanoya, Kanoya East and Kushira, all targets being hit weekly by our carrier forces at the present time…

Phyl phoned me in the late afternoon to read a letter from F. Cyril James, Principal of McGill University. The Principal said that they are trying to fill the chair of Modern European History, left vacant since the retirement of Professor Fryer. They want a man "whose teaching and research ability would enable him to make a major contribution" to their future work in the fields of the Humanities and the Social Sciences. Wallace Notestein had suggested my name, and the Principal wanted to know whether I would be willing to be considered a candidate.

Nothing I can do about this, of course; but the letter pleased me. I'll get other offers as good—*après la guerre finie*…

The news is very good throughout the war. Organized resistance on Okinawa ended yesterday. Our losses have been very high, but the value of the island has already been shown. Since early May, planes from Fleet Air Wing One have been using Okinawa as a home base for strikes against Kyushu and the Korean Straits; and there will be more and more flights from Okinawa in the next weeks… The general public does not yet understand the difficulties of the Pacific War or the strength of the Japanese resistance. I think it indicative of civilian lack of knowledge that [columnist] David Lawrence should be able to call the Okinawa campaign "a worse example of military incompetence than Pearl Harbor." Lawrence is steamed up because losses were so high as a result of the direct attacks pushed by [General Simon] Buckner. The alternative to Buckner's plan was to make new landings in the Japanese rear with marines of the Third Amphib Corps. As George Fielding Elliot says today, the relative advantages of the two plans could—and probably will—be debated for years.[30] But aside from the strategical debate, the point that is important to me is that Lawrence and others seem to find high losses in the Pacific disgraceful. The same howl

[30] For an overview of the controversy surrounding the Battle of Okinawa in the American press in June 1945, see Nicholas Evan Sarantakes, "Warriors of Word and Sword: The Battle of Okinawa, Media Coverage, and Truman's Reevaluation of Strategy in the Pacific," *Journal of American-East Asian Relations*, 23:4 (2016): 334–67.

went up after Tarawa and Iwo—the same charges of military incompetence. In Princeton I found them echoed even by such an eminently reasonable man as Dave Bowers. If the alternate strategy had been employed at Okinawa, there would also have been high losses—and complaints by the armchair strategists. It is good to see that both the *Times* and the *Herald Tribune* are making every effort to convince the public that the war is not yet over, and that there's lots of tough stuff ahead...[31]

Meanwhile, at San Francisco, the Russians have agreed to a compromise on the right of the General Assembly to discuss any question within the scope of the charter. This assures the success of the conference and is very good news indeed.

Reston outlined the history of the last dispute in yesterday's *Times*. . . . Evatt appears to have been the key figure in the negotiations. The man is as hot as a two dollar pistol. . . .

Bert Andrews in the *Herald Tribune* today says that frequent talk of a dangerous crisis or "blowup" at San Francisco was far more than real newspaper talk, and that most observers agree that it was real but that the Russians and Americans have learned to understand and appreciate each other's point of view at the conference and that this augurs well. He says also that members of the American delegation believe that [Secretary of State Edward] Stettinius deserves praise for standing firm on the three issues contested by Russia and the U.S., namely: the problem of working the inter-American security system into the world security organization, the right of discussion in the security council, and the right of discussion in the general assembly. Until more proof is brought forward, I shall continue to

---

[31] Craig added a "Note on the Okinawa Campaign" to his diary on August 27, 1945: "History will probably support Lawrence's view of the campaign. According to people at Ewa, Buckner's idea was to sit tight and blast at the Japs with artillery, and he did this while the Marines mopped up the north and the neighboring islands. Eventually Buckner began to run out of artillery, and he sent a request to General [Roy] Geiger for Marine artillery. Geiger said he would be glad to supply it if he could also bring his infantry south also, and pointed out that the campaign was behind schedule. Buckner refused these terms but repeated his request for artillery. Geiger stuck fast, saying that, if the guns were sent, he was going to bring all his boys along. Buckner finally appealed to Nimitz who upheld Geiger, and so the Marines came south and the drive really got underway. Relations between the Army and the Corps were bad from highest to lowest echelons, and it is said that there was fist-fighting between units relieving each other at the fronts. As Marines came out of the lines they would shout: 'Naha by Sunday, you yellow bastards!' Not the sort of thing that will get into the history books, I'm afraid." Gordon A. Craig, "Tagebuch Vol. V: Journal 1941–1945," 180.

believe that we handled the first of these badly…

Saturday, 22 June 1945. Quonset, RI.
The news continues good. Moscow has announced that a new Polish Government has been formed—one which should please everyone but the London Poles. If this works out, Hopkins certainly deserves great credit. He must have talked long and fast to Stalin during his recent visit.

On the home front, the Republicans, advised by that intellectual corpse Hoover, have almost upset the apple-cart by cutting the power of the Office of Price Administration. It looks, however, as if the Democratic majority has things under control again. . . .

Monday, 24 June 1945. Quonset, RI.
. . . Last night I spent making another blowup for my Kanoya briefing. The briefing itself was today and was pronounced one of the very best of the current school… The school is just about over now, and a couple of nights catching up on navigation, recognition, anti-sub warfare, and foreign air forces should see me through. Already I'm beginning to think of the imminent parting from my family. It won't be pleasant…

Sunday, 30 June 1945. Quonset, RI.
It looks as if the charter will get a very good reception in the Senate. No one quite dares come out against it, and even [Wisconsin Progressive Party Senator Robert] La Follette [Jr.] has announced his support. [Ohio Republican] Senator [Robert A.] Taft, however, has announced that the powers of the U.S. delegate to the new League must be more clearly defined, and this angle will have to be watched. . . .

[In July 1945, Craig traveled by train to San Diego, California, where he reported for duty at Marine Corps Air Depot Miramar. He spent some weeks waiting to be shipped out to Pearl Harbor.]

Wednesday, 1 August 1945. San Diego.
The Big Three meeting at Potsdam ended today and we can now expect the final communiqué. I dreamed last night of Stalin. Characteristically, I was lecturing him on something or other. He was a good listener. . . . The Pétain trial becomes more exciting daily.[32] [Maxime] Weygand's testimony was

---

[32] Marshal Philippe Pétain (1856–1951) was put on trial for treason after leading the collaborationist government of Vichy France during the war years. Charles de Gaulle, who was President of the Provisional Government of the French Republic at the end of the war, commuted his death sentence to life imprisonment due to Pétain's age and his military contributions during the First World War.

given ably—in fact, the general seems to have stolen the show. Now [Pierre] Laval has been captured and [William D.] Leahy has sent a letter praising Petain's patriotism. I have a feeling he is going to beat the rap. . . .

Saturday, 4 August 1945. San Diego.
Alerted today. [John] Shartel and I are shoving off on Monday. . . .

Tuesday, 7 August 1945. At sea.
Up early, had chow, and went topside to see our departure from the States. Recovered some of the thrill of my first ocean trip in 1935—a feeling which kept recurring throughout the day. The absence of deck chairs, women, and—most of all—a bar, however, keeps this within limits... Spent most of the day in the wardroom, drinking coffee and reading Charles Grayson's *Stories for Men*, which Walt Rostow took to England in 1936... The pilots, all considerably younger than Shartel and I, have broken out the cards and are playing poker. We limit ourselves to a little cribbage, at a cent a point...

The big news of the day is the dropping of the first "super-atomic bomb" on Hiroshima. If the reports on its effects are true, it is a terrible weapon and I sincerely wish it had never been discovered. It is worse than gas, and no one can foresee the uses to which it will yet be put. We are tempting providence.

Wednesday, 8 August 1945. At sea.
Russia has declared war on Japan! The Japanese ambassador was told that his country alone was preventing the return of world peace and that, in consequence, Russia must take up arms against her. And so all the wailing of the Hearst press about Truman's failure at Potsdam has proven without foundation. There seems to be a considerable strength to the bond between the United Nations, and I don't think Japan will be able to hold out for very long now. It would be interesting to know where China fits into the new set up and what Russia will ask in the Far East when the war is done. Had a long talk with my bunkmates about American-Russian relations and discovered the usual fear of Russia and the usual irrational arguments about democracy and communism and what might happen 50 years from now. . . .

Thursday, 9 August 1945. At sea.
. . . Listened to the President's speech on Potsdam and found it a very good review. On the atomic bomb, he is less satisfying—a lot about our terrible responsibility and the like. We apparently are going to go on dropping it.

Saturday, 11 August 1945. At sea.

Yesterday morning at 0600 the announcement that the Japs had surrendered, and a certain amount of mild excitement. As the day wore on, it became apparent that the Japs had merely sent a note laying down conditions which would govern their surrender and that this would have to be considered by the Four Powers. Nevertheless, the excitement continued. The wags put up notices offering their uniforms for sale; the drinking brethren, like myself, regretted that the war should come to an end with bars so remote and celebrations so impossible; and all of us began to think intensely of home and to wonder when we would get out of the service. In my own case, the news of the imminent collapse of Japan brought an unreasonable depression of spirits, perhaps because it made my present journey rather pointless. In this, I was at one with the cards who went about chanting "Is this trip necessary?"...

This morning came the news of our answer to the Japanese note, again magnified by the ship scuttlebutt so that it appeared like the end. The negotiations will, however, go on for a few days yet and then the armistice will be set. . . .

Tuesday, 14 August 1945. MCAS Ewa.

We docked yesterday afternoon [in Oahu] and, after an orderly disembarkation, were carted off to Marine Corps Air Station Ewa and set down in a rather messy TOQ [Transient Officers' Quarters]. . . .

Up early feeling rather good. . . . Checked in and was assigned with Shartel, to duty with HQ Squadron, Aircraft Fleet Marine Force, Pacific—which means that no one knows what to do with us at the moment. The best part of the deal is that we are shifted to the BOQ [Bachelor Officer Quarters]—very good quarters and very close to the center of the base... Went to the TOQ and shifted our gear; and, just as we moved into our new quarters, the word came that the Jap note had been received and the war was over. It was 1335 local time. All hell broke loose. . . .

Saturday, 18 August 1945. MCAS Ewa.

Major McFarlane told me today that General Moore has authorized my going to Bougainville, to write a report on the last phase of Marine operations in the Solomons. After talking with him and Col. Robertshaw, it seems to me that no one knows exactly what I am supposed to do when I get there. Somewhat vaguely they talk of my reporting on the transfer of command to the Aussies or NZAF, of my going into Jap held territory and finding what damage we did in our bombing and night hecklings and the like. This looseness of assignment has some good features but it has a great many disadvantages. I am supposed to be attached to MAG 25, and I know dam' well that they'll try to make me a mess officer or something and that I'll probably have to fight them and the Australian and New Zealand Governments to get into places like Buin, Emirau, Kavieng, and the Shortlands. Perhaps it's all a pipe dream. We'll see…

Monday, 20 August 1945. Ewa.
Informed today that the Bougainville deal is off. I guess someone with brains took a couple of peeks at it and decided that it would accomplish nothing.

Tuesday, 21 August 1945. Ewa.
The word is now that I'll replace McFarlane here as Asst. Chief of Staff G-2. It would be a dullish job, devoted mostly to folding up the work of this unit; but at least it would be work. At the moment I am working on odd award cases, which are interesting to a point. . . .

Tuesday, 18 September 1945. Ewa.
With [R. H.] Griffin to see General [Lewie G.] Merritt[33]—the eyes and almost the profile of the young Wellington—a man who looks as if he means business. He gave us the word. We are connected with the U.S. Strategic Bombing Survey—i.e., "a group of highly qualified specialists selected and appointed by its chairman under authority of the President of the United States to conduct an impartial and expert study of the effects of our aerial attack on Japan… The great importance of this undertaking to national postwar security imposes grave responsibility upon those engaged in this fact finding study."

Our job is to go to Kwajalein, set up an HQ and then make a survey on Wake. Then we come back to Kwajalein and move by Auxiliary Personnel Destroyer to Majuro, from which point we make trips to Wotje, Mili, etc. The more the general talked, the better I liked it.

My job, apparently, is to put the report in its final form, since—as the general pointed out—I had had some experience in doing that sort of thing. Griff is to help me. He and I will probably take off in two days. . . .

Friday, 28 September 1945. Wake.
Picked up Wake by radar at 6:45; visual contact an hour later; hove to in anchorage about 9. With sublime indifference to the historic scene, all

---

[33] Lewie Griffith Merritt (1897–1974) was an aviator who served with the Marines for thirty years and saw action in both World Wars, reaching the rank of Major General.

hands immediately began to fish over the side, catching dozens of small flounders… At about 12:30, the General's plane arrived, carrying him, Lt. Col. [L. B.] Robertshaw, four majors, a captain, and two lieutenants from Washington. We joined them at 1, lunching and going to the Marine camp, pitched at the end of the strip on the main island. Here we met our confreres and there ensued a confused reorganization meeting during which everyone was assigned to a division or section, except Griff and I, as we are "Compilation Officers."

As soon as the organization was complete, everyone took off like a ruptured duck, capturing Jap officers as they went. Griff and I stayed behind and horned in on a conversation between our doctor and the ranking Jap medical officer—a cheery little chap in white shirt and shorts, gay knee socks and white shoes. He answered all questions eagerly, slapping our interpreter gaily on the shoulder at intervals. According to him the Japs first felt the pinch as far as food was concerned in April 1944. All men were encouraged to plant gardens of their own and a central garden of 30 m. square was planted. Subs brought food, mail, and medical supplies occasionally—never oftener than once a month. Total casualties from malnutrition were 1500, but there were only two psycho cases and 5–6 suicides. The last sub arrived 18 April 1945.

The Japs on Wake today seem pretty well fed and wander about doing various jobs. One pathetic sight I saw as we shoved off at 5 for the ship—a Jap colonel and two enlisted men were in a battered little launch trying to maintain their dignity as they puttered through the basin…

We returned to the ship, where a Marx Bros. scene ensued as the new hands fought for bunk space. We're overcrowded in the *Rednour* now. I've written this in the middle of a muddled briefing by Friedberg on "How I Bombed Wake."… It's very hot…

Saturday, 29 September 1945. Wake.

Ashore at 8. Preliminary brush with Col. [Marion L.] Dawson and the General on writing of the introduction to the report. They seem to think we can start from scratch and dream up something from thin air… So with Major [C. L. T.] Gabler to set up an intelligence center in the basement of the operations tower; and later, to sit in on an interview of the Jap engineer, who spoke of difficulties of maintenance, and of food shortages, and of morale… So with Griff to look over the records of the War Crimes Investigation here, regarding the deaths of 100 civilians during the raid of 6–7 October 1943. Very interesting reading, but not for our purpose. The Japs claim that 50 were killed when a shelter suffered a direct hit. The others overpowered their guards, seized arms, and were killed in the ensuing fire fight.

In the afternoon a tour of Wake and Peele Islands with Gabler, [First Lieutenant M. M.] Sutherland, Griffin, the Jap engineer, an interpreter, and three enlisted men—all in one jeep. The Jap underground machine shops were very interesting and the admiral [Shigematsu Sakaibara]'s OP [Observation Post] even more so. After visiting the latter, we were invited to visit the admiral in his quarters and had some sake with him—he very cheerful and full of grin. Reminded me of the general [Samuel] Pepys saw drawn and quartered "and he as cheerful as could be in the circumstances." The admiral may well be shot yet for the Oct '43 affair, so the comparison is not too far fetched. On leaving he gave our interpreter 11 green tomatoes from his private garden… So to Peele Island and found it a honeycomb of dugouts—mighty glad we didn't have to fight over it. . . .

Sunday, 30 September 1945. Wake.

Spent the day on Wake and very hot too, by all odds the hottest place I've ever been. Perhaps it's the combination of sun and coral, but whatever it is we're all blistered and red, and even at night we burn… Wrote a draft introduction in the morning and, this afternoon, took another ride on the jeep, this time to inspect the defenses on the west shore of Wake proper. Very complete…

In an interview today, the Jap admiral attributed 90% of his difficulties to blockade and only 10% to aerial bombardment…

Some Emerson and bed…

Monday, 1 October 1945. Wake.

A grey rainy day. The General left the ship at 7 to fly back to Ewa. The eager fact-finders left for shore at 8, to pursue their researches. Griff and I stayed aboard and have had a pleasant day of it. This morning we re-wrote our introduction. Since then we have been reading and resting…

It has been a good day to observe the normal life of the ship, for it never is normal when all the passengers are here. We had lunch today with the ship's officers and listened to their prattle. It is the first of the month and they all have chores and cares. The captain (a navy lt. of about 35 years, probably the oldest officer) and the exec are worried by the slow settling of the ship, and think they may have to seal off another compartment if they are to get us to Majuro and themselves to dry-dock at Eniwetok. The doctor is concerned about a growing shortage of food. (All officers complained bitterly of short rations at lunch, although we had soup, welsh rarebit, iced tea, and ice cream with chocolate sauce—a heavy enough lunch, I should think.) All hands are worried about inventories—a monthly worry—and about points and getting home. Here the mess men—three Negroes—occasionally interjected themselves into the conversation. Since the *Rednour* is now the personal ship of Admiral Harrill, Commander of the Marshalls and Gilberts Stations, getting home may be delayed for them for some time.

Meanwhile on deck, the men fish over the sides. Yesterday two five-foot beauties of the mackerel family were brought aboard; and now everyone wants to fish, and everyone has his own ideas about tackle. We are flanked today on the starboard by a Destroyer Escort (which according to rumor, is going to be decommissioned and is consequently the object of envy on board the *Rednour*) and, on the port, by a Geodetic Survey ship which arrived this morning. A bit further out is an Attack Cargo Ship, which arrived during the night; and that is all the shipping at Wake, except for a couple of Medium Landing Ships and the bombed and beached Fox Tare Freighter Transport and the Jap Destroyers, which rust on the coral…

For the first time in my life, I am reading Emerson with enthusiasm, finding in him much that I have believed myself and much of the spiritual and intellectual arrogance that I believe a man must maintain in this world. I wish Dave Bowers were alive. I feel guilty for not having buckled down to Emerson before, as he advised, and I should like to tell him so. Also, it strikes me that I have no one now to whom I can convey my enthusiasms in reading. Dave's greatest gift was his possession of an eagerness and fire which matched my own, no matter what the subject on hand…

Thursday, 11 October 1945. Majuro.

A dispatch this morning has ordered us to survey Rabaul when we are finished with the Marshalls. Merritt will fly to Tokyo at the end of October and, when he returns, we will shove off for Rabaul by Auxiliary Personnel Destroyer. This means that we will not get back to Ewa before 1 December and the Lord only knows when we'll get home. Everybody pissed off…

Tuesday, 23 October 1945. Majuro.

Up betimes and off to Taroa Island, Maloelap, by Martin PBM Mariner.[34] Found it very hacked up by bombs, although—according to the boys—not so badly as Mili or Wotje. After a brief tour, I sat around and listened to the interrogations. In the afternoon I listened to Ed Williams carrying on with the Jap junior officers and getting them to teach him to tell time and count in Japanese. In return he told them that [Warrant Officer Harry C.] Short

---

[34] The Martin PBM Mariner was a patrol bomber seaplane.

had six children and that I taught in a university of the stature of Purdue and Rutgers. According to him, they consider the worst threat to world peace "history professors. Zey fuck up works…" Home by six and, in the evening, a long disquisition to Sheeks and Williams on Tudor and Stuart history…

Monday, 29 October 1945. Majuro.
25 pages of the Lower Marshalls report finished… Started participating in a moustache-growing contest…Wrote Strayer, intimating that he might give another push about December… In the evening gave the boys the GA Craig Memorial Literary Quiz. No one passed…

Saturday, 3 November 1945. Los Negros.
Left Majuro yesterday at nine in three planes. Reached Kwajalein for refueling at 11. Our Commando had a leaky fuel tank which was not repaired till 4 in the afternoon. Shoved off then. Very cold trip and bucket seats most uncomfortable. Magnificent cloud formations at sunset. Reached Los Negros at 12:30 Majuro time, 10:30 Admiralties time. Reflecting that I had now crossed the equator, shaved around my incipient moustache, showered and hit the sack…

Up this morning to a very good breakfast and a conference with the general before he left for Rabaul. The Wake report, with only minor corrections, has been approved by the Big Wheel in Tokyo…

Monday, 5 November 1945. Los Negros.
We've had our typists going day and night to get a fresh copy of the Wake report for the Admiral in Tokyo. Last night we wrote a new conclusion—the fourth—and this morning the general rejected it and accepted our first. He also approved our section in the Marshalls report on Japanese strategic plans. (Sample comment. M.: "People, where did you find this material?" G.: "Uh-ah-well, sir, we just talked it over and decided that was the Jap plan." M.: "Well, you're exactly right. I found out in Tokyo—") . . .

Wednesday, 14 November 1945. Rabaul.
Today we drew samurai swords—by rank. Mine not bad… Got an October 22 copy of *Time*, my first contact with the outside world in weeks. The outside world seems to be a rather dreadful place. The Truman Administration seems to be coming apart at the seams. I'll admit that trying to handle the labor mess is a ticklish business, but there is no reason for the lack of leadership in domestic affairs generally. And FDR never would have allowed the London Conference to fail. In any event, conferences never fail except because of inadequate preliminary work. [Secretary of State James

F.] Byrnes and his boys seem to have done little preparation, and apparently there were no exploratory talks… Meanwhile, the atomic bomb has gotten to the stage that it is everyone's plaything and pet argument; but no clear line is being taken as to its disposition and control. The loss of FDR was a grave blow to the nation. That becomes clearer every day. And what if we lose the peace this time? Are we a nation capable only of fiddling with gadgets and incapable of applying our brains to human problems?

Time reports that Christian Gauss has retired and that Frisco Godolphin is the new Dean of the College of Princeton University…

Saturday, 17 November 1945. Rabaul.
Our last day at Rabaul. A good day of work—25 pages of the Marshalls report done, bringing the total past the hundred mark… A movie on the fantail in the evening with Greer Garson, a lovely woman…

[Over the following days, Craig travelled back to Hawaii and completed his report.]

Saturday, 24 November 1945. Hawaii.
Gave the general the first draft of the Marshalls report—178 pages. So he left for Washington in a good humor this afternoon and we expect to follow in a few days.

Some desultory work today but a good evening in Ed's room, where Science and Religion fought until the neighbors complained.

Tuesday, 27 November 1945. Hawaii.
. . . Having finished another year of my life yesterday, I should, I dare say, have waxed reflective last night. I was, at that time, too full of steak. I am tonight not in the mood. I have, however, had 32 very full years of life. Since the days when I wrote

"Gordy Craig is 24
I don't want to grow no more"

I have been blessed with much good fortune and have been enabled to accomplish a great deal. I have a beautiful wife, two lovely children, a third child on the way, a good reputation at my university, in the State Department and in the Marine Corps, a fair reputation in my field, some publications to my credit and a lot of fine friends and good memories. I am, for these blessings, very thankful. . . .

Later: The reflective note creeps in. What I should have written last night is that a happy 32 years have taught me that all young men, and especially young men of my calling, should ponder seriously Ulysses's great speech to his men.

non vogliate negar l'esperienza
di retro al sol, del mondo sanza gente.
Considerate la vostra semenza:
fatti non foste a viver come bruti,
ma per seguir virtute e canoscenza'

[Do not be willing to forgo the experience
Of the uninhabited world, as we follow the sun.
Reflect on your ancestry:
you were not born to live like brute animals
but to pursue moral perfection and knowledge.][35]

Wednesday, 28 November 1945. Hawaii.
Everyone in a big stew. There is a good chance that we shall leave Honolulu at 3 a.m. tomorrow morning. We are fussing around getting our transfer pay accounts and our orders and are busy packing all the gear. I'll be glad to get home as soon as possible. Phyl's Thanksgiving letter said she was feeling ill and was afraid the baby was going to jump the gun. I want to be able to call her from the coast within the next few days. I wish she wouldn't cram so much activity into her days, but that is the way she is and—all things considered—I wouldn't want her to change in any respect. . . .

The journal will be discontinued here and mailed to Princeton this afternoon. As in the case of the jottings on the survey, I shall keep the interim record and paste it in later...

28–30 November 1945.
Big rush Wednesday getting orders etc. All squared away by mid-afternoon. Sent my diaries and money orders for $150 to Phyl and proceeded to get fried in club with Griff. Packing, after that, somewhat difficult, especially since I inadvertently packed my wallet in the bottom of my kit and had to repack while the car waited. Arrived Naval Air Station Honolulu, however, safe and sound at 11 and, after fond farewells to [Major Robert "Bob"] Hatton, [Major W. H.] Powell, [Major W. B.] Hagenah and Robertshaw, shoved off in a C-54 at 12:15 a.m.

Arrived Oakland 1400 Calif. Time and through some inspired finagling by Gabler caught a plane at 1600.

---

[35] From Canto 26 of Dante Alighieri's *Inferno*. Dante, *The Divine Comedy: Selected Cantos: A Dual-Language Book*, translated and edited by Stanley Appelbaum (Mineola, New York: Dover Publications, 2000), 82–83.

Arrived Olathe, Kansas at 2400 and at 8:30, 30 Nov. came in at National Airport, Washington—down through the overcast to a very gray but good town.

Checked in at Headquarters. Rushed off to buy a pair of green pants. Grabbed 2 o'clock train and at 6:30 was with my wife and kids again. Happy day!

[In the following weeks, Craig busied himself by spending time with his family, working further on the Marshalls report, and socializing with various friends.]

Thursday, 20 December 1945.
With every trip to Princeton I become increasingly desirous of getting back to civilian life. It's not that the Marine Corps has not been a fine experience for me, but there is a *fin de siècle* feeling about it now. It is gratifying to know that I could stay in the Corps if I wanted to. About ten days ago a Col. Snedecker at MarCorps propositioned me. On Col. Twining's suggestion, he wanted me to sit down and write my projected history of amphibious operations. This, he felt, could be used as ammunition to oppose the unification of the services. Thereafter, with a spot promotion, I would move into the Historical Section. Phyl was temporarily attracted by this proposition, but not very seriously; and I would not consider giving up history for a lifetime in the Corps.

All I want now is to get back to teaching—and to my wife and kids—the third of whom will be arriving momentarily. . . .

Wednesday, 26 December 1945.
. . . In today's *New York Times*, I found the following item:

> "Eleven Japanese Sentenced to Hang
>
> Commander at Wake Is Found Guilty— He Urges Trial of Americans for Atom Bomb.
> Kwajalein, Dec. 25 (U.P)— The former Japanese commander of Wake Island, his executive officer and nine other Japanese were sentenced to death by a naval court today for the mass execution of ninety-six Pan American Airways civilian employees in 1943. . . ."[36]

No comment necessary; except that Bob Hatton and the others who had such a high regard for the Admiral, must feel a little abashed. I drank

[36] See "Eleven Japanese Sentenced to Hang," *New York Times* (December 26, 1945), 4.

his whiskey, but reserved judgment and certainly did not go in for back-slapping like Thorlaksson.[37]

The news from Moscow sounds pretty good, especially with regard to the question of peace treaties. . . .

Friday, 28 December 1945.
A letter from Ed Earle, enclosing an earlier clipping on [Admiral] Sakaibara.[38]

The final *communiqué* on the Moscow Conference has just been issued and I am enclosing it here mainly because I shall want to refer to it sometime and this is one place where I'll be able to find it. Besides this has been an important conference and it is well worth holding on to the record. Now, as [Walter] Lippmann says, if we can only find the right men to do all the work forecast in this statement, we may get somewhere, solve some of our problems, and patch up the world. (The *communiqué* does not mention Iran, or Russia's claims on Turkey, or Palestine where riots broke out yesterday; but surely they too are questions not incapable of solution.)

Saturday, 29 December 1945.
Called home last night at 8 and found Phyl had just gone to hospital. Rushed into town and caught the 9 o'clock train. Had to take a taxi from Trenton to Princeton and arrived home at about 1:30. By then it was all over. Phyl had been delivered of a girl—MARTHA JANE CRAIG—at about fifteen minutes after midnight, weight 8 lbs. 2 oz.
At ten this morning went to the hospital and saw Phyl, who looks very well, and my new daughter, who looks the spitting image of Susan at her age. Very happy.

Leaving my mother with the kids, went this evening to the Palmers to see Felix Gilbert who is just back from Germany.

[1946]

Monday, 7 January 1946. Washington.
A good day's work on the Rabaul text. We knocked off at 11:30 and the job is now almost finished...

Much talk about the demonstration on the part of the GIs in Manila, which approaches the dimensions of a mutiny—marching men howling

---

[37] See Craig's diary entry of 29 September 1945 about meeting Admiral Shigematsu Sakaibara.

[38] See "Japanese Admiral Admits Wake Killings," *New York Times* (December 24, 1945), 5.

down their commanding officer, GIs subscribing for an advertisement in the *Times* in order (presumably) to blast the brass hats, organized petitions to Congress and the like—all spiced with general criticisms of our foreign policy in China and demands that all troops be withdrawn with the exception of garrisons in Japan and Germany.

The explosive nature of this business is terrible. It will have a direct effect, I should think, upon the position of our UNO delegation which has just arrived in London, and since that delegation is already apparently weakened by an internal division of opinion on the atomic bomb, I am most discouraged. Our times are a living argument against Harold Sprout's theory that foreign policy is merely a matter of material power. Here we are—the greatest nation in the world from the standpoint of material power—and yet our foreign policy is completely ineffective because of lack of brains in high places, Congressional irresponsibility, popular sentimentality, selfishness and/or indifference, lack of moral stamina, and demonstrations like the one in Manila (which is, by the way, being duplicated in La Havre, Guam, and points at home).

Wednesday, 9 January 1946. Washington.

The agitations of the GIs continue and have spread to Honolulu, Paris, Yokohama, and Frankfurt. As Griff says, we have now shown the whole damn world what a deplorable state we're in. In Yokohama, the Provost Marshal disbanded the agitation by telling the boys that he would slap the next joker to sing "I wanna go home" into the jug. In Frankfurt, however, a guard with bayonets had to repel a mob which marched on General [Joseph T.] McNarney's headquarters. At home, the papers are showing remarkable reluctance to discuss the question, and most of them blow hot and cold alternately and then say, "Isn't it a shame?" The whole mess is deplorable and the only encouraging feature is that it may put a spoke in Army plans to take over and run all the services…

This afternoon to DivAv to arrange for my release to inactive duty. So back to Gravelly Point where we worked until midnight. The Rabaul report is finished—after a tremendous working spree of two weeks—and we are starting the proof-reading…[39]

Thursday, 10 January 1946. Washington.

Today marks the opening of the first meeting of the Assembly of the UNO. . . .

---

[39] *The Allied Campaign Against Rabaul* (Washington, D.C: United States Strategic Bombing Survey, Naval Analysis Division, 1946).

There are some signs that are not exactly encouraging for the UNO at this time. The GI agitations certainly will not help the prestige of our delegation, nor will the way in which we are apparently muddling in Germany. The U.S. delegation itself is a curious one. I have no great faith in the intellectual acumen or international aspirations of men like [Senator Tom] Connally, [John Foster] Dulles, and [Senator Arthur] Vandenberg. (Drew Pearson today says that the first social event for these three after they landed in England was a weekend at Cliveden, and that is scarcely an auspicious omen.) Worst of all has been the split within the delegation on the atomic bomb issue which was trumpeted aloud all over the world for a week and is now reported to have been cleared up by an assurance by Byrnes to Vandenberg. Here again we show a curious conception of diplomatic technique and I think Walter Lippman is quite correct in his views, as published in this morning's *Post*. . . .

Meanwhile at home we have more strikes than ever. The District telephone operators went on strike this morning. Western Union is on strike, too. For all my sympathy for labor and my disgust with the intellectual shenanigans shown in the propaganda advertisements of GM and GE, I don't like strikes in the wire services when I am away from home…

Wednesday, 16 January 1946. Washington.
Phyl's birthday, but no way of getting in touch with her because of the Washington phone strike. A visit to MarCorps to straighten out my orders. Back to the office to find the typing job just about finished. . . .

In the evening to the Wards in Chevy Chase, taking Griff with me. Paul in excellent form, with some quite frightening stories about the Truman administration. He maintains that Truman is quite out of his depth and dreadfully handicapped by the fact that he has few nation-wide contacts and must, in consequence, rely on Missouri high binders. Paul says that T. has no close friends even in the Senate and that he has come to rely, for advice regarding the Senate, upon a certain Les Bivell, Secretary of the Senate—(a kind of glorified doorman). His lack of comprehension of even ordinary English seems to be indicated by a story concerning the recent mix-up regarding the bomb. The Senate committee on the bomb saw Byrnes before he left for Moscow and, after an hour's conversation, concluded that they did not like Byrnes's ideas. So they rushed over to the White House and protested vigorously against all of Byrnes's ideas. Harry said: "I agree with you 100% and, to prove it, here is an executive order that I have just signed, embodying those ideas." It was only after the

Senators got outside and had a chance to read the order, that they found it was a mere recapitulation of all the views that Byrnes had outlined to them the night before... Paul feels that Truman's domestic advisors are stupid but, on the whole, honest—with the exception of [Robert E.] Hannegan who, he feels, may get Harry into serious trouble. Hannegan, like most of the others, is thinking almost exclusively in terms of the elections and has let it be known that Civil Service employees in Interior, Labor, and Agriculture will have to deliver or else. The greatest mistake so far has been the appointment of a statistician to compute electoral figures in close districts. The expert turned out to be an agent for the Soviet Embassy...

On our foreign services personnel past and present Paul was particularly scathing. Cordell Hull, from the beginning of his service, was actuated largely by personal jealousy. Paul told us how he put the skids under [Raymond] Moley after the London Economic Conference and came out of the White House saying to a friend "I cut the sonuva bitches [sic] throat from ear to ear!" The dismissal of [Sumner] Welles was the result of Hull's fear that Welles was usurping his position. Not that Welles can ever be expected back under this administration. His sexual deficiencies make him *persona non grata* in any mid-Western administration...[40] Of Byrnes, Paul is not sure. He heard Byrnes say flatly before going to Moscow that Russia must have no part in the administration of Jap affairs, that the atom would not be discussed, and that the main purpose of the trip was to persuade Molotov to come to the UNO meeting in London. Yet what happened in Moscow was in complete contradiction of all those statements...

Paul filled out the evening by a running criticism of our delegation to London and an imitation of Stettinius presiding at San Francisco. All very funny, but most discouraging...

Thursday, 24 January 1946. Washington.
The work on the Survey, as far as we are concerned, is finished, and Griff started checking out today. In the last two days we have written an article on "The Reduction of Rabaul" for which Pierre Leblanc of *Marine Corps Gazette* asked. It appears now that there may be some question of getting it cleared by the Survey, but I'll let Pierre handle that...

Wednesday, 30 January 1946. Princeton.
Up early and bade farewell to M. & C. The latter drove me to the Raleigh

---

[40] Sumner Welles (1892–1961), an Undersecretary of State and a major foreign policy adviser to Franklin Roosevelt, was forced to resign in 1943 because of a scandal involving homosexuality.

where I checked my bags and had a second breakfast. So to the Naval Recruiting Station on G Street, where I was given a complete physical check and declared strong enough to return to civilian life. . . .

Then off to Arlington Annex, where I had to fiddle for some two hours and sign innumerable vouchers but finally got my *per diem*, my pay, my travel allowance, and the first installment of my mustering out pay. I walked out a completely checked-out man and realized, to my surprise, that I was—all of a sudden—on inactive duty.

I took a bus back to the Raleigh, where I ordered an old fashioned, a sandwich and some coffee and, feeling the occasion demanded celebration, wrote the following—

Lines Written in the Raleigh, 30 Jan. 1946.
I sit, a mournful solo, in the place
Where Griffin mocked at the whole human race.
Lacking their last ingredient (Griffin's bile),
The drinks are not the same. But, to beguile
My last sad moments in the Corps' proud green,
I drink them, a demobilized Marine.
(Meanwhile in Princeton my exultant wife
Charts my *per diem*-less civilian life.)

Going to the cigar counter, I bought a postcard of the Washington Monument, scribbled the lines on it and dropped it, with Griff's address, into the post box. Then I collected my bags, got a taxi, and caught the 3 o'clock train at Union Station…

I reached Princeton at 7:30 and took a cab home. The driver asked me if I was "just out of the Army." Somewhat nettled, I corrected him, but he was deaf as a post and my acerbity was unnoticed. I reached 24 Edwards Place to find Susan and Debbie still up—the former cutting out things, the latter full of a birthday party she is going to tomorrow. They were packed off to bed and Phyl and I had a drink and dinner and sat and talked until she had to go off to feed Martha. And so I sat and drank coffee and played Offenbach's "Gaîté Parisienne" and Gershwin's "American in Paris" to myself, reflecting upon my good fortune in being safe home again. And mighty thankful too, although equally thankful for the experience of being a Marine…

Now some of Evelyn Waugh's *Brideshead Revisited* before bed…

Thursday, 31 January 1946. Princeton.
Up at 9 to see Susan go off to school. With interference from Debbie,

sorted out my civilian clothes, and then shoved off to town with Phyl. I first went to Nassau Hall for an interview with President Dodds. A queer business—he wants me to be co-chairman, with John Foster Dulles, of one of the conferences to be held during the bicentennial celebrations, but he doesn't seem to know what the conference is all about or when it will be held. However, after seeing Dodds, I bumped into Mike Oates, who told me that *he* would give me the word at some future date. . . .

Saturday, 2 February 1946. Princeton.
An interview with Mike Oates on the coming conference... Bumped into Alba Warren, whom I last saw in Oxford many long years ago... In the afternoon Ed Earle came in with two jobs which will keep me busy this month and also a story of how he had sold Carleton Hayes a bill of goods on me and that I might very well get an offer from Columbia soon. Since Joe Strayer told me yesterday that I might be asked soon to be a kind of junior dean of the Graduate School, I am wondering just what will come of all these putative offers... In the evening Alba came in and we talked of past and future. He has worn well.

[At an unspecified time later, Craig wrote: "Remainder of February devoted to two jobs: one at the Institute doing some research on origins of Munich crisis for Ed Earle and making a précis of [Werner] Sombart's *War and Capitalism*; the other working on the Bicentennial Conferences. The latter necessitated a trip to New York to interview Harlow Shapley. I combined this with lunch with Bill Dougherty. I also had to run up to New Haven where I saw all the Department and stayed overnight with Hajo Holborn. ([Leonard W.] Labaree, acting chairman, asked me to consider possibility of coming to New Haven as visiting lecturer next year.)]

Monday, 11 March 1946. Princeton.
Received an offer this day from Cornell University—to come to Ithaca in Sept. as Associate Professor at $5000. [Cornelius] De Kiewiet, whom I met in the Public Record Office in 1936, very persuasive. [George] Cuttino's hand in this, I see. Also Ed Earle's. Phyl very excited and quite prepared to go.

Tuesday, 12 March 1946. Princeton.
Saw Joe in morning and gave him news. Said I was seriously considering accepting. Joe said he thought Princeton would meet offer... Lectured on "American Policy 1848–66."... In afternoon to Institute to discuss pros and cons with Ed... Jack with Mike Oates on Bicentennial business and Cornell offer. He all for my staying here... Spent evening with Palmers

trying to learn how to play GO.

Wednesday, 13 March 1946. Princeton.
Princeton offering me Associate Professorship as of 1 July at salary of $5500—a $2000 jump over present salary. In view of advantages here for work, think I'll stay. . . .

4

Princeton and Stanford, 1946–1960

During the period from March 1946 to September 1954, I was too busy to keep a diary but contented myself with reasonably explicit notes in my pocket appointment books. These books I have kept, with the exception of the one for 1954, which was lost in a restaurant in Munich in the late fall of that year. . . . What follows here was written in October 1974 on the basis of the remaining pocket diaries, the notations of the years covered being supplemented, whenever possible, by my memory.

During my last weeks of service in the U.S. Marine Corps, when Griff and I were sitting in Gravelly Point (in what is now called Pentagon City), trying to finish the report of the Marshalls-Gilberts Task Force of the U.S. Strategic Bombing Survey, I was called in, during one of my long weekends in Princeton, by Harold Dodds.[1] He told me of the forthcoming Princeton Bicentennial Celebration and said that he wanted me to direct one of the most important of the twelve or so conferences that would highlight this shivaree. I expressed suitable gratitude and asked what the subject of the conference would be. This seemed to embarrass him and, after much paper-shuffling, he had to admit that this had slipped his mind but that his chief aide for conference affairs, the Secretary of the University, Arthur Fox, would fill me in. Which, in due time, Arthur did, telling me that it was to be a conference on "The University and its World Responsibilities." I was still young enough to think that that was a damned original subject and formidable enough to require the services of *two* directors. So Cy Black[2] and

---

[1] Harold W. Dodds (1889–1980) was the fifteenth president of Princeton University, serving from 1933 to 1957.

[2] Cyril E. Black (1915–1989) began his career as a scholar of Russian and Soviet history at Princeton in 1939, and, after service in the Second World War, continued to teach those subjects until his retirement in 1986.

I did most of the not inconsiderable amount of legwork.

The latter part of 1946, for which I have no record, . . . must have been given over to preparations for this conference, and these labors became almost all-consuming in January 1947. In the end, we attracted a remarkable cast of characters for the meetings, which were held in the Princeton Inn on February 19–22. It included Garrett Mattingly of Columbia, William Rappard of the Geneva Institute, Roscoe Pound (that enormously learned man who responded to a quotation from *Faust* by quoting the whole passage), G. A. Borgese (brilliant but objectionable—so incredibly vain that he wanted all of his titles listed on his name tag), David Daiches (of Oxford days, shrewd Scottish critic and admirer of Robert Louis Stevenson), Ben Cherrington and Waldo Leland, old friends like Filmer Northrup and Hajo Holborn and George Cuttino, and assorted horse-holders. . . . I have a picture showing them all in formal stance in my Stanford office. What they all talked about for three days I forget. I remember arranging an evening lecture on a snowy February evening for Arnold Toynbee who spoke inaudibly to an overflow crowd in McCosh 50; I remember taking all the conferees to tea at the Institute, and introducing Toynbee and Rappard to Albert Einstein; and I remember a pleasant Saturday on which Phyl and I took old Rappard to one of the great convocations that studded the year; then to lunch, and finally to a basketball game, which he seemed to enjoy hugely. . . . The conclusions of the conference, if any, will doubtless be found by anyone curious about them in Charles Osgood's book on the Bicentennial Year.[3]

While this was going on, other things were happening, of course. During 1946–47, I taught History 101, 102 (later I, II) "Europe since the Renaissance," a brand-new course, which like History 1, 2, 3 at Stanford (1973–74) which resembles it, was part of one of those recurring educational reforms. It was in this course, incidentally, that Jerome Blum,[4] who came to Princeton in the fall of 1947, gave his first lecture (on the Enlightenment, 9 December 1947) and began a distinguished career as teacher/scholar.

During the last flurry of preparations for the conference, in January

[3] Charles Osgood, *Lights in Nassau Hall: A Book of the Bicentennial Princeton 1746–1946* (Princeton: Princeton University Press, 1952).

[4] Jerome Blum (1933–1993), a leading economic and social historian of rural Europe, with particular emphasis on Central and Eastern European history, joined the Princeton faculty in 1947 and was among Craig's closest friends for nearly half a century.

1947, I got another offer, this time an associate professorship at Columbia. Since I was already, thanks to my offer from Cornell, at that rank, there was no good reason to accept this, and I did not.

In January 1947, also, I began a long career of reviewing for the NY papers by writing a review for the *Times* of the first of those revisionist books designed to prove that FDR arranged the bombing of Pearl Harbor in order to get us into the war. This was a book called *Pearl Harbor* by a *Chicago Tribune* reporter called George Morgenstern.[5]

The conference was hardly in its grave when I became involved in another project, the history of the USMC in WWII. Bill Twining approached me on this early in the year, asking me to write a single-volume work. I was already at work on the preliminary researches for my Prussian army book, and was prepared to say no when Bob Albion,[6] who always had a good money sense, persuaded me to take on the project with Jeter Isely and Phil Crowl[7] as authors who would receive summer stipends for their labors. This took a lot of negotiation in Washington and inside the university but, on 26 March 1947, at a dinner at the Princeton Inn attended by Generals [Gerald] Thomas and [William] Riley, Cols. Bill Twining and Bob Heinl, Datus Smith of the University Press, George Brakely (Financial Vice President of the University), Crowl and Isely, and Bob Albion, Joe Strayer, Frisco Godolphin,[8] and me, The Princeton Marine Corps History Project was established, with an editorial board composed of the last four named above, and was authorized to prepare a book for publication by the press. The Corps undertook to provide freedom from censorship, except in security matters . . . , the necessary documents, and $45,000, the sum that I, in my innocence, set. I could have asked for three times as much, and got it. But why? The $45,000, which arrived on Monday, 31 March, sufficed.

In the end, a fine book, *The U.S. Marines and Amphibious War* (1950),

---

[5] Craig's review of George Morgenstern's *Pearl Harbor: The Story of the Secret War* (New York: Devin-Adair Company, 1947), entitled "The New Mythology for the Critics of FDR," appeared in *The New York Times Book Review* on February 9, 1947.
[6] Robert G. Albion (1896–1983), a pioneering maritime historian at Princeton and later at Harvard, was Assistant Director of Naval History and Historian of Naval Administration for the Department of the Navy from 1943 to 1950.
[7] Philip A. Crowl (1914–1991) was a military historian who taught at Princeton, the U.S. Naval War College, and the University of Nebraska, an intelligence officer during the Second World War, and later in his career a prolific travel writer.
[8] Francis R. B. Godolphin (1903–1974), known to his friends as "Frisco," was a classics scholar and Dean of the College at Princeton from 1945 to 1955.

came out of this, and a lot of good stories.[9] Also plenty of nervous work maintaining the friendship of the collaborators, since Jeter couldn't tolerate Phil's *modus operandi*, was always wanting to go through his index cards (which didn't exist), and had a tendency to resign every Monday morning. Poor Jeter! He made life so hard for himself, hag-ridden by ambition and by the knowledge that I, who had gone to Graduate College with him, was already an associate professor and he was not. . . .

The spring of 1947 seems to have been convivial enough. Life was filled with cocktail parties given by people like Ted Mommsen,[10] who had come to us from Groton School, and the Viners[11]; we used to go to New York for wonderful dinners given by Ted's friend Jakob Goldschmidt, director of the Darmstädter Bank of unfortunate memory (there is a note reading "March 4: Lecture Nationalism; Goldschmidt dinner NY (Gromyko)," but I cannot recall the Soviet diplomat's coming, which I would have done, for I recall most of those wonderful gatherings among Jakob's fantastic collection of Impressionist paintings and can still see him presiding gracefully and wittily at the head of that long table with the great Courbet "La Source" above his head); and the academic year ended with a wonderful bust at the Bellers's on 31 May 1947, when the staff of History 101–102 presented my play "Once over Lightly," with Bob Palmer[12] as the Spirit of History and, among other notable thespians, Aud Wicks as Red Wing, chief of the Cedar Rapids Scavengers, a production that ended with a wholesale distribution of degrees à la Bicentennial Year counterparts. Phyl and the kids and I then disappeared to Westport, Mass. for a two-week vacation, missing the Final University Convocation of the year, at which Truman, Hoover, and Eisenhower were the stars, and a Rhodes Scholar Reunion which featured Felix Frankfurter, Ambassador Winant, and Senator Fulbright...

---

[9] See Jeter A. Iseley and Philip A. Crowl, *U.S. Marines and Amphibious Warfare: Its Theory, and Its Practice in the Pacific* (Princeton: Princeton University Press, 1951).

[10] Theodor Ernst Mommsen (1905–1958), grandson of the German classical historian Theodor Mommsen and nephew of the great sociologist Max Weber, was a medievalist and Petrarch scholar. See Robert E. Lerner, "Ernst Kantorowicz and Theodor E. Mommsen," in *An Interrupted Past: German-Speaking Refugee Historians in the United States After 1933*, ed. Hartmut Lehmann and James J. Sheehan (Cambridge: Cambridge University Press, 1991), 188–205.

[11] Jacob Viner (1892–1970) was a renowned political economist and economic historian.

[12] Robert R. Palmer (1909–2002), an eminent historian of eighteenth-century Europe, taught at Princeton for nearly three decades, from 1936 to 1963.

Before closing out our Princeton year and getting away, I had one other duty to perform. I had agreed to examine the Honors Seniors at Swarthmore and, early in May, had dispatched the written examinations to the candidates. On Friday, 6 June '47, I went to Swarthmore to give the orals. Strictly speaking, I went on the 5th and spent the evening listening to George Cuttino's Claudia Muzio records while Mary Albertson worried about the examinees and argued with Larry Lafore,[13] who wanted to take them all off to play The Game. I found this comic, but on reflection concluded that the whole Swarthmore Honors bit was a bit precious and not worth the effort. Certainly, the students were not all that wonderful when I examined them on Friday, with one exception, a young man named Lyman[14] who actually came down to Thirtieth St. Station to say goodbye to me as I left on Saturday morning. He is now the President of Stanford University. . . .

We were back at Princeton on 1 July and I was soon teaching again, this time in summer school, for these were catch-up years, and lots of people wanted to work in the summer. I gave a new course I had devised—History 320: European Social and Economic Policy after 1848, in which one lecture, on parvenuism as a social and political force, based on my reading of Dickens and Proust, and inspired also by [Ernst] Kohn-Bramstedt's *Aristocracy and the Middle Class*,[15] was the first formal expression of a growing interest in the use of literary materials. Other ideas generated during this course were fruitful later, and I still use some of the problems we posed on exams to startle my graduate students at Stanford. (I say "we," because Ted Mommsen was my constant adviser as I went ahead, and some of the best ideas were his.) It was a lovely course in lots of ways—all new and shining. You can do that sort of thing easily when you're young. Later, you're like Ole Satch; you have to rely on other things than speed, and, when they run

---

[13] Laurence Lafore (1917–1985) was a historian at Swarthmore College and later at the University of Iowa, best known for his work on the origins of the First World War.

[14] Richard W. Lyman (1923–2012) served as the provost of Stanford University from 1967 to 1970, and then as the university's seventh president, from 1970 to 1980.

[15] See Ernst Kohn-Bramstedt, *Aristocracy and the Middle Class: Social Types in German Literature, 1830–1900* (London: King, 1937). Ernst Kohn-Bramstedt (1901–1978), a student of Friedrich Meinecke and Karl Mannheim, was a pioneering historian and sociologist of literature.

out, you're done.[16]

With three new lectures to write every week, the summer passed quickly enough. I played a little golf with Paul Strayer and Ralph Greenlaw (I was trying to learn the game in those days and persevered for a couple of years and then said the hell with it) and I had four days in Washington in September, working in the National Archives. This was to finish up odds and ends of research which had been done earlier in the spring when (thanks to a tip from Alina Luckau, forwarded by Ray Sontag)[17] I had found a treasure trove of captured German materials in the Archives (Moltke, Manteuffel, Seeckt, and, especially, Wilhelm Groener). Much of this I had had photographed, and out of it was to come three articles, the first of which, on Groener's tenure as Reichswehr minister, which was later to be prominently mentioned in a front-page review in the *Times Literary Supplement*, was now in the gestation process. (It was to be finished on 4 January 1948.)[18]

Before that, there were mountains of work to be done. Starting in late September, I was teaching three courses a week—History I, and the course I was to teach until 1961, History 317: European Diplomacy since the Crimean War (Sontag's old course), both at Princeton, and a lecture course on German History at Columbia University, which I gave on Wednesdays. (I never again gave a lecture course on German history until I went to Stanford in 1961, and the Columbia lectures were not very useful by that time.) This load does not seem to have deterred me from undertaking new jobs, particularly when there was money involved. I seem to have lectured on successive evenings in October at Montclair and Maplewood on "the German problem," and in December I was in New Haven, conferring with Tom Mendenhall, Duke Henning, and Archie Foord about putting together a new source book on Europe since 1715. All of this must have been hard on my family.

---

16 This is a reference to baseball pitcher Satchel Paige, who gained fame for his fastball, but later developed a large repertoire of off-speed pitches to compensate for his gradual decline in pitching strength.

17 Raymond J. Sontag (1897–1972) was a distinguished historian of European diplomacy at Princeton University from 1924 to 1941, and then at the University of California, Berkeley.

18 Gordon A. Craig, "The Reichswehr and National Socialism: The Policy of Wilhelm Groener, 1928–1932," *Political Science Quarterly* 63:2 (June 1948): 194–229. For the front–page review in the *TLS*, see "The German Army and Hitler," *Times Literary Supplement* (9 June 1950), 349–351.

[1948]

The new year began with all of the courses begun in the fall reaching their appointed ends, for both Princeton and Columbia were on the semester system, and the first semester ended at the close of January. A lot of graduate work was being cleared up at the same time. In January 1948 I was sitting on doctor's orals at Columbia with people like Lindsay Rogers, John Hazard, John Wuorinen, Carlton Hayes, and Franz Neumann, and at the beginning of February I sat in on similar exams at Princeton for Jeremy Blanchet and Ed Katzenbach, both of whom were protégés of the Earles (especially Beatrice) and had promise, which was, sadly, not to be realized.

During the spring semester I was teaching History II at Princeton (Europe since 1815) and Germany since 1890 at Columbia. The Yale project was launched, which involved another trip to New Haven, where I met Lennie Krieger[19] for the first time—(he and I were to be associate editors of the Mendenhall, Henning, Foord reader, *The Search for Authority*)—and the Marine Corps project gathered momentum. Indeed, the first weekend conference was held at the Princeton Inn on March 12–13, when a group of Marines flew in to discuss the Crowl-Iseley chapter on Guadalcanal. This was so successful that General Riley of the U.S. Marine Corps public relations department insisted we do a repeat, this time with General Vandegrift and the current Commandant, General Cates, on hand. . . . We gave way and on April 15–16 had the damnedest shivaree Princeton ever saw. There was so much brass that brigadiers were being sent out for sandwiches, and so much real liquor (the local ROTC commander, Major Horace Knapp UCMC, sent to Lakewood Naval Air Station for bonded stuff) that, at the formal reception in the Dean of the College's home, my colleagues, unused to anything in recent years that was more potent than Schenley's Black Label, were falling in damp heaps in corners. Among the Marines, floods of reminiscence were loosed. At 2 in the morning I heard Cates saying to Vandegrift, concerning the battle of the Coral Sea, "Christ! If Kelly (Turner) had had the sense to put his hand out, he could have had a capful of stars!" Some of the recollections were usable, which was the point of this, and all similar, exercises.

This semester marked the birth of the W. P. Hall-Craig wandering

---

[19] Leonard Krieger (1918–1990), was an eminent intellectual historian at Yale and the University of Chicago. He and Craig were fellows at the Center for Advanced Study in the Behavioral Sciences at Stanford University in 1956–57.

debate team,[20] and in March we were displaying our wares in Montclair and Maplewood again ("Conflicting Ideas in American Foreign Policy"). Knockabout comedy, always with large audiences. It was a period also when old friends surfaced. In early March Tommy Ballogh[21] of Balliol, an old pal of Phyl's in London, was in town, and we had dinner with him at the Win Rieflers and an evening at the Nass with him and E. H. Carr. (Carr was at the Institute at Ed Earle's invitation, although Ed soon came to detest him heartily.)[22] At the end of March, B. H. Sumner came to the States for a month and spent a good deal of it in Princeton. We saw him frequently at the Earles and with the Viners, and I had one good private talk with him in the Nass; he huddled in his overcoat looking gaunt and ill. We talked about our own profession and our own work, and he gave me a good subject (Freycinet) for Ed Katzenbach, which Ed didn't do much with. It was in this period also that Phyl and I got to know Hans Kohn,[23] meeting him for the first time at the Bellers on 20 March, along with the novelist Hermann Broch, author of *The Sleep-Walkers*, who was living with Erich Kahler and being supported by that generous man. (I saw him several times, a large, sad man who never said a word or even appeared to be interested in the company.)[24] There were many remarkable people floating around Tigertown in those days. In April, I had cocktails at Lucius Wilmerding's

---

[20] Walter P. Hall (1884–1962), one of the most popular members of the Princeton Department of History from 1913 until his retirement in 1952, was known affectionately as "Buzzer" because of his noisy, early-model hearing aid.

[21] Támás (Thomas) Balogh (1905–1985), born into a wealthy Budapest Jewish family, became a Fellow of Balliol College, Oxford in 1945, and later served as an economic correspondent for the *New Statesman*, an economic advisor to the cabinet of Harold Wilson, and a member of the House of Lords.

[22] Edward Hallett Carr (1892–1982) was a British historian, diplomat, journalist, and international relations theorist, best known for his influential book *What Is History?* (New York: Random House, 1961) and his controversial 14-volume history of Soviet Russia from 1917 to 1929.

[23] Hans Kohn (1891–1971), born into a German-speaking Jewish family in Prague, became a leading figure in the Zionist movement during the period between the two world wars, and published his major work, *The Idea of Nationalism: A Study in Its Origins and Background,* in 1944.

[24] Hermann Broch (1886–1951), an émigré novelist from Vienna, wrote his second major book, *The Death of Virgil* (1945) at Erich Kahler's home in Princeton. Erich Kahler (1885–1970), an émigré literary scholar and essayist from Prague, was the linchpin of a circle of German expatriate writers and scholars in Princeton (the Kahler-Kreis), which included not only Hermann Broch, but also Thomas Mann and Albert Einstein.

and heard Arthur Koestler quizzing Johnny von Neumann[25] about computing and other machines. (K.: "Do you mean that you could conceive of a machine that could build another machine?" Von N.: "We could build a machine that would build another machine that would then produce five locomotives and five gold watches every 24 hours. At least we could draw the plans. It would be pointless to execute them." A loud click at this point, caused by the simultaneous dropping of the jaws of Julian P. Boyd and GAC.) And on 1 May, Ted Mommsen and Oskar Morgenstern gave a large party in honor of Jakob Goldschmidt and his new wife (a very flashy number—a kind of international jet setter who didn't work out) and of the nuclear scientist Niels Bohr. . . .

The academic year ended in a muddle of activity. . . . I was involved, with Jack Viner and Harold Sprout, in a faculty-alumni forum, an innovation in the reunion format; there were meetings of a new committee designed to make preparations for the dedication of the new library; and there was the final History II party, with guitar and song. But by mid-June we were at Westport Point, Mass. *en famille*, in a house rented to us by an elderly original named Crippen, like the murderer.

. . . By day I worked in the Library of Congress or in the Archives and I got through an enormous amount of stuff that was not available in Princeton. The town was full of friends—Ray Sontag was in State, working on the captured German documents, Rod Davison had by now begun his career at George Washington, Phil Kaiser was at the Labor Department and was soon to be Assistant Secretary, Rudy Winnacker was at the Pentagon, and Kent Roberts Greenfield[26] was Chief of Military History (and I was soon to be on his board), Charlie Wiltse was working on Polk at the Library of Congress, and other types were wandering about. I saw all of them, having lunch with Ray Sontag frequently at the Cosmos Club, on one occasion with Bernadotte Schmitt and General Cromwell, who had once been British military attaché in Berlin. . . .

During the fall semester I was on leave, and my only lectures were voluntary ones on contemporary world affairs, given on Wednesday

---

[25] John von Neumann (1903–1957), an émigré scientist and polymath from Hungary, did pioneering work in mathematics, physics (quantum mechanics), engineering, computer science, and game theory, and was a key figure in the development of the atomic bomb during World War II.

[26] Kent Roberts Greenfield (1893–1967), a specialist in Italian history and chair of the Department of History at Johns Hopkins University, became chief editor of the official United States Army history of World War II in 1948.

evenings in a high school in Trenton. I did a bit more with the girls. . . . We had a more active social life, seeing a good deal of the Aud Wicks in New Hope and, in Princeton, Jerry Blum and Ted Mommsen, the Bellers, the Sayres, the Palmers, the Stevens, the Herman Weills. On election day, we gave drinks to those great liberals the Bellers and the Chernisses. I cannot remember that they, or for that matter Jerry or I, expected the upset that kept Harry Truman in office, although it is recorded that I won $1.80 on election bets of some kind.

I was at this time overseeing the Marine Corps project, which was making progress, writing my article on military attachés,[27] and pursuing my researches on the Prussian army book. I was interested in getting as much dope as I could about the attitude of our own people in Germany to Hitler's policy in the 30s, particularly as it affected the army; and this took me back to Washington in December, to interview Generals Joe Collins and Wedemeyer in the hope of getting the right to quote from military attachés' reports from Berlin, which I had, thanks to the friendly offices of Jake Beam (later our ambassador to the USSR, in the 30s in the Berlin embassy) already seen. I got nowhere with Collins, and Wedemeyer was no better, although he seemed glad of an audience to whom he could tell the story of his attendance of the German War College and his great social success there. Since General Eisenhower had recently got a lot of publicity by announcing the opening of army files to serious researchers, the runaround I received was annoying, but instructive enough for anyone as interested as I in the ways of bureaucracy. In any case, I had what I wanted, and the permission to quote verbatim was not essential. I improved the shining hour by talking with our Assistant Military Attaché in Berlin before 1934, Percy Black, and by seeing Cocteau's *L'Eternel Retour* with that almost excessively handsome actor, Jean Marais.

I returned home on the 17th of December for a round of Christmas parties and in an important step in the education of Susan and Debbie: on 21 December 1948 I took them to the movies to see the Marx Brothers in "A Night at the Opera," the film with the wonderful stateroom scene that a group of exhilarated Rhodes Scholars tried, with some success, to re-enact on the SS *Laconia* (that noble vessel that carried us to England in September 1936 and was torpedoed by the Germans during the first years of the war).

The year ended with the meetings of the American Historical Association in Washington, where I foregathered with friends like Hajo

---

[27] Gordon A. Craig, "Military Diplomats in the Prussian and German Service: The Attachés, 1816–1914," *Political Science Quarterly*, 64 (1949): 65–94.

Holborn, Felix Gilbert, and Lennie Krieger, and had a business lunch at the New Athens with Phil Kaiser and the later ambassador to Indonesia, Jack Peurifoy.

[1949]

The business meeting had to do with yet another of the involvements of these years that make me, in retrospect, wonder how our marriage survived. I had been approached late in 1948 by Phil Kaiser and asked if I would serve on The Foreign Service Selection Board if the Labor Department succeeded in getting my nomination as a public member approved. He explained that the duties of the Board were concerned with selecting Foreign Service Officers for promotion, and that Labor was interested in seeing that its interests were protected and that officers brought in to the Foreign Service during the war for special duties (labor attachés, agricultural attachés, and the like) were not passed over by a service known for its conservatism. I was interested and, after consulting Phyllis, told Phil to put my name forward. I received my appointment on 6 December 1948, and my lunch at the New Athens at the end of the month was one of a number of enthusiastic briefings by Kaiser, aided in this case by John Peurifoy, who was known as a reformer. . . .

My views about the equity and efficiency of this system can be found in my article "Promotion in a Career Service" (*Foreign Service Journal*, 1950), written after the completion of our work. In retrospect, I think we worked fairly and that our decisions were sound. If Dan Heath had a tendency to give the regular FSOs preference over officers who, because they had come in under the wartime Manpower Act, were johnny-come-latelies in his eyes, this was offset by the insistence of [John S.] Service, backed by me (or vice versa), that the service needed all the variety of mind and specialty that it could get. Generally we worked amicably, and dust-ups were few and inconsequential.

I learned a good deal about the rigors, the frustrations, and the nervous strain that accompany FSOs as they go from post to post, and saw the specific effects of all this in a number of sad case-histories, in which boozing, wenching, and erratic behavior bulked large. I learned that it was not wise to make love to the Chief of Mission's daughter at embassy picnics or to defy local mores by disrobing before open windows. I became impressed by the number of careers that were blighted by timid wives or socially aggressive wives or tale-bearing wives (it was one of the latter that got V. Lansing Collins Jr. transferred from Havana to Tegucigalpa). I was depressed to discover that chiefs of mission were capable of giving officers bad fitness reports because they wore brown suede shoes or were otherwise unorthodox (luckily we were supplied with a list of chiefs of mission who were manifestly irrational or unfair in their efficiency reports, so that we could discount their judgments). I was impressed, on the other hand, by the conscientiousness of most of the chiefs of mission. In the case of George F. Kennan[28] who had written the most recent efficiency reports on those members of the Moscow embassy who were eligible for promotion, one was struck by an almost painful weighing of merits and defects, and Kennan, whom I was to get to know quite well when he came to the Institute in 1950, would often write second and third reports to amplify or correct his original judgment.

All told, I came away from the experience with admiration for our service and the men who made it up, and convinced that most of the attacks upon it were either ideologically inspired (like Robert Bendiner's *The Riddle of the State Department*) or products of ignorance or malice.

Certainly the attacks upon John Service were both malicious and ideological. During the greater part of my time on this job I shared a room in the Roger Smith Hotel (the old Powhatan of my college days) with this gifted officer, and from him I learned the story of his period in China, during which he and his colleagues in the U.S. Mission came to feel that the United States had put its money on the wrong horse and should be making a greater effort to reach an accommodation with Mao Tse Tung. This ran counter to the views of the U.S. ambassador in 1944-45, Patrick J. Hurley, a man with no previous experience in China who was nonetheless confident that he would bring Mao and the Kuomintang together. When his efforts failed, Hurley blamed this on the old China hands in his staff and began to hound John in particular in the Scripps-Howard press. This was, in the end, successful in depriving him of his job, and in forcing him to resort to a laborious appeal procedure which forced his reinstatement, although in a non-sensitive position. It is only in the last few years that John has been completely cleared, the Nixon trip to Peking making his treatment patently indefensible. The dispatches and memoranda that infuriated Hurley have now been published in book form.

In many ways, then, this hitch with the State Department was an interesting and rewarding experience for me, rewarding particularly, I guess,

---

[28] George Kennan (1904–2005) was an American diplomat and historian of international relations who was best known for his early advocacy of a policy of containment towards the Soviet Union.

because my principal work at Princeton was in diplomatic history and because many of my students came to me for advice about going into the Foreign Service or other branches of the government. Life was, of course, rather hectic, what with the commuting to Princeton and the vain attempt every weekend to crowd in everything that had been missed during the week. In Washington, I saw the usual number of people—all the resident types, their number augmented now by Bill Hull in whom the Truman victory had revived all the old Washington excitement and who was, for a while, back in harness. I had lunch with him at the Trois Mousqétuaires on 31 January and frequently thereafter. Dave Bell was back in Washington, and I remember a pleasant lunch with him at that curious place, the Allies Inn. Ed Gullion was at the National War College, and I saw something of him; and it was at this time that I got to know Telford Taylor, who was also working on the German army. John Service and I investigated the good restaurants—Hall's on the waterfront, and The Peking, where we had a memorable Chinese meal. When I had nothing else to do in the evenings, I went to Viviane Romance movies, notably *Carmen*, although I broke out of this pattern once in order to see Harry Baur and Louis Jouvet in *Volpone* and once to hear the Philadelphia Orchestra in Independence Hall. And sometimes I actually read books—that is, real books: Mann's *Dr. Faustus*, Zuckmeyer's *Der Hauptmann von Köpenick*, Raabe's *Chronik der Sperlingsgasse*, Verga's *Cavalleria Rusticana*, Amicis's *La vita militare*. I also finished and read the proofs of my attaché article. And, for some odd reason, in late February I made a one-day *Abstecher* [side-trip] to Pittsburgh to speak to the Yale-Harvard-Princeton Club. I suppose it was a case of yielding to the urgings of Cleve Rea and Ed Trent at the cost of two nights on a train, for I sandwiched it in between Wednesday and Friday meetings of our board (and one did not fly in those days).

I don't know what arrangement I made with Princeton to take care of the classes I missed in February and March. When I got back home at the end of the job, in mid-March, I plunged immediately into the teaching of History II, but I didn't stay put, despite what must have been an effort to catch up. On 7 April, with James G. Shotwell in the chair, I gave a paper on "Germany between East and West" before the Academy of Political Science in New York; on the 25th I was discoursing on the same subject at Smith College (Phyl came on this trip, and we had lunch with the Hans Kohns); and on 2 May I was peddling the same line in Wilmington, staying the night with the John Spruances and receiving a phone call from my old high school sweetie Florence Schote (now calling herself Dagmar).

How this academic year ever came to an end is a mystery; how did I ever find time to examine my graduate students or complete History II? But all things are possible when you are young—even cocktail parties with people with mysterious origins, like the Oppenheim-Herreras, or heavy dinner parties with Herbert Feis,[29] who had come to the Institute, in honor of Arnold Toynbee, who was back in town, being wise in his modest way—or expeditions to New York with the girls to see the circus, accomplished in April. The year did reach its end. . . .

Although not uninterruptedly. For I had learned that there was a good collection of captured German military books in Ottawa in the National Ministry of Defense. I got permission to use it, through the good offices of Colonel Charles Stacey, who had been a member of the Princeton History Department when I was an undergraduate, and I had got a research grant out of the University. So from 6th to 18th July I was in the Canadian capital, which I came to detest as a dull provincial town with lousy restaurants and nothing to amuse the visitor but the Mounties in front of the Parliament Building and the carillon, which I also came to loathe. This jaundiced view was doubtless caused in large part by the dreadful nervous indigestion that was affecting me. Even so, Ottawa is not San Francisco. But I got a lot of work done in books and military journals I hadn't found elsewhere, and I had a pleasant time with the Staceys and a very friendly colonel named Nicholson.

I travelled back to Westport by way of Montreal and Boston and Providence and Fall River, a voyage that took the best part of two days and almost all of Scott's *Redgauntlet*. For the next two weeks I did nothing but act as a *Familienvater* [family man], playing a lot of music on the Martin guitar which I had bought in Washington in March and which I still play occasionally. There were some good parties with the Wicks tribe and some trips to places like Newport and New Bedford.

On 1 August, we left Westport and drove to Mt. Kisco, N.Y., spending the night with the Duane Humphreys and travelling on to Princeton the next day. The month that followed was spent planning for the renewal of History 317 and a course on diplomatic history that I had agreed to give at Columbia, doing some writing (a review article for the *Foreign Service Journal*), working through the correspondence between Edwin von Manteuffel and

---

[29] Herbert Feis (1893–1972) was the Economic Advisor for International Affairs to the State Department during the Hoover and Roosevelt administrations, and the recipient of the 1961 Pulitzer Prize for History for *Between War and Peace: The Potsdam Conference* (Princeton: Princeton University Press, 1960).

Albrecht von Roon (a slow process because of Manteuffel's wretched handwriting, but a rewarding one, since an article emerged from this labor),[30] and taking Phyl to Wilmington and to New York to have dinner with Jakob Goldschmidt.

On 1 September I was in West Point meeting with Cols. Beukema and Abe Lincoln, Grayson Kirk, Don McKay, Ted Dunne, and others. From this session emerged the annual intercollegiate conference that still meets at the Point annually. A week later, Phyl and I went to the Atlantic City Race Track with the Joe Stevenses, who supplied the food services for that and other tracks, and won $3.40 by judicious and very modest betting. . . . Meanwhile, I had periodically been painting and plastering and performing other chores in the building which housed the University League Nursery School, Phyl's creation, which opened its doors on 28 September and which she ran until we left for Stanford in 1961.

By this time, my courses in Princeton and Columbia had begun. At Columbia I had 232 students at my first lecture and held most of them; in Princeton the numbers were more modest but substantial enough. At Columbia, General Eisenhower had become President, and Phyllis and I were invited to dinner at the Faculty Club on 26 October and heard him give one of his first speeches to his faculty, a speech that showed that he was no slouch as a politician. This invitation was, although I did not realize it at the time, the beginning of a campaign to bring me to Columbia; it was followed by invitations to lunch by John Krout, and Shep Clough, and Schuyler Wallace, and a seminar on Germany in McMillin Theater with Wallace and Franz Neumann. All of this came to a head on 16 December when I received a definite invitation to go to Columbia as full professor at $9,000, a princely sum at that time.

As in the case of the Cornell offer, my inclination was to accept. Columbia was an exciting place in those days, and I liked the thought of having Franz Neumann as my colleague.[31] New York itself was an attraction. I had been meeting regularly with the Century Club as a member of a Carnegie Commission on Captured German Documents, and I was

---

[30] Gordon A. Craig, "Portrait of a Political General: Edwin von Manteuffel and the Constitutional Conflict in Prussia," *Political Science Quarterly* 66:1 (March 1951): 1–36.

[31] Franz Neumann (1900–1954) was an émigré political scientist and member of the Institute for Social Research in New York, best known for his pioneering book *Behemoth: The Structure and Practice of National Socialism* (New York: Oxford University Press, 1942).

involved with the German study group in the Council of Foreign Relations. Most of all, I figured I had been in Princeton a long time. Phyl was willing to go along, although she didn't want to leave her nursery school. We spent the weekend touring the environs of Princeton, looking for housing to replace our university house at 12 College Road.

All of this was wasted energy. On Monday, 19 December, the Dean of the Faculty [at Princeton], J. Douglas Brown, described all the disadvantages of working in New York and made me a counter-offer ($8500, as I recall the figure, which, given the potential housing differential, was hard to turn down) and, in the afternoon, Mike Oates lent his persuasive tongue to the cause. I struck my colors, while perhaps, subconsciously, resolving that the *next* time an offer came I would not be so easily deterred from following my instincts. But I said No to Columbia, and No to Jim Rowe in Washington, who wanted me to come into the government in order to work on Foreign Service reform. As the year ended, I was content. I was a full professor at 36, although it wouldn't become official until September. And Phyl was happy enough. She would not have to leave her school, nor would the girls have to leave theirs.

[1950]

. . . Almost the first experience of this summer was a shocking one, learning, as we sat on the beach on a Sunday morning (June 25), that the North Koreans had crossed the parallel and that we were faced with an act of aggression. Thousands of younger men, and everybody else who was in the reserve, must have had a sinking feeling that morning, knowing that they were almost certain to be called. As a father of three in my late 30s, there was no danger of this in my case; and my fears were more general—of an expansion of the war to Europe. President Truman's prompt action in the name of the UN, and our subsequent action to build up NATO despite our increasing involvement in Korea, were what prevented this, I am sure. Leaving this aside, there is no doubt that the Korean War, which in its first phase looked like a Western rout, took the edge off the summer. . . .

It was at this time that the University of California Board of Regents, under the influence of John Neylan, its most powerful member, decided to require an oath of loyalty to the United States of all members of the University faculty. When the faculty objected, the Trustees insisted; attempts at mediation between two hardening positions, made by people like my *Doktorvater* [Ph.D. advisor] Ray Sontag, failed; and people who refused to take the oath began to have their salaries withheld and to be forced out of their positions.

This was the beginning of what was to assume uglier forms at the height of the McCarthy assault upon freedom of thought. The embattled California professors appealed to their colleagues at other institutions; and on 7 September, in Whig Lounge, George Stewart of the Berkeley English Department (author of that good novel *Storm*) talked to a group of us about the controversy and asked for our support. The History Department seized on this with enthusiasm (Elmer Beller and Jerry Blum particularly), and I undertook to coordinate the collection of signatures from other departments to a long telegram to the Regents expressing our outrage. It was a sign of the times that some of our colleagues in Modern Languages felt it necessary to clutter up the lists with statements that their signature must not be taken to signify any sympathy for communism. Even so, we collected 340 signatures (plus those gathered at the Institute by Harold Cherniss) which we wired to the Regents and the Berkeley faculty on 22 September. (Whether this had any appreciable effect on the thinking of many people could be debated. . . .)

For some time, I had been involved in giving a course on teaching for our graduate students, a variant of the Instructors Orientation Course at Quantico. I think it was useful, and I continued to believe this was true after I went to Stanford, although it was not until 1973 that my colleagues there decided to try to do something of the sort. Another experiment, which was put into effect in the fall of 1950, was the Thesis Writers Seminar, at which people writing dissertations submitted chapters to their fellows for criticism and to faculty who attended (and sometimes submitted chapters of things *they* were writing). This worked out, I am convinced, to the benefit of all concerned.

There were some interesting new faces in Princeton this fall. Fritz Ernst of Heidelberg was a guest of the Department, a good historian, editor of *Die Welt als Geschichte* (where I was to publish my Schleicher Letters), and a kind and helpful man, who was to commit suicide later, for mysterious reasons, somehow rooted in the Nazi period. At the Institute were Ed Fox of Cornell, a man who was always suspicious of talent, as his juniors in Ithaca were to discover, and Stuart Hughes,[32] who had just learned that he would not get tenure at Harvard. He asked me about his chances at Princeton, and I offered to put his name forward and did so, for I had then, and have now, a high opinion of his talents. But, when I mentioned the

---

[32] H. Stuart Hughes (1916–1999), one of the leading intellectual historians of his generation, left Harvard for Stanford in 1952, but would return to Harvard in 1957.

matter to Cy Black, he made it clear that he would fight the idea, largely, I gather, because Stuart had been active in the campaign to elect Henry Wallace in 1948. This Cy regarded as political naiveté of the worst kind, and he was so outspoken that I saw the game was lost.

The Korean War had led to a decided change of attitude toward Germany and a decision that the rearmament of the Federal Republic was essential for the security of Europe. Many of us were not happy about this, and on 10–11 November Ed Earle presided over a very interesting conference on the subject, which was attended by Henry Byroade of the State Department, Axel von dem Bussche (who once planned to kill Hitler at the cost of his own life, but was baulked by chance), Konrad Mommsen (Ted's banking brother), Hajo Holborn, Sig Neumann, and Carl Schorske[33] of Wesleyan, Felix Gilbert, and others. We didn't stop German rearmament, but we aired our indignation, and we had a very good singing party at our place, at which Sig Neumann taught me the Thirty Years War song "Wir zogen vor Friaul."[34] . . .

[1951]

. . . I began to write *The Politics of the Prussian Army*, finishing the 3000-word preface on 14 March 1951 and starting the first chapter two days later. This was tremendously exciting and tended to dim my enjoyment of other things. . . .

It was clear that the book would take a long time to finish. With a curious kind of logic which I find admirable in retrospect, and which I wish marked the thinking of some of my junior colleagues, I decided that, while the right hand was busy with Scharnhorst and Boyen, the left should be doing something too, particularly since the Marine project was finished, the Crowl-Isely volume having been published on 19 February. On a cold winter night when Felix Gilbert was in town and was having a drink with me, I suggested that we should repeat the collaboration that helped produce *Makers of Modern Strategy* in 1943 by editing a *Makers of Modern Diplomacy* in

---

[33] Carl E. Schorske (1915–2015) was one of America's leading intellectual and cultural historians of modern Europe. Craig reviewed his *Fin-de-Siecle Vienna: Politics and Culture* (New York: Knopf, 1980) for *The New Republic* (February 9, 1980) and *Thinking with History: Explorations in the Passage to Modernism* (Princeton, N.J.: Princeton University Press, 1998) for *The New York Review of Books* (August 13, 1998).

[34] This song is more commonly known as "Wir Zogen in das Feld" [We Marched Towards the Battlefield] but Craig cites a line from the song, "We Marched Towards Friuli."

which those of our friends who, like us, were engaged in long-term enterprises, might have a chance to get something shorter in book form in the interim. Before Felix went home, we had outlined a book covering the period 1815–1939; the following morning, we made a new outline for a book in the post-World War I period and made a list of potential contributors; on 6 April I wrote a letter to Chet d'Arms of the Rockefeller Foundation, explaining the project and asking for $250 to pay for an evening seminar for the contributors; and a week later Felix and I sat down in the Nassau Tavern with Henry Roberts, Stuart Hughes, Dick Challener,[35] Hajo Holborn and others and hammered out the guide-lines and established the deadlines for what was to be *The Diplomats, 1919–1939* (Princeton, 1953), a book that is still in print and still selling copies (the royalties now going into a fund in memory of David Potter).[36]

All this left little time for anything else. On 15 February, I had a rather odd lunch with Ed Earle, Johnny von Neumann, Robert Oppenheimer, and—the guest of honor—General Wedemeyer. The general proved to be as pompous on this occasion as he was when I visited him in the Pentagon. When the plane that was to take him back to Washington ("his plane," as he impressed on us) was late, he put on a fit of sulks that was something to behold. . . .

I was a member of a small group that met with George F. Kennan, who was now in residence; but I cannot remember much about our meetings, except that George had very odd ideas about the origins of World War I. Infinitely more interesting was a quartet that Jinx Harbison[37] organized, under student urging, to participate in the barbershop quartet contest that had replaced Senior Singing. . . .

And rest I did at least from teaching, for I had a fellowship at the Institute for Advanced Study for the fall semester. I made the most of this, not only to push my book ahead but to write a paper for the AHA meeting in New York in December ("The Professional Diplomat and His Problems," which appeared in *World Politics* at the beginning of the new year)[38] and a chapter

---

[35] Richard Challener (1923–2002) taught American and French diplomatic and military history at Princeton for more than half a century, from 1949 to 2000.

[36] David Potter (1910–1971), a distinguished American historian of the Civil War era, moved from Yale to Stanford in 1961, the same year during which Craig arrived from Princeton.

[37] E. Harris ("Jinx") Harbison (1907–1964) was a Reformation historian who had joined the Princeton faculty in 1933.

[38] Gordon A. Craig, "The Professional Diplomat and His Problems 1919–1939," *World Politics* 4: 2 (January 1952): 145–58.

for the tenth volume of the new *Cambridge Modern History* on the diplomacy of the period 1830–1870.[39] I enjoyed the Institute, not only for the relative peace it gave me, but because it gave me a chance to get to know people like Cherniss and Oppenheimer better (although I would never claim to have known Robert very well; Phyl was able to talk much more freely with him than I) and to meet and talk with new faces like Michael Postan, Jerry Brunner, and Bill Deakin. I had become an ardent fisherman, and this fall marked the beginning of my expeditions with Dick Challener, mostly at Grovers Mill Pond, where we fished in all weathers, sometimes breaking the ice to get the boat out. . . .

[1952]

. . . The intervening months had been marked by much hard work, for the editorial labors connected with *The Diplomats* increased at an accelerating pace as the winter gave way to spring, and after the beginning of February I was, of course, teaching again. I was also doing a good deal of reviewing for the *Herald Tribune* and the *US Quarterly Book Review*; and was engaged as usual in other activities. In January, Phyl and I went down to Bryn Mawr, where I gave the Webster Memorial Lecture and where we stayed overnight at the Joe Herkens (Caroline Robbins); I was still a member of the Kennan study group at the Institute; I was a newly elected member of the Board of the Social Science Research Council, which met periodically in New York and where I met people like Roy Nichols (that wonderful story-teller), Pendleton Herring, Bob Sears of Stanford,[40] whom I was to know years later as a dean, and Phil Mosely,[41] with whom I was to work in many capacities.

Figures from the past moved through the scene. George Costopoulos, a firm friend at Quantico in 1944, the gay blade of Marfairwest and Tijuana, surfaced briefly, looking somewhat uncertain and depressed, and then vanished never to be heard from again. The Woodwards, however, returned to Princeton, where Ed Earle had secured an Institute appointment for

---

39 Gordon A. Craig, "The System of Alliances and the Balance of Power," in *The New Cambridge Modern History*, Volume 10, *The Zenith of European Power, 1830–70*, ed. J. P. T. Bury (Cambridge: Cambridge University Press, 1960), 246–73.

40 Robert Sears (1908–1989), a specialist in child psychology and the psychology of personality, was the Dean of the School of Humanities and Sciences at Stanford during Craig's first decade there, from 1961 to 1970.

41 Philip Mosely (1906–1972) was a specialist in Soviet affairs at Columbia University. He served successive administrations as a foreign policy adviser from the Roosevelt era through the 1960s.

Woodward, almost every year from now until Lady Woodward's death, and we became very fond of them and they very fond of the girls. I remember many a pleasant lunch with him, eating oysters out of a paper sack and drinking American Chablis, with which he planned to fill the cellars of Balliol College, where he had become head of the wine committee. Woodward was not universally liked. That clever man, Isaiah Berlin, with whom I dined in the General Wayne Inn in Bryn Mawr with Felix Gilbert in February, likened him to a Restoration abbé and intimated that he was richer in ambition than in talent. I regarded him as a fine historian with a healthy suspicion of cleverness, and a gay companion. I tried to express my feelings on this score in the obituary notice which I wrote for the *Proceedings of the American Philosophical Society* when he died in 1971.[42] But I was unable to recapture the gusto with which he told the story of his having tea with a horse that had fought in the Crimean War or recalled how he and his wife used to make up names of historians in order to confuse G. P. Gooch, who claimed to know all historians and would respond to their requests for his opinion of their inventions by saying things like "Ah yes, an interesting mind, but not quite sound, don't you agree?"

From Oxford too came Dan Davin, whom I had not seen since 1938. I met him in New York during the Social Science Research Council meetings of 29–30 March, had dinner with him at The Old Homestead (9th Av. at 15th) and a lot of drinks in the King Cole Bar of the St. Regis, and then, when my meetings were over, dragged him down to Princeton for two days. A wonderful reunion which affected me with nostalgia for days. But it was to be a good while before I got back to Oxford. . . .

This was a political year, and under the influence of Joe McLean of the Politics Department I became involved in an ultimately fruitless attempt to win a seat in the U.S. Senate for Archie Alexander.[43] Archie's trouble was that he was so much the gentleman that he would not even mention his opponent's age, although that gentleman, the incumbent H. Alexander Smith, was virtually in his dotage. When I suggested that he might use indirection and say that he had the greatest respect for a man who had been

[42] Gordon A. Craig, "Sir Lewellyn Woodward (1890–1971)," *American Philosophical Society Yearbook 1971* (Philadelphia: American Philosophical Society, 1972), 200–202.

[43] Archibald S. Alexander (1906–1979), a Princeton graduate, lawyer, and civil servant, had served with Craig as a member of the State Department's Foreign Service Selection Board during the late 1940s, and subsequently as Under Secretary of the United States Army during the Truman Administration.

the personal friend of Teddy Roosevelt, Archie merely looked pained, and his professional advisers, a bunch of old pols from Trenton, looked shocked. The academic brain-trusters, McLean, Eric Goldman, and I, were of no use in this campaign; but it wasn't a Democratic year in any case. . . .

We settled in and listened to the hijinks that accompanied the nomination of Eisenhower and Nixon at the Republican convention. Then I got down to the last phase of the editorial work in connection with *The Diplomats*. Felix arrived on 29 July, and we vetted the late-arriving chapters together and then wrote our introduction, by means of telepathic communication between his cabin and ours. This 4000-word essay, which was later highly praised and much relied on by the reviewers, was actually written in two days.[44] On 5 August, the manuscript was complete and was sent off from Dublin to the Princeton University Press. . . .

Except for a Social Science Research Council meeting at Arden House (I managed some fishing even on that, with Bryce Wood and Don Price) and a couple of trips to New York to dig up photographs for *The Diplomats*, I stuck pretty close to Princeton this semester. I was teaching full time (History 317, graduate course, teachers' seminar); there were the proofs for *The Diplomats*; and I was doing a fair amount of reviewing for the *Herald Tribune*. Aside from this, Princeton was a rather interesting place this quarter. On 23 September I had lunch with Cyril Falls;[45] two days later, Dean Crystal blew in from nowhere (a man purged of vice but also of much of his humor; thus, even as the grape does us in, so does abstention), and we had a pleasant nostalgic lunch with Alba Warren; a week later I met Basil Liddell Hart[46] for the first time and in the month that followed saw him frequently and introduced him to an overflow audience in McCosh 50; in late October Sir Charles Webster, with whom I had once had breakfast in Sumner's rooms in Balliol, came to the Institute for a few days, and I lunched with him; Paul Kluke was the guest of our department, and on 8 November I met Hans Herzfeld[47] (who was at Columbia on some kind of

---

[44] Gordon A. Craig and Felix Gilbert, "Introduction," *The Diplomats, 1919–1939*, ed. Gordon A. Craig and Felix Gilbert (Princeton: Princeton University Press, 1953), 3–13.

[45] Cyril Falls (1888–1971) was a British military historian and journalist, noted for his works on the First World War.

[46] Sir Basil Liddell Hart (1895–1970) was a British veteran of the First World War who became an influential historian of military strategy.

[47] Hans Herzfeld (1892–1982) was a German historian who specialized in twentieth-century German history. He taught at the Free University in Berlin and

exchange with the Free University); in mid-November I had lunch at the Institute with John McCloy, his aide Shepard Stone[48] (with whom I was to have relations at a later date), Jack Viner, and Ed Earle; and a little later I met that brilliant and unfortunate man, Herbert Rosinski, whose German army book I was to edit for republication years later.[49] To all these visitors were added my uncle Bert from Victoria and his wife Marie, who descended on us on 1 November. Bert was absolutely fascinated by our television set, which we had just acquired, and could hardly be dragged away from it. When he was detached from the tube, however, I noticed that he was a pretty fair trencherman and not averse to a drop.

We all fought and died with Adlai Stevenson, of course. I was prominent in the Princeton Volunteers and not only lent my pen to the cause but did some speaking—notably at an enthusiastic rally in Roosevelt, N.J. on election eve, along with Joe McLean and Warren Moscow. Alas! Roosevelt was no microcosm, and the country was not ready for Adlai. . . .

[1953]

. . . January was all proofs and exams, and the former continued into the spring semester and were not disposed of until mid-February. I celebrated by getting out of town with the family and spending the Washington's Birthday weekend in Nelson, where it was cold but exhilarating and we could see new faces. I returned all geared up for my army book and actually started on Chapter V on 1 March, but this was soon interrupted by the necessity of preparing an index for *The Diplomats*. . . .

I was now involved with civil-military working groups of the Social Science Research Council and the Twentieth Century Fund, and the former led to a speech before the whole SSRC Board in late March—a speech, I recall, that caused me a lot of trouble and was finally written in the Biltmore the night before. Once it was out of the way, however, I had a hearty lunch

---

was a leading force in the establishment of the university's Friedrich Meinecke Institute for the study of history.

[48] Shepard Stone (1908–1990) was an American journalist, foundation administrator, and supporter of the Free University of Berlin.

[49] Herbert Rosinski, *The German Army*, edited and with an introduction by Gordon A. Craig (New York: Frederick A. Praeger, 1966). Herbert Rosinski (1903–1962), a military historian and student of naval strategy, emigrated from Germany to England in 1936, found himself briefly interned as an enemy alien after the outbreak of the Second World War in 1939, and accepted an appointment as a member of the Institute for Advanced Study in 1940. After a peripatetic career as a lecturer, he died prematurely of heart disease in 1962.

at the Marmiton and dinner with Jakob Goldschmidt (who was horrified to learn that I had dared to walk in Central Park). After the second day's meeting, I went across the river to Jersey City, for the first time since before the war, finding it a sad place, and paid Jean Glassford a visit.

In Princeton, the traffic began to slacken a bit in the early spring, and the only notable transient was Walter Lippmann[50] whom I met in March and talked with at some length. We had something in common because, early in 1952, he had borrowed the final quotation in my article on the professional diplomat (Balfour's warning to the House of Commons in 1918 against constant interrogation of Foreign Service personnel)—and shoved it into one of his columns without any acknowledgement to me.[51] He had, however, written to me about this, and about my article as a whole, and we had had a cordial exchange. It was good to see him again and to listen to his assessment of the temper in Washington and his fears that Eisenhower would do nothing to control Senator McCarthy and his supporters. Already the morale in the State Department was at the vanishing point, because neither the President nor Mr. Dulles seemed inclined to check Scott McLeod's heavy-handed administration of personnel matters, which some people regarded as amounting to a purge. . . .

Before leaving for Nelson I learned that I had been awarded a Fulbright Fellowship. I decided that life was complicated enough, and turned it down.

No sooner had we reached our camp than I had something else to turn down, for I received a message from James Conant in Bonn, asking me to become cultural attaché in Germany. This was attractive, but it felt that two years in Germany would be difficult for the girls at this age and would probably kill my army book. So I said No and, when the offer was renewed in the latter part of July, said No again. I got back to the book and finished chapters V and VI before the summer was over. . . .

I also got to know Harold and Lorrie Stein[52] at this time. In these first years, Harold was a vigorous and, on the whole effective, wheeler-dealer in the Princeton community, but these government types always tried sooner

---

50 Walter Lippmann (1889–1974) was one of the most influential American journalists of the twentieth century, as well as a political philosopher and a pioneer in the field of media studies.

51 Gordon A. Craig, "The Professional Diplomat and His Problems 1919–1939," *World Politics* 4: 2 (January 1952): 145–58.

52 Harold Stein (1903–1966), a professor of public and international affairs at Princeton, was responsible for coordinating the civilian manpower programs of the War Production Board during the Second World War.

or later to assert a superior wisdom, as if bringing light to the children of darkness. Harold did not make the mistakes that Steve Bailey made, which cost him a promising Princeton career and the directorship of the Woodrow Wilson School, but he made enemies. I was not one of them, for I found him a cultivated man and an amusing companion, and we were fast friends until his death. I liked Lorrie too, although she drank more than was good for her, but then who didn't?

Dan Sayre[53] and I became very close also, and it was in these last months of 1953 that we talked about a Princeton TV series. I was involved in a minor way with the media, for I had been asked to serve as a consultant for a radio show about Hitler and the Rhineland coup of 1936 in a series called "Stroke of Fate." (What would have happened if the French had marched?) . . .

A week later, we had our official house-warming and 70 people came to drink rum and sauterne punch and wish us well. This was the week of my 40th birthday. I was now earning $9000 a year (it had taken me three years to equal the salary Columbia offered me in 1949) plus about $2000 in royalties and lecture and consultant fees. This, for those days, was more than adequate, for rents in Princeton and Nelson were low, and one could eat in a good restaurant without having to skip three ordinary meals in order to pay for it. Moreover, the girls were all in public schools. I was conscious of the fact that one day they would be in college and that that might be an expensive business. I had a contract with Henry Holt for a European text which I hoped might relieve that burden, but, although I had signed in 1941, I hadn't done anything on the book, aside from having an occasional lunch with Charley Madison, Holt's history editor. . . .

Woodward was back in town and, very briefly, Noble Frankland and Henry Guerlac. December was filled with the usual number of parties (we really did get around a lot, and, although the faces were the same, they were good faces, and, when it came to talk, it was hard to equal Jack Viner or Harold Stein, or, for that matter, Marion Levy.[54] There were also some good listeners, thank heaven). . . .

---

[53] Daniel Sayre (1903–1956), an aeronautics expert, was associate dean of Princeton's School of Engineering and founding director of the James Forrestal Research Center, established in 1951.

[54] Marion Levy, Jr. (1918–2002), a sociologist, was best known for his two-volume *Modernization and the Structure of Societies* (Princeton: Princeton University Press, 1966), and a characteristically witty self-published book, "Levy's Laws of the Disillusionment of the True Liberal," which became a widely quoted classic.

The AHA meetings this year were in Chicago. I gave a paper on "Chancellor and Chief of Staff," which was later published in my book of essays,[55] had a good dinner at the Red Star Inn on Clark Street (a well-known German restaurant, noisy but excellent) and drove back to Princeton with Ralph Giesey[56] and a fellow named Chevchenko. They were both protégés of Ernst Kantorowicz, the medievalist who had come to the Institute in consequence of the oath fight in Berkeley, an original who combined gastronomy (it was from him that I got my recipe for poached sole with sauce Mornay) with rather esoteric research interests, a kind of throwback, one felt, to the days when he was a member of the circle around Stefan George. (Of his book on ceremonial, E. L. Woodward said: "It's really all in Shakespeare, you know.")[57] Kantorowicz liked to bring bright young men with attractive wives to the Institute. He taught these acolytes, for that's what they became, a great deal, while making them do a lot of fetching and carrying. They were always admitted to his parties, which featured excellent food and wine and remarkable coruscations of wit on the part of the host. The attractive young wives were usually in the kitchen making canapés. Giesey was a special problem, because he changed wives almost as often as Eric Goldman. Kantorowicz grumbled to me once: "He's making a business of it." . . .

[1954]

What happened to us in 1954? I cannot say in any detail, for I lost my pocket diary for the New Year somewhere in Munich, and with it went all my notes for the period before September. The journal of my trip to Europe with Blum covers the period from 24 September until 26 November. Before that the only hard data I possess are brief notations in the end pages of the 1953 diary. . . .

---

55 Gordon A. Craig, "Relations between Civilian and Military Authorities in the Second German Empire: Chancellor and Chief of Staff, 1871–1918," in *War, Politics, and Diplomacy: Selected Essays* (New York: Praeger, 1966), 121–31.

56 Ralph E. Giesey (1923–2011), an influential scholar of early modern France, was a pioneer in the study of the relationship between ritual performances and elite thought and conduct.

57 Ernst Kantorowicz's masterpiece, *The King's Two Bodies: A Study in Medieval Political Theology* (Princeton: Princeton University Press, 1957), is one of the classic works of twentieth-century scholarship on the Middle Ages. He had arrived at the Institute for Advanced Study in 1951, and remained there until his death in 1963. In his memoirs, George Kennan described him as "a man of ineffable Old World charm" and "an essential feature of the Princeton of the 1950s."

. . . At the end of 1953, I was still working on chapter IX of the army book. I must have written the last three chapters and got the whole second half of the book ready for the press in the first months of the new year, for I received page proofs in November. That would account for most of the time that was not spent on teaching and my service on the Social Science Research Council Board and military committee. There was an attempt by students to revive the Craig-Hall debates, which had on one occasion jammed Whig Hall to the gunnels, but Walter was crotchety and uncooperative. Probably just as well.

The most shattering experience of this period was the death of Ed Earle, who had become seriously ill in December and never rallied. I was to dedicate my Prussian army book to him, and this was appropriate, for I owed him a great deal. Edward Mead Earle will not be long remembered for his works. Shortly after the completion of his first book, *Turkey, the Great Powers, and the Bagdad Railway*, he was stricken by tuberculosis and had to spend years at Saranac. When he could work again, his teachers, Charles Beard and Carleton Hayes, managed to get him a professorship at the Institute for Advanced Study. How this was managed, I don't know. I have heard that the post was first offered to Beard himself. In any case, Earle was *the* Professor of History at the Institute for Advanced Study from about 1938 to 1954.

His diminished energies would not permit major projects. I suppose his only independent works were his edition of the Federalist Papers and a little wartime book called *Against the Torrent*, which is badly dated. But his services to the profession were nevertheless very great. When he organized his military studies seminar at the Institute in the late 30s, he revitalized a branch of history that had always been regarded with tolerant amusement or patronizing scorn by other historians; and the appearance of *Makers of Modern Strategy* in 1943 was a professional event of major importance. Among other things, it reestablished the kind of military history once written by Delbrück[58] and encouraged a new concentration on the political, economic, and social aspects of military establishments, while, at the same time, encouraging a new sophistication in strategical studies. My own Prussian army book grew out of my work on *Makers of Modern Strategy*, and it was Ed who first encouraged me to undertake it. At least indirectly,

---

[58] Hans Delbrück (1848–1929), a pioneering German military historian, was the subject of Craig's contribution to *Makers of Modern Strategy*, published by Princeton University Press in 1943, an essay of such high quality that it was reprinted in the second edition of the book, edited by Peter Paret, in 1986.

[Morris] Janowitz, [Michael] Howard, and [Peter] Paret[59] also owe a debt to Earle's work; and air force historians (Ed was one of the first to see the importance of air power in history) regard his work on their specialty as almost biblical in authority.

After the war, Ed had other seminars—a highly successful one on France, an unsuccessful one on England, which was attended by, among others, E. L. Woodward and Bill Willcox and was characterized by *burschikös* [boyish] attacks by me upon Jack Viner's positions and skillful ripostes by Jack in which he cited my articles to prove that I was the cause of his errors. These feasts of reason were always fun, particularly for the young. Ed always had his eye on the *Nachwuchs* [new blood], and many a young man, languishing in Buffalo or Carbondale, had his life changed by a letter from Ed expressing interest in his first book or a recent article and asking him whether he might not be interested in elaborating his views during a term at the Institute. Neither of Ed's successors, George Kennan and Felix Gilbert, has been as successful as Ed was in searching out talent—he brought Hughes and Gordon Wright[60] and Schorske and Willcox and Challener and many others to the Institute at just the right moment in their careers—nor have they tried as hard.

I owe him two semesters at the Institute as a member; but my debt is much greater than that. After the experience of *Makers of Modern Strategy*, I was a special protégé of his, and he promoted my interests, getting me into jobs where he thought I might do well and gain prestige, recommending me to Irita Van Doren of the *Herald-Tribune* as a reviewer, watching over my work, and improving its style. Phyllis was annoyed by this, fearing that the Earles were trying to take me over completely (Beatrice and Roz did come on a bit strong) and were seeking to claim credit for my achievements. This, of course, was taradiddle (Phyl never did like the Earle women), for I have never been a very likely Trilby for anyone's Svengali. Ed was not a completely selfless man, but in all of our dealings I am convinced that he was thinking primarily of *my* development. Thus, he belonged among those

---

[59] Peter Paret (1924–2020), a leading historian of war who also did distinguished work in the field of art history, was Gordon Craig's colleague at Stanford from 1969 to 1985. With the great British military historian Michael Howard (1922–2019), he published the standard English-language edition of Carl von Clausewitz's *On War* in 1976.

[60] Gordon Wright (1912–2000), one of the leading American historians of modern France, taught at Stanford from 1957 until his retirement in 1977; as chair of the Department of History, he was instrumental in recruiting Craig from Princeton to Stanford in 1961.

I regarded as my teachers: Bill Dougherty and Jean Glassford, Sontag and Holborn, Sumner and Woodward, Ted Mommsen, and, perhaps, Felix Gilbert. It was natural for me to dedicate my big book to him, and, after he died, I was touched and proud when Bea told me that he had wanted me to have the academic gown that his teacher, Carleton J. H. Hayes, had worn and passed on to him. (When the girls gave me a new Princeton gown when we went west in 1961, I presented Ed's gown to my best student, Henry Ashby Turner, Jr.)[61]

I can't remember when Ed died or even going to his funeral. Perhaps I was away, but where?

The newest of my ventures at this time was television. In the late weeks of 1953 Dan Sayre had surprised me by saying that the idea of a Princeton TV show had been languishing in committee for months and that the time had come for action. "… So you and I are going to throw the hams on the tube." That's just about what happened. Dan and I negotiated with NBC who put up money to support a half-hour Sunday afternoon program, and a bright young producer came down to Princeton to help us plan the programs. . . . He later gave up TV and wrote a novel. I don't blame him, for he had an almost Sisyphean labor in getting the suspicious professors far enough up the hill to get a clear view of the possibilities open to them. With much patience, he taught us that we could not simply put a lot of lecturers on the screen; with much expostulation and academic profanity, we taught him that certain TV techniques simply would not do in our programs and that the Terewth could not be hoked up.[62] On the balance, we got along excellently well and we put about eight shows on the screen during the spring. These included one on perception with Hadley Cantril, one on insects' (particularly bees') sense of time with Colin Pittendrigh, a very effective half hour on utopian novels with Dudley Johnson, and another on the appeal of communism with Gabriel Almond, who had just written a book on the subject. Mo Lee, Jinx Harbison, and I did something on total and limited war, with goofy maps and charts. (The Terewth *has* to be hoked up a bit.)

It was a low-budget show, so the camera work was a bit primitive, with

---

[61] Henry Ashby Turner Jr. (1932–2008) earned his Ph.D. under Gordon Craig's direction at Princeton in 1960 and taught at Yale University for over forty years. *German Big Business and the Rise of Hitler* (New York: Oxford University Press, 1985) was his best-known book.

[62] Dickens's bombastic preacher Mr. Chadband enthuses about "the light of Terewth," i.e., Truth, in *Bleak House*.

a lot of shots of backs of heads. Strange accidents occurred—falling screens disclosing carpenters and other types who were not supposed to be in the act, an actor in Almond's show unwrapping a sandwich and creating a noise like heavy machine gunfire that drowned out the voices. Even so, the program was a success. It was renewed for two years, and, in the second year, won a prize. For that period I was the effective director, and the target first of my colleagues' complaints that we were demeaning the name of Princeton, later of the same colleagues' hints that they would not be averse to performing, still later of their charges that I was discriminating against them by not putting them on the screen.

During the summer the family was in Nelson. So was I on weekends, but the rest of the time I was at Harvard, teaching in the summer session. I can't have liked it much, for I remember more about the boring bus rides between Cambridge and Dublin on Fridays and Sunday than I do about my courses or my digs. But there were pleasant moments—at concerts of the Boston Pops Orchestra; in Fenway Park, watching Ted Williams beat the Yankees; on private rambles in Boston and, once, in Marblehead. I spent an evening with Sidney Monas, a former student, and his description of his work on Nicholas I's Third Section made me interested in the police and, later, inspired a section of my textbook.[63] Dave Owen invited me to dinner (we had been colleagues at Yale), and I saw something of Don McKay. I went to restaurants like Loch-Ober and Jakesy Wirt's with Bob Albion, who had left Princeton to end his career at Harvard, principally, we gathered, because it was close to Maine, where he had a boat; and I got to like a couple of quite ordinary joints off Harvard Square, to one of which I always repaired when I got off the Sunday night bus, because it had good dark bread and better dark beer.

I knew that I was going to Germany in the fall, for I had persuaded the University Research Committee that the University's only German historian should get over there and get to know something about the German academic scene. I had got a grant but was very nervous about the German language in which I had no speaking ability except a faint residue of what little I commanded in 1935 and 1938. Out of the goodness of his

---

[63] Sidney Monas (1924–2019) was a professor in the Departments of Slavic and Eurasian Studies and History at the University of Texas for forty years, and the author of *The Third Section: Police and Society in Russia under Nicholas I* (Cambridge: Harvard University Press, 1961).

heart, Klaus Epstein,[64] who must have just finished his graduate work, undertook to help me. I think I also hired a nice but very homely German girl, and we three met two or three times a week and conversed. It was very painful but useful, and it made Klaus and me friends. We remained so until his untimely death in 1967. I last saw him in the Harnack House in Berlin, where I was giving a public lecture. He was unable to stay for the question period and left as it began, waving to me as he did. A few days later, I heard that he had been killed in an automobile accident in Frankfurt.

We returned to Princeton from Nelson at the end of August, and I began to prepare for my trip. I had persuaded Jerry Blum to come with me at least for the first part (he flatly refused to go to Germany), and now I buckled down to the job of preparing an elaborate strategical plan for the junket. (I hadn't been an intelligence officer for nothing.) Jerry did a lot of jeering about this, but it was effective, saving time and helping us plan activities in advance. Jerry never complained about the restaurants we visited, which had in fact been listed before we even left the States. I always knew ahead of time, in the case of cities I had never visited, where we were going to sleep and eat and what we ought to try to see. . . .

For the period that extended from my return from Europe in 1954 until my next trip abroad in 1958, I kept no regular *Tagebuch*. What follows is based on my pocket diaries for the period [GAC, October 1974].

[1955]

The return home on the *Queen Mary* was my last Atlantic crossing by ship and perhaps the dullest, equaled in this only by the trip home in 1938. All of the others were memorable. The first was in April 1914 on the SS *Grampian* of the White Star Line from Glasgow to Montreal, a dreadfully stormy trip during which weather and fog caused the death, off the Grand Banks, of a ship that left the dock on the same night as we, the SS *Empress of Ireland*, a tragedy second only in loss of life to that of the *Titanic*.[65] While I have no personal recollection of this voyage, I heard of it often in the course of my childhood and was always told that I comported myself well,

---

[64] Klaus Epstein (1927–1967) left Germany as a child with his family after the Nazi seizure of power. At the time of his death at the age of forty, he was the chair of the Department of History at Brown University.

[65] RMS *Empress of Ireland* was a Scottish-built ocean liner that sank near the mouth of the Saint Lawrence River following a collision in thick fog with the Norwegian collier *Storstad* in the early hours of the morning of May 29, 1914. Of the 1,477 people on board, 1,012 died, making it the worst maritime disaster in Canadian history.

laughing heartily during the ship's most desperate curvetting. Equally tempestuous was the 1936 crossing in the SS *Laconia* from New York to Liverpool, with most of that year's class of Rhodes Scholars. The ship unaccountably stopped in Boston and then headed straight into a storm that lasted for five days and incapacitated everyone except hardy souls like Rostow and me, a fact always held against me because I had headed the committee that chose the ship. The rigors of the voyage were alleviated on the last two days by a continuous party that culminated in Phil Kaiser's attempt (not wholly unsuccessful) to reproduce the famous stowaway scene from *A Night at the Opera* in my stateroom.

The two crossings in 1935 were less rambunctious and I remember them fondly because they were filled with moonlight and singing and pretty girls. The home voyage in 1938 was not interesting, and the one with Blum on the *Elizabeth* wasn't either, despite some mildly amusing experiences with the two Scottish ladies who were our tablemates. Jerry likes to tell the story of how, annoyed by the experience of having my quotations from *Tam-o-Shanter* corrected by these old biddies, I took my revenge by pretending to find a pearl in one of my oysters; but no trip in which something like that was the high-point would be considered, by any fair-minded man, as a gasser.

Still it was not as dull as my voyage home in 1954, during which I met and danced with a couple of pleasant girls and had drinks with a few amiable fellows but never felt like repeating the experience. The only thing I remember distinctly is sitting in the lounge smoking the excellent *Punch* and *Llaranaga* cigars that the steward brought me and wishing that the *Queen Mary* would hurry up and get home. I was at least provided with lots of time to ruminate upon the conversations I had had in Germany and to begin the task that was to occupy me for months, the onerous one of reading the proofs of my book. . . .

. . . In addition to teaching and the TV program, I was doing quite a bit of reviewing for the *Tribune* (Kubizek's memoirs of the young Hitler and Garrett Mattingly's *Renaissance Diplomacy* were among the books I reviewed this semester)[66] and making some short lecture trips to places like the University of Delaware and the Army War College at Carlisle Barracks, Pennsylvania. I had been made a member of the Advisory Board on the History of the U.S. Army in World War II and went to my first meeting of

---

[66] Gordon A. Craig, "Adolf Hitler When Young," *New York Herald Tribune Book Review* (13 March 1955): 1, 10, and "Diplomats—Spies or Peacemakers?," *New York Herald Tribune Book Review* (26 June 1955): 3.

this group at the beginning of April, having cocktails with General Matthew Ridgway and dinner with the lesser brass at the Metropolitan Club.

Another general of some renown whom I met was Hasso von Manteuffel, who had played a prominent role in the Battle of the Bulge in December 1944. He came to New York later in April as part of a group of parliamentarians and members of Amt Blank[67]; and Shep Stone arranged a luncheon at the University Club to which I was invited.[68] Axel von dem Bussche was also in the country doing Amt Blank business in Washington, and I had seen him at the time of the OMH Board meeting earlier in the month. . . .

After the department party and an appearance in a Faculty-Alumni Seminar at reunions ("Problems of Modern France": Gardner Patterson, Ed Furniss, Ed Katzenbach and I), we took off for Nelson and had an uneventful and entirely satisfactory summer. Perhaps not wholly uneventful. I came back from fishing one day and, while automatically straightening some books in a shelf so that their spines would be aligned, discovered that the offending volume was *The Politics of the Prussian Army, 1640-1945*, which Phyllis had artfully positioned to catch my eye. There is nothing quite as exciting, among intellectual things, as first seeing the book that you have labored on for years. That was a good day! . . .

The big event of the fall—aside from the publication of my book in October and its choice as a selection for members by the History Book Club a month later—was my mother's 70th birthday which we celebrated in the grand style on 10 December with all the old gang. . . .

We were beginning to get some good graduate students in these years. My Ph.Ds Katzenbach and Aandahl were now finished. In 1954–55 Stanley

---

[67] The Amt Blank was a West German government office headed by Theodor Blank, which served as a provisional defense ministry until the Allies allowed West German rearmament and a formal Ministry of Defense was established in 1955.

[68] In Volume XXXIII, p. 43 of the diaries, Craig described this meeting in greater detail: "Spier has in his manuscript a report of a luncheon in New York given by Shepard Stone for the members of the Bundestag's European Security Committee, a group that included Fritz Erker and General Hasso von Manteuffel. Gabriel Almond and I were among the American participants in this luncheon discussion and so was Walter Millis, who astonished the German guests and embarrassed and infuriated the American ones, by erupting with a harangue about the imminent takeover of the American government by the Pentagon. Millis, a rather nice man ordinarily (I knew him when he was collaborating with Harold Stein) was a little nuts on the dangers of American militarism, and he certainly chose the wrong place to show it."

Mellon, Burdette Poland, Gene Brucker, and Dick Dunne, all of whom took my colloquia, finished their degrees. Ivo Lederer,[69] Gus Alef, and Peter Sugar, with whom I was to work closely, had just begun their studies. Richard Ullman[70] was also doing graduate work now and did a paper on U.S. diplomats in the 30s that was so good that I urged him to publish it in *World Politics*. He later claimed that this advice, and my bringing him together with George Kennan, had a determinative effect on his career.

[1956]

The New Year started pleasantly with tea with the Woodwards and some skating on the lake, but there were sadder notes. In February Bill Koren died, and even before then Dan Sayre had been stricken with lung cancer and, after an operation that seemed likely to succeed, had a recurrence. He was to die while we were in California, remaining gay and optimistic until the very end.

Life was almost routinized in this first half of 1956. Phyl did her work at the school, sometimes asking me to participate (there was an evening panel discussion in February on sibling rivalry at which I spoke) and I did my teaching and continued to work at the Church. Apart from a trip to Exeter, to give a lecture to the school, in January, another one at Iowa City to give a paper on "Bismarck and his Ambassadors" at a conference arranged by Bill Aydelotte, and a pleasant trip with Phyl to Lexington, Virginia to give the Phi Beta Kappa Address at Washington and Lee, I stayed close to home. The TV series was in its third and last year, and Eric Goldman[71] and I did a show with George Kennan on the origins of the Marshall Plan, which the timorous TV people did not want to shoot because George had changed his script at the last moment, and there was no time for their lawyers to look it over. The fact that George was telling the story of the origins of the Marshall Plan for the first time was of no importance to them, and they went ahead only when I threatened to cancel

---

[69] Ivo J. Lederer (1929–1998), born in Zagreb, Yugoslavia, fled with his Jewish family to Italy in 1941, survived three years in hiding there, and reached the United States as a refugee in 1944. A specialist in Russian and East European diplomatic history, he was Gordon Craig's colleague at Stanford from 1965 to 1977.

[70] Richard Ullmann (1933–2014), a diplomatic historian and foreign policy scholar, taught at Princeton's Woodrow Wilson School of Public and International Affairs from 1965 until his retirement in 2002.

[71] Eric Goldman (1916–1989), a professor of American history at Princeton and later an adviser to President Lyndon Johnson, published his most influential work in 1952: *Rendezvous with Destiny: A History of Modern American Reform.*

the rest of the series. It was a rare dust-up, which nearly drove Goldman to apoplexy, but George never turned a hair. The show turned out to be a good one, and we viewed it on 21 April, with the Kennans, the Goldmans, the Ed DeLongs, and the John Rudds.

In May, I went to Washington for a meeting of the Office of the Chief of Military History Advisory Board and, in the same month, to Rutgers for a conference on coalition diplomacy, where I met Paul Nitze, whom I liked, and Louis Halle, whom I didn't, largely because of his contemptuous attitude toward the UN. I later discovered that he was really more intelligent than he appeared, but his attitude was congruent with another tendency that was common to the government intellectuals at this conference. They were all fond of quoting Thucydides and of using his world picture to rationalize the Cold War. Years later, in a lecture at Tucson on "The Dangers of Thinking Historically," I was to recall this and to cite it as a dangerous example of imposing a dialectical pattern upon current affairs, using Thucydides to justify a policy based upon unconditionality and disrespect for the rights of neutrals. . . .

And now came the great and fateful adventure. I had been invited two years earlier by Ralph W. Tyler to become a Fellow of the Center for Advanced Study in the Behavioral Sciences in Stanford, Calif., and when I was forced to decline the invitation, he postponed it until 1956–57. We now set out for California, an enormously exciting business for us all because, except for Phyl we knew nothing of the west, and even she had not been to California.

So we cranked up the Ford Country Sedan and, after dropping my mother, who had been visiting us, at Keene, took off at noon on 13 August. . . . We settled in quickly and were greeted with western hospitality by the Easton Rothwells of the Hoover Institution, and Stuart Hughes, who was to leave Stanford this year, spend six months at the Center, and then return to Harvard.[72] On 10 September we made our first visit to San Francisco. . . . It was the damnedest city we had ever seen. It still is.

The idea of the Center was a stroke of genius, and I trust the founders have realized that by now. Bringing a job lot of 50 scholars together in a beautiful setting and giving them freedom to do what they wanted to do,

---

[72] The Hoover Institution is a public policy and research institution located on the grounds of Stanford University. It was founded by and named for President Herbert Hoover. Because of its reputation as a bastion of conservatism and its regular appointment of former government figures as fellows, its relationship with the faculty and students of its host institution has often been contentious.

alone or together—what a noble conception! Freedom is, of course, a tricky business, and there were those among us who were made nervous by it and missed the comfort of their own telephones and their usual comfortable load of committees, which they cursed but cherished as a buffer against the challenge of scholarship. Some developed anxieties as the year went on and became subject to nervous tics or writing blocs from which they vainly sought release by sniffing a magic bottle contrived by Joe Wolpe, which merely affected its users with euphoria, so that writing no longer seemed important. Some took refuge in seminars, some of which turned out to be quite educational (like the one on social stratification that I attended), although most petered out inconclusively. A few were disjointed by the whole experience and ended up in divorce or, in the case of one wife (although a bit later), suicide. But most Fellows got adjusted fairly quickly and got down to their work, while at the same time learning from people in other disciplines. There was a preliminary period of testing each other and experimenting with pecking orders. The historians were rare birds. There had been none in the Center's first year; there were only five in this, its third. But they were a pretty feisty five (Bridenbaugh, Craig, Hughes, Krieger, and Metzger), at least the first four were, and defended themselves against queries about their method. (My answer was always "We search for truth"; Bridenbaugh, *à corsair un corsair et demi* [it takes a thief to catch a thief], would reply, not wholly relevantly, "We write for the great public instead of each other, like you.") Eventually, this interdisciplinary suspicion abated, and we began to profit from being together for lunch and morning and afternoon coffee, and at the same time we pushed our own projects forward. I got a tremendous amount of work done for my German history which later fed my Stanford lectures; I got a good start on my Johns Hopkins lectures; and I wrote the first four chapters of my *Europe Since 1815*. In the last, my approach was certainly influenced by my daily talks with people like Chully Halsey and Hans Speier and Karl Deutsch and Gay Almond, as well as my close association with Carl Bridenbaugh,[73] whose well-stocked mind I picked for many things, including the words of the ballad that asks

Who takes care of the caretaker's daughter
When the caretaker's busy taking care?

Intellectually, the Center could hardly have been busier. . . . Even so,

---

[73] Carl Bridenbaugh (1903–1990), a prolific and influential historian of colonial America, was elected president of the American Historical Association in 1962.

1956–57 went down in Center history as "Good Time Charlie Year," and the secretarial staff members who were working on the hill at that time always greet me, on my rare visits there, with some recollection of a time that obviously stands out in their minds as a halcyon season of feasts and frolics. And in truth there were many of these. . . .

Occasionally, the outside world intruded into this happy existence of hard work and hard play. The Hungarian revolt and the Suez crisis shocked us and touched off a wave of meetings on Soviet strategy (Hans Speier's brilliant paper on nuclear blackmail[74] came out of this) and on the uses of games theory in foreign policy analysis. I was once more intrigued by the thought of returning to the world of affairs, for in December I was again offered the position of cultural attaché in Germany, and it was harder to turn down this time. But Phyl thought too much of her school to want to stay away from Princeton for at least another two years; and I was caught up in new scholarly projects which I was encouraged to pursue by learning that my last one, *The Politics of the Prussian Army*, had won the H. B. Adams Prize of the American Historical Association. My intimate knowledge of the new Germany was to be gained in a different way and not for another six years. . . .

[1957]

. . . In February, Adlai Stevenson visited the center, and my stock went up when Ralph Tyler, in the awkward first moments after his arrival, called me over and introduced me, on the strength of our Princeton connection. I had, as a matter of fact, met the governor in Princeton at a reception given by the county Democratic leader Troy Lord, and he had told me a very funny story of having to spend the night in Prospect with Tom Dewey. I reminded him of this, and he laughed heartily, to the awe of the assembled liberals and their wives, who plainly regarded the occasion as a religious service and Stevenson as a deity. It was funny to watch the women straightening their garter belts as they made their way down the line to meet him and then collapsing in nervous giggles as they moved away.

We saw Stevenson again two days later in Burlingame where the Robbins Millbanks were giving a reception for Bob Goheen, who had just been appointed president of Princeton in succession to Harold Dodds and was to take over his duties in September. Stevenson told me that it was a nervous business having to appear without preparation before a large group

---

[74] Hans Speier, "Soviet Atomic Blackmail and the North Atlantic Alliance," *World Politics* 9:3 (April 1957): 307–28 .

of people described as distinguished scholars. I told him that they were not as formidable as all that. . . .

The year at the Center gave us everything that anyone could have desired, and a little bit more, because there was a middling earthquake on 22 March, which was serious enough to cause rock slides that cut off cars travelling on the ocean highway between Half Moon Bay and Pacifica.[75] . . .

I had to be back in Princeton for a conference on NATO sponsored by the Center for International Studies and directed by Ed Furniss, so I left the family in Wilmington and went on alone, arriving in time to march in the commencement procession on 18th June. The conference brought to Princeton leading ministers and parliamentarians from all the NATO countries, and in the week of our meetings, which dealt with every aspect of NATO's activities and all its numerous problems, I got a chance to talk intimately with people like Fritz Erler and General von Sänger und Etterlin, from the Bundesrepublik, and Denis Healy of the Labour Party, who had been up at Balliol in my time. The speakers from outside were excellent: General "Lightning Joe" Collins, the Italian ambassador Brosio, C. E. Woodhouse, Paul Nitze, Lester Pearson (a wonderful man with whom I had a long talk about the need for a good book on modern diplomatic technique), and Christian Herter. Under the leadership of General Gallois, we had an excellent meeting on security questions. On the last night, there was a pleasant *Bierabend* [beer evening], but not much in the way of song. . . .

I started off the new academic year impressively by getting my classes going, giving a lecture at the Army War College, and beginning to lead a class on the New Testament in the First Church (something that John Bodo had conned me into when we were in the West). All this paled before the impressiveness of Phyl's performance, for, on 1 October, she gave birth to a 6 lb. 10 oz. boy whom we named at once Charles Grant Craig. I was in a state of complete euphoria for days. Jerry Blum was not too badly pleased either, for he won the Faculty Lounge Pool that had been stimulated by the imminent blessed event. . . .

[1958]

. . . On 17 March I began my Johns Hopkins Lectures, "From Bismarck to Adenauer: Aspects of German Statecraft," which were successful as

[75] This earthquake, measured at 5.7 on the Richter scale, struck close to the San Andreas fault near the San Francisco Peninsula. Damage was minimal.

presented and amazingly so in print,[76] the press making money out of the original edition, which had to be reprinted, and, I dare say, getting a percentage of the sales of the Harper & Row paperback and the Droste Verlag edition (translation by my student Wolf Helbich). Indeed, the paperback edition went out of print only last year. Of the presentation of the lectures in Baltimore, I remember that the weather was foul and that the fourth lecture had to be postponed because snow shut the whole university down for a day. I compressed it and gave it and the fifth lecture together on Friday the 21st. It was, despite the weather, a pleasant week. I got to know Vann Woodward and Hans Gatzke better; Fred Lane gave a very nice party for me; and I had an interesting evening at the Woodwards with Sidney Painter and Owen Lattimore, the embattled Far East expert who was soon to become an exile from his country because of the kind of attacks that John Service had had to suffer. (In Lattimore's case, they were not entirely unjustified.)[77]

In April, I went to Washington for the meeting of the Office of the Chief of Military History board, and this time met General [Lyman] Lemnitzer (the army is always good at trotting out the high brass) and had a good dinner with Lou Morton (soon to leave the Office of the Chief of Military History, baulked of a chance at Bob Greenfield's top spot because his colleagues considered him brutal in his ambitions, which, indeed, had gained him the name "The Barracuda"), Byron Fairchild, and Fred Aandahl, who was quietly making his way up the ranks in State. In May, I was back in Quantico, speaking to the Senior Class, and watching a two-hour presentation of the class solution to that year's Advanced Base Problem. . . .

In mid-June, . . . I performed by marching at commencement, and then we went off to Nelson. I had only two days there, for I had to go to Germany. The previous summer, when I was alone in the house and was sleeping late, I dreamed that I had received a telephone call from the German Consulate General in New York, inviting me to become the guest of the Foreign Office for a month in Germany. When I awakened, I called New York back and found it had not been a dream. The *Auswärtiges Amt* [Foreign Office] had been, for some time, inviting groups of Americans (journalists, school teachers, etc.) to go to Germany and see what life in the

---

[76] Gordon A. Craig, *From Bismarck to Adenauer: Aspects of German Statecraft* (Baltimore: Johns Hopkins University Press, 1958).

[77] Owen Lattimore (1900–1989), an influential scholar of China and Central Asia, was one of the principal targets of Senator Joseph McCarthy's hunt for Communist agents within the State Department during the early 1950s.

Bundesrespublik [Federal Republic of Germany] was like. This time, it was to be a group of social scientists, presumably (although no list was sent to me). I later found out that the various consulate generals were asked to come up with candidates and consulted their friends. The fellow in New York called Axel von dem Bussche, who gave him my name, and I was invited. Naturally, I accepted. Now, on 21 June 1958, I travelled by train to New York (eight hours!), stayed overnight at the Statler, killed the next day doing this and that, and at 7 p.m. was bound for Germany on Lufthansa.

Tuesday, 24 June 1958. Cologne.
Up betimes and had breakfast with Miller of Washington State, Maser of Oregon State, and [Fritz] Epstein of Library of Congress. Read news in *Frankfurter Allgemeine Zeitung*—repercussions of Sunday's riots before Soviet embassy here in protest against the Hungarian executions, rumors of a heightening of the Lebanon crisis, restrained articles on the halting of desegregation in Little Rock, advance dope on today's football match in Gödesburg between Germany and Sweden, etc.

Started day with a general briefing by Dr. Thiery. Tried then to call one of Magathan's friends at the *Verteidigungsministerium* [Defense Ministry]. No luck—apparently not there. So to the university where we were welcomed officially (champagne, biscuits, and cigars) by the Rektor Magnificus. Afterwards I had a good talk with Max Braubach and W. Hubatsch, both of whom I met four years ago. Braubach showed us over his seminar.

Lunch at the *Gasthaus im Stiefel* [Restaurant] on Bonngasse (separated only by a Chinese restaurant(!) from Beethoven's birthplace)—*Kasseler Rippchen* [ribs] and *viertel Mosel* [wine]—very good. Then off in rain to buy guitar *Bänder* [books] at Braun-Peretti's in the Hähnchen Passage. Some good guitars and harmonicas, very cheap...

Later: This afternoon a conference with two secretaries of the *Westdeutsche Rektorenkonferenz* [West German Rectors' Conference] at Bad Godesheim, where we asked questions about the state of education in the *Bundesrepublik* and the East Zone—mostly the former.[78] We learned nothing revolutionary, but the meeting was interesting. It confirmed my impression that, essentially, the traditional system has remained intact. Although efforts have been made to open the high schools to anyone qualified who desires

[78] At this time, the German Democratic Republic (East Germany) was not officially recognized by most Western countries, and was instead referred to as the *Ostzone* (Eastern Zone) or, more simply, as the "Zone," as a way of emphasizing its temporary or illegitimate character.

to enter, and although some *Länder* [federal German states] give free high school education, it is still true that only about 15% of the total school population get to the university. Our discussion leader admitted that it is still virtually impossible for anyone who stays in the *Volksschule* until he is 14 (i.e., anyone who does not go to the *Gymnasium* or the *Realschule* when he is 10) ever to get to the university.[79]

On the other hand, about 40% of those who *do* go into the high schools at 10 eventually apply for college; and students whose parents have only moderate means can, in their last two university terms, get grants up to 200 DM a month. Yet only about 4% or 5% of worker and peasant children ever get to college for reasons made clear above.

We talked about the social sciences, which are not doing particularly well here, because of the pressure of the traditional faculties,—and about student societies which are still a source of concern to the *Rektoren* (who are against them but are handicapped by a recent court decision which holds that corporation colors may not be worn in the university but that students who wear them may not be expelled(!)—and about academic freedom, which is as healthy here as at home—and about a number of other things. All in all, a good meeting. . . .

Wednesday, 25 June 1958. Cologne.
. . . At 9:00 to the *AA* [Foreign Office building in Bonn], "*das Haus der tausend Fenster* [the House of a Thousand Windows]," for a conference with a Dr. Dietrich on NATO questions. Tucker (Hopkins) and I got him into a corner on strategical questions and finally invited him to lunch to carry on further. Before that, however, we had a most interesting two-hour session on refugee problems, led by a *Ministerialdirigent* [Ministerial Director] Werner Middelmann, who laid out the problem and the human aspects of it in the first years, admirably.

The lunch—with Dietrich and one of his colleagues at the *Königshof*—was expensive, but not particularly useful to me, since I had to dash off at 1:30 to drive with Epstein and Dr. Erich Matthias of the German *Commission für die Geschichte des Parlementarianismus* [Commission for the History of Parliamentarianism] to Koblenz. It was a beautiful drive—past Rolandeck, where we saw painters covering up the damage done to the

---

[79] The German public school system was divided between three major types of schools. The *Volksschule* (People's School) was a kind of basic primary educational institution. Promising students are able to attend the *Gymnasium* (a university preparatory school) or the *Realschule* (a secondary school from which the best students can transfer to the *Gymnasium*).

front of the Soviet Embassy the other night, and on to Remagen (where the bridge isn't), Andernach, and finally Koblenz. I had not been to Koblenz since 1935, when I remember standing by the Deutsche Eck [German Corner], where the Mosel flows into the Rhine, and giving a few pfennigs to a kid of six or seven who accosted me. He would be 30 years old now, if he survived the war, all of which proves that I am getting old. I remember also that there was a white swastika, done with paint or whitewash, rather crookedly, on the rock face of the Ehrenbreitstein. I looked carefully, but there was no trace of it.

We had a long talk with Dr. Winter, the head archivist of the *Bundesarchiv* [Federal Archive] and with two of his assistants, one of whom was Wolfgang Mommsen, Ted's cousin.[80] Everyone interested as to whether I was going to write another volume on the German army. . . .

Sunday, 29 June 1958. Hamburg.

. . . Then by train to Lübeck where we saw the things pictured in the pages that follow, had lunch at the Schiffer Gesellschaft, with Sommer of *Die Zeit* and J. P. Marquand's daughter who drove here with Hopper, visited the Soviet border, and talked with an officer of the Customs Service who was stationed there. The paved road from Lübeck to the border simply ends when it reaches that point. There is a barbed wire barrier and a wide green ploughed strip, studded with watch towers (two of which we could see) which stretches all the way from the Baltic Sea to the Czech border. No East German guards were in sight, and the only sign of vigilance on the W. German side was a green-clad officer of the Customs service with a large dog. We talked with him for a while, and learned that there is absolutely no fraternization between the guards on both sides of the border. The East Germans want to be left alone so that they have no trouble with their bosses. The whole thing is ghastly and gives point to the verse which Sommer's grandmother found scribbled on the wall of her cell in E. Germany when she was arrested for three days a few years ago:

Hier sitz ich als Deutscher in
Deutschland gefangen
Weil ich von Deutschland nach

80 Wolfgang A. Mommsen (1907–1986) was a German archivist and historian, not to be confused with his relative, Wolfgang J. Mommsen (1930–2004), a historian of Imperial Germany and biographer of Max Weber.

Deutschland gegangen.[81]

. . . .

Saturday, 5 July 1958. Heidelberg.
. . . Yesterday up betimes and with the group to Karlsruhe where we were driven to the former palace of Prince Max von Baden, now the headquarters of the *Bundesverfassungsgericht* [Federal Constitutional Court]. Here we were received by members of the court and instructed in the differences between federal and local courts in Germany. It was all most interesting. Afterwards the justices took us by car to Ettlingen where there is a famous gourmet restaurant, the Restaurant Erbprinz, where we lunched magnificently. . . . I talked especially with justices named Katz and Heck, both of whom had some American experience. It emerges from their talk that the court is the real keystone of the German constitutional system, and one hopes that it is not asked to decide too many hot political questions until the *Bundesrepublik* is solid. For, after all, as Arnold Brecht said today, what Germany really needs is about thirty years of uninterrupted constitutional rule. . . .

Thursday, 17 July 1958. Berlin.
. . . Today up early and off in a group to the Refugees' Reception Center where we were briefed about the ways in which refugees come over and how they are processed when they do.[82] With a couple of others I sat in on a most moving interrogation of a father (a philologist) and daughter who had just come over, after a series of difficulties (involving troubles over his party and church membership, and his failure to give a Marxist twist to Plato's *Crito*), leaving behind a son who is an ardent Communist. . . .

Sunday, 20 July 1958. Berlin.
In the last two days I have had a chance to see two styles of commemoration, and the contrast has been striking. On Friday morning, after a briefing at the U.S. Mission by an intelligent young man named Peter Smith, we drove in an army bus into the Soviet sector. We started by driving through the Brandenburger Gate and then, very slowly, around what used to be the old gov't quarter—now mostly ruins, among which the heap of rubble that was Hitler's bunker is prominent. There is little left of the Berlin I saw 23 years ago; and, where the old royal palace was, there is now nothing

---

[81] This verse can be translated as "Here I sit as a German in Germany, caught because I went from Germany to Germany."

[82] Craig is referring here to East German defectors to West Germany.

but a great big square, Marx-Lenin Platz, where we dismounted and took pictures. We then drove via Potsdam Platz and Alexander Platz—mere shadows of what they had been—to Stalinallee, very fancy, not unimpressive, but bogus.[83] Then, finally, we went to the Soviet war memorial at Treptow, with its monumental bad taste—bad taste erected in colossal scale. Through the whole trip, the subdued air—indeed, the silence—of East Berlin had a melancholy effect on us—not relieved by the heightened crisis in the Near East.

Yesterday, we went to Plötzensee Prison, where the members of the *Widerstand* [Resistance] met their death, and stood in front of the simple tomb to their memories and heard a short memorial service—the finale of Schubert's Symphony in D minor op. 120; a *Gedenkrede* [Speech of Commemoration] by Senator Lipschitz of Berlin that was superb, and short speeches by Minister Schröder (subbing for Adenauer, who cancelled, because of the mess in the Near East) and Emil Henk, a survivor; and finally, the *allegro marciale* from Liszt's "Mazeppa," played, like the Schubert, by the Berlin Orchestra. All this was impressive in its simplicity, and there were no false notes…

There have been other things to fill the last days, the most interesting of which was the Senate reception for resistance survivors and their families. Epstein wrangled invitations for Eugene Anderson and me, and I guess we were the only non-Germans except Harold Deutsch. About 250 people over a hundred of whom were under 20—a good way of keeping a good tradition alive. I met *Gräfin* [Countess Marion] Dönhoff again, and she was very nice; and I bumped into Axel von dem Bussche, who admitted that he was responsible for my coming on this trip.[84] I dined with Dr. and Mrs. Poelchau (he was the prison doctor and knew all the victims), Countess York von Wartenburg, Frau Tilmann (whose husband was in the diplomatic service), and several others. Later I had a long talk with Frau Suhn, wife of the former *Bürgermeister* [mayor]. She told me stories about Adenauer, whom she admires, despite the difference in their political opinions, and she expressed the fear that there was a latent fascism in Germany. Most

[83] The Stalinallee was a showcase boulevard in East Berlin.

[84] Countess Marion Dönhoff (1909–2002), a leading participant in the resistance against Nazism during the Second World War, was a German journalist, publisher, and editor-in-chief of *Die Zeit*, Germany's most prestigious liberal weekly newspaper. Baron Axel von dem Bussche (1919–1993) was the last surviving member of the group of German Army officers who tried to assassinate Hitler in 1943 and again in 1944.

interesting were her criticisms of Schröder's appearance today. He was a *Parteigenosse* [Party member], she pointed out, and neither his youth nor the fact that he had a Jewish wife could excuse this. . . .[85]

P.S. Countess Dönhoff gave me a nice saying of Luther's to pass on to my melancholy students: "If I knew that the world was going to be destroyed tomorrow, I would plant an apple tree today."[86]

Saturday, 26 July 1958. Nelson, N.H.
Got up early on Tuesday and went shopping. Bumped into Fritz Epstein in street and he told me that Ted Mommsen was dead—(by his own hand, I learned later). There was a notice in the *Frankfurter Allgemeine.* I returned to the hotel and wrote a short letter to Konrad Mommsen in Cologne. . . .

[On June 29, 1985, Craig added the following: "Note: This diary gives little indication of the shock that Epstein's information represented. Only a couple of days earlier, at a reception in the *Senatsaal* [Senate Chamber] of the Free University, I had found myself staring at the [Franz von] Lenbach portrait of Theodor Mommsen that hung over Ted's desk in his home in Princeton and later on the wall of the faculty—a portrait so melancholy—indeed, brooding—that I was sure it must have contributed to his not infrequent depressions. He must have sent it to Berlin (where it now hangs in the Berlin Museum) when he decided to kill himself. He had been scheduled to go to Germany in 1958–59 and found the prospect unpleasant (again, the shadow of his grandfather). He prepared for his death like a Roman gentleman, disposing of his effects, making gifts to special friends ($1000 to our Susan for a piano, his library to Norman Cantor). He was a good friend from whom I learned how to be a teacher.

Between July 1958, when I came back from Germany, and May 1963, I kept no regular *Tagebuch.* What follows, written in October and November 1974, is based upon my pocket diaries for the years in question and upon other clippings and documents that I preserved.]

[1958]

. . . We were back in Princeton by 1 September and Phyllis was soon hard

---

[85] Gerhard Schröder (1910–1989), not to be confused with the Social Democratic Chancellor of the same name, was a prominent member of the Christian Democratic Union political party and headed a series of ministries during the chancellorship of Konrad Adenauer. He had joined the Nazi Party in 1933, but left it in 1941 to marry his half-Jewish wife.

[86] This quotation is thought to be apocryphal.

at work in her University League Nursery school, which was just entering the tenth year of its existence. I had my usual course load, plus my New Testament class at the Church. In place of my TV job, I was now chairman of the Public Lectures Committee, which was not uninteresting, and was becoming involved with a committee that was designed to do something about reviving McCarter Theater by putting a repertory theater into it.

It was at this time also that my lectures at the superior schools of the armed services began to increase in number. On 5 September I flew to Montgomery, Alabama, to lecture to the Air University on "Traditional Policies and Objectives of Small Powers." On 9 September I was in Washington, lecturing to the National War College on "The Current Struggle." On the 19th I was in Newport lecturing to the Naval War College on "Classical and Modern Strategic Concepts." On 21 October, I was at Carlisle Barracks again, telling the Army War College what I knew about "The Role of Diplomacy in the East-West Struggle"— (There was no doubt in the service schools in this period that the Cold War was real and serious, for it should be remembered that the launching of the Sputnik in October 1957 had caused a small panic among the security-minded and that Khrushchev's Berlin note of November 1958 made things look very grim indeed)—and on 10 November, at Quantico, after watching the Marine birthday parade from the reviewing stand, a ceremony that honored Bill Twining, who was retiring as Commandant of the Schools, I lectured to the senior class. This schedule was to continue into the next year.[87] In January, for instance, I flew to Norfolk to give a lecture to the Armed Forces Staff School.

I always enjoyed lecturing at the staff schools (and still do). The audience was composed of professionals of middle rank (majors, lieutenant colonels, commanders, in most schools; colonels, naval captains, class I FSOs, in the National War College), so that the discussions were somewhat more informed than they were in university classes. And there was *lots* of discussion and damned little silence. The routine was always the same: 20 minutes over coffee with the Commandant; introduction to whole student body; lecture; cigarette break; 20–30 minutes of questions on platform; cigarette break; seminar 1½ hours with group of students with a particular interest in the subject of the lecture; formal lunch with a hand-picked group of students; transportation to point of departure. The questions were

---

[87] In November 1958, Khrushchev issued an ultimatum to the Allied Powers demanding that they conclude a peace treaty with the two German states and withdraw their forces from Berlin, making it a free, demilitarized city.

intelligent, although sometimes loaded (but these last could be turned aside amid general laughter if you said something like "You don't really expect me to answer that, do you?"). The seminar discussions were lively and sometimes heated; the luncheons pleasant and sometimes an occasion on which I met an old student or an old friend. . . . On this Quantico trip, for instance, I lunched with Brute Krulak and John Chaisson of IOC days, both destined to rise to the top of the Corps.[88] I generally came away exhausted but always with a sense of having learned something and generally with some interesting gossip and a couple of good stories. The Marines were the best storytellers, but I discovered that nearly every one with a star on his shoulder, regardless of his service affiliation, was a pretty good ear-bender.

In addition to everything else, I was doing a good deal of reviewing for the *Tribune*—generally bad biographies of General Marshall or accounts of this or that military operation in World War II, but occasionally something a bit more interesting. In September, for example, I reviewed the first of Barbara Tuchman's books to receive any real attention, *The Zimmermann Note*, and was soon engaged in correspondence with her, for she wanted information on the "Perdicaris alive or Raisuli dead!" affair.[89] She never got around to a book on this, turning instead to the work that established her name, *The Guns of August*, but the results of her researches she incorporated in *The Proud Tower*. I was to review the former of these for the *Herald Tribune*, and the latter for a magazine that I first started writing for in 1958, *The Reporter*.[90]

[1959]

I imagine, looking back on it all, that it was early in this year that we began to think that it might be interesting to move to another university. For some time I had been flirting with this idea and had, for this reason, been very interested in the renewal of the offer of the cultural attaché's job

---

[88] Victor H. "Brute" Krulak (1913–2008) served with the Marines in World War II, in Korea, and in Vietnam. In 1958, he was director at Quantico. John R. Chaisson (1916–1972) achieved the rank of Lieutenant General and served as Chief of Staff of the Marine Corps. (For Chaisson, see also, p. 45, n. 23.)

[89] "Perdicaris alive or Raisuli dead!" refers to the Perdicaris Affair of 1904 in Morocco. Ion Perdicaris, an American citizen, was kidnapped by local tribal leader Mulai Ahmed er Raisuli. This led to an American intervention amid demands for Perdicaris's safe return.

[90] Gordon A. Craig, "Summer, 1914: Curtain Up on World War I," *New York Herald Tribune Book Review* (28 December 1962): 5; and "Before the Deluge," *The Reporter* (10 February 1966): 53–54.

in Bonn. Phyl had been opposed to a move, largely because of her devotion to the school that she had created. In February 1959, however, something happened that effected a subtle change in her thinking. *Town Topics*, the local newspaper edited by Dan Coyle, honored her as Woman of the Week for her ten years of hard work in making the nursery school a Princeton institution, and other honors were paid her at the tenth anniversary party on 2 March. Now, automatically, Phyl's work became as repetitious as mine had become, and she began to feel that we should look for fair fields and pastures new, particularly now, she argued, since we had, in effect, a new family to bring up. I explained to her that to move would be more difficult than she thought, given my salary, and library needs, etc. But as the year went on, our travel lust grew, and by December I felt strongly enough about the desirability of a change to intimate to Carl Bridenbaugh that I could be moved. . . .

The Public Lectures Committee was presenting some good things at this time. In February Harold Dodds gave the Stafford Little Lectures on "the Governance of the University" and in April Paul Henri Spaak gave the Edge Lecture on problems of European security and integration. There was also a Princeton conference of some interest, on the subject of neutrality and neutralism, in March. The principal speakers were E. L. Woodward and that old ass William Yandell Elliott of Harvard.[91] I gave a paper on "Neutralism in the 19th Century," which I printed later in *War, Politics, and Diplomacy*.[92]

I was to see Elliott again almost immediately, for a week after the conference, I was in Cambridge as a member of an *ad hoc* committee appointed for the purpose of deciding whether Stanley Hoffman[93] and Henry Kissinger should receive tenure. Apart from Phil Mosely of Columbia, I cannot remember any of the other committee members. The president of Harvard, Nathan Pusey, sat with us but contributed nothing; the man in charge was the provost, McGeorge Bundy. Stanley's promotion went through without trouble; in Henry's case the department was divided, those opposed taking the view that he was more interested in politics than

---

[91] William Yandell Elliott (1896–1979) was an American historian at Harvard for over forty years and an advisor to six American presidents.

[92] Gordon A. Craig, *War, Politics, and Diplomacy: Selected Essays* (New York: Frederick A. Praeger, 1966).

[93] Stanley Hoffmann (1928–2015), an émigré scholar from France, joined the Department of Government at Harvard in 1955 and became one of the foremost experts on French politics and society, European politics, U.S. foreign policy, and international relations.

in scholarship. Adam Ulam came before the committee to argue against promotion. Elliott appeared on Henry's behalf. The committee was split too but was finally persuaded by Bundy's argument that Henry was an honest man and would resign if politics began to take up too much of his time.

We had, as usual, lots of visitors. Peter Laslett of Cambridge came by, an amusing man, as I discovered in an evening at the Graduate College with Jerry Blum, who was his host. Less amusing was Dean Acheson,[94] beside whom I sat at a dinner in Prospect on the evening of the Spaak lecture. He was non-communicative to the point of rudeness and left me feeling (1) that he disliked academic intellectuals and (2) that he had drunk too much or too little. Pleasanter all round was a visit from Dan Davin in April, despite the fact that he announced that he was a nervous wreck and couldn't eat. We went to a party at the Kingsley Amis's (the novelist was spending a semester in Princeton) which I found a bit wild by normal Princeton standards but also a bit strained (warmed-over Scott Fitzgerald stuff). After Dan had insulted a few people and was feeling better, I took him home and heated up some turkey pot-pies, which reminded him so powerfully of the meat pies we used to buy through the window gratings in Balliol that he ate two of them and recovered. The next day we had a civilized tea party at the home of John Brett Smith, head of the Oxford Press in New York, and then Dan left for home.

In May, the case of Mo Lee[95] was decided by the department in a way that marked the end of Mo's Princeton career and caused a kind of inter-departmental friction that had been unknown in the past. This was a pity, but the days of the All-Pals-Together department were due to end sooner or later, and professionalism had to be given precedence over personal factors. I was now becoming increasingly involved in my own writing and in May and June wrote four chapters for my European history, an achievement that still fills me with astonishment. . . .

Christmas was merry, but was followed, as usual, by the wearing and expensive American Historical Association meetings, this time in Chicago. I saw lots of old friends, including the Gieseys and the Lees (I asked Mo if

---

[94] Dean Acheson (1893–1971), lawyer and statesman, was President Harry Truman's principal foreign policy adviser, and Secretary of State from 1949 to 1953.

[95] Maurice D. Lee, Jr. (1926–2020) a prolific historian of early modern English and Scottish history, joined the Department of History at Rutgers University in 1966, and went on to become the chair of that department.

he blamed his failure to get tenure on me and said I was afraid Elmer did); and I saw Carl Bridenbaugh and let him know I could be moved from Princeton. (He asked me whether Cal should hire Hans Rosenberg. I asked, "Why not hire me?" I then told him that they couldn't find a better man than Hans for the German spot. He pressed me on my own position. I said I was getting ready to shift-ho. He pointed out that Sontag would be retiring soon. I said etc. etc. He tottered off happily, saying that bringing me to Cal would be his last achievement before retirement). . . .

[1960]

During the first part of the new year, I fell into the hands of a mad periodontist in Trenton . . . , who undertook to save my choppers by slicing the gums to ribbons—a fiendish operation which he performed in a series of painful sessions with gusto, making loud intellectual small talk as he buried his knives in my flesh, and adjusting the Muzak to drown my prayers and imprecations.

This might have had traumatic effects had it not been for powerful distractions. It was at the most painful phase of these operations that Victor Lange of the German department suggested that Princeton might give Konrad Adenauer an honorary degree. I was scheduled to direct a two-day Faculty Alumni Conference on German Affairs, and I persuaded Bob Goheen that a special convocation for Adenauer might put this conference on the map. We went ahead, despite the considerable amount of negotiation this involved and the horrendous security problems that had to be solved. The upshot was that Adenauer, with a large suite that included his son, the Foreign Minister Brentano, Felix Eckart, and others, came to Princeton on 14 March, had dinner at Prospect, where Phyl and I met him, went to the Chapel, got his degree and gave a speech, and took off for his plane to Washington.

All of this was beautifully managed and was a fine introduction for the conference, most of the members of which had front-row seats at the convocation. Adenauer's speech raises some intriguing historical problems. We had an advance copy, so that Victor Lange could translate it and read it to the audience after the Chancellor sat down, and this was sent to the newspapers. But the Chancellor, perhaps recollecting belatedly that this was John Foster Dulles's university and being moved by this into new trains of thought, gave a quite different speech which bore little relation to the one that Lange doggedly read in English once the old man sat down. *Frage* [Question]: what speech did Adenauer give in Princeton? *Antwort* [Answer]:

The one that was printed in the *N.Y. Times*, namely Lange's. . . .

All told, that was a crowded week. On the day before Adenauer's convocation, Martin Luther King had preached in the Chapel, and that evening we had with us the distinguished German theologian and resistance figure, Bishop [Hanns] Lilje, with whom I had appeared on a NBC TV show in February. . . . When the conference ended, on Wednesday, and I had said farewell to my friends, I had two lectures and three preceptorials to give, another session with Chilton, and a trip with Phyl to Philadelphia to hear Susan sing in choir with the Philadelphia Orchestra. . . .

We were all too busy to pay much attention to what I kept calling, in my public lectures, "the East-West struggle." In retrospect, the years 1957–1962 still strike me as having been very dangerous, but at the time it seemed best to regard the situation as desperate but not serious. . . .

. . . Late in October I received a telephone call from Gordon Wright in Stanford asking whether I would be interested in accepting a job in German history. I said I could be moved but that it would cost a bit, and that I would write and describe my situation. I did so, and he answered, telling me that he thought Stanford might go as high as $18,000, plus moving expenses, benefits, etc. When the matter assumed actuality in this way, I felt I had no perspective and needed advice. Blum was not helpful. When I told him, in secrecy, that I was considering a job at Stanford, he said, "Oh well, if you want to consider the minor leagues." It was Jim Perkins,[96] who gave me what I needed, talking about the matter objectively, pointing out the strength I would take to Stanford and the opportunities it would bring, and telling what kind of letter to write to Stanford. I sat down and used all my knowledge of diplomacy, pointing out the things that would have to be taken care of before I could think of moving, urging Stanford to put its terms on paper, and promising that I would not bargain but would give them a definite answer within ten days. Later, someone in the Dean's office in Stanford said I had put them over the barrel. However that may be, on 1 November 1960, as I came back from a painful visit to my dentist, I found a letter on my desk, meeting my terms on things like transportation and fringe benefits and offering me a salary of $20,000. I immediately phoned Phyl, who asked, "What are you going to do?" I answered, "I'm going upstairs and tell Joe I'm going to Stanford."

And that is what I did. It was a cruel shock to Joe, and it was a long time

---

[96] James Perkins (1911–1998) was a political scientist and university administrator who trained and taught at Princeton and later became president of Cornell University.

before he forgave me for having kept him in the dark, which I had done, of course, with the best motives in the world, in order to prevent myself from getting caught up in the pressures that Princeton would have exerted in an effort to persuade me to stay. Douglas Brown understood this when I talked with him. "You think you have a call," he said. "Let's see if it's a good call or a bad." He apparently concluded that it was good, for he did not persist in an attempt to dissuade me.

I was perhaps less shrewd in my bargaining than I might have been. I did not try to make Stanford grant me my accumulated sabbatical time, and I gave up my plan to spend all of 1961–1962 in Berlin, where I had been invited to become Theodor Heuss Professor, agreeing to begin teaching in June and to postpone my departure for Germany until spring quarter 1962. But we were happy. The Stanford offer was higher than we had dared hope, and we were off to California.

The worst aspect of the business, aside from Joe's wounded feelings, was the necessity of explaining interminably that we weren't mad at anybody and that we were moving because we had only one life to lead and wanted it to be different now and then. When I told people that I was fleeing the dreadful prospect of becoming a Princeton Mr. Chips, they always looked as if they knew better. It was deplorable to note how many people seemed to feel that Phyl and I possessed so much "power" and "influence" in Princeton that we were mad to give it up. My colleagues at other eastern universities—like Sid Burrell of Barnard—were just as bad when I met them all at the American Historical Association meetings in New York in December. To leave Princeton and go out to that strange place founded by a railroad tycoon in a land peopled with Indians and actors seemed to them to be a dubious enterprise, and I seemed to be less considerable for embarking on it. . . .

5

The Sixties: Stanford and Berlin, 1961–1969

[1961]

I noticed as the new year began that I was no longer privy to much of the internal business of the department. This was probably natural, but it reached the point of nonsense when Jerry Blum, after two drinks and much apparent wrestling with his conscience, told me that he had been named Joe Strayer's successor as department chairman, doing so in a manner that intimated that I was being informed of this only because we were old friends. I didn't take this too seriously or the fact that a news release by the Department of Public Information about my forthcoming lecture series in California carefully omitted any mention of my imminent transference to Stanford. Still, it was an odd feeling after all these years, being on the outside.

But then *our* thoughts were outside too. At the end of January, Phyl flew out to California in order to find a house for us and in an astonishingly short space of time found a marvelous house in College Terrace at 2050 Dartmouth St., in which we were to live happily for ten years. (The difficulty was finding money enough to start buying it, for we had no property to sell. We managed by taking two mortgages, an advance against the royalties of my text, now finished, and advances on other books still to be written, *Koniggrätz* for instance. It wasn't easy.) In April, I flew out and had a long reunion with San Francisco, staying at the Fairmont and dining royally at the Buon Gusto on the 1st, going down to Stanford the next day to see the Wrights and the house and returning to the city to dine with Tom Elliott, doing a radio show and my speech at the University Club the next day and topping off the day with a pub crawl with Tom. On 4 April I flew down to Los Angeles and made my way to Riverside and stayed there for a week, giving my lectures in the evening and teaching classes by day, going on side trips in free time to Beaumont and San Bernardino and Claremont. I met lots of old and new friends—the Laues (Theo was chairman of the department at UCal Riverside in those days),[1] Arthur Turner, a Scot and a political scientist, Douglass and Virginia Adair at Claremont, Malcolm Cowley, the critic in residence, the girl who played the piano at the Caravan Motel where I was staying, and all the boys and girls in my classes at the University. Now that I had decided to become a Californian I liked them all and found everything that I saw exciting and beautiful. There was, to be sure, an excitement in Riverside in those days for the University was brand new and going places and everyone was filled with the old zip. Later, the smog was to take over and blight some of those hopes. . . .

Life was not uninteresting in these last months of my Princeton career. I filled out my term as chairman of the Committee on Public Lectures and brought a number of interesting people to Princeton. . . . I also continued my work in the Church, arranging programs on thermonuclear war for the Committee on Social Concern, with speakers like John Shy and Dick Challener.

Things got very busy after my return from California. I had been invited by Theodore Ropp to give a lecture at Duke University and went down to Durham on the 24th where Ropp took care of me, and Bob Durden, one of our former graduate students, piloted me about and took me over for a look at Chapel Hill. During this trip I met once more the man who had been my first German teacher at Princeton, a nice man and good scholar, Herman Salinger. In the same month I gave two lectures, based on the Haynes Lectures, to the International Relations Club, which reciprocated by presenting me with a beautifully lettered message of appreciation and regret which I later had framed. On 5 May came my last lecture in History 317, an affecting occasion. . . .

Later in the month there was a departmental dinner for the departing professors (Dana Munro was retiring, and Joe was handing the reins over to Jerry), and I was presented with a handsome lithograph of Princeton as it looked in 1837.

After that things moved rapidly. . . . There was a final flurry of parties in Princeton—one for the Bill Dougherties *et al.*, which we arranged, one given by Jerry, others at the Palmers and the Harbisons, and a final meeting

[1] Theodore H. Von Laue (1916–2000), sent to Princeton in 1937 by his father, the Nobel Prize-winning German physicist Max von Laue (who did not want his son to grow up "in a country ruled by gangsters"), became a leading historian of Russia and later a pioneering world historian.

of the Twentieth Century Fund at the Cravens—and a very pleasant 25th reunion of my class and, in that reunion weekend, a final performance with Jinx Harbison, an Alumni Seminar on "History as a Vehicle of Liberal Education." That done, we left for California on 11 June.

. . . It was an exasperating trip, and I remember little of it and that in confusing patches—a picture of the car standing on a desert road and me in search of water amid signs reading "Watch out for rattlesnakes!" By today's standards, however, the trip was not expensive: $476.79 for the lot of us ($196.69 for gas and repairs; $280.10 for bed and board).

The main thing was that we had arrived. We put the house in order quickly and happily, and we loved it from the very beginning and worked hard to improve it. . . .

. . . For me it was not an easy year. I had never given lectures on German history since my first hitch at Columbia in 1946–47, and I now had to write entirely new lectures, first for the period 1914 to the present, then for the period from the 18th century to 1914. I always seemed to be writing lectures this year, and it was only after I had got to Germany in April 1962 that I realized what a lousy father and husband I had been in the preceding months. I had received such a buildup in the local press (most popular lecturer at Princeton, and all that nonsense) that I felt I had to prove that it was true. I succeeded all right, but it was hard on the family. . . .

The summer passed in a kind of blur. I gave a lecture course on 20th-century Germany and a graduate course on European diplomatic history 1919–1939. . . .

. . . At the end of September, I was writing lectures again, and there were fewer diversions, unless one counts the rush that Sigma Nu (the "intellectual fraternity") put on me, so that, for a brief time, I became an associate member of the house. . . .

In October I gave a paper before a curious faculty organization (long since dead, happily) called the University Research Club, which had been founded by Ray Lyman Wilbur and was now run by an archaeologist named Hazel Hansen. Doughnuts and fruit juice and papers about the osmosis of plants. My paper was supposed to be entitled "On Bismarck Scholarship" but this had been printed in the program with an apostrophe and an s added to the Chancellor's name, and I bitterly offended Professor Hansen by suggesting jocularly that, while Bismarck was well enough fixed to do without financial assistance, he could probably have won an athletic scholarship by his prowess at *Mensur* or saber-fighting. The faculty who had been at Stanford before the incursion of Potter, Hastorf, Guérard, Craig *et al.* were bitterly suspicious of us new boys and tended to feel that our humor was always at their expense.

Through George Knoles, I was invited to belong to another curious organization, a men's glee club that met at frequent intervals in members' homes and sang four-part harmony from tattered sheets.[2] We were never very good except when we were getting the beer from the kitchen, where we sang barbershop. The formal stuff was pretty awful, partly because some of the members were too old to sing very well (one of them had been retired since 1938).

Aside from these diversions and an unexpected visit early in December from John Garrett and his wife (the former *femme fatale* of Balliol days, Helen Coates), I worked hard on my courses and learned the ropes. When we got to exam period, I agreed to do an alumni affair and ended up in the same place where I had spoken to the Princeton alumni in 1956. It had not improved. . . .

[1962]

Everything after the first of January pointed to Berlin. I was worried by the state of my German and by the thought of finding it impossible to teach in another language, and, when I had free time from my lectures and graduate work, I haunted the *Sprachlaboratorium* [language lab] or took conversation [lessons] from a tall German girl who taught me to drop my r's and correct other dreadful faults.

There was time for a few junkets before the big one. In February I went to Northwestern University to participate in a symposium on "Commitment in an Age of Anxiety," in which I heard a very funny discussion in which Stuart Hughes chivvied Saul Bellow for having no interest in politics and was chivvied by Hannah Arendt in return, and in which I participated in another panel with Arthur Lansen, James Landis of the Harvard Law School and Harold Taylor, the President of Sarah Lawrence (who, not knowing anything about my work, played it safe by introducing me to the audience as "the historian's historian"). During the trip I saw Lacey Smith and Gray Boyce and Dick Snyder and I went into Chicago and participated in "Kup's Show," a midnight talk show in which my colleagues were Norman Thomas, Ralph de Toledano, the right-wing publicist, Nancy Walker, the actress, Janet Leighton (who wrote *I Was Jacqueline Kennedy's Dressmaker*), and a fellow named Bill Gresham who was

[2] George Knoles (1907–2014), an American historian at Stanford, was the longest-lived member of the faculty, reaching the age of 107.

silent for a long time and then talked at length about geeks. All very edifying. . . .

It is difficult to compress the story of my first Berlin hitch in a few pages, because it was a crowded period, filled with new experiences and new friends. I went to Berlin as Theodor Heuss Professor. . . . Horst Hartwich, head of the Free University's *Außenkommission* [Foreign Commission], which handled relations with foreign institutions and scholars, was interested in strengthening the ties with Stanford, the first university abroad to establish a student exchange with the Free University. There were signs that the Stanford ASSU [Associated Students of Stanford University] was becoming more interested in Africa than Berlin. Hartwich wanted to see that the tie was not snapped, so he found funds to establish a graduate student exchange and also persuaded the *Senator für Wissenschaft und Kunst* [Senator for the Arts and Sciences], in May, to appoint me to the Free University faculty as *Honorarprofessor* [Honorary Professor]. I have been proud of this appointment and have tried to live up to it by being active in my professorship.

That first *Sommersemester* [summer term], I stayed, until the family arrived, in the *Gastehaus*'s [Guest House's] second building (Geffertstr. 51), now in private hands, and took my meals in the comfortable villa where I have stayed so often since. At the breakfast and mid-day dinner table, in a comfortable room well-stocked with Edgar Wallaces in German and a statue of a child reading a book through enormous spectacles (the *Bücherworm* [the Bookworm]) I met the other permanent guests under the excellent Fraulein Wedding's care—a young Italian named Ferrari, whom I remember chiefly because, when he forgot his key, his voice would rise plaintively through the soft E. T. A. Hoffmann spring night to my window: "Herr Krike! Herr Krike!," and a collection of *Strohwitwer* [bachelors]: Franz Schick from Utah, a political scientist, Wolfgang Baumgart, director of the Institut für Theaterwissenschaft, and Michael de Ferdinandy, a Hungarian who now taught in Puerto Rico. . . .

I arrived in Berlin two weeks before the start of term and had lots of time on my hands. I had to write my lectures in diplomatic history (which Hartwich was having put into German for me) and to plan my colloquium on the period 1919–1939, but there were lots of empty hours, and I had to fill them up. I began, therefore, systematically to conquer the city by foot. I soon established a network of routine stops—my bank on the Baslerstraße in Lichterfelde West, and my *Friseur* [barber] across the street, the Kindl restaurant opposite Rathaus Steglitz, Elwert and Meurer, my bookstore on Hauptstraße near Innsbrucker Platz and the restaurant on that square, my two homely *Stammlokale* [hangouts], Schilling's in Dahlem Dorf and an *Eckkneipe* [corner pub] (now sadly transformed into a *Wienerwald* chicken house) at Thiel Alle and Unter den Eichen, the *Historiker Kneipe* [Historians' pub] run by Herr Greinert opposite the Meinecke Institut, and the places on the Kurfürstendamm where I sat and read newspapers on Saturdays. But I ranged far beyond this—to the *Hufeisensiedlung* [Bruno Taut's Horseshoe Estate] out in the direction of Britz, to Wedding and the Plötzensee prison, to the Wannsee and to Tegel, to the Hasenheide and Spandau, to the Dahlem Museum and the *Nationalgalerie* at *Schloß Charlottenburg* [the National Gallery at Charlottenburg Palace], and, of course, to East Berlin, to prowl about in the Bode Museum and the Pergamon [Museum] and to hunt down places like Alexanderplatz, Gendarmenmarkt, the Sperlingsgasse, and other places that appeared in favorite novels.

Because I was alone a great deal of the time, particularly in the first weeks, I was subject to fits of melancholy and homesickness. I took to writing verse again, but it didn't come out right, and the damned lectures made it impossible to do any other kind of creative writing. Once the term got started, the business of giving classes and getting to know students helped me to regain my perspective, and, when the university got going full swing, I began to see something of colleagues like [Gerhard A.] Ritter,[3] Kurt Sontheimer of the Otto Suhr Institute, Herzfeld and [Walter] Bußmann[4] of the Meinecke. Soon there were demands for talks, like the one before the *Studentenhaus* [Student Union] on the Goethestrasse, and the best of my students . . . had things for me to do. . . .

I soon discovered that everything that had been written about the excellence of the theater and music in Berlin was true; and this first term in

---

[3] Gerhard A. Ritter (1929–2015) was a leading figure in the development of postwar German social history. His scholarship focused on the working class, trade unions, and the development of the modern welfare state. Ritter is perhaps best known for *Der Sozialstaat: Entstehung und Entwicklung im internationalen Vergleich*, which was first published in 1991. He is not to be confused with the conservative historian Gerhard Georg Bernhard Ritter (1888–1967), who specialized in Prussian history and wrote his magnum opus on the development of German militarism between 1740 and 1918.

[4] Walter Bußmann (1914–1993) was a German historian whose scholarship focused on the politics of Imperial Germany and the resistance to the Third Reich. He taught at the Free University in Berlin, at the University of Munich, and the University of Karlsruhe.

Berlin was a valuable period of education and re-education. . . .

In the midst of all of these diversions, I learned that my old teacher and colleague and fellow-debater and friend, Buzzer Hall, had died in Texas. I have thought of him quite often since and talked of him often to my students, particularly when I am trying to tell them what makes a great teacher.

Contributing to the zest of life in Berlin was the uncertainty of its political future. The Wall had been built only seven months before I got to Berlin, and there were many people among those I know who believed that it was only a first step to something worse. The first lunch I had in the *Historiker Kneipe* with colleagues in the Meinecke Institut was a gloomy one, with people like Dietrich and Helbig making the darkest kind of prophecies about how soon the red flag would float over all of Berlin. Gerhard Ritter's wife worried constantly lest her two small sons might have to grow up in a totalitarian state, and her fears contributed, I imagine, to his decision, a bit later on, to go to Münster.

Nor were such fears confined to the Germans. When I first came to the city I decided to make my presence known to the people at the U.S. Mission, so that I might get on their cocktail party list. This worked, and I used to get invitations to things like the Commandant's 4th of July party and the cultural attaché's receptions. I also got invited to lunch by the U.S. Minister, who was a former Princetonian called Alan Lightner,[5] and who, in conversation before Shep Stone arrived, expressed the most gloomy forebodings because he felt that President Kennedy did not understand the importance of Berlin and was surrounded by people who were no better on this score than he was himself. Lightner was afraid that JFK might be spooked or conned by the Soviets into giving the city up. He told me that he had gone back to Washington in an attempt to persuade the President that the United States would suffer irreparable damage if she allowed Berlin to be lost but that JFK was non-committal, saying only that he would read the Minister's reports. Lightner said, "We've just got to get Bobby over here to see what the situation's really like."

It is my impression that Lightner's fears were not illusory. Certainly, if one reads [Arthur] Schlesinger's *A Thousand Days*, one senses that JFK was worried that Berlin might trigger a nuclear exchange and was anxious to eliminate it as a problem. If the Soviets had used the right mixture of menaces and promises early in 1962 they might have nobbled Berlin. But

---

[5] Edwin Allen Lightner (1909–1990) was a Foreign Service officer who served as the State Department's representative in Berlin from 1959 to 1963.

they seem to have been made apprehensive by the confrontation of tanks at the Wall in November and perhaps didn't realize that the Kennedy boys were just as apprehensive as they, if not more so.

. . . Some time in the course of these [assorted activities and travels], I had a luncheon with Fred Burkhardt[6] and Horst Hartwich in the Luignan Restaurant on the Kurfürstendamm which is interesting if one thinks of what was soon to happen in the Free University. Hartwich was complaining about the way in which professors resisted all proposals for reform of any kind, barricading themselves in their institutes, which they had made independent kingdoms. Fred, who had been active in getting funds for the Free University when it was founded in 1949, groaned: "My God! We thought we were founding the most progressive university in Germany and here it is, less than 15 years later, trying to go back to the age of William II." Much of the trouble that was to descend on the university five years later came from the entrenched conservatism of the professors, who played right into the hands of the extreme left.

[Craig returned to Stanford at the end of the summer in 1962 and resumed his usual activities.]

. . . The Cuban missile crisis momentarily threatened to put an end to the even tenor of this way, and it certainly shook the whole community, shaking the English Department, indeed, out of its collective wits, so that it importuned the President by telegraph to stop threatening them poor Russians. The President happily paid no attention to them and the crisis subsided and, indeed, ushered in a period of relaxation in Soviet-American relations in which, among other things, the Berlin ultimatum of 1958 and the threats of unilateral action since that time were quietly jettisoned. We returned, in Stanford, to our academic and related concerns. . . .

Despite occasional unorthodoxies . . . , we were becoming establishment figures. I was placed on Dean Sears's Appointments and Promotions Committee at the beginning of the academic year; and Phyl and I were invited to join a Discussion Group whose membership included the Carl Spaeths, Mike Villards, Jack Hilgards, Dave Farilles, Paul Hannas, John Dodds, and Wilbur Schramms, all sound conservative pillars of society. We

[6] Frederick Burkhardt (1912–2007), the editor of the papers William James and the correspondence of Charles Darwin, was also a gifted academic administrator, serving as the president of Bennington College and then the American Council of Learned Societies. A veteran of the OSS, he participated in the American administration of Berlin in the aftermath of the war.

accepted and found we were regarded as the obligatory Young Turks of the Group. (We also, for a time, belonged to an awful play-reading group led by the George Knoleses, the Bob Walkers, and the John Loftises. In this Phyllis was always given the part of the other woman or the whore and I was generally an amiable drunk.)

. . . [We] closed out a very crowded and rich year decorously. In the course of the year, I had been admitted to the membership both of the American Philosophical Society and the American Academy of Arts and Sciences, so that I now belonged both to the club of Franklin and Jefferson and that of their New England opponents.

[1963]

[After a trip to the East Coast in January, Craig returned to Stanford.] . . . As soon as I got there I began to write my book on the battle of Königgrätz. I had the whole thing laid out in a multi-columned schema which showed what units on both sides were where when. Guiding myself on this and reams of notes that I had made, I wrote like a fury, finishing the introduction on 11 February, the second day of composition, and finishing the book on 27 April, 70,000 words in 76 days.[7]

Tuesday, 18 June 1963. Beethovenweg (Nundorf), Vienna.
. . . The subject of the [*Daedalus*] conference—the New Europe—was fascinating and, as I listened to the presentations, I became more aware of the kind of difficulties brought by change.[8] Europe is not being Americanized. What is going on is almost self-generating and is finding its own forms, some of which encourage anti-Americanism. Those who dislike change and do not want European unification are given lots of opportunities to complain that the United States is forcing them in directions they don't want to go. Western Europeans are thus somewhat ambivalent about the concept of a New Europe. On the other hand, as [Zbigniew] Brzezinski pointed out in our last session, "New Europe" has, in Eastern Europe, assumed an attractiveness that threatens to drive orthodox Marxism from the field, so exciting is it to the Poles and Czechs and Rumanians. But precisely because we have done so little hard thinking about the East European problem, *our* conceptions of the New Europe are apt, when expressed, to drive the Yugoslavs, etc. into the capacious bosom

---

[7] Gordon A. Craig, *The Battle of Königgrätz: Prussia's Victory over Austria, 1866* (Philadelphia: J. B. Lippincott Co., 1964).

[8] The papers presented at this conference can be found in *Daedalus* 93:1 (Winter 1964).

of the Soviet Union. It is interesting that there was no discussion of the Oder-Neisse issue or Berlin or German re-unification until the last morning of the conference, and that was not very enlightening. . . .

On Sunday the 16th, it was all over. We had an interesting morning session and a good lunch, and then I motored with Erich Weil and the Adornos to Milano, this time by the mountain road past Lecco. If one wanted a revelation of the new Europe, none was better than the approach to Milano from the north. The contrast with the sort of thing I saw nine years ago during a bus trip from Milano to Bergamo over roughly comparable country was dramatic. The traces of the old economy of Lombardy, as described in Bob Greenfield's book about pre-Risorgimento Lombardy, which we could still see in '54, are now gone.[9] What one sees is literally acres of new buildings rising—great modern houses for light industry (furniture, for example)—with apartment houses to go with them. I have seen no concentration of building like this, even in America, and can consequently understand the volume of traffic that was moving toward Bellagio as we came down, all in good-looking small cars, or the statistics which say that Italian motor production rose 25% in the first half of 1963, or the more dramatic figures which show that in a few years, unless something changes, the Italian agricultural population will be down to about 15% and there will be deserts around places like Siena, as Rossi d'Orio pointed out in an eloquent speech at the conference. All of this does not explain the presence of a large baseball stadium outside of Milan, with a game in progress as we passed. . . .

From the Gloriole, Schönbrunn: Vienna looks so wonderful, compared with its condition in 1935, that one finds oneself saying that the best way of making a country go is to have a totalitarian regime for a while and then a World War… I am here principally to talk about exchange fellowships with the gov't, but this has foundered on typical Austrian *Schlamperei* [sloppiness]. . . .

Apart from these talks, I have gone to the University and called upon Hugo Hantsch,[10] in the interest of my students, and [Friedrich] Engel-

---

[9] Kent Roberts Greenfield, *Economics and Liberalism in the Risorgimento; A Study of Nationalism in Lombardy, 1814–1848* (Baltimore: Johns Hopkins University Press, 1934).

[10] Hugo Hantsch (1895–1972), confined by the Nazis to Buchenwald in 1938, survived the war by serving as a parish priest in a small village in Lower Austria. After the war he resumed his career as a professor of history and retired as director of the Historical Institute of the University of Vienna in 1965.

Jánosi[11] from respect. The former was pleasant but lethargic—a spent force; the latter, spirited and energetic and eager to speak for Stanford at the Washington Embassy and the *Bundesministerium für Unterricht* [Federal Ministry of Education]... I have also done all the things I did in 1935—*Volksgarten* [People's Garden], *Stephansdom* [St. Stephen's Cathedral], Schönbrunn [Palace], etc., collected pictures of the buildings on the Ring mentioned in my text, visited the Karl Marx Hof (a truly provocative building. One can understand the position of the Right with respect to it, while not sympathizing with it)—and walked from Nussdorf via the Beethovengang and the vineyards to Grinzing. I have bought a hat at Habig, had a drink (with Fred Burkhardt and Henry Kissinger) at Sacher's, eaten in a Gösser brewery restaurant (excellent food, but *so noisy*—the waiters running at top speed and shouting at each other), had coffee in various cafes, and been twice to the opera. . . .

. . . Today (19 June) I spent part of the morning writing a report of my negotiations to Brooks, went to a bank (where the same Slavic confusion that lost the battle of Königgrätz seemed to reign), saw Engel-Jánosi, visited the Kunst-Historisches Museum, lunched in the Opern Gasse, and went out to Schönbrunn where I climbed the Gloriette, which I can't remember doing in 1935. From the top, one gets a panoramic view of the whole city that is worth the climb. I was exhausted when I got back to the Kummer but recovered after a hot bath and went back to the Sacher for a Campari and soda with Burkhardt and Henry Kissinger, followed by a very good dinner and a very interesting talk about foreign policy, with some startling revelations by Kissinger of the Kennedys' "trickiness in matters of policy." (The speech by Bobby, which so heartened the Berliners and which seemed a pledge to them, was described by Bobby himself as no pledge at all, but merely a "speech written by Arthur Schlesinger." According to Kissinger, the President is great in detail but not on directions, is rather anti-German, and has been aptly described by Dean Acheson as possessing "a lt. colonel's mind." . . .

. . . While I have been doing all this, the Russians have put their first woman into space and she has brought *Kitsch in dem Weltraum* [Kitsch in space] to a point of perfection. She is reported to have said: "*Mütterchen, mach dir keine Sorgen! Ich habe in mein Raumschiff das grösste Vertrauen. Sag es auch*

[11] Friedrich Engel-Jánosi (1893–1978), born into an ennobled family of Austrian-Jewish industrialists, converted to Catholicism, and became a leading expert on the relationship between the Holy See and the Hapsburg monarchy and on Austrian foreign policy more generally.

allen Müttern der Welt, dass mir nichts geschehen wird. Mein Schiff ist eine ausserordentlich präzise Maschine" ["Don't worry, mother! I have the greatest confidence in my spaceship. Also tell all the mothers of the world that nothing will happen to me. My ship is an extremely precise machine"] (*Express*, Wien, 18 June). In Russian this probably sounds even more banal... In England the unedifying Profumo scandal continues to claim all attention.[12] [Prime Minister Harold] Macmillan has weathered the first storm, but just barely. . . .

Saturday, 22 June 1963. Berlin.
. . . So via Munich (Air France) to Berlin (Pan Am) arriving on Thursday 20 June in time to have dinner at the *Gästehaus*, which I found filled with the usual collection of odd types. . . . Of a quite different order of magnitude is Reinhard Bendix[13] whom I now meet for the first time, and who talks interestingly about things that matter. There is no better index to a man's intellectual character than the themes he chooses to work on. Men who take big subjects or big men seem to grow with their subject, if they were not grown before. . . . In any case, Bendix's *Max Weber* is a book of weight, and so is he. . . .

. . . Yesterday I started my official visits with the Otto Suhr Institut, whence I took Gerhard Ritter, Franz Ansprenger, and Hans Rosenberg, who is here for a few days, to lunch at the Forsthaus. Then I called on Hartwich, who is up to his neck in preparations for President K's arrival and visit to the Free University on Wednesday. I had the amusing task of re-casting the English version of the award of membership in the academic community that will be made to JFK, collaborating with G. N. Kruger and wife whom I met at Princeton recently. The Latin and German (I'm not sure which came first) had been Englished by Fränkel, and the result was shattering. I gave a new version, less close to the German text but *English*. Even my rhetoric could not overcome the repetition in substance, but it was pleasant (in view of Kissinger's story about Bobby) to underline those

---

[12] The Profumo Scandal concerned British Secretary of State for War John Profumo's extramarital affair with nineteen-year-old Christine Keeler, which he dishonestly denied during a hearing in the House of Commons. Adding to the seriousness of the scandal was public speculation that Keeler was simultaneously having an affair with a Soviet naval attaché, Yevgeny Ivanov, thus creating a national security risk.

[13] Reinhard Bendix (1916–1991) emigrated from Germany to the United States at age 22 and had a long and productive career as a professor in the Departments of Sociology and Political Science at the University of California, Berkeley.

sections in which the address spoke of JFK's "unambiguous declaration" of the U.S. determination to defend Berlin... Hartwich is fatter but in good fettle. He is paying all my expenses here and giving a big party for me tonight... After this talk, I went to Elwert und Meurer and bought too many books, and came back to the *Gästehaus* for a good talk with Bendix (and the confused Texan, who doesn't know why Truman was a good president) about the American diplomatic style, and the elements of Hollywood and Madison Ave. in JFK's style, and charisma, and creeping sexuality as a threat to the American young. I suggested that if we could remove the *Alpdruck* [nightmare] of sex from the shoulders of our young, they would thank us. He agreed and talked of how a few months in a Swiss school changed the values of his kids in this respect. . . .

Sunday morning, 23 June 1963. Café Thiel Ecke, Berlin.
. . . JFK's approaching visit crowds everything else out of the papers. According to H. v. Borch [of *Die Welt*], reporting from Washington, a good part of the press at home feels that, in view of what is going on in various capitals, the trip should have been postponed, and that this view was shared by some of K's advisers. . . .

. . . When I do the new edition of my textbook, I may have to point to this year as the great turning point—the change of generations. In every country from the Atlantic to Moscow, there is some kind of internal crisis, with the possible exception of France, Scandinavia, and Switzerland. But here the Adenauer era is at an end; in England, Macmillan is tottering to a fall; and there are crises in Spain, Italy, Austria, Greece, Turkey, and heaven only knows where else. In Moscow, one prepares for the "ideological confrontation between what *Christ und Welt* calls the Rome and the Byzantium of communism. Only one crisis has been cleared up in these last days: we have a new Pope. That change, which highlights the general state of flux, was accomplished expeditiously and without, apparently, a change of direction, for Montini (now Paul) is reputed to be a liberal and is expected to continue the work of the late Pope (whose short reign, incidentally, eclipsed that of his ambiguous predecessor, currently the target of Germany's most sensational play, [Rolf] Hochhuth's *Der Stellvertreter* [*The Deputy*], which accuses him of collaboration with the Nazis. We shall have to change the name of Pacelliallee in Dahlem—perhaps to Hochhuthallee!).[14]

I would not know, and could not guess, what Kennedy's private motives are in coming over. I should like to believe that Borch is right. But it seems

[14] The Pacelliallee was named after Eugenio Pacelli, who became Pope Pius XII.

charakterisch [in character] that he should come to Berlin during the Film Festival. . . .

Monday, 24 June 1963. Gästehaus, Berlin.
. . . The Kennedy visit so far is a tremendous success, and his reception at Cologne was so tumultuous that it seems to have induced him to go very far indeed in his commitments to Germany, which will probably annoy our English friends. Everyone here is enraptured—the trade in American flags is brisk—and rocking chairs are beginning to sell. . . .

Wednesday, 26 June 1963. Frankfurter Hof, Frankfurt am Main.
. . . Up early this morning and off to Frankfurt, arriving at about ten. Not my favorite city. Although the shops are often more impressive than those in Berlin, nothing else is. . . .

. . . JFK's speech at the Paulskirche yesterday was both a reaffirmation of the "Interdependence Speech" at Philadelphia last 4 July, and a slap at de Gaulle (JFK's warning that divisive tactics merely play into the hands of communism). The Gaullist papers are speaking of a "war for Germany" and Mr. [Walter] Lippmann, writing *before* the speech, has some very curious ideas on the same subject (which strike me as far-fetched, as does his interpretation of Adenauer's welcome). [Joseph] Alsop has something interesting to say, and something that explains the *London Daily Express*'s attack on the Germans today. . . .

The President's reception in Berlin was apparently stupendous. Walking here in Frankfurt, I got an occasional look at a TV screen, and the crowd at *Rathaus Schöneberg* [Schöneberg City Hall] was enough to impress anyone. JFK may have been induced by it to make the greatest commitment that he could possibly have made: his declaration that he considers himself a Berliner. This was greeted with what can only be described as rapture… In the face of all of this, the Communists seem curiously embarrassed and inept. The [East German] Ulbricht regime's answer to Kennedy was (1) to widen the Wall and to create a forbidden zone behind it; (2) to put a curtain behind the *Brandenburger Tor* [Brandenburg Gate] so that JFK and the East Berliners could not see one another; and (3) to put a Brigitte Bardot film on TV at the time of JFK's arrival. Khrushchev's answer was to declare that he is coming to East Berlin on Friday, ostensibly in connection with Ulbricht's birthday…

Not that there is any lack of confusion in the West. We have now a new scandal, this time in Sweden where a highly placed colonel, who has filled a whole series of staff jobs, has just confessed that he has been spying for

Russia since 1948![15] . . .

Friday, 27 June 1963. Frankfurt-am-Main.
I asked Hartwich about the future of Berlin, the mood of the population, the prospects of growth, etc., and he seemed reasonably optimistic. He pointed out, however, that of the 20,000 workers who had come to Berlin from West Germany since August, 7% or more had had to return because there were neither jobs nor homes for them; and, for much the same reason, the Free University this year had to turn down 4000 West German students seeking admission. It is clear that [General Lucius D.] Clay (who received a tumultuous reception yesterday—even signs—or one sign—reading "Clay for President") is right in pleading for more capital for Berlin…[16] Bussmann was perhaps less optimistic, although his were private grouses. He feels a sense of isolation in Berlin, and he says it's not always easy to get out of, for the delays on the *Autobahn* of late have been interminable, and the planes are often full. Aside from this, Bussmann does not believe in all the talk about making Berlin a Culture Center—or rather *the* Culture Center of Europe. He says, probably rightly, that one cannot make culture centers. In this talk, and in the *Rummel* [hype] of the yearly Film Festival, and in the frenetic excitement over the JFK visit, he finds signs of a growing provincialism in Berlin…

In our last talk in Berlin, Hans Rosenberg said that in the letters he is receiving as he pursues his extensive search for a successor to Sontag at Cal, my name keeps coming up. He asked if I might be interested in moving to Berkeley. I gave him a careful answer, since I want to be able to keep my leverage at Stanford (for which the threat of leaving might be useful in many ways—scholarships, library, etc.) and because I am *not* perfectly happy at Stanford (colleagues, *usw.* [etc.]) and *might* be seriously interested if the job were right. It would, of course, depend on Phyl and how her job at the Health Council develops. If all goes well there, there is little chance of our going…

Later: At ten went to the Diesterweg Verlag to talk to a Herr Bautsch about the forthcoming Oxford edition of Hannah Vogt's *Schuld oder*

---

[15] This incident refers to the case of Stig Wennerström (1906–2006), who was eventually convicted of treason.

[16] General Clay had served as the military governor of the American zone of occupation in Germany from 1947 to 1949 and had orchestrated the Berlin Airlift.

Verhängnis.[17] The book is a result of a decision by the *Ländesregierung* [state government] of Hesse that there should be more *Zeitgeschichte* [contemporary history] in the schools, a decision triggered by the anti-Semitic outrages in Cologne a couple of years ago.[18] This interested the press, because it specializes in schoolbooks, and it approached Hannah Vogt, who works at the *Bundeszentrale für politische Unterricht* [Federal Agency for Political Education] in Wiesbaden and had independently reached the conclusion that it was more important for her to write a book about Germany's immediate past than the book that she had projected on communism. So she got to work, and her labors were given form by the questions she kept hearing from school teachers, who said they were raised by their students or by their students' parents. This accounts for the "question-form" that impressed me when I read the book, and it gave a freshness and directness to the book which apparently accounts for its success. In any event, it has been approved by the 10 *Länder* [German states] and Berlin and has been used in school programs all over Germany. And not only there, for parents have bought and read the book on their own account, and it has done well in book stores and, by October, will have sold some 400,000 copies, which is good in any league.

Diesterweg is an old family firm, now being run, as one of Bautsch's colleagues said, by *our* generation (the class of 1913 etc.). Another manifestation of the New Europe! . . . Frau Vogt, a spirited and witty type, came over from Wiesbaden, and she, Bautsch, and I had lunch and some more talk at a place called the *Kupferpfanne*, where I had the "Hubertustopf"—(venison), and she "Reis Orientale." It will be a pleasure to write an introduction to her book. . . .

I walked back to town, confirmed my ticket at Pan Am, had a haircut that left me looking like Yul Brynner, and then had a few beers and sausages at Fat Julius's where I read all the papers on JFK's triumph in Berlin yesterday. *Die Welt* in its editorial said that after the President's statement "Ich bin Berliner"; "kann es bei uns und in der Welt keinen Zweifel mehr geben an der Entschlossenheit des amerikanischen Präsidenten." [I am a Berliner; there can no longer be any doubt in our country or in the world

---

17 Gordon A. Craig, introduction to Hannah Vogt, *The Burden of Guilt: A Short History of Germany, 1914–1945*, trans. Herbert Arthur Strauss (New York: Oxford University Press, 1964).

18 A newly dedicated synagogue was defaced by vandals on December 24, 1959. This was followed by a series of copycat incidents in western Germany involving anti-Semitic and Nazi graffiti.

about the determination of the American President.] The speech was a confirmation, it added, of the declarations made after 13 August by Clay and Johnson. Most papers printed the speech *in toto*, and most commented on the great moment of silence when JFK retired into Rathaus Schöneberg to sign the Golden Book, and the Freedom Bell began to ring, and the crowd stood quietly and then slowly dispersed.

At the Free University, all seems to have gone as planned. The *Ehrenbürgerbrief* [Honorary Citizen's Letter] which I helped turn into English was read although none of the newspapers I have seen has reproduced the English version. The pictures of the bestowal of the honor all show my friend Hartwich looking very stern and dignified. I recognize none of the faces in the background.

The proper verb for the activities of the average German in the last few days was supplied for me by Frau Dr. Vogt, who said that she had "ge-Kennedy'd.".

Now then—

es, es, es und es, es ist ein
harter Schluss
weil, weil, weil und weil, weil
ich aus Frankfurt muss.[19]

Tomorrow, early, I go on to London and start speaking English again. . . .

Wednesday, 10 July 1963. Palo Alto.

A lot of gardening and some reading. Since I have to think about doing my Anvil book on Bismarck (180 pp. text; 100 pp. docs.), I have started reading the Rothfels edition of his letters, many of which are known to me but some of the most famous of which (the *Werbebrief* [suitor letter], for instance) I have never read in their entirety.[20] The letters to [Gustav] Scharlach still strike me as amazing letters… Also reading the essays of Robert Minder on French and German literature—last night the one on *Einbürgerung* [naturalization] which argues that G. writers retreated from civil life, and,

---

[19] Craig is quoting a nineteenth-century journeyman's song. Roughly translated, this verse reads:

It, it, it and it,
This ending it is hard
For, for, for and for,
From Frankfurt I must part.

[20] The *Werbebrief* is the 1846 letter Bismarck wrote to Heinrich von Puttkamer, expressing his interest in marrying the latter's daughter and declaring himself worthy as a suitor.

indeed, from the real world as such to the home and to God, whereas all major French writers dealt, even if only indirectly with the world of politics and social problems… I must return to Harry Levin's *The Gates of Horn* which deals with the last idea at length…[21]

Thursday, 11 July 1963. Palo Alto.
Coffee this morning with [Kurt] Müller-Vollmer, with whom I shall give a Humboldt seminar in the fall.[22] Preliminary discussion of scope and content, which inspired me to start rounding up some reading. Started checking the index of [Friedrich] Meinecke's *Ausgewählte Briefwechsel* [Selected Correspondence] and to read the Kaehler-Meinecke discussion of Humboldt, which followed the publication of [Siegfried] Kaehler's book.[23] Might be a good idea to think a bit of [Wilhelm von] Humboldt's importance in German historiography in the eyes of [Johann Gustav] Droysen (who called H. the [Francis] Bacon of German history-writing), Droysen's student Meinecke, and Meinecke's student Kaehler… It soon proved impossible to confine myself to Humboldt references, and I began to read the wonderful M-K exchanges during the second half of the 1939–45 war, when the big raids began to hit Berlin, and both men had to face up to defeat and the destruction of all the values they had lived by. Some of the discussion of Christianity and the *deus absconditus* [hidden God] in history fascinating. For the Vienna paper, it would be well to re-read all of this… In Kaehler's remarks on the first volume of M's memoirs, there are also some useful hints—e.g., his description of the book as an ideal source for an understanding of the typical small town in the Wilhelmine period, and for a realization of what European youth was like before it began to think in terms of Nietzsche and the like. If I do a seminar on Wilhelmine Germany, I must remember to include the memoirs—and the plays of [Carl] Sternheim, which seem to be enjoying a vogue in the Bay Area these days. . . .

---

[21] Harry Levin, *The Gates of Horn: A Study of Five French Realists* (New York: Oxford University Press, 1963).

[22] Kurt Müller-Vollmer (1928–2019) was a German American professor of German Studies at Stanford from 1962 until his retirement in 1995. His many fields of expertise included hermeneutics, philology, and the philosophical and empirical work of Wilhelm von Humboldt.

[23] Siegfried A. Kaehler (1885–1963) wrote his dissertation on Wilhelm von Humboldt under the direction of Friedrich Meinecke, and published *Wilhelm von Humboldt und der Staat. Ein Beitrag zur Geschichte deutscher Lebensgestaltung um 1800* in 1927.

Saturday, 20 July 1963. Palo Alto.
A week of teeth, losing the last of my uppers on Tuesday and trying to cope with china choppers ever since. Not the pleasantest of experiences.

A mixed bag of reading. Read all of the Meinecke-Kaehler wartime letters. Very exciting stuff and required reading for young historians. Bussmann, who has been given K's correspondence to put in order, says that K. wrote too many letters—that he was, in fact, *always* writing letters and that this left him no time to write history. There is something in this—K's output was not great—but perhaps the letters are better than the unwritten monographs would have been. K. is often wrong-headed in his reflections on the cause of the disaster, but always provocative; and his reflections on the return of *Angst* and *Furcht* [fear] to human experience after they had been expelled from our consciousness by science and liberalism are exciting. For the young historian his comments on M's memoirs and on the *Catastrophe* book should be a model of how scholars should talk about each other's books and a demonstration that friendship does *not* depend on bland compliments.[24]

A typical Kaehler sally: In answer to all those historians who began to talk of Bismarck's tragic mistake of 1866 (the exclusion of Austria and the organization of Germany under Prussian hegemony), he asks what the result would have been if G had had to face up to the European and imperial problems under Austrian leadership, as described in [Heinrich] Srbik's third volume (K. to M., 20.9.1949)... M's frank appraisal of the formative influences in K's thinking also good (M. to K., Mai 1950)... Finally, some wonderful suggestions for reading: [Ina] Seidel's *Lennacker* (also discussed by Minder), [Hermann] Heimpel's *Jugendroman* [Youth Novel], *Die halbe Violine* [The half violin], *eine Münchener Jugend* [A Munich Youth]— I met Heimpel last year in Göttingen, and have been quoting his essay "On Dying for One's Country" ever since)—Paul Fechter's *Menschen und Zeiten* [*People and Times*] (1948), for its pictures of Berlin in the Wilhelmine and Weimar period, the biographies of Weber and Harnack (to go with M's second), and much else...

Aside from this, I have done most of Erich Marcks's *Bismarck's Jugend* [*Bismarck's Youth*] (to go with the letters), [Johann Wolfgang von Goethe's] *Hermann und Dorothea* (because I want to read Humboldt on it) and the remarkable *Novelle* of Günter Grass, *Katz und Maus* [*Cat and Mouse*], which packs as big a wallop as *Die Blechtrommel* [*The Tin Drum*]. I am also making

---

[24] Craig is referring to Friedrich Meinecke's short, pessimistic postwar book *Die Deutsche Katastrophe* [*The German Catastrophe*] (Wiesbaden: E. Brockhaus, 1946).

some corrections and elaborations in my Königgrätz ms. for Baldwin and Lippincott, who seem to like it, although without raving. . . .

Wednesday, 4 September 1963. Palo Alto.
. . . The work with Humboldt goes well, and I have some main lines sketched for our seminar. I have been reading G. P. Gooch, Jacques Droz, [G. de] Ruggiero, [Walter M.] Simon—all helpful, although Simon does not understand Humboldt and oversimplifies the crisis of 1819—[Friedrich Carl] Sell's German Liberalism book (a silly performance) and Lenny Krieger (harder to understand than Humboldt, and not as provocative). I have also pushed ahead with Humboldt's diplomatic stuff and his constitutional writings. The [Friedrich von] Gentz tie may be useful to investigate for seminar purposes. Paul Sweet's book is not very good, but the Gentz *Tagebücher* [Diaries] are, and there is lots of Humboldt stuff. [W. H.] Bruford says that Talleyrand thought very highly of Humboldt's diplomatic talents. This would be good to hunt down—and perhaps a good theme would be a survey of diplomats' opinions of H. in the Rome, Vienna, and London periods and during the Wiener Kongress [Congress of Vienna]... Other reading: [Heinrich] Böll's *Ansichten eines Clowns* [*The Clown*], which is causing a row in Germany—a good example of contemporary *Kulturpessimismus* [cultural pessimism], and the best book of Böll's I have read; and [Wilhelm] Raabe's *Das Odfeld*,[25] a tremendous achievement and a good book for a historian to read... Robert Minder tells us that Schiller's *Geisterseher* [*The Visionary*] was influenced by Choderlos de Laclos and that it, in turn, influenced *The Charterhouse of Parma*. I find myself becoming increasingly interested in Schiller, and will probably get into him more deeply, *Geisterseher* at least. . . .

Monday, 23 September 1963. Palo Alto.
Registration Day, and the usual madhouse preceding the opening of term. The summer now officially over, and I have relatively little to show for it, although the Humboldt seminar may prove the time spent on him was not entirely wasted. The last two weeks have been spent reading Kaehler on *Humboldt and der Staat* [Humboldt and the State], more Schiller, Humboldt's *Tagebücher* [Diaries] (his travels in France during the revolution), and most recently his *Letters to a Female Friend*. Very odd stuff, with a tremendous

---

25 For a translation, see Wilhelm Raabe, *The Odin Field: A Story*, trans. Michael Ritterson (Rochester: Camden House, 2001). This historical novel, published in 1888, tells the story of an aged former teacher at convent school in Lower Saxony at the time of the Seven Years' War.

amount of talking about how independent he was and how impervious to the sort of thing that worries other men. I think there is something to Kaehler's emphasis on the erotic in H's thought and the way in which his tendency to aestheticize and idealize was both a retreat from reality and an admission of dislike of responsibility. Certainly people who boast of their strength and independence have been known to be less strong than they advertise themselves as being. An interesting monograph by [Franz] Bertram ties the summer's reading together nicely by arguing that [Adalbert] Stifter's *Nachsommer* [*Indian Summer*] is an expression of H's *Bildungstheorie* [*Educational Theory*], and that, in fact, S. was much impressed by the *Briefe an eine Freundin* [*Letters to a Female Friend*]. . . .

The letters to Charlotte Diede are not, therefore, without interest (although one cannot help wondering whether basically they were not a form of titillation). Perhaps they appealed to Stifter (who did not get on with his wife) because he admired H. as much for having found a correspondent as pliant (while intelligent) as Charlotte, as for the high moral sentiments expressed… In large doses the letters to Charlotte are tedious, for the sentiments are too noble and the tone too lofty. And one misses the change of pace which one finds in the letters between H. and his wife, where one can always count on Li to pep things up—with a suggestion that H. persuade Castlereagh to cede her an island, or a firm warning to H. that the peace treaty (of 1814) must not be written in French, but in Latin. H. wrote better letters to Li, partly because he was (one suspects) a little frightened of her.[26] So much for idealization…

I am tired of talking to myself. But with whom does one talk about the things he reads? No one here and—perhaps to be honest—no one if I were back at Princeton…

Ernst Kantorowicz died of an aneurysm last week. . . .

Thursday, 26 September 1963. Palo Alto.

Lunch at the Red Cottage with Peter Duignan,[27] who tried to convince me that we should collaborate with the Hoover in a joint appointment in Russian History, appointing Leopold Haimson as Mazour's successor. Not a bad idea for Haimson, who is working on the Menshevists, and is probably as good as Cy Black and Theo von Laue, both of whom are in any

---

[26] "Li" was a nickname for Wilhelm von Humboldt's wife, Caroline.

[27] Peter Duignan (1926–2012), a fellow at the Hoover Institution for more than half a century, began his career as a specialist in the history of sub-Saharan Africa, and later expanded the range of his research and publications to include the Middle East, immigration history, American foreign policy, and the European Union.

case unavailable. Tried idea out on Gordon Wright who as usual closed up as soon as the Hoover was mentioned and actually admitted that he was "unregenerate," whatever that means. I was angry and showed it. We'll never get anywhere while this attitude to the Hoover persists, and any good Russian man who comes to us will want to work at the Hoover anyway. Gordon seems to think we can appoint a junior man in Russian studies, a silly idea... I am fed up with Stanford politics. . . .

Friday, 27 September 1963. Palo Alto.
Today resumed one of my more pleasant routines, possible only on days on which there are no committee meetings: a swim at the gym and then lunch in my office by myself, during which I read [Peter] Kropotkin's *Memoirs of a Revolutionist.* I started this last term and I now plan, when Kropotkin is finished, to turn to Victor Serge's *Memoirs of a Revolutionary.* Just the right kind of change of pace from my usual pabulum...

Today wrote a letter for the memorial volume to be given to Jinx Harbison celebrating his 30th anniversary as a Princeton teacher—in a wheelchair, poor fellow...

Reading Hannah Arendt's *Rahel Varnhagen: Lebensgeschichte einer deutscher Jüdin aus der Romantik* [*Rahel Varnhagen: The Life of a Jewess*] (Munich, 1959). . . . Very good on Rahel's salon, to which all cultivated people went at the turn of the century, even those who, like the Humboldt brothers, detested their hostess. Arendt says that the Jewish salon, "the ever repeatedly dreamed idyll of a mixed society," was a chance constellation in a time of transition between a declining and a not yet stabilized society. The Jews were the *Lückenbüsser* [stopgap]: "because the Jews stood outside society, they were for a short time a kind of neutral ground on which the cultivated met." They (and the actors and the nobility, like Prinz Louis Ferdinand, who came to Rahel) helped give resonance and assurance to the intellectual bourgeoisie represented there. As soon as the latter felt firm ground under their feet, they dropped the Jews... A curious passage (67–70) on Humboldt as a romantic who learned to value *Glück* [serendipity] and to accept *Unglück* [misfortune], to accept what was given him in life, and who, because of this, was the only one to conquer "*die romantische Verwirrung* [the Romantic confusion]." He didn't try to do things as much as let them happen to him. Thus (I suppose) the indecisions upon which Kaehler had so much to say... Book is also good on Gentz and his relations with Rahel; and on anti-Semitism in Germany in this period (Grattenauer's *Wider den Juden* [Against the Jews] of 1800–1801, apparently as all-inclusive a racial attack as that of the Nazis, the pogrom of 1819, etc. etc.). Rahel, who spent her life trying to escape the consequences of being a Jew and to liberate herself by marriage, ended by venerating Heine who accepted Jewishness. (One sees in this book, incidentally, the attack upon Jews who seek to join the enemy which runs through Arendt's Eichmann book and has made fools like [Judge Michael A.] Musmanno and weaklings like the editors of the *Times Book Review* accuse her of anti-Semitism)... The Jewish salons, incidentally, were killed off by the defeat of 1806 which put an end to the Frederician atmosphere in which the rich Jews had flourished. The second generation of Romanticists—Brentano, Müller, Arnim—tended to be anti-Semitic... The Prussian Jews were nevertheless emancipated by decree in 1812, and thousands of them fought in the wars of liberation... Arendt on Humboldt's comments concerning Rahel's parvenuism in 1814/15 (when she married Varnhagen: "*W.v.H. ist hier wie auch sonst die beste, scharfsinnigste und mechanteste Klatschquelle seiner Zeit* [W.v.H. is here, as elsewhere, the best, most astute and most malicious source of gossip of his time]." (s. 188) ... If anti-Rahel, he did not become anti-Semitic, although his wife did and broke a decade-long friendship with Rahel in 1815 by addressing her, before a large company, as '*Sie.*" (pp. 195f.)...

Wilhelm von Humboldt und die Nation, ed. by Rudolf Freese (Verlag der Nation, East Berlin (?) n.d.)—an admiring communist anthology of H's writings with an introduction that praises him as the representative man of his time and the ablest antagonist of the Frederician State, while warning readers that his arguments must not be turned against the Ulbricht state and reminding them that H's individualism was not the selfish kind that one finds in late capitalism but one whose ultimate consequences were to serve society. Humboldt the nationalist working for German unity, rather than for Prussia, is stressed here, and the modern parallel is pointed out. A thousand pages of selections, with good pictures—pasted in by hand!

Wednesday, 9 October 1963. Palo Alto.
A luncheon at the University Club for [Kurt] Kiesinger, Minister-President of Baden-Württemberg. I drove Willi Strothman and Herzfeld out and found the place filled with Germans including people from the Washington Embassy and the Consul General and Cultural Attaché (Sommer) from San Francisco. A rather heavy lunch for the middle of the day, ending with Napoleons which were hardly in keeping with the Teutonic tone.

Thursday, 17 October 1963. Palo Alto.
Yesterday was given over to the visit of Waldemar Besson of Erlangen. I met him when he was [Hans] Rothfels's assistant at Tübingen in 1958. R.

appears to have wanted Besson to be his successor but this sort of thing is not done, so B. moved on. I owe to Besson a long article about me in the *Deutsche Rundschau*, which amused Fred Burkhardt greatly.

[Wayne] Vucinich,[28] [Lew] Spitz[29] and I met Besson at the Southern Pacific Railway station and took him to lunch at the Ramar Oaks in Atherton—a good lunch but with cocktails, which made the afternoon difficult and work impossible. At 4:15 went to Tresidder Union to hear Besson speak on current tendencies in German politics. Most interesting. He pointed up the dilemma confronting Erhard (who became chancellor yesterday) and Schroeder who want to follow the Atlantic (Kennedy) line in foreign policy but are confronted with a strong Gaullist wing inside the Christian Democratic Union and the Christian Social Union. (Besson says that *all* of the leading Catholics—but none of the leading Protestants—in his part of the world are Gaullists—which shows an interesting correspondence between religion and foreign policy which might be elaborated. The Social Democratic Party of Germany includes virtually no Gaullists, except in Bavaria.) The appeal of de Gaulle is that he promises grandeur of a kind (not German but European) and an escape from threatening provincialism and dependence on America. He intimates to the Germans, and the German Gaullists echo this, that to follow the western line is to betray the cause of re-unification. The effectiveness of the argument is shown by the Bonn gov't's long hesitation with respect to the test ban and the muttering about the wheat deal. Besson's view is that Erhard and Schröder will have real trouble unless they (1) make Washington understand that Bonn must be a full member of the Atlantic alliance, which means that Germans must be given a share in strategical planning. (This the Kennedy gang don't seem to be [able to] face up to, although writers like [name omitted] have been arguing the necessity of this for a long time.) Erhard and Schröder must (2) find a way to follow the Atlantic line while finding a way to keep the possibility of progress towards re-unification; and—to increase the chances of this they must (3) be more active in foreign policy than Adenauer in the last three years, seek a new

---

[28] Wayne Vucinich (1913–2005), one of the founders of Russian, Slavic, East European, and Byzantine Studies at Stanford, taught at the University from 1946 until his retirement in 1978, and was director of the Center for Russian and East European Studies from 1972 to 1985.

[29] Lewis W. Spitz (1922–1999), a prolific scholar of Reformation history, arrived at Stanford, along with Gordon Craig and David Potter, in 1961, and taught early modern European history there until his retirement in 1993.

approach to the satellites (by revising the Hallstein Doctrine), in short *find* a German policy of their own. (The Kennedy boys have been saying this themselves.) Above all they must (4) strive to make West Germany acceptable to the Soviet Union by trade, cultural exchange, and any other means that come to hand. If they can do this, they may actually in time be lucky in finding an acceptable alternative to Ulbricht—which or who does not exist today.

In the present thaw, with the two World Powers moving towards a comprehensive arrangement, the Germans fear a freezing of the status-quo which will delay reunification indefinitely. Besson argues that it would be morally impossible for a people to accept the imprisonment of 17 million of their own kind. So Erhard and Schroeder have to keep the door open – or Gaullism will get even stronger. . . .

Friday, 18 October 1963. Palo Alto.
Yesterday afternoon Humboldt seminar on his aesthetics—the "Hermann und Dorothea" essay. Heavy sledding, but fun.

In the evening to the Herzfelds for dinner. George Mosse[30] on hand. Good time. Mosse is burning up the campus, and Lew Spitz and I feel he can be picked off the Wisconsin tree. Whether the conservative members of the Department would agree to making him an offer is perhaps questionable. I find it hard to believe, but it is true that some of the fraternity feel that the new blood (Potter, Spitz, Craig) have brought too many students to the department and that this means too much work for everybody. John Johnson, who has other reasons for resentment, would prefer the appointment of dull young men, rather than bright oldsters. How Blum would jeer if he knew this! . . .

Friday, 25 October 1963. Palo Alto.
I have agreed to write an essay on doctrine and training in the Austrian army in the 19th century for the Liddell Hart Festschrift which Michael Howard is editing.[31] The other contributors are as distinguished a group as the one that did the G. P. Gooch seminar and include Alastair Buchan,

[30] Born into a prominent German Jewish family in Berlin, George Mosse (1918–1999) became an innovative and prolific scholar of German history and the history of nationalism at the University of Wisconsin–Madison. With Walter Laqueur, he founded the *Journal of Contemporary History*, to which Craig contributed, in 1966.

[31] Gordon A. Craig, "Command and Staff Problems in the Austrian Army, 1740–1866," in Michael Howard, ed., *The Theory and Practice of War: Essays Presented to Captain B. H. Liddell Hart on His Seventieth Birthday* (New York: Frederick A. Praeger, 1966).

Norman Gibbs, Maury Matloff, Peter Paret, J. M. Mackintosh, Henry Kissinger, and Hans-Adolf Jacobsen. I am fired up over the prospect, and am thinking of a piece that will start with the reforms of Archduke Carl during the Napoleonic period and run on to Conrad's time. Out of this in time will come, I hope, a book on the politics of the Austrian Army, or something of the sort… Meanwhile, Peter Paret (who will write a piece on Clausewitz for the Liddell Hart book) is pursuing negotiations with Klaus Knorr and Herb Bailey for our long dreamed of international edition of Clausewitz in five volumes.

Friday, 1 November 1963. Palo Alto.
. . . Lecture this morning, after which I got reports of yesterday's dept. meeting, which I had to miss. Dave Potter told me with amusement that dept. decided to authorize an offer to George Mosse, despite speeches by Bill Bark,[32] who argued that bringing outsiders to dept. made it impossible to give the insiders decent raises. David said there was little doubt that these shafts were aimed at us late-comers, but he didn't seem worried. . . .

Monday, 4 November 1963. Palo Alto.
Lecture at 9. Swim at noon. Office Hours. Dept. Library Committee—how to get more books for library without money… In the evening, the Mosse seminar in which George was more evasive and rigid than usual and did not distinguish himself. Drinks afterwards at the Wrights where discussion continued, and Bracher,[33] [Juan] Linz, and [Heinz] Eulau continued their prodding, with an occasional tart addition from Dick Lyman. George apologized to me(!) for having forced me to reveal myself as a narrow political historian, and I told him Ed Earle's way of handling muddled methodologists by insisting that he was not very bright in the esoteric fields but that he did know the simple hard political facts which the ideologues ignored. To talk about German conservatism, as George did tonight, with no appreciation of the political facts—and to wave them away when they are called to his attention—is not very impressive.

Tuesday, 5 November 1963. Palo Alto.

---

32 William C. Bark (1909–1996), best known for his book *Origins of the Medieval World* (Stanford: Stanford University Press, 1958), directed Stanford's Western Civilization program from 1947 through the mid-1960s.

33 Karl Dietrich Bracher (1922–2016), a political scientist and historian of the Weimar Republic and Nazi Germany, was a champion of liberal democracy best known for his pioneering account of the collapse of the Weimar Republic, and his critical analyses of totalitarian ideologies and dictatorships.

. . . After the seminar a talk with Dave Potter who was disturbed by Mosse's performance and believes we should hold off in the question of inviting him to join the department. I sensed last night that George had lost ground—that Lyman and Potter were dubious and that even Spitz was less enthusiastic than he had been. I confess to feeling strong doubts myself, but I called Gordon and argued that we should not swing too quickly in the anti-Mosse direction and that, if—after another such performance—we decide not to invite him, we should nevertheless go after a top man, rather than a young one. Peter Gay of Columbia is one possibility. Another, suggested diffidently by Gordon Wright because he feels I might be sensitive about competition in my field, is Fritz Stern. To the latter suggestion, I reacted warmly, pointing out that I didn't care what I taught in the way of courses, that in any event, I was a political historian and Stern an intellectual one, and that Fritz was a fine fellow. Gordon seems very pro-Stern, so Mosse may have done himself in…

This evening introduced Karl Bracher in the Tuesday Evening Lecture Series. He talked on problems of parliamentarianism, a gloss on his Bellagio paper. Very good, indeed. Reception in Stern Hall afterwards.

Thursday, 14 November 1963. Philadelphia.
Arrived in Philadelphia last night at about 10 and went to Benjamin Franklin Hotel. On road read first hundred pages of Günter Grass's *Hundejahre* [*Dog Years*].

This is being written at the first session of the Philosophical Society's meeting. . . .

There is a remarkable gathering of old buffers here, and as the program shows a very varied intellectual menu. The most striking thing, perhaps, of this meeting is the assumption, which hangs over the audience that sits in this handsome room under the portraits of Washington and Jefferson and the bust of Ben Franklin, that any cultivated man should be able to understand serious papers on any serious subject and that no concessions need be made to non-specialists. An 18th-century idea that is heartening in an age in which we too easily accept from some of the brethren the suggestion that their specialty is a mystery not capable of comprehension by the layman. This allows many fakirs to get university chairs and foundation grants. Goethe and Franklin would have seen through them in a minute. . . .

Friday, 22 November 1963. Palo Alto.
. . . At about 11 o'clock this morning President Kennedy was shot and killed

in the streets of Dallas. Everything here came to a grinding halt, and a good many people—particularly the students—are in a state of semi-shock. It is interesting that the immediate conclusion drawn by all men of liberal persuasion was that it must have been a Bircher fanatic—(a view to which I inclined myself, although I thought it might equally well be a Cuban refugee brooding over the Bay of Pigs incident). Others suggested that it might be a violent segregationist. At present moment, it appears that it is none of these, but a Castro-ite and Communist fellow traveler. If this is confirmed, the consequences for national sanity may be very grave indeed. Let us hope that the murderer is obviously mad and worked by himself. This will not undo the blow to the country, but it will prevent even worse from occurring. . . .

Tuesday, 26 November 1963. Palo Alto.
A harrowing weekend. Friday, as I say, was a day of numbness. Dick von Wagener, who was in town, dropped in in the evening, and we talked a while, but no one made much sense. Saturday was—like the two days that followed—spent before the TV set. On Sunday morning, George Wilson gave a fine sermon at the First Presbyterian Church in which he pointed out that the President's murder (and the shooting of his assassin, which we heard about from Wilson for the first time and which shocked and disgusted me even more—if that is possible—than the assault on the President) was the logical result of the violence that has come to characterize our society and the hatred that has begun to inspire our domestic politics. Other people have pointed to this since (Richard Nixon, for example, in a TV interview yesterday), but none that I have heard as eloquently as Wilson. The newspapers today are talking of the assassination as an event which may shock us back into sobriety and decency and mutual forbearance and political moderation and national unity. Perhaps if enough men of goodwill get down to work, this can be so, but it will require a few other things too: a little more speed from Congress in civil rights legislation, a little more attention to the kind of smut that is peddled by Hollywood these days and advertised luridly in family newspapers, a little more insistence about the abolition of violence in TV programs and the suppression of comic books that idealize it, a few more laws governing the sale of firearms, and the substitution of improved education for the Moon Shot Program as our first national objective.

The TV coverage of the church services and funeral yesterday was magnificent! The collaboration of the Catholic Church and the military gave the networks material that was unbeatable, and they made the most of it. I hope our schools and colleges will make the most of this to teach a few simple values to the young. (Not that they need it as much as their elders, if I can judge from Marty and her contemporaries.) The funeral coverage was varied with a series of excellent musical programs—indeed, there was more good music to be found on TV in these four days than in months previously—and some good biographical essays on Johnson, the assassin Oswald, and the like. There was also a rather odd British program "That Was the Week That Was"[34] (usually a satirical show) that was embarrassingly maudlin—(it included a dreadful poem "To Jackie," delivered by Dame Sybil Thorndyke)—and which showed a rather worrying tendency to feel that the world had come to an end because their hero had been removed. This disturbs me because I should like to see the English have a bit more confidence in themselves and, I might add, a bit more confidence in us. JFK's passing is going to cause trouble but it is not going to paralyze the energies of this nation, and it is disturbing to find our allies thinking this might be so. . . .

Today I am 50!

Monday, 2 December 1963. Palo Alto.
A lecture in the morning, a swim at noon, and an afternoon of students. In the evening, the Mosse seminar, with George holding forth on Hitler, not too effectively, to my way of thinking, or (to judge by some dissatisfied snufflings on my right hand) to Gordon Wright's. Afterward I dodged a party at Wayne Vucinich's place, but was captured by Milorad Drachkovitch and taken off to his place for a drink of Metaxas with his charming wife and a discussion of his projected conference in celebration of the 100th anniversary of the First International…

In the afternoon, took Peter Duignan my criticisms of the Lutz-Burdick manuscript on the German Revolution of 1918—an amateurish job; and had a talk with Gay Almond,[35] who will become chairman of the Political Science Department in September and wants the historians to launch a series of case studies on democratization in Europe in collaboration with his boys—whom he will, he hopes, strengthen by the addition of Sidney Verba and Bernie Cohen. . . .

---

[34] *That Was the Week That Was* was a BBC satirical television program that aired in 1962 and 1963, with David Frost as host.

[35] Gabriel Almond (1911–2002), a political scientist who did pioneering work in the fields of comparative politics, political development, and political culture, taught at Yale and Princeton before moving to Stanford in 1963.

Thursday, 5 December 1963. Palo Alto.
Last Humboldt seminar on linguistics. On the whole, I think the experiment has worked. If Vollmer is smart, he will try to parlay it into a symposium volume.

Today Bob Sears asked me to become Assoc. Dean of Arts and Sciences, in succession to Virgil Whittaker, who has just become Dean of Graduate Studies. Phyl thinks I should accept, but, although the offer is flattering, I shall not do so, for professional reasons which I explained to her... I am reminded of the story about the cannibals who captured a whole college faculty and sold the meat. Deans fetched higher prices than professors or instructors and the butcher explained this by asking "Did you ever try to *clean* a dean?" I am a teacher-scholar and that's all I want to be. The only dean-ship that would ever tempt me would be that currently occupied by Doug Brown at Princeton, and that is not likely to be offered to me. . . .

Friday, 13 December 1963. Palo Alto.
Nettled Gordon Wright today by telling him there was an unhealthy mood of retrenchment in the Department and that, while our decision on Mosse may have been right—(and after having read the muddled paper of one of my students who took his course, I lean to the belief that it was)—the reasons many had for voting against him—(too many Chiefs, not enough Indians)—were signs of dry rot. I instanced Don Fehrenbacher's[36] recent memo, proposing that all professors limit themselves to two graduate student advisees a year as another case in point, and said that, with students coming West to work with me, I could not and would not accept any such nonsense. I told him the Department had been standing still for three years, and that it had better start moving again, and I urged action to bring Fritz Stern and Cy Black here. I was perhaps vehement to the point of rudeness, but I may have done some good... Made same speech to Potter, who agrees with me... Rest of day spent in papers, this being end of quarter...

The Clausewitz project has been accepted by the Princeton University Press... I have also just been made a member of the editorial board of the *American Historical Review*. . . .

[1964]

Tuesday, 25 February 1964. Palo Alto.

---

[36] Don E. Fehrenbacher (1920–1997), a preeminent Lincoln scholar, won the Pulitzer Prize in History in 1979 for his definitive study of the Dred Scott case.

Another sack lunch dept. mtng., this time on graduate program. Shot down a Lyman-Fehrenbacher scheme for reforming first-year graduate study, finding such unlikely allies as Bark, Wright, and Miller. . . . Home to listen to Liston-Clay fight on the radio—a sad performance.

Monday, 9 March 1964. Palo Alto.

. . . At six set off with Phyl (suffering from a bad cold) to Belvedere across the Golden Gate Bridge for dinner with Consul General [Siegfried] von Nostitz. After some difficulty were led to his home by a police car one hour late. Here we found the Brachers, the Herzfelds, and the Rosenbergs. Talked about the case of Fritz Fischer who was to come to U.S. on a German gov't grant which has now been taken from him by FM Schröder, presumably as a result of protests by Gerhard Ritter and other conservatives who dislike his book *Griff nach der Welt-Macht* [published in the United States as *Germany's Aims in the First World War*].[37] A stupid thing for Schröder to have done, and one which will have most unfortunate repercussions here. Rosenberg says that the American Council of Learned Societies will now pay his passage and that Berkeley will invite him to speak. I promised to try to get him an invitation and a fee from Stanford... Left party early and drove to Hilton Inn at Airport to spend the night. [Craig added later: "Our host Nostitz comes from an old Saxon military family and he claims that one of his relatives commanded the Austrian horse at Trautenau in 1866."]

Wednesday, 11 March 1964. Washington DC.

A day spent in the State Department, the first meeting of the Arms Control and Disarmament Agency (ACDA)'s Soc Science Advisory Board—a day largely given over to briefing but most interesting. Most of the board were old friends, for I knew them all except Osgood, Heard, and Branfenbrenner and I discover that not only Archie Alexander is in the outfit (as Assistant Director) but also Jacob Beam,[38] whom I met years ago before he went on to become ambassador in Warsaw and who showed me the military attaché reports sent from Berlin after the Blood Purge of '34, is connected with the ACDA—I gather on [ACDA Director William Chapman] Foster's negotiating staff. Foster briefed us on recent developments at Geneva and

---

[37] The German title of Fischer's book can be translated as "*The Grab for World Power: Imperial Germany's War Aims Politics, 1914–1918.*"

[38] Jacob Beam (1908–1993) was a veteran American diplomat who served as third secretary to the U.S. embassy in Berlin from 1934 to 1940, as ambassador to Poland from 1957 to 1961, as ambassador to Czechoslovakia from 1966 to 1969, and as ambassador to the Soviet Union from 1969 to 1973.

surprised me by saying that, despite Gromyko's recent blast in *Pravda* in which he apparently rejected *all* American suggestions about new lines to follow, the situation is, in fact, better than it was a year ago, and although the Russians cannot be expected to jump for President Johnson's nuclear freeze proposal, one should not conclude that that will be unproductive... Among other things that I learned from Foster's talk is that the new (and apparently less objectionable) term for inspection is verification... Both Foster and Beam spoke of the good results of the continuous dialogue that goes on in the Co-Chairman Organization at Geneva (a contribution made by Krishna Menon to diplomacy) and of the participation of the eight so-called Non-Aligned Nations (India, Burma, UAR, Mexico, Brazil, Sweden, Nigeria, Ethiopia) in the disarmament talks (along with the ten aligned states, 5:5). With respect to the latter, they both believed that the neutrals are becoming much more sophisticated about nuclear matters and that the Russians are finding it less easy to impress them by grand gestures and ringing declarations... The mission of the professors, incidentally, is to suggest research projects that will backstop the American effort in this field, to maintain liaison with the academic community, and, where possible, to facilitate the flow of information about ACDA's work to the general public. The last must be done, however, without resort to "propaganda," for the people on the Hill are apprehensive of the possible results of disarmament.

At luncheon, a most interesting talk with Mosely and Beam about the Berlin access problem. Both of them worked with the European Advisory Commission and they are highly critical of Bill Franklin's recent article on the subject in *World Politics*, which they regard as a kind of cover up for the State Department.[39] The State Department, they hold, had a horror of having to make any decisions in Germany and had a habit of losing proposals which might have forced them to make some. Mosely claims that the Russians would have been glad to sign an access agreement if it had been shoved at them before the troops were withdrawn to their own zones and that he had worked out an arrangement with all necessary safeguards. It was simply lost and the problem handed over to our soldiers, who screwed everything up... Mosely talked also of the false legal argument underlying Khrushchev's Berlin note of 1958, which embarrassed the

[39] The European Advisory Commission was established by the foreign ministers of the United States, the United Kingdom, and the Soviet Union in 1943 to study postwar potential problems and make recommendations to the respective governments. See William M. Franklin, "Zonal Boundaries and Access to Berlin," *World Politics* 16:1 (1963): 1–31.

Russians when it was discovered. . . .

Monday, 23 March 1964. Palo Alto.
A call from Phil Crowl in Princeton in connection with Dulles papers. He asked me to interview Adenauer, Erhard, Brentano, Brandt, *et al.* for the project. Accepted.

Lunch at Red Cottage with Ken Culver of Holt. Says my text is far out in front in field and has seriously reduced sales of Thompson.

Thursday, 2 April 1964. Palo Alto.
. . . Today lunch with Henry Kissinger at Red Cottage. Some interesting stories about JFK's disingenuousness and how much Adenauer disliked him.

Wednesday, 15 April 1964. Berlin.
I have typed my Liddell Hart piece (on Austrian staff) and shipped it off to Howard. I am thinking now of a piece for *The Reporter* on the new literature on Hitler: the [Percy] Schramm intro. to the new edition of Picker's *Tischgespräche* [*Hitler's Table Talk*], which has caused a controversy here because it has so much of the "human" Hitler in it (as opposed to the *dämonisch* [demonic]), the new biography by [Hans Bernd] Gisevius, the study by [Joachim] Fest, the Becktenwald medical study, "What was Hitler suffering from?" *usw* [etc.]. It should be interesting... Then I must get down to the intro. for the Vogt book and the new edition of my Bismarck-Adenauer book. Willi Strothmann wants me to go to Stuttgart to make a speech to Stanford in Germany, but I have decided that this is plain exploitation and that I haven't the time. My first classes are not until 6 May and will be confined, after that time, to Wed., Thurs., and Fri. It would be a crime to piddle that time away doing the sort of thing and I don't intend to do so. I have worked my fingers to the bone for Stanford students during the past two years. Enough is enough.

I am not moving around much and have not even gone to my old haunts on the Ku'damm or in Steglitz. I am not sleeping well and my stomach is off. My new radio is a joy, however, and keeps me amused.

The news sensation of the day is the row over the false report of Khrushchev's death, a mistake apparently made by the Deutsche Presse-Agentur [German News Agency] on Monday night (the 13th). Aside from that, Cyprus is threatening to blow sky high; there are more desegregation riots in the USA; NATO is threatening (again) to fall to pieces; . . . The Southeast Asia Treaty Organization is on its back; etc. On the other hand, "Let me hold your hand" and "Old Shatterhand Melody" are one-two on the Hot Platter List here and they are selling Beatle wigs in the KaDeWe [department store].

Friday, 17 April 1964. Berlin.
The Soviet gov't has now kicked the Deutsche Presse-Agentur agency out of Moscow on the grounds that the release of the Khrushchev story was an act of provocation; and Marguerite Higgins writes in *Die Welt* this morning that there are officials in Washington who believe that Moscow may be right. She adds, however, that the number of those who believe the Germans capable of anything has been sharply reduced. Johnson being decidedly friendly to Germany, particularly since Erhard's Texas visit... The clipping across the way [*Christ und Welt*, 10.4.6, on the mistrust among the hardline East German military leadership of Khrushchev's liberalization policies, pasted in the Diary] refers to a recent visit of Marshal Malinowski to East Berlin. Interesting. It may be that what is left of Prussian military politics is in the East German army. Which would surprise the hell out of the types who write me about the revival of militarism in *West* Germany... The escapes from East Berlin and the Zone continue—two boys got across in a stolen sports plane yesterday and, a few weeks ago, eight students managed to escape separately from East Berlin by jumping off interzonal trains. The refugees are bringing some interesting information. A 27-yr. old doctor whose father, also a refugee, worked in the East Berlin gas company, has given some very striking data on the rise of suicides in East Berlin since 13 August 1961—200 to 250 yearly by gas alone. The suicide rate in West Berlin, incidentally, is also high, and the suicides by gas about the same, but then the population of East Berlin is only about half that of the western half. . . . Years ago, in a post-lecture seminar in the National War College, an army officer said to me that the way to get the Soviets on the hip was to collect all the anarchists and bomb-throwers in the world, stick them on an island with press and radio facilities, and let them spend their time attacking the Soviet Union for betraying the Revolution. This is just what the Chinese are doing with great effect. They seem to have taken the bloom off Khrushchev's recent trip to Hungary and, perhaps, to have prevented him from announcing an imminent withdrawal of Soviet troops. They are also worrying the satellites, and the Rumanians are now playing a very odd game... On the other hand, the Chinese approaches to France, and French willingness to entertain them, have ruined the Gaullists in Germany, who are too conservative to put up with this and are left without a program, while Schröder is stronger than ever before. . . .

Thursday, 23 April 1964. Berlin.
The last two days have been given over to writing my introduction for the Oxford Press edition of Hannah Vogt's *Schuld oder Verhängnis* [published in English as *The Burden of Guilt*]. It is now finished—about 3000 words which make some sense—and is off in the mail to Sheldon Meyer. . . .

A correspondent writing in the *Tagespiegel* over the weekend reported that certain private associations in West Germany intend to present a Leopold v. Ranke prize and an Ulrich v. Hutten prize to David Hoggan[40] when he comes to Germany in May and that other honors can be expected from Right Radical groups. This will cause a bigger stink in the USA than the [Fritz] Fischer business. The correspondent was very angry about the misuse of Ranke's and Hutten's names to honor a *Geschichtsklitterung* [historical misrepresentation]. He gave a very fair picture of American criticisms of the book and promised details about the people (Rhine Ruhr Klub) behind this demonstration… With respect to the Fischer business, the current issue of *Die Zeit* has an editorial, the letter which Epstein, Stern, Snell, and I (among others) sent to the paper, a very weak Foreign Office statement, and selections (unsigned) from letters to Fischer from American historians, including me. . . .

The New York World's Fair opened yesterday with only minor racial demonstrations… On Monday, Pres. Johnson spoke on foreign policy and pleased everyone here (except the Springer press: *BZ* asks today whether USA becomes *weich* [soft]) by announcing a cutback in production of fissionable materials, which the Soviet Union will match. Wednesday, the Pres. gave a press conference and *dis*pleased everyone here by announcing that U-2 flights over Cuba will continue, to watch for erection of middle-range rocket sites… *Die Welt* of today reports that the Republican Party has released a report of a "committee of experts," including Gens. [Lauris] Norstad, Al Gruenther, Cortlandt Schuyler, plus Ted Achilles and Randolph Burgess, in which the gov't is accused of causing a crisis of confidence in NATO by its inconsequent behavior. It calls on U.S. to stop withdrawal of troops from Europe and to build up conventional forces instead. Moreover, instead of relaxing our allies by talking about a period of *Entspannung* [détente] with the Soviet Union, we should be pressing them to make greater sacrifices, or at least to carry more of the burden. Question

---

[40] David Hoggan (1923–1988) was an American historian, anti-Semite, and apologist for the Nazi regime whose most famous book, *Der erzwungene Krieg* [The Forced War] (Tübingen: Verlag der Deutschen Hochschullehrer-Zeitung, 1961), argued that Nazi Germany was a victim of foreign aggression.

of control of atomic weapons should be looked into by an international group of experts, working independently of the NATO Council... Gen. Gallois has also a critical essay on American NATO policy. . . .

Friday, 24 April 1964. Berlin.
Today is the publication day of my book on the battle of Königgrätz. Let us hope for reviewers who know something of the literature and can compare what I have done with what has been done before.

Last night, I saw the film made of the [Gustaf] Gründgens production in Hamburg of *Faust I.* A marvelous piece of work! And Gründgens tremendous as Mephistopheles. . . .

Saturday, 25 April 1964. Berlin.
I have just returned from about 8 hours of *Bummel* [strolling] about Berlin, and I'm tired. I started off this morning to the Ernst Reuter Platz (or Knie, as the Berliners call it) to see the parade of the Occupying Powers, which I duly did and found very dull—long pauses between the units and a fearful wait between the infantry units and the mechanized. Berlin, as usual, turned out in thousands. It was impossible to get near the edge of the street, and enterprising youngsters were climbing up the sides of the new building of the Technische Universität [Technical University] and standing on the ledges and—when chased by the police—escaping through the windows *into* the building... The British marched best and the U.S. Air Force units worst. The British bands played regimental songs; the French bands things like *Sambre et Meuse*; the American bands "America the Beautiful" and "Wenn i komm, wenn i komm, wenn i wieder wieder komm"—and, of course, the Air Force Song... Before the armor had finished rolling, I walked to Bahnhof Zoo [Zoo Station] and took the train to Putlitzstr. whence I walked along the Westhafenkanal to Seestraße and then, past the turn-off to the Plötzensee prison, to the beginning of Heckerdamm, and out this much torn-up path through garden colonies, for what seemed miles, until a block from Kurt Schumacher Damm, Heckerdamm became a wide street lined with new apt. houses, still a-building. Here stands the new Maria Regina Martyrum Church, dedicated (by Pius XII) to the men who lost their lives in Plötzensee, and the *Konzentrationslager* [concentration camps]. The church and its surroundings are a bit too too—the altar painting does not quite come off, and the way of the cross does not impress me. The *pietà* I think is effective. The whole worth seeing, but not from the direction I travelled—a weary way by foot... After leaving the church I took the 62 bus to Schloss Charlottenburg where I dismounted and visited

the gallery in the Orangerie to see the Liebermanns, Slevogts and Lovis Corinths, and the Spitzwegs and Caspar David Friedrichs. Nothing much new, except a couple of Menzels, one of which—William I leaving to join the army in 1871—I should like dearly to own. I walked through the gardens and visited the *Grabstätte* [gravesite] of Friedrich Wilhelm III and Queen Louise (with marble sculptures by Rauch) and Wilhelm I and Augusta… I then walked down the Schloss str. to Ranke str., where I finally succumbed to weariness, hunger, and thirst and stopped in a small restaurant and had two Doornkaats and two glasses of pilsener beer, while I ate a bockwurst and a roll and sketched in my green notebook the article on Hitler literature that I will write for *The Reporter*. I then walked on past all the second-hand stores to Joachimstalerstr., made a *Biegen* [turn] and visited the Amerika Haus to see the exhibition of the history of the U.S. Army and the photographic history of the Wall. Then I walked down the Kurfürstendamm as far as Uhlandstr., passing two types with Beatle wigs sitting at a table in front of Kempinskis, and all sorts of girls who reminded me of the passages I copied out of the Luther Bible (Song of Songs) for the letter I sent to Blum last night. Kept thinking how nice it would be if Phyl were here. Got into U-Bahn and went back to the Gästehaus, reading the grammar that I carry with me on subways… A good day…

On way home in U-Bahn was astonished to see a 17-year-old girl roll a perfect cigarette. Must be the influence of the new Western shop in the KaDeWe, which sells Levis, hats, etc. and looks like a cow country general store, except that it is too clean, and that a barrel, prominently displayed, is labeled, "Wine." In San Francisco, yes; but not out among the cows. . . .

Sunday, 17 May 1964. Berlin.

A lot has happened since my last entry. . . . *Thursday*, I worked all day on my opening statement for my seminar and put the finishing touches to a list of seminar topics (which included "Aristocracy and Middle Class in the Novels of Vicki Baum" and some 40 others). This last proved quite inadequate. When I got [to] class at four, I found 62 students. How I shall handle this number, I do not know. I have always held that teaching is a matter of arranging furniture properly, but there is little possibility of good arrangement in the Institut. I am stuck with a hopelessly clumsy room. Fiddled about with possible solutions without achieving much. . . .

Wednesday, 20 May 1964. Berlin.

I am in the throes of reviving the Bismarck-Adenauer book and have written a new preface and introduction. I hope that I shall have little to change in the first two chapters except footnotes. In the third, both the Stresemann and the Bruening stuff will require some alteration, and in the fourth I should like to beef up Hitler a bit. The big job will be the writing of a new Adenauer chapter... All this would go fast if it were not for the fact that this seminar of mine will soon be taking a good deal of my time again. It has involved me in a not inconsiderable number of book bills also, as I discovered today when I got my bill from Elwert and Meurer (which did not prevent me from spending another seven bucks, however, on a collection of Georg Lukács's essays on the sociology of literature). Ah well! Perhaps I shall learn something useful from it all... The *Reporter* piece will appear in the issue of 28th May, and [the editor, Philip] Horton now wants a review of Herman Finer's book on the Suez crisis, which I shall do. . . . Phil Crowl has written about the Dulles interviewing which I guess will go forward; and Agnes Peterson[41] writes to say that the DDR has "in principle" agreed to let me visit the Potsdam archives. Lots to do! . . .

Thursday, 21 May 1964. Berlin.
The news from Laos is not good. The Communists have broken the neutrality agreement and seem on the point of capturing the whole central plain. Much fuss in Washington... More amusing, because it casts light on the excellence of our security service, is the discovery in the walls of the U.S. Embassy in Moscow of over a hundred listening devices... More alarming is the news that over a thousand people turned out in Munich to hear Hoggan who actually said that Britain would start a third World War if she had the power, and called upon the crowd to agree with him that Germany was guiltless in 1939... Finally, we have the juicy item ["Seebohm fordert erneut Rückgabe des Sudetenlands [Seebohm renews call for the return of the Sudetenland]," *Tagesspiegel*, 20 May] opposite, a speech by a federal minister [Hans-Christoph Seebohm], claiming that the Munich agreement was a legal international treaty, and hence should still be in power! . . .

Monday, 25 May 1964. Berlin.
. . . With every German politician in the upper bracket heading for Washington, the piece above, "Die deutsche Frage" [The German Question], from *Die Zeit* [22 May 1964], is apt... Johnson has just made a good speech at the dedication of the George C. Marshall Research Library

---

[41] Agnes Peterson (1923–2008) served as Curator of the Central and Western European Collections of the Hoover Institution from 1958 until her retirement in 1993.

at Lexington, Virginia, during which he talked of advancing towards reunification of Germany by way of increased contacts with Eastern Europe. Hence the talks which Harriman is holding with the Rumanians, and Ruski pressure (which has annoyed Schroeder) for a shift in the West German line towards Yugoslavia. Conrad Hilton now intends to build a hotel in Budapest. No one can say that U.S. policy doesn't move… The Laos-*Sudvietnam* business is ugly, and probably will become more so. I do not think we will stand much more shoving around without doing something pretty serious in return. . . . Seebohm has had his wrist slapped by Erhard, and rather more firmly than the papers seemed to expect; but he has not been fired (as the *Washington Post* and other foreign papers demanded). The displacee vote is, I imagine, too strong…

I have been having a lot of fun with Gregor von Rezzori's *Maghrebinische Geschichten* [*Tales of Maghrebinia*], which is filled with old Jewish stories that I have been telling for years, plus many wonderful new ones. Recommended by Manger-König… It has inspired me to try to tell stories in German myself, and tonight I tried out the one about the spinster who was afraid of ostriches. M. K. laughed. . . .

Wednesday, 17 June 1964. Berlin.

Last night Fraulein Wedding, good soul, came up with a bottle of *roter Sekt* and drank my health and that of my family on my 25th anniversary. A very nice thing for her to do, and I was very touched. I should have enjoyed more, however, a card from Phyl.

. . . Goldwater has won the California primary by a nose and is close to having enough votes to get the nomination in San Francisco on the first or second ballot. I say close because I have a feeling that he might still be stopped, and the liberal Republicans and party pros, scenting a disaster in November, are making a last-minute drive to put Scranton over. But the Republicans are as usual *so* stupid, and their great leader Eisenhower is *so* incapable of decision that they'll probably botch the job…

Last Friday's treaty between the USSR and the DDR is still being analyzed by the pundits. It is not the separate peace treaty that was haunting my thoughts during the last three weeks, and which Ulbricht doubtless wanted. But the clause insisting that West Berlin is not a part of the *Bundesrepublik* could cause some stickiness. Aside from that, Khrushchev was very careful to inform the Western Powers *before* the treaty was signed and, in the text, to stipulate that Four-Power rights were still in force… Ulbricht has got himself another Treaty of Rapallo, which will doubtless be useful to him…

Sunday, 21 June 1964. Berlin.
The current issue of *Die Zeit* speaks of the treaty as an acknowledgement by the Soviets that they "am Checkpoint Charlie im atomaren Fingerhakeln mit den Amerikanern unterlegen [sind]" [are inferior to the Americans at Checkpoint Charlie in atomic finger-wrestling].The Berlin crisis which was introduced by Khrushchev's November 1958 ultimatum is now in fact over, writes Theo Sommer, and both the treaty text and the fact that Khrushchev informed the Western partners before the treaty was signed, show that the "normalization" of the situation in West Berlin has become a distant goal. Article 6 says that West Berlin will be *betrachtet* [regarded] (but not, as Ulbricht would have liked, *behandelt* [handled]) as an independent political unit; and Article 9 insists on the validity of the rights and duties of the Powers as spelled out in treaties, including that of Potsdam... On the other hand, if Ulbricht didn't get what he wanted in Moscow, neither did Erhard get his way in Washington for LBJ has put the "German initiative" on the ice, and it looks as if the *status quo* has been confirmed, and Germany will remain in its present form for a long time to come. On this last point, Sommer gets agreement from H. Studnitz in the current *Christ und Welt*...

Also in the news: Admiral Hayes's article in *Quick*, claiming the *Bundeswehr* will become a *Staat im Staate* [state within a state] unless present tendencies are halted. Big row in the Christian Democratic Union. . . .

Thursday after my seminar, a reception for the foreign professors at the Club House in Goethe St. ... Friday, after my two lectures, called on Günther Gieraths,[42] former *Wehrmacht* colonel, historian, and aide to Beck[43] (whom he describes as having been almost wholly incapable of leading a conspiratorial putsch successfully, even in the most favorable circumstances). Told me some interesting tales about his detention by the Russians in Potsdam and how, in the end, he was rowed across the Havel by Glienicke bridge by his *Bursche* [fellows], and escaped to the West. It was Gierats who gave Herzfeld cover in the Historical Section for so long and

---

[42] Günther Gieraths (1898–1967) was a German librarian and military historian who served as Director of the Army Library in Berlin from 1936 to 1945. His *magnum opus* was *Die Kampfhandlungen der brandenburgisch–preussischen Armee, 1626–1807; ein Quellenhandbuch* (Berlin: De Gruyter, 1964).

[43] General Ludwig Beck (1880–1944) was Chief of the General Staff during the early years of the Nazi regime. He resigned in August 1938 after failing to organize army opposition to Hitler's plan for war against Czechoslovakia, and later participated in the unsuccessful attempt by disillusioned army officers to eliminate Hitler in July 1944. After the failure of the plot, he was arrested and executed.

protected him against the anti-Semitic laws. His is now a shattered existence—his only son dead in the Polish campaign, his property and books long gone, his health ruined. He has, nonetheless, done his book on *Kampfhandlungen* [combat operations]. I must go see him again. . . .

Church and communion this morning. This afternoon tea with Annedore Leber, wife of Julius Leber.[44] She now runs a small press which has brought out [Klaus] Epstein's [Matthias] *Erzberger*, and she is interested in doing a German edition of Henry Turner's *Stresemann* with an introduction by me. I said I would do it if she got rights… We talked a bit about Dulles, and she expressed great admiration, which rather surprised me. Her reasons were good…

Finished Richard Goold-Adams, *John Foster Dulles: A Reappraisal*, a good book, and began Herman Finer's *Dulles over Suez*, which I must review for *The Reporter* and which will have to be considered in the public lecture I have agreed to give at the Otto Suhr Institut on 23 July, on the subject "John Foster Dulles und die Amerikanische Staatskunst [John Foster Dulles and American Statecraft]."

Monday, 22 June 1964. Berlin.

Tape recorder business. Back business. Negotiation with Shep Stone (along with Bendix and Hartwich) in hope of persuading him to beef up Heuss Professorship program…

The U.S. gov't has gotten very tough in the Far East and is actually talking about the possibility of war with China. This had to come, and it will now be up to the Chinese to make up their minds about what they really want to risk. *Pravda* has just told them that, in view of their campaign against the Soviet Union, they can expect no help from that quarter. At the same time, in what may be an indication of an intention to back up, the Chinese Foreign Minister has said Red China will push ahead toward development of a nuclear capacity so that it will no longer be subject to "atomic blackmail."…

Thursday, 25 June 1964. Berlin.

On Tuesday I had a long interview with the *Bundesbevollmächtigter* [Federal Representative] Felix von Eckardt in the *Bundeshaus* [Federal Parliament]---one and a half hours on tape, and all interesting—particularly on

---

[44] Annedore Leber (1904–1968) was a publicist and SPD politician, as well as the widow of Julius Leber (1891–1945), an SPD parliamentarian and a leader in the anti-Nazi resistance movement. Arrested by the Gestapo in July 1944, he was executed on 5 January 1945.

Adenauer's reaction to the European Defense Community breakdown in '54 and his temporary belief that France must be excluded from any future military arrangements—a dramatic exception to the main line of his French policy, which I should add to my Adenauer chapter in the revised Bismarck/Adenauer book. Eckardt also good on Dulles, whom he regarded as a man who did not come up with brilliant strokes but was always well prepared and always a good negotiator in the sense that he was always prepared. Also he had guts and knew when to hold on. (All this denied, of course, by Herman Finer's book which I think very bad and, in sections, cheap.) Dulles's reaction to Khrushchev's Berlin note in November 1958 – the suggestion that the gov't of the East Zone might be considered as "agents" of the USSR—he considered a very shrewd stroke—a reaction, I gather, that was not immediately shared by Adenauer... Mrs. Eleanor Dulles, whom I saw yesterday at the American Mission, said she had criticized John Foster Dulles after he talked about the "agents" and after his additional suggestion that free elections might not be the only way to re-unify Germany and found him in a rather defiant mood—("I was right in what I said, wasn't I?" he asked her). She explained that, even if he was, there would be a flap in Bonn; and there was. He finally allayed the recurrent German nervousness in his trip to Bonn in February 1959, at which time he knew he was dying... Mrs. Dulles expressed the opinion that 1958 was the year in which JFD really came into his own. His method and his style began to work at their peak efficiency—as the Far Eastern and Lebanon crises showed, and the shrewd response to the Khrushchev Berlin note. (Goold-Adams agrees with this, and so does Eckardt—who feels, as I did in 1958, that the Lebanon stroke was a masterpiece)...

I am beginning to feel that the Suez crisis (an undeniable demonstration of all that was worst in Dulles) is retrospectively a Godsend to all of the bleeding-heart liberals who hated his guts on wholly irrational grounds—(because he was too religious, for example, a point which Finer feels compelled to make on every page)—as well as to those of our Allies who were embarrassed by his insistence on firmness vis-à-vis the USSR—and who can protect their weak positions by pointing to Dulles's defeat. Yet what guts there is in the Western alliance is in the good ole US of A, when we have men who know how to apply it, and Dulles knew pretty well. . . .

Friday, 10 July 1964. Berlin.

. . . Thursday morning I flew with Pan Am to Frankfurt, travelling with Herzfeld, to take part in [a panel discussion on "the Causes of the First World War in the History-Writing of the Present," put on by the Amerika

Haus Frankfurt in conjunction with the Historical Seminar of Frankfurt University.]

We put up at the Metropol-Monopol, near the Hauptbahnhof, which was comfortable and not too expensive and dined at the Restaurant Schultheiss im Westend with [Paul] Kluke, Vossler (always nice), the other participants, and the Amerika Haus people. The discussion itself was nothing much to speak of, although it was apparently successful—some 550 people showing up and listening earnestly. The trouble was that [Erwin] Hölzle (a former Nazi and an old-fashioned nationalist still and an unpleasant and opinionated man in any case) would talk only about Russia, upon whom he seemed to want to place all of the blame for the first World War, and [Fritz] Fischer would talk only about Fischer. (The man is absolutely obsessed with his book and the attacks made on it.) As a result, whenever Herzfeld and I tried to broaden the discussion, the other two would drag it back to the July Crisis.[45] In the end we were reduced to making jokes or taking cracks at these two fanatics. I spoke German at the beginning, but then lapsed into English, which is just as well, for in my own language I can speak with authority and a certain vivacity as well, and the latter quality was badly needed. I came away from the discussion convinced that Fischer's book is worse than I thought and that [Klaus] Epstein's praise of it merely points up Epstein's weakness. I think that both have little understanding of men—particularly political leaders in crisis—and that they overestimate the importance of documents (or perhaps are too willing to take them at face value). Both are wrong, I am sure, about [Imperial Chancellor Theobald von] Bethmann-Hollweg—or, at least, further from the truth than [Karl Dietrich] Erdmann. Old Herzfeld was wonderful in the discussion, and kept Fischer under decent control. It was interesting to note that the audience was pro-Fischer and seemed to like Herzfeld and me, but was noticeably anti-Hölzle. (Hölzle is probably an embittered man. His engagement with the Nazis barred him from a university chair and might, indeed, have kept him out of all higher education if [Gerhard] Ritter had not been a bit soft and found employment for him in Freiburg, which was

---

[45] The July Crisis was the diplomatic crisis that followed the assassination of the Archduke Franz Ferdinand, heir to the throne of the Austro-Hungarian Empire. The failure to find a diplomatic solution to the crisis led to the outbreak of the First World War. In contrast to Erwin Hölzle, who placed primary blame with the Russians, Fritz Fischer, in his controversial book *Griff nach der Weltmacht*, had proposed that Germany's leaders had sought an expansionist war in order to neutralize domestic opposition to the Imperial regime.

a stepping stone to Konstanz)... Ritter, by the way, had a very good and balanced piece on the causes of the war in the *Frankfurter Allgemeine Zeitung* for 8 July. . . .

Up betimes and had a heavier breakfast than usual, the last part of which was shared by Fischer, who talked more about his book. I diverted him to the Heye affair, and he told me a discouraging story about a discussion club he belongs to in Hamburg, the membership of which is filled with leading businessmen, civic leaders, bureaucrats, and scholars and where he heard a discussion of the Heye affair in which the only people to speak favorably of Heye were the soldiers (or at least *one* soldier, Graf Kalckreuth), whereas all of the civilians criticized his action (giving his views to *Quick* magazine) and seemed indifferent to the seriousness of what he had to say...[46]

Leaving Fischer, I pushed off to the Zeil, to the offices of S. Fischer Verlag, where I had coffee with Herr Janko von Musulin, a charming man who comes from an old Austrian family and has written a book on Eugene of Savoy. He wants me to write a history of Prussia for him and/or a cultural history of the Weimar Republic. I hedged, but admitted that I would rather like to write the latter. . . .

Wednesday, 15 July 1964. Berlin.

On Saturday Phyl and I had lunch with the [James Bryant] Conants. The Lyons and an educationist named Robinson who is moving here from Hamburg were also there, and we had a lively time. Afterwards, I interviewed Conant on Dulles (and got some interesting stuff, especially on Dulles's role in the sticky period after the collapse of the European Defense Community, and on Conant's own dislike of him and feeling that he treated his ambassadors badly—which did not prevent Conant from saying at the end that he considered him "a great Secretary of State"). Conant then "interviewed" me about my thoughts on German politics (which, in view of the Seebohm and Heye cases are not as rosy as they tended once to be, as I shall say in a talk to the *Deutscher Akademischer Austauschdienst* [German Academic Exchange Service] tomorrow) and about my opinion on the question whether he should write his memoirs. I said, sincerely I hope, that in his case I thought it was a duty, which seemed to please him.

In the evening a largish party at the Herzfelds at which a very good

---

[46] The Heye Affair concerned Hellmuth Heye, who was named Commissioner of the German Armed Forces in 1961. Heye, a high-ranking naval officer in the Second World War, criticized the constitution of the *Bundeswehr* in the periodical *Quick*, and found himself politically isolated. He subsequently resigned.

accordionist and I made music. . . .

Monday, I went to East Berlin to arrange my trip to Potsdam. Getting attended to at the *DDR Reiseburo* [East German travel bureau] (after an hour's wait at the Friedrichstrasse control) was so frustrating that I tore up my form and abandoned the whole enterprise. After a walk, along the Wilhelmstrasse past Hitler's bunker to Leipziger Str. and then back to Friedrichstr., my conscience got to work, and I returned to the travel bureau and filled out a new form, got waited on, and went to Alexanderplatz to the Police Praesidium for my visa. Everything now moved so smoothly that I had time to do a little sightseeing—seeing the nice Platz der Akademie, and the Sophienkirche, and the old Jewish Burying Ground where Moses Mendelssohn lies and where the Nazis in 1942 used the Jewish Old Folks Home as an assembly point for sending people to Auschwitz. Leaving East Berlin has been made a lot easier and, clutching an Insel Verlag 2 vol. [edition of Wilhelm] Raabe, which I bought in the Karl Marx Buchhandlung in the Alexanderplatz, I was home by 6:30. . . .

Tuesday, I rose early (5:30 a.m.) and was in a train to Friedrichstrasse at six. Remarkable how many people are afoot at that hour. I was through the control at seven and caught the 7:26 to Karlshorst (a ridiculous way to have to go to Potsdam).[47] Here the station was filled with young people and delegations from the East on day excursions. The streetcar from Potsdam station to the center of town (the Platz der Nationen) was so full that I felt by the end of the trip that I should propose marriage to the woman standing next to me… By 11 o'clock I was at the Central Archives in Potsdam, where I was greeted warmly by the Asst. Director Braher and given every courtesy while I looked through the documents in which Agnes Peterson and the Hoover [Institution] are interested. Braher himself confessed sadly, when I asked what he was writing, that there was no point in writing, since there were few outlets for the sort of thing he was interested in, and, even if he could find a publisher in France or England, it might involve him in trouble… I was amazed at the freedom given Western scholars at the Institute and, more so, because my student Hopwood was able to go from Potsdam to the archives at Merseberg; but Braher said that all this depended on the political situation, intimating that the present freedom—or relative freedom—could not be counted on to last. In Braher I found the same sad resignation and shabbiness that I saw in the people crowding the trains and streetcars. The Zone is a sad place, and I think Kessel's article in today's

[47] Potsdam is 16 miles southwest of central Berlin as the crow flies, but during the Cold War, trains from East Berlin were routed circuitously around West Berlin.

Welt is a good one... After my work was done, I went into town and walked a bit in the gardens of *Sanssouci* [Palace] and then tried to find something to buy for Phyl. There are no gift shops or attractive restaurants or bars or even very well-stocked stores in the Zone, and I could get nothing to eat till I got back home. In East Berlin I went to the Polish and Czech shops at Friedrichstrasse, which are showplaces of Volk-art, and bought a bracelet and some wooden figures, and then to a bookstore for a copy of Erich Mühsam's *Unpolitical Memoirs*, and then went home. . . .

Friday, 17 July 1964. Berlin.

Today, 39 years ago, I entered the United States for the first time. . .

The Reporter, which published my piece on Hitler literature in its issue of 16 July, has sent me a letter from Franz Schoenberner (formerly of *Simplicissimus*) expressing surprise that I didn't know that Schramm was a Nazi. Schramm is a rather foolish man, but a Nazi he is not and never was...[48]

The press today—the European press, that is—is filled with dark forebodings about the nomination of Barry Goldwater by the Republicans—the British press, naturally, being most extreme. We can expect the nomination to feed all the forces of anti-Americanism, which are strongest in England. Here, unfortunately, we will see Gaullism strengthened and the right radicals encouraged. The *NY Times* the other day said that, according to information from its Bonn correspondent, Goldwater and Seebohm were in correspondence, and Seebohm has repudiated this so energetically that there may be truth in it. Certainly Goldwater's statements are calculated to please *some* people here—his *Spiegel* interview, for instance, in which he said that Germany could have won both world wars if her generals had been a little better. My radical student [Hermann L.] Gremliza tells me that the *National Zeitung* had a big spread on Goldwater some months ago...[49]

Monday, 20 July 1964. Berlin.

Saturday was largely given over to trying to prepare for a discussion in

[48] Percy Schramm (1894–1970) had a difficult relationship with the Nazi regime, and opposed some aspects of Nazi ideology, but he became a member of the SA and the Nazi Party, and he served as the official historian of the German High Command Operational Staff. On the basis of his access and wartime experiences, he published books in the postwar period about Nazi Germany's military leadership. See Craig, "What the Germans Are Reading About Hitler," *The Reporter* (16 July 1944): 36–37.

[49] Hermann Gremliza (1940–2019) became a prominent left-wing journalist in Germany and was the founder of the magazine *Konkret*.

which I really should not have been involved—a panel discussion at the Urania Hall on moral quandaries of the conspiracy against Hitler. My German is not so good that I can simply improvise in a question-answer situation before a large audience. Even at Frankfurt, where I was completely on top of the situation and the subject, I confined myself to a few opening remarks in German and then went over to English. Here that was impossible, and I had to guess how the discussion might go and plan things to say in German. But, of course, one can't guess the way a heated, emotional, and highly personal discussion will evolve, let alone how the questions from the audience will go; and when I found myself before a thousand people with Bußmann, et al., it soon transpired that my guessing had not been very good. The panel discussion was a good one enlivened by some fine exchanges between Pastor Bethge (Dietrich Bonhoeffer's friend) and *Generalstaatsanwalt* [State Prosecutor, Hans] Günther who argued that the killing of Hitler was justified by the *Notwehrparagraphen* [Self-defense clause] (as is the shooting of rabid dogs). This is a popular position, but one that overlooks many of the serious moral problems with which the conspirators had to grapple. Moltke and Bonhoeffer were both Christians, the latter a man of the cloth—but on the right to kill Hitler they differed, and Moltke was the one who was opposed. On these issues, I had little to say, confining myself to a few badly constructed remarks on the illegality of the oath and on the justifiability of killing a man who at Marigaux showed that he was deaf to reason and, at the end, to a brief speech on the importance of 20 July in making possible a reconciliation with America. The proceedings were enlivened by the eruption on the platform of a madman who attacked the hierarchy of the Church for weakening the will to resistance... In the hall afterwards I met *Staatssekretär* [State Secretary] [Hans Heinrich] Herwarth [von Bittenfeld] again (who made some kind remarks about my Bismarck-Adenauer book), Gräfin [Marion] von Dönhoff of *Die Zeit*, and Helmut Krausnick of the *Institut für Zeitgeschichte* [Institute for Contemporary History] in Munich, along with assorted madmen who wanted to make speeches about obscure grievances...

Afterwards, to the home of Friedrich Georgi, who is the son-in-law of General der Infanterie Friedrich Olbricht, who was shot in the Bendlerstrasse courtyard along with Stauffenberg on 20 July. Georgi, as a young *Luftwaffe* [Air Force] staff officer, was in the office of his father-in-law at the time. Lots of stories about the macabre aspects of the aftermath of the revolt—of the way in which the *Luftwaffe* tried to protect Georgi, of the way in which his complaints about misuse of his personal effects in prison led to the imprisonment of the people who had been stealing his cigars, of the bogusness of the stories told by Eugen Gerstenmayer about his role in the fracas at the Bendlerstrasse on 20 July, etc., etc. I drank *Kalte Ente* and listened and occasionally talked to Annedore Leber. . . .

[On 30 July 1964, Craig traveled to Belgium to interview Walter Hallstein.]

Sunday, 2 August 1964. Berlin.
. . . I arose at 6:30, breakfasted and made my way out to Common Market headquarters on the Avenue de la Joyeuse Entrée, which is out among the triumphal arches and the ruins of the buildings built for the Exposition of 1883. Hallstein, the President of the Common Market, and before that Adenauer's Foreign Minister and author of the Hallstein doctrine, was most cordial and as informative as he could be about Dulles, although his own experience with him lay six years back. He was better on Adenauer and particularly on the Old Man's trip to Moscow in 1955 where he told me a marvelous story about Molotov's willingness to deny publicly a promise he had made in the presence of 12 witnesses, without even blushing, and another of how a telephone call to Bonn ordering the return of the Chancellor's plane to Moscow, a day sooner than it was supposed to come, got action out of Khrushchev on the prisoners issue on which he had refused to yield until, apparently, the report of his intercepting officer reached him... Hallstein was interested in my recent lecture on Dulles, and I promised to send him a copy. . . .

Yesterday was a day of work in which I wrote a review for the *Tribune* of Donald McCormack's book on Lloyd George (a bad book) and another for *The Reporter* of Herman Finer's *Dulles over Suez*, a much worse one.[50] In between, Phyl, Charlie, and I went to town and had a pleasant dinner at the Tegernseer Tönnchen on the Mommsen Strasse. Afterwards, at about 12:30, while I was putting finishing touches to my assault on that nice man Finer (with whom I got on so well one night at David Harris's), I heard a hell of a crash and went downstairs to find that my car had been side-swiped and thrown across the sidewalk by a French military vehicle which was banged into a tree nearby, without driver. With the aid of a young American and two girls, who happened by, we got the police, who then produced a drunk American soldier in mufti, which necessitated the calling of the American Military Police, who were closely followed by the French. A real international incident, as one of the German policemen said to me happily,

---

[50] Craig's essay "Dulles as Villain," a review of Herman Finer's *Dulles Over Suez*, appeared in *The Reporter* on September 10, 1964.

and all rather amusing (since, *Gottseidank* [Thanks be to God], no one had been hurt). But it took a lot of time. I finally go back upstairs and back to my review of Finer, which I finished, I should imagine, about four. . . .

[On August 3, Craig flew to Darmstadt to interview Heinrich von Brentano.[51]]

Tuesday, 4 August 1964. Darmstadt.
. . . I had a light lunch in the Weinhaus Bockshaut on the Kirchstrasse and returned to my hotel to gather my traps and take a cab to Steinbergweg 25 where Heinrich von Brentano was waiting for me. A beautiful house with an extensive garden, filled with roses and begonia and phlox and a fine lawn running off toward the Odenwald, which begins here. Brentano looking gaunt from his illness—(I suspect he has had an operation for lung cancer: he reminded me of Dan Sayre after his operation)—but hearty. We chatted for a few minutes about the Princeton visit of Adenauer, where Brentano and I sat with Mrs. Goheen, and then repaired to his study, where, under the photographs of Adenauer and Dulles, I turned on the machine, and we got down to work. The interview lasted until Brentano's doctor arrived at 5:50, almost two hours. As in the case of Eckardt and Hallstein, Brentano was full of admiration for Dulles and, while expressing some criticism of his handling of the Suez affair, had no hesitation in pronouncing him a great Secretary of State. The most interesting aspects of our talk had to do with Dulles's reaction to the defeat of the European Defense Community, which—according to Brentano—Dulles blamed on the British rather than the French. He corroborated Eckardt's story of Dulles working behind the scenes to push the British toward the solution that saved the day. Brentano was also most interesting on the Adenauer trip to Moscow—the experience of treating with men who could simply not understand why Adenauer should care about saving 10,000 prisoners of war. In this connection, Brentano says that he (as Maj. Leader accompanying the Chancellor) was the one who suggested calling the planes back to Moscow early, a threat which brought the Soviets into line. The end result of the conference—the treaty of friendship—apparently surprised and annoyed Dulles, but, once Brentano had explained the nature of the Moscow meeting, he was mollified. On the question of Dulles's "agents theory" Brentano also had

[51] Heinrich von Brentano (1904–1964) was a Christian Democratic Union politician who served as West Germany's Foreign Minister from 1955 to 1961.

some interesting notes.[52] All in all, a fine interview, with some good stories. . . .

Thursday, 5 August 1964. Berlin.

Yesterday Phyl, Martha, Charlie, and I spent most of the day in East Berlin. We took the car and went through Checkpoint Charlie and then drove to the Wilhelmstrasse where I pointed out Hitler's bunker and the spot where the *Reichskanzlei* [Imperial Chancellery] stood. Then we drove back up the Leipziger Strasse, made a slight detour to see the Gendarmenmarkt with its two little Doms, and then went on out to Treptow to see the Soviet Memorial Cemetery with the two gigantic wings made from the marble of the old *Reichskanzlei* and all the *Kitsch* that the Communists insist on putting into their art. Treptow is one place where the memory of Joseph Stalin is ineradicable. His name is on every one of those ugly stones, coupled with uglier pictorial reliefs, which commemorate the accomplishments of the Red Army and the partisans…

It was a beautiful day and, having come this far, we decided to go further, and drove all the way out to Köpenick and through it to the area around the Müggelsee, where we visited (and Charlie and I climbed) the Müggelturm. Then we retraced our steps, detouring a bit to drive through the industrial area along the Spree [River] which is damned impressive. I have lost my scorn of the accomplishments of the German Democratic Republic. In ten years East Berlin will be a flourishing city. The progress made in the last two years is most impressive.

We got back to Unter den Linden in time to watch the changing of the guard in front of the Old Watch, which Charlie (sitting on my shoulders) liked, although he said that it was kind of scary when the soldiers did the goose step. The crowd watching was a bit odd, for a film was being made in the university area about Karl Liebknecht and the war of 1914, and extras were wandering about in 1914 costumes and there was a 1914 horse-drawn omnibus standing by…[53]

---

[52] The "Agents Theory" refers to Dulles's belief that if the Soviet Union turned control of Allied access to East Berlin over to the East German authorities, that the Allies could accept that if there were guarantees that the East Germans were acting as agents of the Soviet Union, rather than on the basis of their own sovereignty, which was not recognized by the Western powers at that time.

[53] Karl Liebknecht (1871–1919) was a leading radical politician in the Social Democratic Party who opposed German participation in the First World War. He abstained in the August 1914 parliamentary vote to approve war credits to the Imperial government at the outset of the war, and he voted against the renewal of

We had a good lunch at the Opera Café and I drank a Polish vodka (which I don't like) and a Czech beer (which was undistinguished) with it. I should have liked to visit the Invalidenkirchhof and to have paid my respects to Scharnhorst and Boyen, but it was getting late, so we paid a brief visit to the Hedwigkirche instead, where Phyl took some pictures, and then came back home.[54]

We arrived in time to hear a re-broadcast of President Johnson's speech explaining the bombing attack on the North Vietnam bases, which we have made as a reprisal for the PT boat attacks upon our fleet units in the Bay of Tonkin. A good speech which we must hope will warn the Chinese not to go too far. . . .

[After making a side trip to London and Edinburgh, Craig and his family returned to the United States on August 23, 1964.]

. . .

Thursday, 24 September 1964. Washington D.C.

Meeting of the Social Science Advisory Board of the Arms Control and Disarmament Agency. Of the Board, Dean Griswold, Ed Mason, Urie Bronfenbrenner, Phil Mosely, Phil Davison, and Mrs. [Alice] Hsieh present; of the agency, Foster, Beam, Alexander, and various smaller fry. An interesting day. Much talk of possible proliferation if and when China detonates a bomb—the likely nations being India, Sweden and Switzerland, UAR and Israel, Japan and Indonesia. A nice prospect! This is why the next year will be such a crucial one in negotiations. Let's hope the Russians see it the same way… Report by Bronfenbrenner on how worried the Russians are about Goldwater and China. . . .

Tuesday, 20 October 1964. Palo Alto.

Tumultuous times. Last Thursday Khrushchev was fired, the Chinese exploded a nuclear device, Labor defeated the conservatives by four votes, and the Jenkins Case gave Barry Goldwater an issue which he needs but which probably (because of the other things) won't help him much.

Today Herbert Hoover died.

---

war credits later that year. A founding member of the German Communist Party, Liebknecht was assassinated during the suppression of the German Revolution of 1919.

[54] Gerhard von Scharnhorst (1755–1813) and Hermann von Boyen (1771–1848) were prominent Prussian army officers in the Napoleonic and post-Napoleonic periods.

Today, we offered Cy Black Mazour's spot in Russian history.

I still struggle with my Vienna paper… Social life at a minimum, except for the History Party on Friday last (at which I played some guitar) and dinner Saturday at the McAfee Browns. I simply teach, read, and go to committee meetings. . . .

Wednesday, 28 October 1964. Palo Alto.

Finished the ten-page précis of my paper for Vienna. I wonder when I'll write the paper… At any rate, I can now get down to my paper for the American Historical Association meeting, which has to be in Robert Kann's hands on 1 December if he is not to be thrown into a thundering apoplexy.

The election campaign winds its weary way to climax. At this point, neither candidate looks very impressive, although the Goldwater crowd has certainly gone further than any political group in recent times in the use of plain dishonesty as a campaign tactic. Goldwater himself is plainly a fool, and Miller a rogue, and I think this must be plain enough to the average American to make the election outcome a certain Democratic sweep.

My seminar on World War I goes wonderfully well, thanks to a nucleus of extraordinarily knowledgeable students. . . .

Sunday, 15 November 1964. Palo Alto.

The newspapers report the death of Heinrich von Brentano. I'm sorry. He was an able man and a gentleman, and I liked him when I saw him in July. . . . [55]

Tuesday, 17 November 1964. Palo Alto.

A visit from Vann Woodward, who is apparently out scouting for Yale. I got my students Hopwood and Gillis in to see him, and he was interested in them; but I do not expect them to get jobs in a place which already has three German historians—Holborn, Gatzke, and my student Henry Turner. I gave Vann a drink after his labors, and we talked about Russian historians, for whom Yale is searching with no more success than we. I have pretty well convinced myself that Ivo Lederer should be our man, but that depends upon whether he is going to devote himself to Russian rather than to Balkan history…

At noon today, a meeting of Bob Sears's advisory Appointments and Promotions Committee, and a long discussion of our functions and prerogatives. An afternoon full of students. Tonight—pursuing my researches for my American Historical Association paper—read Winston

---

[55] See above, entry of 4 August.

Churchill's *The Unknown War*, a remarkably good book for half its length but a very unbalanced one which is curiously vague about the Gorlice-Tarnów [military offensive] and stops abruptly with the Russian Revolution.[56]

Thursday, 19 November 1964. Palo Alto.
Lunch today at the Pioneer Inn in Woodside with Herbert Mann of the California Press. In the afternoon and evening worked on Ludendorff and Falkenhayn. My research is just about over, and I'd better get down to the paper itself...

Yesterday I signed a petition supporting the free speech movement in Berkeley, where the University administration has made any number of foolish moves in combating campus radicals. Today a letter in the *Daily* made much of the fact that Wright, Pease, [Charles] Drekmeier, and I had signed and said that this might reassure students who are afraid of guilt by association. . . .

Saturday, 26 December 1964. Palo Alto.
. . . I forgot to record here that about two weeks ago I had a call from David Donald in Baltimore, asking if I would consider moving into the spot left vacant when Gatzke went to Yale. This was amusing, since I was asked to take the spot in Yale before Gatzke got it. However, I played it seriously and pretended to consider the offer and waited three days before turning it down on the grounds that I couldn't leave my grad students and Phyl couldn't leave her school. (I did not mention the weather or the fact that the salary mentioned by Donald as the highest possible one that I could expect was $2000.00 less than what I'm getting here.) . . .

In free moments, I have read Fontane's *Schach von Wuthenow*, a fine novel which has some good things to say about the decline of the Frederician army. . . .

Thursday, 31 December 1964. Palo Alto.
Almost the last minutes of the old year. I am recovering still from my exertions in Washington during the last three days. The American Historical Association convention was much as usual. My paper went over well; even R. J. Sontag came to hear it, along with 800 other people, including many students. I saw all my old friends—Blum, Aandahl, Lee, Loewenheim, etc.,

---

[56] Winston S. Churchill, *The Unknown War: The Eastern Front* (New York: Charles Scribner's Sons, 1931). This was the sixth and final volume of *The World Crisis*, Churchill's monumental history of the First World War.

etc.—and much of Julian Boyd, the retiring president. I was also urged by the new president, Fred Lane, to take the job of Executive Secretary of the Association at $25,000, and asked by Dick Morris if I would like to go to Columbia as professor. I shall do neither. . . .

[1965]

Friday, 22 January 1965. Palo Alto.
. . . Last night to hear Eugen Weber[57] lead the second session of the inter-departmental seminar on Rumanian Fascism. Some interesting stuff on the relatively recent origin of anti-Semitism in Rumania (no Jews there till after the Treaty of Adrianople [of 1829]) and upon the romantic nationalists who were [Corneliu] Codreanu's teachers—Alexander Couza and Nicholas Jorga. Although I didn't wait for the discussion, I thought Weber more impressive than on his first appearance...

In connection with my Air Force Academy Lecture, read Gerhard Ritter's chapter in *Staats-Kunst und Kriegshandwerk* I [*Statecraft and the Art of War*] on [August von] Gneisenau and [Klemens von] Metternich (a brilliant job), Franklin Scott's 30-year old monograph on [Jean] Bernadotte, and the memoirs of [Karl Freiherr von] Müffling (most interesting in their criticism of Gneisenau). . . .

Reading more of Fontane's *Vor dem Sturm* [*Before the Storm*]. Remarkable passage on the reaction in Berlin to [Ludwig] Yorck's capitulation to the Russians at Tauroggen, which struck some as a breach of loyalty. Obvious parallel to attitude to oath to Hitler in 1944, although I've never heard Fontane cited in this connection... A fine passage also on Othegraven's reaction to Marie's refusal to accept his offer of marriage: "*Und so ist mein Los beschlossen. Trag ich es; nicht nur weil ich muß, auch weil ich will. Tue, was dir geziemt. Aber ich hatte es mir schöner geträumt; auch heute noch!*" [And so my lot is decided. I bear it; not only because I *must*, but also because I *want it.* Do what is right for you. But I had dreamed it better; even today!] . . .

Thursday, 28 January 1965. Palo Alto.
My Roosevelt University lecture will be published, Roth writing to say that the contract has been signed. Praeger has written also to say they would be interested in a volume of my essays, so I shall tailor all incidental pieces with that in mind. This will be a good publishing year for me, what with the introduction to the Vogt book, the piece in the Liddell Hart Festschrift and

---

[57] Eugen Weber (1925–2007) was a Romanian-born American historian of modern France who taught at UCLA for nearly forty years.

the Harmon Lecture which should appear in April, the revised edition of Bismarck/Adenauer, which will be published 24 February, a reprinting of my *Reporter* piece on Hitler in the [*Princeton*] *Alumni Weekly*, my Vienna paper which is already in print, and some solid reviews in the *Tribune* and the *Times*. The *Journal of Modern History* is looking at my Washington paper too; but if I were an editor, as I am on the *American Historical Review*, I'm not at all sure I would accept it. It is interesting and even amusing—more so than most articles in our historical journals; but I do not think it advances the frontiers of knowledge very far.

Felix Gilbert and I are both annoyed at the way Lennie Krieger and Fritz Stern are handling the proposed Festschrift for Hajo Holborn, which is to be called "The Responsibilities of Power." The table of contents shows neither balance nor imagination, and is almost wholly oriented to the 20th century, which is not Hajo's strongest period. I have been asked, successively, to write on Seeckt, Hindenburg, Napoleon (?!), and Frederick the Great. Only the last tempted me, although I decided in the end that, in view of Meinecke's chapter in *Die Idee der Staatsraison* [*Machiavellism*], there was nothing *I* could write that would be interesting. I have suggested a piece on the Great Elector, but the editors have now countered with a proposal that I do Ludendorff, which I don't want to do…

Winston Churchill died this week. So did Harry Stuhldreher, quarterback of Notre Dame's Four Horsemen of 1924–25. From the tone of the green pages of the *Chronicle*, one would imagine the two men of equal stature, with Stuhldreher getting the edge…

Today, at noon, a committee meeting—a new offspring of the Committee on International Relations—to determine, apparently, whether we are spending too much on area studies and too little on the tried and true investigation of diplomatic and related subjects. . . .

Monday, 1 February 1965. Palo Alto.

A wearying day—lecture, correspondence, seminar—and now we have already reached the time for mid-term exams. Disturbing to my writing plans, which are in any case always a bit unrealistic. I have, in point of fact, so many commitments that it is depressing to contemplate them. I meet my deadlines only by expending as little energy as possible on teaching. Yet I never stop teaching and haven't had a term off since 1957. (That is what Berlin has done to my life.) … Ah well! Reading the English version of

Werner Richter's *Bismarck* for the *NY Times*. . . .[58]

Tuesday, 9 February 1965. Palo Alto.
Last Wednesday Ivo Lederer came to town to receive our offer of Mazour's spot in the department. Result: three days of arranging interviews for him (which was rather artfully done, I think) and giving him food and drink—here, at the Potters, at the Drachkovitches, etc. After three days of this I was worn out, and I am still not at my best. It will have been worth it if he accepts our offer, for he is a good man... Certainly he charmed *all* members of my department and Carl Spaeth as well (which may be useful financially). . . .[59]

In the university, the current sensation has been the publication of a report of a committee of the student government, accusing the Dean of Women, Lucille Allen, of trying to convince students to spy on young instructors in the English department who were allegedly reading salacious passages to their classes, encouraging the young bucks to deflower maidens, and using their grading power to seduce virgins. Not unnaturally the newspapers have taken this up, as have the campus radicals who would dearly love something comparable to the Berkeley Free Speech mess to erupt here. A good faculty committee, which includes Ken Arrow and Sandy Dornbusch,[60] is investigating and it will come before the Advisory Board, on which I am currently serving, on Friday. . . .[61]

Thursday, 11 February 1965. Palo Alto.
. . . Things in South Vietnam are approaching full crisis, and I see no great success and much potential danger in the Johnson policy of tit-for-tat retaliation unless it is coupled with a willingness to negotiate while our position still has some strength. Not an easy business in any event, and public opinion curiously uncertain. . . .

---

58 Gordon A. Craig, "Iron and Rust," *The New York Times Book Review* (28 March 1965): 6–7.

59 Carl Spaeth, Dean of the Stanford Law School from 1946 to 1962, was a specialist in international law.

60 Kenneth Arrow (1921–2017) was a major contributor to neoclassical economic theory and a recipient of the Nobel Prize in Economic Sciences in 1972. Sandy Dornbusch (1926–2016) was a sociologist renowned for his research on adolescence and a founder of Stanford's Program in Human Biology.

61 For a more detailed description of the Lucille Allen affair, see Richard W. Lyman, *Stanford in Turmoil: Campus Unrest, 1966–1972* (Stanford: Stanford University Press), 28–32.

Tuesday, 16 February 1965. Palo Alto.

Yesterday the *Stanford Daily* announced that the Dean of Women had submitted her resignation, so that's that… A heavy day, filled with lecture, correspondence, seminar, meeting of Tenure Sub-Committee, and in the evening—in pursuance of my Harmon Lecture—Regele's *Radetzky*…

A batch of reviews of the Königgrätz book has come in, all clipped from papers like the New Bedford, Mass. *Standard Times*, the Charleston *Evening Post*, and the Duluth *Sun News Tribune.* My favorite is the one in the *Navy News* for May 1964, where Lillian E. Robinson, Book Review Editor, writes: "Mr. Craig is a specialist in modern European history, and is the author of other novels, one of which won the H. B. Adams Prize of the American Historical Association in 1956." . . .

Thursday, 18 February 1965. Palo Alto.

Assistant Dean Bonnie Fitzwater has now resigned in protest against the recent administrative action and the failure to hear Lucille Allen's defenders. She departs with a blast against the committee of the faculty and the irresponsibility of the students. I have received a derisive letter from Phil Crowl about our classroom methods, and doubtless will receive others…

I have accepted John Dodds's invitation to be Phi Beta Kappa Visiting Scholar next year which will involve four weeks of travelling to and lecturing at small colleges and will pay me enough to have a summer in Germany if I want it—(*without* having to teach)…

My American Historical Association piece on the Austro-German military alliance has been accepted for publication by the *Journal of Modern History*. . . .[62]

Thursday, 18 March 1965. Palo Alto.

Last Wednesday afternoon, having given my last lecture for the quarter in the morning, I took the 2:05 United flight to Baltimore, arriving there at about 11 and bussing into the city with Paul Hanna who was on his way to a meeting from his hq at the East-West Center in Honolulu. As usual, I spent the night at the Roger Smith… In the morning of Thursday I repaired after breakfast to the State Department and was sworn in (after formally receiving my clearance), a ceremony which will entitle me to a per diem and a consultant's fee of $100.00 a day… At the meeting of the Arms Control and Disarmament Agency's Social Science Advisory Board, we spent the

---

[62] Gordon A. Craig, "The World War I Alliance of the Central Powers in Retrospect: The Military Cohesion of the Alliance," *Journal of Modern History* 37:3 (September 1965): 336–44.

morning listening to the staff story of Senator Fulbright's attack on the agency's budget. Since his attack seems to have been directed principally against an implausible Johns Hopkins Research Center Project which cost $87,000 for seven think-pieces by people like Arnold Wolfers, Livy Merchant, and that ass [name omitted] who was in Germany with me, I did not feel the attack unjustified and said so. Archie Alexander seemed a little hurt, but told me privately that it was not *his* project. We all felt that a bit more care might be spent on selection of projects, and that the utility of the greater part of them should be demonstrable… In the afternoon (after a wretched lunch) we discussed proliferation of nuclear weapons with Adrian Fisher, the no. 2 man in the agency and then moved on to a discussion of the U.S. White Paper on Viet Nam, a topic raised by [Urie] Bronfenbrenner, who—apparently on the strength of letters from some acquaintances in the Soviet Union—felt that the White Paper falsified our image because it did not stress our love of peace. After a meandering speech by B. which went on interminably, I pointed out that White Papers have specific purposes, that I for one did not believe that every American note should be filled with rhetorical invocations and protestations; and that I figured Secretary Rusk and his staff were smart enough to have done all the things which B. seemed to think had not been done. Nor did I believe in negotiation for the sake of negotiation or to gratify the *amour propre* of the French. This was supported very strongly by Alice Hsieh and by Phil Davison, but particularly by Phil Mosely, who cited examples of things done already which made B's suggestions look naïve, and who added that, if we had to leave Viet Nam, he would advocate our doing so unilaterally and with a declaration to the effect that we had tried and failed to build local support, rather than after a conference at which the Russians and Chinese sat and shouted "Get Out! Get out!"… After the meeting Tom Longh of the staff gave us all copies of I. F. Stone's critique of the White Paper—an action which must have cost him a lot of sleep, for he called me after my return here and said someone on the Hill had found out that we had discussed Viet Nam and received the Stone piece and would I please regard the latter as a private gift… In our debate Dean Griswold and the staff all seemed to be with Bronfenbrenner; Chancellor Heard and the others already mentioned being closer to the hard line. . . .

Monday, 29 March 1965. Palo Alto.

Thursday early I was off to Denver by United Air Lines and thence by Continental to Colorado Springs where I was met by my escort officer, Capt. Charles M. Cooke, Jr., who turned out to be the son of the Admiral

Cooke who was Erny King's planning officer in WWII. I persuaded him to let me sack out in the Bachelor Officer Quarters for the balance of the afternoon. The weather was too lousy to make sitting up profitable in any case, the clouds so low that one could not see the mountains and snow over everything. So I slept in a great suite with five beds and (as I discovered in the morning) leaky window fittings, but comfortable and fitted out with lots of mirrors and a good bathroom and a kitchen with a good range and a refrigerator and lots of ice-cubes and coffee. At 5 Cooke came for me and took me to the Club where the History Dept. gave me an informal cocktail party, during which Col. Will Ruenheck (whom I met during my last trip here in 1960) arrived. He and Cooke and a Captain named McIsaac and a major whose name I missed took me to dinner afterwards and then sent me to bed with a very rosy glow. . . .

Rose early with a slight *Katzenjammer* [hangover] and at 8:45 gave my lecture to the whole cadet corps and some guests—about 2500 people, all hiding in the dark behind the klieg lights. Not an easy job, but it went all right. Afterwards, there was coffee at the Club where my old high school pal Irene von Borstel (now Posner) showed up, as she did in 1960, and where I also had a good talk with a 75-year-old colonel named Kloepfer, who used to work with Pershing and saved Pershing's son from the fire which killed the rest of his family. . . .

Tuesday, 27 April 1965. Palo Alto.

Left for Philadelphia on morning of 21 April after a most successful colloquium the night before. . . . Uneventful trip. In Philadelphia at 5 and time to buy magazines and bourbon before dinner. Quiet evening with Anthony Eden's second volume which I am reviewing for the *Virginia Quarterly*...[63] The doormen at the Benjamin Franklin are now dressed in cocked hats, red coats, and short breeches. Some of them don't have the legs for it...

On Thursday the 22nd rose at a leisurely hour and had brunch of sorts, after which I went on to the Philosophical Building, where I found Roberta and Carl Bridenbaugh, and had a reunion. Then to the afternoon session of the American Philosophical Society, at which I heard a wholly incomprehensible paper by Carl Cori, a most intelligent one on David Rittenhouse by a nice man named [Brooke] Hindle, and a very silly one by the editor of the *Scientific American*, who was worked up about federal grants

---

[63] Gordon A. Craig, "Hectic and Peripatetic Years," *Virginia Quarterly Review* 41:3 (1965): 474–77.

for scientific research, which he believed imposed a pressure upon the university which destroyed its freedom. This was so foolish that I rose in the question period and protested—so eloquently, apparently, that Erwin Griswold and Carl Bridenbaugh were moved to congratulate me. . . .

I decided to skip the Mendel papers, and I had seen all my old pals—(Col. Wertenbaker ["There's nothing wrong with me except that I'm so old!"], John Wheeler, Wilbert Moore, Elmer Butler, Sir Ronald Syme, Fritz Machlup, Harlow Shapley, Wallace Notestein, Lyman Butterfield, and Roy Nichols—to say nothing of Chief Justice Earl Warren, who asked me to carry his best wishes to Wally Sterling.)[64] . . .

On Saturday up at 6:30 and off to the Metropolitan Airport and a 9:15 plane to Chicago, sending my bag straight onto St. Louis. Called up Lennie Krieger and had a drink with him and allowed him to persuade me to write on Schiller in the Festschrift he and Fritz Stern are preparing for Holborn, which is to be called *The Responsibilities of Power*. . . .[65]

Tuesday, 11 May 1965. Palo Alto.
Balance of yesterday spent discussing the so-called "teach-in" on Vietnam which will be held next Monday and which seems to be shaping up as a protest meeting against the administration. I don't like this and, since I have now been asked to participate, I have a right to be concerned. . . .

Wednesday, 12 May 1965. Palo Alto.
Withdrew from participation in the "teach-in" after a discussion with Sandy Dornbusch and a guy named [name omitted] who was one of the organizers. Flushed them out into the open, so that today's *Daily* quotes [name omitted] as admitting this is a protest meeting pure and simple, an admission that seems to have caused some divisions in the original list of sponsors. Meanwhile, I am sponsoring a telegram to LBJ, supporting our Vietnam policy as expounded in the Baltimore speech. I am in some curious company since my co-sponsors are Hoover Institution people or Goldwater supporters; and it will be interesting to see how many people sign my telegram and how many people find excuses in the text or the sponsors to refuse…

---

[64] J. Wallace Sterling (1906–1985) was the fifth president of Stanford University, serving from 1949 to 1968, the crucial years of the university's transformation into a world-class teaching and research institution.

[65] Gordon A. Craig, "Friedrich Schiller and the Problems of Power," in *The Responsibility of Power: Historical Essays in Honor of Hajo Holborn*, ed. Leonard Krieger and Fritz Stern (New York: Doubleday, 1967), 138–56.

A wonderful colloquium today with my undergraduates on Kierkegaard and Nietzsche and Dostoevsky. . . .

Friday, 14 May 1965. Palo Alto.
I now seem to be back in the so-called Teach-In. Impressed by Claude Buss's work to make it a more academic and objective enterprise than it started out to be (or perhaps was designed to be), I promised to come to his end of the show; and then Milorad Drachkovitch and I agreed to appear on a panel after Morgenthau's talk, provided we had a strong chairman and no guitar-banging or revivalism. Meanwhile, we are collecting signatures for our telegram of support to the President. A good number of people (who are not definitely opposed to our policy) are sitting on their hands. Intellectuals tend in these matters to be Lacedaemonian or sentimental. But in my own department, Pease, Spitz, Bailey, Potter, Fehrenbacher, Liu, and Gatell have signed, and that is a pretty strong representation. . . .

Sunday, 23 May 1965. Palo Alto.
. . . On Monday, 17 May we had the much touted Teach-In on Vietnam. Thanks to the efforts of Claude Buss and others, it was not badly unbalanced. The big feature of the day was the 8:00 meeting before an overflow crowd in Memorial Auditorium (with about a thousand people outside), at which a State Dept Public Relations type named Horner and Hans Morgenthau[66] spoke. Since Dept. spokesmen can only say the official lines and cannot speculate, Morgenthau had the better of it, although I found him woefully weak, imprecise, and illogical. For the panel that followed the set-pieces, Milorad Drachkovitch and I were prepared to prove how weak his arguments were, but Sidney Verba, the chairman, styled the discussion so that we had no opportunity, having—along with Morgenthau, Horner, Leopold Haimson, and Shnurmann of Cal—to take a position on an essentially false set of questions. We got a couple of licks in, and I took occasion to remind the crowd that jeering whenever gov't spokesmen mentioned the complexity of the problems facing their country did not show intelligence. I also suggested a negotiating formula, but no one seemed to want to talk about specific things, moralizing and breast-beating being the order of the day… Afterwards, to the Drachkovitches for drinks, where Peter Duignan, under the influence of a couple of shots of rifle whiskey, was very indiscreet about internal politics in the Hoover. . . .

---

[66] Hans Morgenthau (1904–1980), another of the great refugee scholars who escaped from Nazi Germany during the 1930s, became one of the leading theorists of the "realist" school of international relations during the postwar period.

Friday, 16 July 1965. Seattle.
It was announced yesterday that Adlai Stevenson had died of a heart attack in London. An unexpected and grievous loss. S was a cultivated and witty man who worked hard for his country in positions where cultivation and wit helped. He was one of the few men at the level of gov't whom I met on more than one occasion—(I can always remember the awe with which some of the bleeding hearts at the Ford Center regarded me in 1956 when he and I talked for some minutes about trivial things; and I remember earlier how Phyl and I met him at Thorne Lord's in Princeton and he told us about the difficulties of being a guest in the same house with Tom Dewey). What we shall do in the UN without him I do not know. . . .

Later: Thanks to Sol Katz, got a copy of the *Times Literary Supplement* of 8 July, in which my Königgrätz book is reviewed. Aside from the fact that the reviewer finds the book "rather heavier going than the others in the Great Battles of History series" (presumably because "Professor Craig's account is based on profound reading") "the only grumble" he has is "that he (me) has not put a scale on any of his maps." All told, the review is intelligent, although the reviewer is mistaken in thinking that I have not been kind to Moltke in the matter of his extended battle order. Why can't there be reviews like this in our journals? Perhaps because editors assign books like this to people like Laurence Steefel, who reviewed it in the *Journal of Modern History* and—not understanding military affairs—said nothing negative and nothing positive, except that I was well-known. In the *Sunday Observer* of 23 May, A. J. P. Taylor reviewed the book along with some others and said some nice things about it, including the fact that I was briefer and brisker than Friedjung. . . .

Tuesday, 10 August 1965. Seattle.
Gave public lecture tonight on "Germany since Adenauer." Large crowd; good response; few questions. Speech taped for local radio. Now I must do World Affairs interview and TV show, all of which takes time. However, text revisions are being typed; yesterday, I mailed my revised intro. for Rosinski, which seems to have pleased everyone, including his close friend Dick Stebbins (of OSS days) who has written me. Tomorrow, I shall write my opinion of the [Alfred] Vagts manuscripts on military attachés which the Princeton Press has asked me to do. Then I shall go all out to do these last two chapters in my remaining time. It will be very tight, what with exams and dinner engagements.

Wednesday, 12 August 1965. Palo Alto.

Mailed my critique of Vagts to the Press and said, on the whole, I approved publication...[67]

This evening a call from Phil Crowl. In view of uncertainty with respect to my getting interviews with Adenauer and any Englishmen, he suggests that I might talk about Dulles with our ambassador [James Williams] Riddleberger in Vienna and with [Paul-Henri] Spaak in Brussels. He asked if I would object to shuttling around a bit. I said of course not, provided I got some time in Berlin. . . .

Thursday, 26 August 1965. Palo Alto.

. . . The revision of my text is on its way to New York. It has taken so much of my time that I have been barely conscious of other things in these last weeks, although some dreadful things have been happening, like the race riots in Los Angeles. . . .

The Vietnam war goes rather better. John Fischer has a fine piece in the current *Harper's*[68] which comes as close as anything I've seen to expressing my own position on the war and my objection to the intellectuals who keep chanting "Get out of Vietnam!" I imagine that I shall be listening to English intellectuals saying the same thing pretty soon. I expect to encounter lots of anti-Americanism on this trip. . . .

Saturday, 11 September 1965. Berlin.

The trip from Budapest to Berlin was broken by long pauses in Vienna and Munich, and I used them to catch up on the news, and, particularly, to read about the shameful war in India. Two of the most self-righteous nations in the world are now demonstrating that they don't deserve to be governing themselves at all. As the *Süddeutsche_Zeitung* of 9 Sept. said: "*Ein Prestigekrieg Indiens mit Pakistan um den Besitz von Kaschmir—das muß in den Augen eines freiwillig in sich gegangenen Europas nicht anders bedeuten als eine Rechtfertigung des Kolonialismus, unter dem solcher Krieg niemals stattgefunden hätte.*" Every bomb dropped on Lahore, it continued, "*jeder solche Rückfall aus den politischen Sitten dieses Jahrhunderts in die nationalistischen des vorigen bedeutet eine Trumpfkarte in den Händen der Reaktionäre von Südafrika bis Alabama.*" ["A prestige war between India and Pakistan for the possession of Kashmir—in the eyes of a voluntarily withdrawn Europe this cannot mean anything else than a justification for colonialism under which such a war would never have taken place." Every bomb dropped on Lahore, it continued, "every such relapse

---

[67] Alfred Vagts, *The Military Attaché* (Princeton: Princeton University Press, 1967).

[68] John Fischer, "James Bond, Mr. Johnson, and the Intellectuals," *Harper's Magazine* (August 1965).

from the political customs of this century to the nationalistic customs of the previous one means a trump card in the hands of reactionaries from South Africa to Alabama."]

Fully as disturbing, although not unexpected, was de Gaulle's press conference in which he made it clear that further French cooperation with the Common Market would depend on revision of the Rome Treaties and, further, that he would, by 1969 at least, demand a reform of NATO. The press comments here are almost resigned to Big Charlie's antics. . . .

Compared with these events, the German election campaign is not only tame but dull. I wish everything was because I shall have a week's work to do, revising my revision and saying new things about Austria, Hungary, India, NATO, SEATO, de Gaulle, and the Common Market already, and I don't want any more. . . .

I think the young are going in for he/she hairdos. At least I saw a couple at the play wearing identical hairstyles, his hair falling to his shoulders like hers. The only way you could tell that he was male was that he had a slight moustache, not an infallible guide in this country… Earlier, at my barber's, I was shattered to observe a young man in the chair next to mine having his trimmed and oiled hair wrapped in a tight net and then submitted to the treatment of one of those hair setting machines that women use. I realize that other ages have had their dandies, with similar and even more exotic ways, but I am not at all sure that this form of dandyism was not always a sign of national degeneration and decline. I always become gloomy when I compare this sort of thing, and the other, uglier forms it assumes in the States, with the more spartan qualities of youth in the East. I know that the comparison is unfair and not even accurate, but I get unhappy even so…

Monday, 13 September 1965. Berlin.
. . . At 4 to . . . have tea with Annedore Leber, finding her worried about my use of [satirist Kurt] Tucholsky in the first paragraph of my introduction to her edition of Turner's book. She seems to feel it may alienate her conservative friends. I tried to reassure her and said I would think it all over when I got back to the States. She also talked of the possibility of my doing a book on "*Braun, Preußen und die Weimarer Demokratie* [Otto Braun, Prussia, and the Weimar Democracy]." Not a bad theme, and apparently Weyman, the *Oberbürgermeister* [Lord Mayor] of Hamburg, has a lot of Braun papers… Spent the evening at Henry Turner's along with Gottwald, who is translating Henry's book, and his wife, a nice Californian girl. . . .

Later: Went over to East Berlin with Henry Turner, who had to make some arrangements for his trip to Potsdam tomorrow. I hoped to see the

German Romanticism show in the National Gallery but it was closed. So was the Invaliden Kirchhof where I wanted to see Scharnhorst's grave. *Faute de mieux*, we drove through the rain to the Friedrichshain and saw the *Märchenbrunnen* [Fairytale Fountain]. Then back through Check Point Charlie to West Berlin, where we sought out [Gustav] Stresemann's grave. Then to the Tegernseer Tönnchen, Mommsenstraße, for a relaxed dinner. . . .

Friday, 17 September 1965. Amsterdam.
Discovered at 9 a.m. that the tape recorder, which has served me well, was dead—definitively. Since I had an appointment with Ambassador Tyler in the Hague at 12:45, this posed a problem. I took off in a rush and found a shop which confirmed my diagnosis but agreed to buy my dead machine and sell me a new one. At the cost of seriously cutting into my cash reserve, I went along and dashed off to the Hague with a new Sony machine. I made my appointment: the ambassador, William Tyler, turned out to be a chap who had come to the Princeton NATO conference of 1957 (Ed Furniss's show). We soon turned up enough mutual acquaintances to establish a basis of confidence. He took me home to lunch and then gave a very well-prepared and balanced assessment of Dulles, which I hardly interrupted. An able, if rather over-cultivated, man. . . .

Thursday, 23 September 1965. Oxford.
. . . Tuesday I arose early and went off to see George Weidenfeld the publisher who tried to persuade me to plan and edit a multi-volume history of Germany, reminded me that he and [Janko] Musulin of Fischer [Verlag] wanted a short history of Prussia from me, and, finally, suggested I write a 25,000 word book (with 65 illustrations) called *The Junkers*. I avoided committing myself on any of these, although I was interested in the last, but used Mr. Weidenfeld's mood to get a free telephone call to Bonn from him. I called [Josef] Selbach, who is *Ministerialdirigent* [Ministerial Director] in the *Bundeskanzleramt* [Federal Chancellor's Office] and learned from him that Adenauer is so busy with post-election consultations (the Christian Democratic Union won handily) that he cannot see me now. . . .

Yesterday, I rose late, had a big breakfast and took my recorder off to Worcester College. Here after an excellent light lunch *en famille*, I interviewed the Provost, Sir Oliver Franks. He was interesting but careful, avoiding all my snares and pleading lack of memory on those aspects of the Japanese Treaty negotiations which are most interesting, particularly the question whether Dulles misled [Anthony] Eden in the matter of the

Yoshida letter or whether the misunderstanding which poisoned later relations between Dulles and Eden, was really caused by Franks's failure to brief his own foreign minister...[69] Despite this (or because of it) Franks struck me as a very able man. He is presently directing the Oxford University Enquiry...

Leaving Franks, I went for a walk in the beautiful Worcester gardens and off in the distance descried a familiar figure, my friend and mentor E. L. Woodward walking with his sister. I caught them up and we did five turns of the Gardens talking about Vienna and related subjects. Then he took me home to tea. . . .

Thursday, 30 September 1965. Palo Alto.
First meeting of the NEW history dept—with all the new boys on hand. . . . The dept has the opportunity now to become what the Princeton dept was in the years 1948–1955. . . .

[1966]

Saturday, 1 January 1966. Jenner.
The American Historical Association conference is over. The weather was dreadful, and our eastern friends hardly got a chance to see us at our best. I did my best to counteract the elements with restaurants. . . . The conference itself was rather better than most. I listened to a most disappointing session on "The Writing of History," in which I thought that Jack Hexter, Theo von Laue, and Norman Cantor did no good to their reputations; and, in a session on German thought of the early 19th century, only Charlie Gillespie made sense while two young men *and* Stanley Mellon

---

[69] The Yoshida Letter was a letter dictated by John Foster Dulles and signed by the Japanese Prime Minister, Yoshida Shigeru, in which Japan pledged to sign a peace treaty with the Chiang Kai-Shek regime in Taiwan as soon as possible. Dulles failed to disclose the full nature of the letter to Eden, then Britain's Foreign Minister, during a visit to the United States. Britain had hoped that the Japanese would maintain an attitude of equidistance from the two Chinas, fearing that if Japan were completely barred from trading with communist China, it might challenge the British for commercial primacy in southeast Asia. The British Ambassador to the United States, Oliver Franks, had seen the contents of the letter, but failed to relay the contents to Eden before Eden's meeting with Dulles. When Yoshida's letter was publicized shortly after Eden's return to Britain, it was a source of embarrassment and consternation for the British government, and soured relations between Eden and Dulles. See Kevin Ruane, "The Origins of the Eden-Dulles Antagonism: The Yoshida Letter and the Cold War in East Asia 1951–1952," *Contemporary British History* 25:1 (March 2011): 141–56.

were brilliant but unsound, the last demonstrating, in some unfortunate remarks about French realism, that he understood neither Balzac nor Georg Lukács. At least, this was the conclusion drawn by Felix Gilbert and me, who had a drink together afterwards… In contrast, Carl Schorske's paper on Morris and Wagner, at the Modern European Section's Luncheon was brilliant—a marvelous piece of analysis. . . .

Sunday, 30 January 1966. Palo Alto.
To Memorial Church with Phyl to hear William Sloane Coffin of Yale give a most intemperate sermon on the Vietnam situation. Admitting that we could not simply pull out (because of our pledge and because of the indiscriminate killing that would be sure to follow a takeover by Ho), he argued that the U.S. gov't was refusing to do the one thing that would assure negotiation: namely, granting the Viet Cong a seat at the table. It is by no means clear that we have refused this; we have merely refused to grant it in advance, and rightly so… We went up afterwards to say hello (Mel went to Mississippi with Coffin) and found an indignant couple reproaching him for misusing the pulpit. "I brought my children to hear about God, etc." Curious American belief that politics profanes the church…

Monday, 31 January 1966. Palo Alto.
American bombing of Vietnam resumed early today after a pause which has lasted since Christmas. Before dawn, [name omitted] of the English Department and other young activists were at work trying to organize a kind of academic strike in protest and, after my nine o'clock lecture, three students brought me an ill-written announcement of a series of protest meetings. Aside from its bad style, this was distinguished by ignorance of the U.S. Constitution and a high degree of disingenuousness, reflecting the current communist line that the bombing pause and the peace offensive represented a gigantic hoax. Asked for my opinions by the *Daily* over the phone this evening, I said I regretted the resumption of bombing but must assume that the President was acting on the basis of a full assessment of the situation and in the belief that negotiation would not be promoted by further waiting, and, furthermore, that I regarded the idea of an academic protest strike as "a kind of sentimentality." During the course of the day, I declined the opportunity to appear with Coffin on a program this evening, but agreed to appear on the 16th together with Stanley Hoffman of Harvard. . . .

Wednesday, 16 February 1966. Palo Alto.
Tonight at 8 to Dinkelspiel where Stanley Hoffman spoke on Vietnam and

Lyman Van Slyke and I commented. A brilliant job by Hoffman, who dismissed the moralists and the breast-beaters and the Lippmann/ Morgenthau geo-politicians (who want to divide the world into spheres of influence) and the legalists in a few well-chosen words, and then proceeded to deal with the matter as a strictly political problem. His conclusions were a bit vague, and he is inclined to be defeatist to the point of wanting to hand everything over to the Viet Cong. On those points and others we criticized him. Afterwards a woman came up and said it was the best meeting on Vietnam she had ever attended and the first in which all of the speakers had not talked only about napalm and the bombing of innocent civilians. It is perhaps significant that only about 150 people came to the meeting, and none of those who tried to stampede the faculty into a strike when bombing resumed. Claude Buss, who does not support the Administration policy but is trying to educate Stanford undergraduates in foreign affairs, was disgusted. . . .[70]

Tuesday, 5 April 1966. Palo Alto.

In the morning mail, a letter from Jerry saying that at yesterday's faculty meeting in Princeton Bob Goheen announced that Bob Palmer will succeed Doug Brown as Dean of Faculty in July '67 when Doug retires, and that Bill Bowen, who was at the Pittendrigh dinner a week or so ago, will be Princeton's first Provost. The news surprised me and left me with curiously mixed feelings, partly, I guess, because I always believed that Dean of Princeton's Faculty was one position *I* could fill and the only administrative job I would ever seriously consider. So I dare say there was a strong admixture of jealousy in my reaction to the news, which was silly, since I would, in all probability, be a very bad dean of anything, since I would very soon be bored with any administrative job, and since—even if *I had* received the offer—I would, in view of Phyl's job and my commitment to scholarship, have turned it down. I guess what I was subconsciously wishing was that they had asked me or at least considered me for the job (which, in all probability, they did not).

As for Bob's appointment, I think it is a good one in all probability, and that, if Princeton is lucky, he will quickly turn into another Robert Root, a dean with character and color and ideas. It is a decided loss to the historical profession, for the job will leave him no time to write.

---

[70] Claude Buss (1903–1998), whose diplomatic career included service in China and the Philippines, was one of the principal American experts on East Asia for more than half a century.

Jerry ended his note by urging me to see the light and return. A fat chance! . . . I don't believe that one should double back on one's trail that way. . . .

Thursday, 14 April 1966. Palo Alto.

I have been reading the Communist press upon my paper at Vienna in September. Both the *Bulletin des Arbeitkreises 'Zweites Weltkrieg'* (Deutsche Akademie der Wissenschaften zu Berlin DDR) Nr. 4, 1965 and *Einheit: Zeitschrift für Theorie und Praxis des Wissenschaftlichen Sozialismus* (hrsg. V. Zentralkomitee der Sozialistischen Einheitspartei Deutschlands) agree that I was attempting a rehabilitation of the German military but that I suffered an "*eklatante Niederlage*" [striking defeat].[71] Both make much of the fact that only three historians supported me (Kraußnick, Vogelsang, Carsten—they apparently don't count [Eberhard] Jäckel of Kiel, although his thesis was the same as my own), whereas 13 spoke against me. Of these 13 they mention only a few and say little of their speeches, which were both dreary and irrelevant. *Einheit* makes much of that fact that I was attacked even by two *Western* historians—[Philippe] Contamine of France (who made a very obvious point, with which I had no trouble in agreeing but which had nothing to do with my paper, and who made it with that ineffable French air of superiority which comes from reading nothing that is not published in Paris) and George Hallgarten (whose remarks were obscure and erratic and who is, of course, mad). . . .

Thursday, 28 April 1966. Palo Alto.

. . . Today, I left the house at 9:30 and was in Los Angeles at 11:45, in Chatsworth (via Hertz rented car) at 2, closeted with General Curtis LeMay USAF ret., on the plane for SF at 5:15, and back in my home having a drink at 7:15. Twentieth-century style! LeMay was like a caricature of himself. He has some ill-defined position at the head of something called Networks Electronics, where I had to get a special visitors badge and sign in and out as if I were going into G-2 in the Pentagon. Patriotic emblems all over the place and exhortations to rally to the cause. LeMay himself was not interested in Dulles, and aside from making cracks about the State Dept., talked mainly about himself and his strategical views, which boil down to

---

[71] The first of these two publications can be translated as "Bulletin of the 'Second World War Working Group," published by the Berlin (GDR) Academy of Sciences. The second, "*Einheit*," is "Unity: Magazine for Theory and Praxis of Scientific Socialism," edited by the 5th Central Committee of the Socialist Unity Party of Germany.

the precept "Bomb everybody now, if not yesterday." His views on Korea, Vietnam, Lebanon, Matsu and Quemoy, and Berlin were unenlightening. He *did* opine that we should have done nothing during the Suez crisis to hamper the British and French, and he expressed a low opinion of people who take a moral view of political questions. Not a very rewarding day. . . .

Tuesday, 10 May 1966. Palo Alto.
Yesterday, a call from Charles Frankel's office in the State Department to ask if I would be interested in going to Bonn for two years as Cultural Affairs Officer. As, in the year 1957, when Conant asked me the same question, I had to say no, because of commitments to the University, and particularly to my graduate students. . . .

Monday, 16 May 1966. Palo Alto.
On Friday, Günter Grass came to town to read from his works. Walter Sokel[72] had asked me to have dinner with him at the club and, since Martha wanted to meet him, I arranged for her to be having a drink with me when he arrived. This ruse worked, and Grass (who turned out to be a shorter, plumper, and *liebenswürdiger Mensch* [more amiable person] than I had imagined he would be) sat beside her, obviously charmed, and even introduced her to a late comer as his daughter. After cocktails, she left, and we dined and then went to Cubberley where Grass read four new poems and the conclusion of Part II of *Hundejahre* [*Dog Years*] to an overflow audience. The questions afterward were, for the most part, stupid—along the line of "Why do you always write about the past when the future is so demanding?" or "Why didn't you sign the anti-U.S.-Vietnam-policy manifesto of the West German intellectuals?" He answered generally by stressing the fact that writing is a trade that has to be learned and practiced and that there are no universal experts, least of all among writers. The questions about contemporary German politics were even stupider than the more general ones. Indeed, the only question that made sense had to do with writers who had influenced Grass or for whom he felt an affinity, and his answer—Alfred Döblin—was lost on the non-*Germanisten*... As he came off the platform, I picked him up and took him to the club, tailed by a queue of undergraduates who asked much better questions than those asked in the hall. We then had a pleasant faculty reception, and as it faded Grass and I had a chance to talk about the Wallenstein novel of Döblin and

---

[72] Walter Sokel (1917–2014) an émigré scholar from Vienna, was one of the leading authorities on German literature in the United States, and a major figure in the field of Kafka studies. He was Craig's colleague at Stanford from 1964 to 1973.

other things. He says that he and I should give a joint seminar when next I come to Berlin, on military style and the German language. Unfortunately, this has already been written up in the passage from *Hundejahre* which he read tonight. Perhaps we can find something else. At least I have made another Berlin contact. . . .

Two personal items: the article opposite from today's *Stanford Daily* and an article on the History Department in the *Stanford Course Review* (an undergraduate publication), which says some nice things about me but adds that, because of the difficulty of my courses, my insistence upon hard reading and attendance at lectures, and my "dynamic lecturing style," I am "often called 'the little Prussian general.'" *Sancta simplicitas*![73] By whom, I wonder? . . .

Thursday, 26 May 1966. Palo Alto.
Lunch at the club with Stuart McLean, Campus Presbyterian Pastor, and a long talk about how to get through to the student activists, whose latest caper, last weekend, was to stage a sit-in in the President's Office in order to protest against the University's giving Selective Service exams. The sit-in was a flop, but even so a deplorable by-passing of the normal chain of communication; civil disobedience for the sake of civil disobedience... In the afternoon persuaded Walter Sokel and Hans Speier to join with me in a program to be given in the city under the auspices of the West German Consulate General on the subject, "The 17th of June, Bert Brecht and Günter Grass." Wrote Grass and told him about it, while sending him a copy of the German edition of my Königgrätz book.

Monday, 6 June 1966. Palo Alto.
A packet of reviews from Zsolnay Verlag, all from German, Austrian, and Swiss papers, and uniformly complimentary. The *Frankfurter Allgemeine Zeitung* printed whole of introduction in its Sunday edition two weeks ago. Berlin and Bavarian radio networks will have programs during first week of July on Königgrätz with my book as basis, latter with [Alexander] Lernet-Holenia and [Hans-Joachim] Schoeps. All very nice, but why must they describe me as "the English historian," "the British military expert" or "the distinguished Scottish historian"? . . .

Thursday, 9 June 1966. Palo Alto.

---

[73] "Sancta simplicitas" is a Latin expression meaning "Holy Simplicity," used to express ironic astonishment at one's own naivete or innocence, or simply "The times!"

An interesting meeting at noon in Bob Sears's office, on the possibility of setting up a Humanities and Sciences Council—a faculty body distinct from the Academic Council. I strongly favor this, for we need a more effective parliamentary body than we have. I pointed out, however, and was strongly supported by Phil Rhinelander, that no change would work that wasn't thorough, and that the new Council would have to be given real power. The General Studies and other committees would have to be subordinated to it. And the upshot would be that the Academic Council would be changed into something like the Delegations of the Austrian-Hungarian Empire. . . .

Saturday, 11 June 1966. Palo Alto.
Spoke at Class Day on history and its perils—in short, about the importance of maintaining historical perspective in a changing world. Al Guerard[74] was a bit unbuttoned, identifying himself somewhat too emphatically with student activism and giving too many hostages to fortune. (Rab Minto opines that all this rises from a desperate desire not to be abandoned by the young, which may not be wholly wrong.) Bob Brown very good and very funny, particularly in wondering whether, in choosing their class day speakers, the committee had been influenced by a book he once had a part in, called *God, Sex, and War.* This was not the only reference to my supposed martial proclivities. In a remark about Guerard's opposition to the war in Vietnam, Brown said that it was "an opposition of which Professor Craig would not approve," which I thought unnecessary but interesting. People will be calling me "Old Blood and Guts" next. . . .

Wednesday, 15 June 1966. Palo Alto.
Lunch with Walter Sokel and a long talk which has given me an idea for a new book: "German Intellectuals and the Problems of Power, 1770–1830" with chapters on Schiller, Kleist, Uhland, Humboldt, Clausewitz, and Hegel. Exciting idea. . . .[75]

Sunday, 4 September 1966. Palo Alto.
. . . I have been trying to rationalize my commitments by agreeing to do a book on Dulles for Simon and Schuster for an advance big enough to liquidate my commitments to Van Nostrand (for an Anvil book on Bismarck) and Hold (for a diplomatic history). This deal has just about jelled... Finally, I have been cleaning up my desk. Reading my mail (Krieger

---

[74] Albert J. Guerard (1914–2000) was a novelist and literary critic who, like Craig, began teaching at Stanford in 1961.

[75] Gordon A. Craig, *The Politics of the Unpolitical: German Writers and the Problem of Power, 1770–1871* (New York: Oxford University Press, 1995).

likes the Schiller piece; Gilbert likes the German intellectuals project; the Darmstadt jury has chosen my K book as book of the month, and Elvert and Meurer are going to play this up in their *Schaufenster* [display window]; Zsolnay has made an offer to Praeger for German rights to *War, Politics. and Diplomacy*; etc.); and answering it has taken a lot of time and so has the always onerous job of going through accumulations of German newspapers and clipping them, and reading back issues of *Der Spiegel.* I want as quickly as possible to get down to the planning and writing of my *Germany, 1865–1945* for the Oxford series and, for this, it is important to clip wisely and to note that *Spiegel* Nrs. 32–35 of this year have interesting analyses of *Mein Kampf.* Before this, however, I must write six long delayed book reviews and revise one of my Phi Beta Kappa talks for publication in *The Key Reporter.* . . .

Wednesday, 14 September 1966. Palo Alto.
Wrote diplomatic note to Herbert Hoover, Jr., outlining questions I hoped he would discuss when I talk with him about Dulles on 26th. Aided in this by phone call by Dick Challener who also encouraged me to go ahead with my own Dulles project by saying that the forthcoming Gerson book will provide no competition. The Simon and Schuster contract is here and I will sign it (after I read it)... Wrote review of Ronald Clarke's book on Sir Henry Tizard for *The International Journal*... Finished Rudi Blesh's *Keaton*, a very good book... Can't make any headway with John Barth's *Giles Goatboy.* Despite the advertising blurb it is *not* the answer to Günter Grass. . . .

Friday, 16 September 1966. Palo Alto.
A pleasant afternoon with John Service, whom I interviewed for the Dulles project. I hadn't seen him since the spring of 1949, when we served together on the Foreign Service Selection Board. Later that year because of pressure by the Scripps-Howard papers and the growing McCarthy madness, his appointment to the mission in India was stalled and at the beginning of the next year he was dismissed on loyalty charges rising out of the *Amerasia* case.[76] He appealed but was not reinstated (after a Supreme Court decision) until 1957. He was in the department in a non-security job for a time and

---

[76] *Amerasia* was a journal specializing in Asian affairs. After an investigation and raid, the journal staff was found to be in possession of hundreds of classified government documents without authorization. John Service was one of the government officials suspected of leaking the documents to *Amerasia.* See Harvey Klehr and Ronald Radosh, *The Amerasia Spy Case: Prelude to McCarthyism* (Chapel Hill: University of North Carolina Press, 1996).

then was told he was going to Bonn as Chief Administrative Officer but after 11 months intensive German language work, this was washed out for unknown reason, and he was sent as consul to Liverpool where he finished his service. He is now curator of Berkeley's Far Eastern Collection, and has a son in the Foreign Service—which shows courage, or stubbornness on the young man's part... Since Jack was fired by Acheson he had little first-hand stuff to put on the tape about Dulles, but his second-hand material was interesting—reaction inside Department to various policies, morale, etc. After the machine was shut off, he said that, after Dulles had told John Carter Vincent that he was fired, he leaned back and said, "Now what do you think of the situation in the Far East?" Similarly, after firing John Patton Davies, he offered to help him find a job. Davies said, "No, thank you." . . .

Thursday, 22 September 1966. Princeton, N.J.
The second day of the Arms Control and Disarmament Agency board meetings more interesting than the first because Adrian Fischer gave us a morning-long summary of recent developments in the 18-Nation Disarmament Conference at Geneva, the upshot of which was that the Soviets are not terribly far apart from us on substantive matters and particularly on the guts of a non-proliferation treaty, but that they simply will not (perhaps cannot) sign any kind of treaty with us while the Vietnam war is going on. During Fischer's talk, word came in that Nicholas Katzenbach will replace George Ball in the No. 2 spot in the State Dept., that Gene Rostow will take over Tom Mann's old No. 3 job, and Foy Kohler will move from Moscow to take No. 4. All in all, a strengthening... In the afternoon, Urie Bronfenbrenner reported on the Psychological Congress in Moscow in a way that indicates that the historians in 1970 may find more *Schlamperei* [sloppiness] there than in Vienna; Janowitz gave an interesting talk on the Sociological Conference in Evian (and its arms control aspects: Soviet interest, but backwardness in military sociology); and Griswold gave a talk about his recent trip to the Far East (which struck me as being over-optimistic with respect to currents of thought in Japan—cf. Claude Buss). . . .

Monday, 26 September 1966. Washington, D.C.
. . . An interesting evening in which I had a few words with [West German Chancellor Ludwig] Erhard (reminding him of the *Feier* [celebration] for Prof. Oppenheim, his teacher, where I first met him) and where I had at my table Mrs. McNamara and Mrs. Dean Acheson and Mr. George Ball.

Saw the Rostows . . . and Nicholas Katzenbach and Bob Bowie and Dean Rusk and had drinks afterward with the Jim Perkins and the Meredith Wilsons (who will take over Ralph Tyler's spot in the Ford Center). . . .

Tuesday, 27 September 1966. Washington, D.C.
The final edition of today's *Washington Post* has a story on the dinner party and a guest list, and I find that all sorts of types (like [the actress] Merle Oberon) were there. . . . My table mates were Mrs. [Alice Stanley] Acheson and Mrs. [Margaret] McNamara with the first of whom I talked about the iniquities of the present director of the Smithsonian and the even greater sins of John Foster Dulles. Mrs. Acheson said that, because of what Dulles did to the Foreign Service, her husband could only be persuaded with difficulty to attend the funeral services and that he refused, all too audibly, to sing the last hymn, "Come all ye saints!" . . . After dinner Walt Rostow, who had earlier introduced me to State Secretary Carstens, told me that he had played "The Claustrophobia Blues" to Mrs. LBJ at the Ranch last week. I had a word with Nicholas Katzenbach, about his brother Ed, who is my Ph.D., and another with Mrs. LBJ about her recent trip to San Francisco, which she said was "a dream." Jim Perkins asked how her German was, and she answered that she hadn't understood a word of the *Bundeskanzler*'s response to LBJ's remarks after dinner. I told her that this was because Erhard has such a lousy Bavarian accent, but she didn't recognize this as a joke or a compliment. . . . I did not see Miss Oberon or the two Gemini II astronauts [Pete] Conrad and [Richard] Gordon; I recognized but did not meet McCloy, Taylor, Fortas, Dirksen, etc. On the strength of my Berlin connection, I introduced myself to General Clay, and Jim Perkins introduced me to Secretary of the Treasury Fowler; aside from these contacts, I floated with the throng pleasantly. . . .

The Perkins hired a limousine to take them to the White House. I walked over from the Roger Smith in a dark coat borrowed from Fred Aandahl and was passed through the SW Gate by the police at 7:50. I walked up the drive to the house, was checked and had my ticket taken away by a young man who asked if Mrs. Craig was not coming, so that he might be sure that no peacenick with bomb claiming to be my wife got upstairs. For a few minutes we all stood about uncomfortably in the round lower hall where we had handed in our tickets and top-coats. Then, promptly at 8, we all went up the marble staircase into a room I could not identify, each of us being announced in a loud voice (I simply as "Dr. Craig"). This system allowed us to escape isolation by pouncing on the first people whose names we recognized, as I did first in the case of the Rostows and then in that of the Perkins. Servants brought drinks around and an orchestra played popular music in the background, which changed to a ruffle of drums and the first strains of "Hail to the Chief" when the President's party was announced and came in behind an honor guard bearing flags. The young Marine captain who was my escort officer, (a former student of mine at Princeton, as he told me) placed me and his other charges in appropriate places in the line, and we all moved forward slowly to meet the President, the *Bundeskanzler*, Mrs. Johnson, and Mrs. Erhard, in that order. While we moved forward, . . . the music reverted to the popular, discoursing "My Funny Valentine" as I reached the President. Once through the line, we were seized by other White House aides and taken to our tables, and dinner began. Music continued through this, and at one point four violins invaded the Blue Room and serenaded the *Bundeskanzler*, with Hungarian tunes, for some reason, and an odd version of "*Du, du liegst mir im Herzen*" [You, you are in my heart]. When we reached the coffee and cigars, the President gave a short speech which was carried to us by a public address system from his table in the State Dining Room and was accompanied by the mutter of Erhard's interpreter at the table behind me. Then Erhard responded in German, and then we got the translation. We then rose, said polite things to our tablemates, and went outside to have a brandy and mill about for 15 minutes, those of us with weak bladders using this time to find the john, which was a long way away. Then we gathered in the East Room for the concert, which I thought very good, despite the heroic stance and expression adopted by Mr. Kroll during the Bach. This lasted half an hour, and then, after a glass of champagne, we went downstairs, and cars were brought. I left in the Perkins limousine. . . .

Tuesday, 11 October 1966. Palo Alto.
I have spent most of the time since coming back from Jenner drawing up a record of my professional career for the Guggenheim Foundation in the hope that they will unbelt with some cash to help close the gap between what I will give up here by going on leave and what Berlin will give me. A silly and probably an unrewarding business. I had to tell them that I couldn't list all my published works since, in addition to my books, I have published 40 articles and 235 reviews since 1944. . . .

Tuesday, 8 November 1966. Palo Alto.
. . . In evening listened to the sad details of Ronald Reagan's victory in the California gubernatorial election and the pronounced Republican gains throughout the nation. All due to white backlash, unhappiness about high

taxes, impatience with beatniks and defiance of decency, and—I am afraid—dissatisfaction with the policy of restraint in the Vietnam war. This is not a victory for the peace party; it may be a victory for those who, like Curtis Le May, want to "bomb them back into their caves." If so, a sad outlook for us all... Shut off TV and wrote a new lecture for tomorrow on Religion and Politics in Germany after 1871. . . .

Friday, 11 November 1966. Palo Alto.
Lunch with Walter Sokel at Red Cottage. We vetted the list of novels we will use in our two-quarter seminar and pretty well settled on, for the first (autumn) quarter, Spielhagen, *Problematische Naturen* [*Problematic Characters*], Gustav Freytag, *Soll und Haben* [*Debt and Credit*], Raabe, *Der Hungerpastor* [*The Hunger Pastor*] (or possibly *Abu Telfan* [*Abu Telfan: Or, the Return from the Mountains of the Moon*]), Fontane, *Irrungen, Wirrungen* and *Der Stechlin* [*A Suitable Match* and *The Stechlin*], Hesse, *Peter Camenzind* [*Peter Camenzind*], Leonhard Frank, *Die Räuberbande* [*The Robber Band*], Heinrich Mann, *Der Untertan* [*Man of Straw*], Ernst Toller, *Ein Jugend in Deutschland* [*I Was a German*], and, for the second (spring) quarter, Arnold Zweig, *Der Streit um Sergeaten Grischa* [*The Case of Sergeant Grischa*], Ernst von Salomon, *Die Geächteten* [*The Outlaws*], W. Speyer, *Kampf der Tertia* [*Galahads and Pussy-Cats*] or Frank Thiess, *Abschied von Paradies* [*Farewell to Paradise*], Alfred Döblin, *Berlin Alexanderplatz* [*Berlin Alexanderplatz*], Vicki Baum, *Stud. Chem. Helen Willfuer* [*Helene*], Hans Fallada, *Kleiner Mann, was nun?* [*Little Man, What Now?*], Ernst Wiechert, *Das einfache Leben* [*The Simple Life*], Ernst Jünger, *Auf den Marmorklippen* [*On the Marble Cliffs*], and Hermann Kasack, *Die Stadt hinter dem Strom* [*The City Beyond the River*]. Some of the books we would have liked to use—other Spielhagen novels, Max Kretzer's *Meister Timpe* [*Master Timpe*], Hermann Löns—are not readily available. Afterwards, we talked of my projected paper and Sokel was, as usual, filled with good ideas. The political views of many of the main literary figures can, he thinks, be found in the journals, particularly in *Die neue Rundschau* [*The New Review*] and *Die Schaubühne* [*The Playhouse*] and *Die Aktion* [*The Action*]; and the political essays of [Alfred] Döblin should throw particular light upon the mutual antipathy of the *Linksintellektuellen* [left-wing intellectuals] and the Social Democratic Party of Germany. Basic to the whole problem is the fact that the incapacity of the German bourgeoisie for democracy was as true of the intellectuals as it was of the businessmen, so that instead of reconciling themselves to the compromises of politics and the realities of power they lost themselves in *O Mensch*! enthusiasms, various kinds of utopianism, or abstractions in the first phase and negative criticism and satire in the second—if they did not

simply relapse into aestheticism and other forms of neutralism. In this last connection, Sokel reminded me that there was a neutralism on the right as well as the left, and that some attention should be paid to people like [Ernst] Wiechert and Gertrude von le Fort.

I suspect myself that the realization that there was a gap between their knowledge and the world of action accounts for the frustration and over-eager, excessively incautious behavior of a man like Bronnen, as it does for the curious behavior of [Gottfried] Benn in 1933.[77]

One of the tragic aspects of the behavior of the intellectuals during the Weimar period was that even when they intended to strengthen the republic by their attacks upon its weakness, they were apt to confirm its enemies in their hostility and even gave them new weapons. Who knows how many anti-Semites took comfort in [Kurt] Tucholsky's [Herr] Wendriner pieces, or how many of his barbed comments were used for their own purposes by people who hated him?[78]

Must look up [Frida] Rubiner and [Hermann] Heller, the real utopians. . . .

Wednesday, 16 November 1966. Palo Alto.
Lectured on Bismarck's foreign policy and gave seminar on literati and polities in the years 1813–1815, with particular references to Fr. Schlegel and Gentz and with much discussion of the sociology and the psychology of intellectuals (Schumpeter, Weber, *et al*). Interesting to note, in connection with my article, that when Schlegel dedicated his lectures on literature to Metternich in 1812, he said that it was his purpose to close, or help close, the gap that existed between the world of letters and the world of politics... With respect to that article, have read today Heinrich Mann's essays "Geist und Tat" and "Voltaire and Goethe," Walter Sokel's essay on Kurt Hiller, the pages on Hiller, Rubiner, and the expressionist drama in Soergel-Hohoff (and the long section on Carl Sternheim), and some

---

77 Both the Austrian playwright and director Arnolt Bronnen (1895–1959) and the German poet Gottfried Benn (1886–1956) were disillusioned with the Weimar system and initially welcomed the advent of the Nazi regime, signing the "vow of most faithful allegiance" to Adolf Hitler. However, both men eventually turned away from the Nazis, as their earlier work was banned and they were prevented from publishing.

78 Kurt Tucholsky (1890–1935) was a satirist who created a fictional character named "Herr Wendriner," a Jewish nouveau-riche businessman obsessed with money and status. Although Tucholsky was himself Jewish, and his defenders argue that the Wendriner pieces primarily satirize the excesses of German society, his critics argue that he provided ammunition and confirmation to anti-Semites.

Tucholsky. I can see the beginnings of my piece (some reflections on Robert Minder's essay on French *Sozialierung* and German *Innerlichkeit* and then a discussion of Mann, Hiller, the war, and the beginning of literary activism, followed by an analysis of its utopian character and its ineffectiveness (rooted in a refusal to study the political process and learn about power)). What comes after that I don't know. I shall have to find some way of bringing in neutralism (aestheticism/*Innerlichkeit*), satire (the self-defeating weapon) and frustration (utopianism taking flight in blindness (Becher, Renn) or in *Schicksalsrausch* (Johst, Benn)). All this still fuzzy... And where does Döblin come in? . . .

Wednesday, 23 November 1966. Palo Alto.
Lecture in the morning. Gave lunch to Herb Mann, Anatole Mazour, and Sam Knoll at the Club. Afterwards Sam came to my seminar and talked for two hours about the work of the Mainz Commission in carrying out the Carlsbad Decrees.[79] Took him back to the Club afterwards, gave him a drink, and left him with Josie Mazour while I went home to dress for dinner. This we had at the Club again as guests of Glenn Campbell, the occasion being a do for Eleanor Lansing Dulles, whom I had last seen in Berlin. Had a good talk with her and gave her a copy of my book, which has an essay on her brother. Discussion of German question after dinner, during which she attributed the present cabinet crisis to Erhard's failure to win any concessions on the offset payments issue during his visit to Washington and indicated that she thinks this was a bad mistake on our part.[80] Bertram Wolfe made some sense with his remarks and so, I hope, did I, while Stefan Possony used the occasion to attack McNamara for not being martial enough and Lewis Gann made a gentle speech reproaching the U.S. gov't from writing off Eastern Europe, which he thinks can still be saved. Hoover Institution parties are always a bit weird and out of the time-space continuum. . . .

It was announced this morning that Dick Lyman will be the new Provost. A very good choice. . . .

[1967]

---

[79] The Carlsbad Decrees of 1819 introduced a series of restrictions on the freedom of assembly, speech, and the press in the lands of the German Confederation in an attempt to weaken popular sentiments in favor of liberal reform and German unification.

[80] During the Cold War, the "German Question" pertained to the issue of Germany's division and eventual reunification.

Sunday, 8 January 1967. Palo Alto.
. . . Finished the Meinecke, a wonderful book conveying the atmosphere of pre-war and war-time Germany better than any that I know, and describing a world of scholarship that is long dead.[81] Meinecke and his colleagues talked to each other about their work and met in the evenings to discuss it in depth. I haven't got a colleague in all Stanford who would be interested in anything I said about any of my projects for longer than five minutes—except perhaps Sokel. . . .

Friday, 13 January 1967, Palo Alto.
Walter Laqueur has sent me a review of my *Königgrätz* from an East German journal which, making allowances for the sort of thing that communists must say (that I am a prisoner of the imperialistic ideology, etc.), is very favorable… The editor of the new *Journal of Central Europe* has asked me to join the editorial board, arguing subtly that, since I opposed the foundation of the journal on the grounds that there weren't enough good unpublished pieces to justify a new magazine, I would be the kind of hard-headed editor they needed. It is hard to resist that kind of appeal, and I guess I'll accept, although I am already a member of the editorial boards of the *American Historical Review*, the *Journal of Contemporary History*, and a new *International Affairs Review* published at Colorado College. . . .

Tuesday, 11 April 1967. Berlin.
. . . Herzfeld came in to see me yesterday afternoon, and we had a long talk in the course of which he promised to make the Clausewitz-Gneisenau correspondence available to me so that selections from it can be used in our edition. We also talked of his projected book on Berlin politics after 1945, and he said new difficulties rise because people have forgotten the situation with the USSR at that time and make up the damnedest new hypotheses without reference to the documents. (E.g., in the USA, the new "We started the Cold War" thesis.) We agreed that the young, in particular, seem almost willfully ignorant of history, as well as very cavalier in the use of facts… In today's *Tagesspiegel*, the above clipping, which deals with the Ruling Mayor's request that the *Allgemeiner Studierendenausschuss (AStA)* [General Students' Committee] disavow the students who were arrested while making bombs to throw at Humphrey.[82] The language of the retort

---

[81] Craig was referring here to the second volume of Friedrich Meinecke's memoirs, *Straßburg, Freiburg, Berlin, 1901–1919; Erinnerungen* (Stuttgart: K.F. Koehler, 1949).
[82] The students in question were actually pranksters who planned to attack Vice President Hubert Humphrey with pudding and yoghurt, rather than bombs.

is worthy of the Stanford Student Legislature, and the reference to criticism of our Vietnam policy by other protecting powers puzzling. The whole statement reeks of argument by imputation... The *Tagesspiegel* also reprints the bulk of an editorial from *The Times* (London) with which I entirely agree. I guess we Americans can learn to be unloved, but there is always the danger of a violent backlash, which would benefit only the wrong people. . . .

Friday, 14 April 1967. Berlin.
Last evening to the U.S. Embassy for dinner and a talk about Berlin attitudes toward the U.S. Besides the ambassador, there were present [John A.] Calhoun's successor as Minister, Brewster Morris,[83] and [R.] Lyons, the cultural attaché, Senator [Werner] Stein (SPD, Bildung), Dr. Jeserich, who edits *Der Monat*, Philipp of the Osteuropa Institut, Horst Hartwich, Becker of the Law Faculty, and several other professors whose names I didn't get. The discussion was animated, ranging from the Free University *Chinesen* to Vietnam and the Oder-Neisse Line. A surprising number of those present seemed to feel that a voluntary repudiation of any claim to the Oder-Neisse lands would have a beneficial effect on Polish opinion, and that the sacrifice of a bargaining counter was not important.[84] I have doubts. No one present felt that the student disorders warranted any change in the "Berlin model." I agree. I chivvied the Germans a bit on anti-Americanism, suggesting that it was not confined in Berlin to the student left. They eagerly denied that this was so, and they may be right. . . .

There was some talk of the possibility of LBJ coming over when, as now seems likely, Adenauer dies. It would do some good, I dare say, but the President is just getting home from the Latin American Presidents Conference in Punta del Este in Uruguay, and I imagine that he has a few jobs to do in Washington... The news in general is hardly heartening—political troubles in Greece, border clashes in Korea and on the line between Syria and Israel, and the coast of Brittany being ruined by crude oil from the sunk tanker *Torrey Canyon*. The only bright note is that Chancellor [Kurt] Kiesinger has appealed to the Socialist Unity Party congress which is about to meet in East Berlin to take practical measures to ease the division of the German people and create a basis for a general

---

[83] Brewster Morris (1909–1990) was an American diplomat who served as Ambassador to Chad from 1963 to 1967. His career in the Foreign Service included postings in Germany before and after the Second World War.

[84] At this time, West Germany had not renounced its claims on its former territory east of the Oder and Western Neisse Rivers, which had been awarded to Poland after the Yalta and Potsdam conferences at the end of the Second World War.

relaxation of tension, and his message has been received without the usual ideological slanging. . . .

Wednesday, 19 April 1967. Berlin.
Konrad Adenauer died today, shortly after noon. So I never got to interview him after all, a pity, for I admired him.

Worked all day preparing for the first session of my colloquium in American history.

Thursday, 20 April 1967. Berlin.
The papers are largely given over to Konrad Adenauer today, *Die Welt* having a whole pictorial supplement, and all the others filled with editorials and feature stories. The *Frankfurter Allgemeine Zeitung* and *Tagesspiegel* leaders, I found particularly good. . . .

On my way back to my room from a morning at the Institut, I passed a large body of police gathered in one of the construction sites on Fabeck Straße near the Museum. I couldn't figure out what they were up to, but I learned from the radio this evening that the excavators have found an unexploded bomb, left over from the war… The police are being kept busy here for they were called into action last night because of a "sit-in" in the Ford-Bau called to protest the Academic Senate's decision to discipline seven of the "*sogenannte Humphrey-Attentäter* [so-called Humphrey-Assassins]."… Johnson's decision to come to Bonn for Adenauer's funeral has—since [Harold] Wilson and [Charles] de Gaulle will also be there—aroused all sorts of rumors of a Western Summit Conference. . . .[85]

Friday, 21 April 1967. Berlin.
. . . In a feature article today, *Die Welt* comes very close to saying that Adenauer was clever even in the time of his death, arranging it so that LBJ could make a European trip and by-pass Paris without causing diplomatic embarrassment, and helping overcome a coolness in German-American relations that has been growing ever since the death of John Foster Dulles…

The U.S. air force has bombed power plants in the port of Haiphong for the first time…

The left wing of the student organization at the Free University had a rare *Schlamassel* [imbroglio] in the Ford Bau yesterday, and police had to be called in. I imagine that, if this goes on, the Senate will intervene. The activists are protesting disciplinary action against the so-called "*Humphrey*

---

[85] See the entry of 11 April 1967.

Attentäter" (among other things), and they are supported by AStA, not on principle or issue, but simply because no student government these days has the guts to oppose another student group that is defying any kind of legitimate authority. . . .

Sunday, 30 April 1967. Berlin.
. . . In the evening [of Friday, 28 April] to the Herzfelds for dinner. Leschnitzers there, and I talked a bit with him about Kleist. But the conversation was pretty well dominated by the Rektor, [Hans-Joachim] Lieber, a man obviously close to the end of his strength and patience, who could talk only of his troubles with the radical students and with the *Allgemeiner Studierendenausschuss* (*AStA*) [General Students' Committee] leadership, troubles which have mounted since the Academic Senate took disciplinary measures against the Humphrey-pudding throwers. He actually intimated that, in certain circumstances, he would throw in his hand, resign, and let the Berlin *Senat* take over, which might mean the closing of the University for the rest of the semester, and would, in any event, mean the end of the "Berlin model." It is doubtful in any case that the model can stand when the great majority of students allow a fringe group of radicals to force crises by a deliberate program of misrepresentation, provocation, and flat refusal to recognize any form of authority. Because of certain features of the original constitution, it is virtually impossible to discipline trouble-makers, and the radicals are protected by AStA out of that odd solidarity of the young which prevents them from ever siding with their elders against their fellows, no matter what the latter might be doing. AStA also has as much money for publicity as the *Rektor*—indeed, the *FU-Spiegel* [Student Newspaper] has more. We may be seeing a kind of analogue to the last days of the Weimar Republic: "democracy" being used to destroy democracy because of the neutrality of the majority. There are some signs that the tide might turn against the AStA leadership. The student assemblies of the Law and Social Sciences Faculties have voted to recommend a check on AStA, but the assemblies of the Philosophical and Mathematics Faculties (after some rigging of the vote, according to Baumgart) have voted to support another sit-in when the Academic Senate has its next meeting. At the last sit-in, the *Rektor* had to call in the police, and—after some squabbling with the students and the carting out of 30 or so—the Police President called off the action for fear that a real riot might take place in the confined area of the Ford Bau, with bloodshed, etc. What will happen this time, no one can foresee. The only real hope lies in the self-mobilization of the neutrals against the people who are manipulating them... This is not

to say that the students who want reform are not right. There are lots of things that should be changed here. Harms [Kaufmann][86] and I agreed on Thursday that the Friedrich Meinecke Institut is in grave need of reform. At present, the university administration is not geared to control the separate institutes and destroy their parochialism. Lieber said the other night that, when he saw what people like Wally Sterling, Kingman Brewster, Bob Goheen, and Grayson Kirk were able to do in American universities, he was convinced that the *Rektorat* should last at least ten years. Such changes are long overdue. Sadly, however, the student leaders who are raising hell are not interested in discussing them. They simply want a row, a breaking-off relations, and a demonstration of their power. . . .

I am increasingly disturbed over the escalation of the Vietnam war (the bombing particularly), and I don't like [General William] Westmoreland's performance before Congress a bit, not because of what he said but because of what he did not say, and because the idea of his addressing Congress is not a good one. . . .

Monday, 8 May 1967. Berlin.

Wednesday evening of last week, I went in the evening to the Meinecke Institute, to sit in on a discussion of the situation in the Free University. I went to the Bar Keller and stood around for a while, but, since I was spoken to by only one student, I became uncomfortable and came home. There was at least one of my "colleagues" there, but he made no attempt to introduce himself. After three full weeks of classes, no one in the Institute, from the Director down, has made any effort to communicate with me or even to say they're glad I'm here. (I exclude Herzfeld, who is no longer active, and Stourzh at the Kennedy Institute who got in touch with me because he wanted a favor. I am fed up and doubt that I will come back to Berlin.) . . .

Friday, 2 June 1967. Berlin.

Up early and to East Berlin, where I found Georg Forster's *Briefe* [*Letters*] in a bookshop in Alexanderplatz. Also a nice two-volume edition of Ludwig Börne… Took pictures of the Marienkirche; had lunch in the *Keller* of the *Rathaus* [Cellar of the City Hall]; went to look again for the Sperlingsgasse, with odd results; then to the Gendarmenmarkt, and then, by *Strassenbahn*

---

86 Harms Kaufmann (1938–2019) studied and earned graduate degrees in history at Stanford and the Free University. He served as director of the Institute for the International Education of Students in Vienna and later worked for international development organizations.

[tram], to the general area of the Invalidenkirchhof. It took a visit to a pub, to figure how to get there, but in the end I managed and took photographs of the graves of [Gerhard von] Scharnhorst, [Hans von] Seeckt, and [Alfred von] Schlieffen (a simple plaque with his name and dates and, above, the words "I know my redeemer lives" and, below, the words "Psalm 23").[87]

Saturday, 3 June 1967. Berlin.
The Invalidenkirchhof lies hard on the Wall, and the attendant warned me against taking pictures and even advised me to put the *Fotoapparat* [camera] in my pocket. I did so, but sneaked it out a couple of times, so as to fulfill the purpose of the trip. On the way to the churchyard, I passed a handsome stone with a bronze plaque which said that here, on 23 May 1962, the Volkspolizist [police officer] Peter Göring was "murdered" while doing his duty along the Wall. The same rituals and incantations prevail on both sides of the barrier… In general, East Berlin was looking better than three years ago—lots of new buildings—the people better dressed (except for the shoes)—the young looking spruce and with hair like the young here. On the other hand, there is not much in the stores—even in *Das gute Buch*, the largest book store in East Berlin, where the books are not only few in number but dirty—and in the *Ratskeller* [city hall cellar], while the vodka and beer were in good supply (except that the latter comes only in half-liter bottles and is not cold enough), the first three things I asked for in the way of food (a ham sandwich, cold cuts, steak tartare) were unavailable, and I had to settle for a herring. . . .

Later: Little that goes on in the world these days is encouraging. The crisis in the Middle East is as dangerous as it was a week ago, and, although there is some talk of a message from Kosygin to LBJ and new Gaullist-inspired rumors of an effective French mediation, [Ahmad] Shukeiri, the head of the Palestinian Liberation Army, is openly calling for the destruction of Israel and the deportation of those Jews who survive to the countries from which they came. The Soviets have meanwhile protested sternly against damage to one of their ships by American bombing in Haiphong harbor. Along the Wall, a young East German was killed trying to escape to the West, and in front of the opera last night a student was killed, apparently by a stray bullet, in lengthy and violent demonstrations against the Shah of Persia, who had gone to hear *Die Zauberflöte* [*The Magic*

---

[87] These three men were all notable Prussian military figures.

Flute] in a closed performance.[88] Thirty-four other people were injured by stones, pieces of wood, etc. (Now the student radicals, with a martyr, are planning to push their protest further, with *Trauerzuge* [a funeral procession] with black flags today, and talk of a university-wide strike.) At home, there are riots of the hippies in New York, and doubtless in other places. Against all of this, there is little good news to cite, except the fact that the Giants are only 3½ games out of first place. Being away from one's family these days is a nervous business…

Monday, 5 June 1967. Berlin.
War in the Near East! Before I went down to breakfast this morning, the radio announced that fighting had broken out in the Negev with tanks engaged and that there have been air battles. Both sides blaming their opponents for aggression. No details…

This is an ironical footnote to the plea made by the narrator in the Piscator-Neumann version of *War and Peace* which Henry Ehrmann and I saw in East Berlin last night. Cleverly cut down to playable size (the masonic scenes and Pierre's marriage are eliminated) and beautifully produced (the battle of Borodino with toy soldiers, etc.) and acted, the whole production was a powerful argument against war—which we nevertheless have. The radio has just announced (10:30 a.m.) that Israel claims the destruction of 142 Egyptian planes (in the air and on the ground) and that Egypt says 42 Israeli planes were shot down. Israeli troops are advancing on all fronts. Syria has declared war; Jordan, a state of siege…

It will be interesting to see what effect this will have on the student movement here. Henry Ehrmann told me last night that the *Allgemeiner Studierendenausschuss* (*AStA*) [General Students' Committee] at Heidelberg had already passed a resolution two days ago, expressing sympathy for the Arabs and blaming the Jews for aggression—(Argument: imperialist lackey Israel, the tool of Wall Street and the genocidal U.S. government vs. the brave socialist Arabs)—and that a similar resolution was made here but tabled. This sickens me, and cannot but increase anti-German feeling at home and in England and France. Implicit in the argument is a covert anti-Semitism, just as, in the charges of U.S. genocide in Vietnam, there is an implicit "You see, we are not the only people who have committed mass murder." The anti-westernism of the student leadership here and in other German universities is in sharp contrast to the mood of '62 and '64, and it

[88] Craig is referring here to the murder of Benno Ohnesorg during demonstrations against the Shah.

is most disturbing in its violence and lack of reason. The picture given of policy in Vietnam is a caricature at best; nothing is said of the atrocities on the other side; and no calculation is made of the consequences of alternate courses of action...

I went down to the Kurfürstendamm on Saturday to see the "Marat-Sade," which I disliked, and walked back from the Lehniner Platz to Bahnhof Zoo afterwards. In the neighborhood of Joachimsthalersallee large crowds composed of knots of students and citizens discussing the opera business and the shooting of Benno Ohnesorg. This was impressive, but the language of the handouts was not, telling the people of Berlin that they were being duped by the Springer press and that the police were seeking to hide the fact of the student's "murder." The police have, it is true, acted less than efficiently for some weeks in confrontations with the students, and there is a marked discrepancy between the police report of the shooting and the testimony of witnesses as given in the press (even the Springer press). This will have to be resolved by a systematic investigation. But there is no breath of self-criticism in any of the student literature; no willingness to admit that demonstrations in which groups, led by people who have said publicly that Berlin needs a "happening" like the Brussels department store fire, throw rocks and bottles and tomatoes and eggs at the police and at citizens trying to enter the opera are irresponsible and are bound to lead to counter-violence.[89] The temper on both sides is ugly; the Springer press is calling for a complete purge of irresponsible elements from the University; even a moderate paper like *Spandauer Volksblatt* wrote yesterday "*Die Demokratie ist nicht die Hure pubertärer Weltverbesserer* [Democracy is not the whore of pubescent do-gooders]"; and the Berlin Senate has forbidden demonstrations of any kind, a move deplored by the *Frankfurter Allgemeine Zeitung* as provocative and unenforceable. Almost anything could happen in the University in the next few days—from a strike to a complete closing of the University.

Tuesday, 6 June 1967. Berlin.

I find, after discussion with my fellows in the Guest House, with my assistant [name omitted] and with my students, that I more and more incline to their side. The police and the city government have acted in a most fishy

[89] The "Brussels department store fire" refers to a disastrous fire at the L'Innovation department store on May 22, 1967, in which 251 people were killed. There was widespread speculation that the fire was started by anti-American protesters.

manner throughout this whole affair, and a TV program has just revealed that, at *Rathaus* Schöneberg, before the Shah's arrival, the police let two *BVG* [*Berliner Verkehrsbetriebe*, the Berlin public transit agency] buses through the barriers which then discharged pro-Shah Persians armed with clubs and pipes, who proceeded to take the initiative in several of the subsequent scraps. If the police have to rely on goons in plain clothes to do their work, things have come to a scandalous state here. Moreover, one of my students, [name omitted], whose father is a member of the Bundestag, is lying in a hospital as a result of having been hit on the head *from behind* by a policeman's club. I still think the students bear a lot of responsibility, but some of them are willing to admit this and are working hard to get through the press barrier to the public and, thus, to effect a closing of the fearful gap that has opened between students and public here. I have now signed a statement drafted by my student in the Friedrich Meinecke Institut, calling for a defusing of the situation and a complete investigation. Löwenthal and Sontheimer of the Otto Suhr Institut have also signed... The reigning *Bürgermeister* [mayor], [Heinrich] Albertz, seems to be a fool, and his "state of siege" (for that is what the *Demonstrations-verbot* [ban on demonstrations] resembles) a dangerous force. Fortunately, the Rektor Lieber had a moment of sanity and announced that the major lecture halls are open to the students for discussion. Most classes are *not* meeting this week, or meeting only to discuss the crisis. I offered my seminar students the latter opportunity today, but they decided that it would be better to use the time to distribute literature on the Ku'damm. So we signed a letter of sympathy to [name omitted] and disbanded. Thursday is a *Trauerfeier* [funeral service] for Benno Ohnesorg, and all classes are called off. Friday he will be buried in Hannover, and there will be a *Sternfahrt* [rally] to Hannover from all the German universities. . . .

In all of this brouhaha . . . the students and most of their teachers have no time to be concerned with the war in the Near East. As far as one can tell so far, the Israelis have had it all their way—winning air superiority, capturing Gaza (and most of the Palestine Liberation Army) and Jordanian Jerusalem, and driving to within 80 miles of the Suez Canal. Nasser has closed the latter to all shipping and is loudly proclaiming that British and American forces are actively engaged. That was to be expected. Let us hope he does not get the idea that he should try to drop something on the Sixth Fleet... The Russian position is not clear, although there was a hint at noon today that they might be beginning to hedge... The Soviet *Dusenjäger* [jet fighters] have been active over the city and one hears long *Booms* every hour...

Wednesday, 7 June 1967. Berlin.
The Israelis have taken Sharm el Sheik (where all the trouble began) and are within 25 miles of the Suez Canal. They are also well within Jordan. They claim to have destroyed 400 Arab planes and 250 Egyptian tanks and at Gaza, apparently, took the town and most of [Ahmad] Shukeiri's Palestine Liberation Army. Meanwhile, the Security Council has called for a cease fire. Israel has announced its willingness if the Arabs go along. The King of Jordan has already announced his readiness, after earlier ordering his troops to fight on—a sign perhaps that Jordanian resistance is nearly at an end.

Now comes the great diplomatic tugging and hauling. It is dangerous to guess what tactics the Russians will adopt, but I should think that, after arranging a cease fire, they might well demand impossible border conditions from Israel's point of view, on the specious grounds that Israel was the aggressor. This would precipitate a crisis in which the USSR would dramatically demonstrate that it was the friend of the Arabs, while testing the will of the West to stand by Israel. If the British and French craw-fished, they would have demonstrated that the Western alliance was weak. They can't expect us to cave in under such pressure, but there is always the possibility that our allies would persuade us to accept terms that would leave Israel unhappy. Meanwhile, all governments in the Near East would have been discredited, and the Soviet chance of replacing both King Hussein of Jordan and Nasser by Communists or at least by more malleable leaders would be good, since they would have pretty well done for themselves anyway. There is also a communist party in Israel that might grow as a result of Israel's disappointment. Meanwhile, all Near East governments would have broken ties with and cut off oil from the West, and the USSR would be able to take advantage of that. So a hard line might pay off richly. Almost *any* line that the Soviets take will bring them profits, for the Arabs will not admit that the Israelis have beaten them and will (as they have been doing already) blame it all on us...

The 6 p.m. news says that, as in 1956, the Egyptian soldiers are putting up no real resistance and are already throwing away their shoes and fleeing. The Israelis have also almost reached the Jordan and are trying to pinch off the Jordanian bulge. (The Nasser press is claiming now that the Israelis have won all of their victories under an American air umbrella.)

This morning, I went to a meeting at the Meinecke Institut on the Free University crisis, which turned into a discussion of a resolution drafted by 34 Meinecke students and signed by a number of *Assistenten* [Assistants] in the Friedrich Meinecke and Otto Suhr Instituten and by a number of

Ordinarien [Full Professors]—Claessens, Ehrmann, Landmann, Löwenthal, Schwan, and Sontheimer of the Suhr Institut, and—Craig of the Meinecke Institut. Some of the students said that events had by-passed this resolution; others wanted to know why the *Ordinarien* in the Meinecke Institut had not signed it. The latter were then given a laborious and quite deplorable explanation by [Heinz] Quirin of how he had signed and then withdrawn his signature because of certain formulations which he had thought were going to be changed and because he wanted to wait until the Philosophical Faculty had taken a position, etc., etc. This rambling discourse did not go down well, one student pointing out that it had taken Löwenthal only two minutes to make up his mind to sign, a remark approved by considerable drumming on desk tops. After an hour and a half, I left them to this profitless debate and went to Elwert and Meurer with some more books to be shipped home. . . .

Thursday, 8 June 1967. Berlin.

. . . This morning it was announced that Jordan had laid down its arms; this afternoon that Egyptian attempts to break out in the Sinai desert had failed with heavy losses; tonight that the Egyptian government has accepted the cease fire. All of the fine talk about the war entering a new phase and Algerian reinforcements and a fight to the end, have ended in this; and now the first rumors of a putsch against Nasser are being heard. Syria has not yet accepted the cease fire, but the Syrians have been doing more talking than fighting in any case. Still the diplomatic struggle is yet to come, and, although the USSR is in something of the position of Napoleon III in July 1866, having made the mistake of betting on a long war with favorable opportunities for mediation of a profitable kind, I should expect the negotiations for a settlement to be sticky, unless the USSR simply settles for a growth of communist party strength in the Arab lands. Israel may well prove to be the most difficult obstacle to a viable settlement in the Near East. Let's hope not…

This evening to the Harnack House where I addressed a large German audience, in German, on the subject of American foreign policy in the 60s. Lively question period afterwards; and the whole show went off well…

Today no classes again—*Trauerfeier* [Funeral service] in the Auditorium maximum for Benno Ohnesorg, after which the cortege passed through the zone (without any checking by DDR guards) on the way to Hannover, where the funeral will be held tomorrow. Thousands of students from all over Germany expected to attend. . . .

Thursday, 15 June 1967. Berlin.

At the height of the war, the USSR apparently made a new proposal on the atomic treaty to the U.S. How does one figure that?

Worked yesterday on Forster until 4, when Harms [Kaufmann] picked me up and took me to the antique shops on the Motz and Eisenach Strassen. Bought a few military lithographs, and then went to the Europa Center for a drink and [the restaurant] Die Schildkröte for dinner. Speculated on state of Red Army and particularly on its intelligence and wondered what would be the fate of the Soviet military attaché in Cairo. Agreed that it was time for the U.S. to be a bit more critical in distributing aid. It might be well to remember India's voting record in the on-going sessions of the Security Council.

Harms tells me that the result of the *Vollversammlung* [plenary meeting] in the Meinecke Institut was quite deplorable. A suggestion by one student that the professors might pay a little more attention to contemporary affairs led to wounded speeches by Berger and Dietrich and a walk-out by all the *Ordinarien.* He says it might be a good idea for me to indicate that I like to talk to students and am always at the Krug after seminar.

In this morning's mail, a contrite note from Ziebura and a letter from David Potter explaining a wire which he sent to Hartwich last week inquiring about my health. He had had a call from Ernest Gordon[90] in Princeton asking about the truth of a rumor, relayed by a Princeton professor travelling abroad, that I had died in Berlin on 1 June. Quite a flap in the History Dept. for a couple of days before a letter arrived from me dated 5 June. Then David called Phyl. . . .

Wednesday, 28 June 1967. Berlin.

This morning's paper reported that Klaus Epstein was killed in an automobile accident in Frankfurt on Monday. Only 40 years old, just about the age Jeter Isely had reached when he died in 1954. A hard blow to the historical profession and a harder one to Fritz Epstein, who was so proud of his son. . . .[91]

---

[90] Ernest Gordon (1917–2002) was Dean of the Chapel at Princeton from 1955 to 1981. Like Craig a native of Scotland and a Presbyterian, he decided on a career in the ministry while in a Japanese prison camp for three years during World War II.

[91] See Gordon A. Craig, "In Memoriam: Klaus Epstein," *Journal of Contemporary History* 3:1 (January 1968): 199–200. On the influence of Fritz Epstein (1898–1979) on Craig's generation of historians, see Carl E. Schorske, "The Refugee Scholar as Intellectual Educator: A Student's Recollections," in *An Interrupted Past: German-*

Saturday, 15 July 1967. Dublin.
Rose early and did my exercises. Breakfasted. Packed. At 11 Felix Gilbert arrived, and we talked history—first, about my Forster piece which he liked and which seems to have excited him to the point that he wants to send stuff to me about Forster and Müller.[92] He likes the idea of the book very much. We also talked about Peter Paret who now has the offer of Michael Howard's chair at London, which neither of us want him to accept. Felix thinks Princeton should make him a big offer, and I agree. Blum, of course, could never see Peter's talent—(the blindness to talent in anyone who is interested in military affairs is very widespread in America)—but Lawrence Stone, the new chairman, may have more sense. In my last lunch with Herzfeld, he expressed enthusiasm for Peter's *Yorck*, and said he was advertising it everywhere... At 11:45 Walter Simon arrived and we talked more about history—Klaus Epstein's death, Gerhard Ritter's death last week, possible replacements for Gordon Wright during his absence in Paris (Ziebura? Mellon? Douglas Johnson? etc.), how to find money to get Walter to Toronto for the Holborn do, etc. Felix left at 12, and Walter and I had a drink, and he said he has written a double review of Peter's *Yorck* and Klaus's *Conservatism*, very damning of the latter.[93] He also said he is interested in someday doing a Humboldt book. . . .

Thursday, 27 July 1967. Oban, Argyll.
We are holed up at the Park Hotel on the Esplanade and are so comfortable that we have scratched Inverness and decided to stay here until next Tuesday. It rained hard yesterday but has been lovely today. This afternoon Phyl and I took the bus to Ganavan Sands and climbed up to the head where we had a finer view of the Firth of Lorn, the Island of Mull, and the approach to Loch Etive. We have stocked up on new reading matter. Having read *Ulysses* in Dublin, I shall read *Kidnapped* here, for it was on the Isle of Mull that David Balfour came ashore after the wreck of the brig

---

Speaking Refugee Historians in the United States After 1933, ed. Hartmut Lehmann and James J. Sheehan (Cambridge: Cambridge University Press, 1991), 140–46.

92 Gordon A. Craig, "Engagement and Neutrality in Germany: The Case of Georg Forster, 1754–94," *Journal of Modern History* 41:1 (March 1969): 1–16. Forster, who died before reaching the age of forty, was a German naturalist, ethnologist, travel writer, journalist, and, toward the end of his short life, Jacobin revolutionary.

93 The books to which Craig refers here are Peter Paret's *Yorck and the Era of Prussian Reform* and Klaus Epstein's *The Genesis of German Conservatism*, both published by Princeton University Press in 1966.

Covenant... This has been a fine trip, but constantly saddened by the dreadful news of the riots in Detroit and other cities and violence that will undo much of the progress made toward better race relations in the last five years. . . . Also in the news the odd de Gaulle trip to Canada, during which Big Charlie acted in a way that indicates he has fallen prey to galloping megalomania, making speeches which combined slurs against America with encouragement to French separatists. [Canadian Prime Minister Lester] Pearson's remonstrance and his statement after de Gaulle cut his visit short and left Canada in a huff, were models of diplomatic style. . . .

Friday, 29 September 1967. Palo Alto.

. . . A most interesting talk by [William Chapman] Foster on the negotiations at Geneva and the considerable progress made toward agreement on a non-proliferation treaty (NPT) with the Russians. (We are much closer to agreement with them than with our allies, especially the Germans.) The Soviets, when they want something, seem to be able to compartmentalize their concerns; and, in response to a question from me, Foster said that they never had, in his negotiations with them on this treaty, mentioned Vietnam. Our allies' complaints about not being consulted by us (cf. the *Spiegel* story of this summer on [Kurt] Kiesinger's sharp handling of George McGhee) are, according to Foster, phony. They were repeatedly informed and consulted. He talked also of the anti-ballistic missile deployment, a disheartening business which is caused by political pressures which the administration cannot withstand... Some staff reports, including a chilling one on U.S. arms traffic: $2 billions of military items and commodities of potential military use exported in 1966. . . .

Today meetings from 9:30 to 3: more staff reports, lunch, reports from Social Science Advisory Board members about their summer activities or findings concerning arms control. We are a traveling bunch. The chairman (Erwin Griswold) had been to Africa, Australia, and New Zealand; Phil Davison to Saigon; Alice Hsieh to Japan; Urie Bronfenbrenner to Russia; Phil Mosely to France; and I to Germany. . . .

Thursday, 18 October 1967. Palo Alto.

More than a week gone by. . . . The Hoover Conference on Fifty Years of the Russian Revolution is over without my having attended any of the sessions...although I went to the Wednesday dinner and met some of the participants, including John Turkevich from Princeton and [name omitted]; I have attended three committee meetings and met all my classes, having good fun in my colloquium, where yesterday we talked communism and surrealism and composed a collective automatic surrealist poem; and I have written a review of two books on the Suez crisis for *The Reporter* (no! That I have reported already) and one of Joachim Kremarz, *Stauffenberg* for the *Canadian Review of History*.[94] My Forster piece has been taken by the *Journal of Modern History*, although I shall have to wait fifteen months to see it in print; and Felix Gilbert likes my Humboldt piece (in the Watt-Bourne *Festschrift* for Medlicott)[95] so much that he has sent me an old lithograph of Humboldt, which is now being framed... For the New Left this is anti-draft week and a lot of skulls were thumped by the police outside the Oakland Induction Center yesterday. The newspapers are filled with maudlin and hysterical letters and Robert McAfee Brown, as far as I can understand him, has come out for civil disobedience.

I am playing Tchaikovsky's *Eugen Onegin* a lot because I admire Wunderlich and Frick, and re-reading *Bleak House*. Tonight finished [George] Kennan's *Memoirs*. A very odd man! . . .

Thursday, 2 November 1967. Palo Alto.
Picked up the framed Humboldt and installed him in my study. An impressive companion for Bismarck and Schiller.

Friday, 3 November 1967. Palo Alto.
Phone call from Eugen Weber at UCLA to ask me if I would like to move there. Money no object. Declined and recommended Paret, Turner, Schroeder. Mailed corrections and additions to my essays book to Zsolnay in Vienna. Bought records of Wunderlich, Tauber, and Gerald Moore—wonderful!... Called Paret in evening and found that Weber had offered him a professorship... Planned new course for spring quarter on "The Diplomatic Revolution of Our Times."

Wednesday, 8 November 1967. Palo Alto.
Der tägliche Kram [The daily stuff]... Yesterday, a most amusing letter from Blum, revealing that his moods are my own—not surprising considering the coincidence of our ages and values... Have become quite excited about my projected course on modern diplomacy, and, last night, drafted a final examination for it; ... have become excited too about Johannes von Müller and want to do nothing but work on him. I should like to do a large piece

---

[94] Craig's review of Joachim Kramarz's book on Claus von Stauffenberg appeared in the *Canadian Journal of History/Annales canadiennes d'histoire*, 3:1 (March 1968): 126.
[95] Gordon A. Craig, "Wilhelm Humboldt as Diplomat," in *Studies in International History: Essays Presented to W. Norton Medlicott*, ed. K. Bourne and D. C. Watt (Hamden: Archon Books, 1967).

of which my talk for the American Philosophical Society would be only a part, and get the whole published in something like the *Journal of the History of Ideas* or whatever it's called.[96] If I can pull this off I shall have four essays—Schiller, Humboldt, Forster, and Müller—and will be on my way toward my book on the period 1770–1830. . . .

Thursday, 16 November 1967. Palo Alto.
This week is being largely given over to writing letters of recommendation for students—a tedious but necessary business.

This afternoon a bad-tempered departmental meeting to discuss Dean Whittaker's planned uses of Ford Foundation funds in a new policy which may seriously cut back the department's graduate program. The bad temper caused by differences over tactics. After I left, this apparently came close to name-calling. Bark, of course, speaking for himself, Miller, Bailey, and Knoles—the conservatives who will never oppose the Company. . . .

Tuesday, 21 November 1967. Palo Alto.
Lunch with Sokel who is worried by Packer Committee's attack on language requirement.[97] Talking of offers elsewhere… Later called Dick Lyman and expressed concern over lack of coordination in university policy. Too many committees; too many contradictory policies on languages, curricular reform, graduate policy, etc.

Sunday, 3 December 1967. Palo Alto.
Worked on Latin which, for some reason, I am learning. Good fun. . . .

Sunday, 10 December 1967. Palo Alto.
Making good progress with my Latin and reading an interminable novel by Fr. Spielhagen, *Problematische Naturen* [*Problematic Characters*], for the Craig/Sokel seminar. 1200 pages! Poor students. Interesting, however. Haven't read Spielhagen since I devised my own graduate course at Princeton and worked with old George Madison Priest. Spielhagen is worth an article. Maybe I'll write it sometime. . . .

[1968]

---

[96] Gordon A. Craig, "Johannes von Müller: The Historian in Search of a Hero," *American Historical Review* 74:5 (June 1969): 1487–1502.

[97] The Packer Committee was named for Herbert Packer (1925–1972), a Stanford law professor and criminal justice systems theorist who served as vice provost for academic planning and programs and received the Dinkelspiel Award for service to undergraduate education in 1969.

Monday, 15 January 1968. Palo Alto.
Lunch with Walter Sokel to talk about our seminar… At 4:15 meeting of Humanities & Sciences Faculty at which David Potter and I temporarily derailed a drive to do away with Western Civ requirement.

Wednesday 17 January 1968. Palo Alto.
The Craig-Sokel seminar started last week with a methodological discussion. Today we discussed our first novel, Raabe's *Der Hungerpastor*, and things went very well, indeed. I hope Walter will restrain himself a bit, and let the students take more of a part in what goes on, but I dare say he will. I must say his explanation of the pietism–anti-Semitism theme and the role of Jacob Boehme in the novel was masterly. The novel itself is much richer and certainly more skillfully constructed than I thought. The *Randfiguren* [marginal figures] (Felix Götz and *Der Fabrikant* [the manufacturer]) are important; the use of *Don Giovanni* to introduce the metamorphosed Moses very adroit. Socially or I should say, sociologically—quite fascinating book. . . .

Thursday, 25 January 1968. Palo Alto.
. . . Meeting of University Lectures Committee at noon. Lot of business done fast. At 3 talked to Holt Rinehart people about 3rd edition of my book. Not too far away, I'm sorry to say. At 4:15, meeting of department with Western Civilization staff on tactics to be used in next meeting of Humanities & Sciences faculty when attack is bound to be resumed. The Western Civ staff have by now carried pluralism and specialization so far, that it is difficult to argue that their course is any more "historical" in nature than other sequences in other departments and that it deserves a preferred place. Thus do the young, given their heads, cook their own goose. . . .

Wednesday, 31 January 1968. Palo Alto.
At noon meeting of the staff of the Alumni College Abroad—an enterprise that seems a bit dubious in these days when the gov't is considering restrictions on travel and when the Far Eastern situation deteriorates steadily. With fighting going on in the streets of Saigon and, indeed, in the U.S. Embassy compound, one wonders what all that build-up was for; and things are likely to get worse before they get better. . . .

Lorenz Eitner[98] told me today that the Nazis claimed that the

[98] Lorenz Eitner (1919–2009), another of the great refugee scholars whose career intersected with Craig's at Stanford, was a leading authority on the art of Théodore Géricault.

Freemasons killed Schiller by means of arsenic in his wallpaper—in short, the sort of thing that happened to Clare Luce when she was ambassador in Rome. . . .[99]

Friday, 2 February 1968. Palo Alto.

Committee meeting at noon, on curricular suggestions in International Relations. Since the University does not appear to be anxious to spend money on new appointments, it would seem to be pointless to carry on discussions of this kind. I said as much and got the approval of the others to wrap up our deliberations in a short report which will throw the ball at the administration's feet. Hard on Ivo, to whom we are an advisory committee, but there are more important things to do than this. . . .

Sunday, 4 February 1968. Palo Alto.

. . . The Craig/Sokel seminar has been going well, but it takes an enormous amount of time. I have managed to go through Balzac's *Splendeurs et misères des courtisanes* [*The Splendors and Miseries of Courtesans*] (part of my Schiller work) and to finish [André] Beaufre's book on the collapse of France this weekend, but I have been prevented from doing anything else by the necessity of re-reading Fontane's *Der Stechlin.* Not that this is not a great pleasure and one that makes me so homesick for Berlin that I made myself a steak tartare for dinner tonight… Since I stopped drinking I have got much more work done daily, but there is so much more to do, and my commitments are so great that I am not sure I am making any progress.

If this is discouraging, it pales in comparison with the news from Vietnam, where the Viet Cong are still holding half of Hue and Saigon is apparently a shambles, with public services at a standstill, food and water supply endangered, and cholera threatening. And the main Viet Cong attack still to come, presumably at Khe Sanh. In face of all this, administration statements to the effect that the Viet Cong attacks have "failed" are hardly convincing. But then neither are Dr. [Benjamin] Spock's explanations of the logic of his position, or his silence about what would happen at home and abroad if we followed his advice.[100] On this last, there is a good, but

[99] Schiller died of tuberculosis. There is nothing to substantiate the claims of the Nazis. Ambassador Luce was not intentionally poisoned by her political enemies, but rather suffered from gradual arsenic poisoning from flaking lead paint on the ceiling of her private quarters. See "Foreign Relations: Arsenic for the Ambassador," *Time* (23 July 1956).

[100] Dr. Spock had publicly called for Americans to resist conscription to fight in what he considered an unjust war.

chilling, piece by John Fischer in the current issue of *Harpers*. . . .

Saturday, 17 February 1968. Palo Alto.

Wrote the review of Woodward's book last night and went to my office this morning and typed and mailed it.[101] Found in my mail a letter from John Snell, inviting me in the name of the Modern European Section of the American Historical Association, to give the luncheon meeting address at the Chicago meeting in December. I feel that I must accept this time (having turned a similar invitation down some years ago) which will mean an even more crowded year and some changes in planning. My projected schedule now looks like this:

March: Nebraska and Missouri: "Problems of Political Leadership in World War I." Arms Control and Disarmament Agency meeting, Washington.
April: American Philosophical Society, Philadelphia: "Schiller and the Police."
May: Air Force Academy Conference: German Resistance.
June: University of California, Davis Conference: Wilsonian Democracy in Europe.
August: Stanford Alumni College (Six Lectures).
September: Arms Control and Disarmament Agency meeting, Washington.
November: Southern Historical Association Conference: "Problems of Political Leadership in WWI" (revised).
December: American Historical Association: "Johannes v. Müller and Frederick II."

What one would call a full plateful, considering the additional fact that spring quarter will be complicated with the second half of the very demanding Craig/Sokel seminar, as well as by the new diplomatic course. . . .

In the last two days have read the seventh and eighth volumes of Anthony Powell's magnificent *The Music of Time*, and have ordered all eight volumes from Blackwell's. One of the few works by a living Anglo-Saxon novelist that deserves shelf space…

Tuesday, 20 February 1968. Palo Alto.

. . . Today, after my lecture and some more [Heinrich] Mann, did what my sub-conscious has been telling me to do for some time. I resigned from the Alumni European jaunt. I have been concerned about this junket ever since LBJ began to talk about necessary travel restrictions because of the balance

---

101 Gordon A. Craig, "Soldiers and Statesmen," a review of *Great Britain and the War of 1914–1918* by Llewellyn Woodward, *The Reporter* (18 April 1968): 49–50.

of payments problem; but the thing that triggered my decision was the recent draft policy announcement. If my graduate students are going to be drafted, I don't want to be taking luxury tours… I think Gay Almond is going to follow suit…

Wednesday, 21 February 1968. Palo Alto.

A very good seminar discussion of H. Mann's *Der Untertan* [*Man of Straw*], a book that is better and more unpleasant than I remember and—in its last chapters—more expressionist than I knew. I wonder how many of the students are aware of the intensity of the Craig-Sokel competition as the session goes forward. It is never unpleasant, and I think it adds vigor and imagination to the discussions, but it is not without its comic aspects too. Academics are, as I said to Phyl last night, the vainest people in the world… In the evening, against next week's labors, read [Arthur] Schnitzler's *Leutnant Gustl* [*Lieutenant Gustl*], a remarkable piece, and began to re-read *Der Weg ins Freie* [*The Road into the Open*], while trying to keep my mind off the bloody fighting in Hue. . . .

In Fontane's *Von Zwanzig bis Dreissig* [From Twenty to Thirty] found a remarkable and quotable passage on street-fighting…

Thursday, 22 February 1968. Palo Alto.

. . . In the afternoon, drinks for Gregory Vlastos[102] and wife (just arrived from Princeton for a term at the Ford Center), the Almonds, the Potters, and Robert Rhodes-James. Pleasant. When the war was mentioned, I was surprised at the emotion with which Dorothea Almond and Dilys Potter talked about Americans killing civilians, Dilys saying she couldn't understand why the American people didn't rise up and demand an end to the war. The greater likelihood is that vox pop will demand a bigger war effort with no holds barred. If Khe Sanh should fall, which God forbid, the demand for the employment of nuclear weapons will become much stronger than it already is, and it will be very difficult to keep the war limited. Let's hope that the heavy enemy losses in this last two weeks will slow Giap down, and that our local commanders have everything they need… Troubled times. . . .

Monday, 26 February 1968. Palo Alto.

Lecture at 9: "Germany under Occupation." Lunch with Sokel. Office

---

[102] Gregory Vlastos (1907–1991) taught ancient philosophy at Princeton from 1955 to 1976, and then at the University of California, Berkeley until his retirement in 1987.

hours. Talk to Stanford-in-Germany group at 4:15. Introduced *Triumph des Willens* [Leni Riefenstahl's *Triumph of the Will*] to a large audience at 8. In between times wrote and typed a review of the Fischer book for the *Political Science Quarterly*...[103] Meanwhile, the situation in Vietnam does not improve. I can't understand why the newspapers can talk so blithely about 5000 Marines being surrounded by 40,000 Viet Cong and North Vietnamese, as if all will go well or (worse) as if it is not very important whether it does or not. In fact, the stove will go up with a vengeance if things go badly, as they can hardly help doing; and then we will be in for the whole treatment—nukes and all. Reading about the decision to resort to unrestricted submarine warfare in Fischer last night, I got the cold grues. After all, what the German soldiers and sailors were saying in January 1917 was not so very different in tone from what we have been getting from our own of late... But why hasn't Westmoreland had anything to say about Khe Sanh? He seems to have lots to say about other things. . . .

Friday, 1 March 1968. Palo Alto.
. . . Today I received a statement drawn up by Stanley Hoffmann and other members of the American Academy, calling for a settlement based on "meaningful mutual accommodations" with the Viet Cong. The statement has no smell of outrage about it, which is good, and is based firmly upon considerations of national interest. I have consistently opposed any deal with the Viet Cong, but it may be time to correct that—or, perhaps I should say, change that. I don't know. I shall have to do some thinking. . . .

Tuesday, 12 March 1968. Lincoln, Nebraska.
. . . Listened to TV report on the New Hampshire primary. Nixon very strong, against no opposition. On the Democratic side, LBJ very weak against [Senator Eugene] McCarthy, who will actually bag most of the delegates. What this means about the war is not clear, since McCarthy's views on that are not clear, and an NBC poll taken before the primaries showed a lot of the voters in NH either confused about his position or voting for him *despite* his dove-like stance for reasons other than the war. One thing is clear, however: McCarthy's stock is up, and all the eggheads in California will be delirious with joy. *Ohne mich* [Without me].

Wednesday, 13 March 1968. Columbia, MO.
. . . The news tonight is that Bobby Kennedy is re-considering his position

---

103 Craig's review of Fritz Fischer's *Germany's Aims in the First World War* appeared in *Political Science Quarterly* 84:4 (December 1969): 700–702.

with respect to the presidential sweepstakes. He has flown back to New York to consult with advisors! An unprincipled man. . . .

Monday, 18 March 1968. Palo Alto.
. . . Afterwards . . . [we] drove home, listening as we did while some smart newspapermen on the *Meet the Press* program made mincemeat of Bobby Kennedy who has just declared that he will run for the presidency but is trying to con the country into believing that he will do his best to help Senator McCarthy too. Help him right into the wilderness no doubt. . . .

Sunday, 31 March 1968. Palo Alto.
Today, the President announced (1) a unilateral de-escalation of the war (no bombing except north of the DMZ) and (2) his decision not to run again. I am glad of the first decision and sorry over the second—sorry because I cannot see another candidate. My first reaction concerning political repercussions is that this will kill Kennedy, but that may be wishful thinking. It may stop Nixon, or at least inspire some new activity in the Rockefeller and Reagan camps. It is—as *every* commentator on TV has said—a whole new ball game. . . .

Thursday, 4 April 1968. Palo Alto.
Martin Luther King was shot and killed in Memphis this evening. God help the Republic!

Saturday, 13 April 1968. Palo Alto.
[The birth of a grandchild] was the only really good news in the last dreadful ten days in which the nation has seen rioting and widespread arson in Washington, Chicago, Kansas City, Baltimore, Newark, Trenton, Pittsburgh, and Cincinnati, and in which the shock wave has now spread to Germany where a madman, inspired by King's murderer, has seriously wounded Rudi Dutschke[104] of the *Sozialistische Deutsche Studentenbund* [Socialist German Student League] and touched off serious disorders in Berlin, Munich, and Frankfurt. Mercifully, the cities of California (as well as New York, Philadelphia, and Boston) have been spared. Not that our campus has been unaffected. The killing of King prompted the Black Student Union (BSU) to formulate a series of demands (doubling black

---

[104] Rudi Dutschke (1940–1979) was a radical left-wing leader of the Socialist German Student League and the extra-parliamentary opposition to the government of the Federal Republic. He was badly injured in the assassination attempt in 1968 and, although he was able to resume his political activities, he suffered from health issues for the rest of his life.

student admissions, increasing number of Negroes on faculty, investigation of certain alleged instances of discrimination, and the like) which they presented in an ultimative fashion in a mass meeting in which they seized the microphone from the Provost, Dick Lyman, while he was in the middle of a speech. He kept his cool, in the modern parlance; and so did the administration in general, jockeying the BSU to a negotiating position and reaching an agreement which gave them virtually everything they wanted but in a way that did not jeopardize the University's decision-making power or its control over admissions. What the University is giving, it should, I am sure, give, but it will cost a lot. Doubling black admissions next fall and starting a pilot program for people who do not meet our normal standards (10 from minority groups next year) will cost something like $1–2 million, which we do not presently have. Still, we can probably get it. We shall also have to build into our system something like a dispersed junior college to handle the new customers effectively without hurting general standards. This won't be easy, but it can be done without too great effort, and in ten years it may pay off handsomely. Meanwhile, the very fact that we are doing it will have a favorable effect and may stimulate action on the part of institutions who can take care of greater numbers than we, as a private institution, can.

On the whole, the University has handled itself well, Lyman particularly who daily looks more like the logical successor to Sterling. Depressing are the intimations of a coming white backlash on the part of alumni and the abundant evidence of overreaction and emotionalism on the part of many of my colleagues and many students. The latter resembles an "*amour de la boue*," a visceral satisfaction in guilt and atonement, an undignified scramble to demonstrate to our black brothers that we will invite abuse and excuse it. When the Academic Council was asked to vote on the President's announcement concerning the new black admissions policy and the pilot program, one of my colleagues insisted that this seemed to indicate that this was *all* we were going to do, and another proposed that these concessions be specifically labelled as "minimal." When Jim Gibbs, a pleasant black anthropologist, made a short speech, my colleagues felt called upon to applaud, although he had spoken only good sense and although applause is not, and should not, be a part of meetings of this kind. Overreaction is, I suppose, an American trait, and emotional responses to political matters an intellectual one; but it is difficult to take any pleasure in manifestations of these truths.

In the midst of all this, it was not easy to carry on normal activities. I insisted on doing so, and, indeed, for my new experimental course in 20th-century diplomacy, it would have been disastrous if I had not done so. I also managed to get my piece for the American Philosophical Society written (I have today finished the revision) and it is in good shape.

Yesterday and today were Days of Concern on the campus with any number of public meetings (addressed, in one instance, by that howling ass Roger Hilsman) and smaller seminars. Last night I went to Fremont House and, together with Dick Lyman, Sid Drell of the Stanford Linear Accelerator Center,[105] and a very intelligent man from Harvard Business School, carried on a discussion of the theme "The University as a Public Arena." I took the occasion to say a few things about [the Free University in] Berlin as a horrible example of what can happen to a good university when it becomes too much so. . . .

Tuesday, 7 May 1968. Palo Alto.

. . . Here we're now caught up in a situation as potentially distracting as the troubles that disrupted my seminar in Berlin last year—a dispute over judicial procedure complete with sit-in at the Old Union and mass meetings on every side. (Last night Dick Lyman tried to plead for reason at Memorial Auditorium; tonight there are marathon speeches at the Old Union.) The only good feature of the affair (and it may not last) is that none of the violence or brutishness that have led to the closing of Columbia is present here. On the other hand, the leaders of the Students for a Democratic Society (especially [name omitted], a former lieutenant of Mario Savio) are real pros and are attempting to infect the students as a whole with the idea that Lyman is not to be trusted. I lunched today at the Ford Center with Cohen of Chicago, Gregory Vlastos of Princeton, and Meredith Wilson. Meredith said Lyman is in a parlous position and that he could end up as did David Truman at Columbia, with his future usefulness destroyed. . . .

Tonight, after dinner, we visited the sit-in and—among others—heard Gavin Langmuir[106] and Walter Meyerhoff of the faculty plead for moderation, without visible effect. . . .

Thursday, 9 May 1968. Palo Alto.

---

[105] Sidney Drell (1926–2016) was a professor of theoretical physics at the Stanford Linear Accelerator Center (SLAC) and a senior fellow at the Hoover Institution. For more than half a century, he was one of the principal American experts on arms control and nuclear nonproliferation issues.

[106] Gavin Langmuir (1924–2005), who taught at Stanford from 1958 until his retirement in 1993, was a preeminent authority on medieval anti-Semitism.

Yesterday afternoon a marathon 3½ hour meeting of the Academic Council in which, by a vote of 285 to 240, we gave amnesty to the Central Intelligence Agency protesters whose trials and sentences had led to the present sit-in, as well as to the sit-in-ers, and moved toward a new judicial system. Vote was carried by the Humanities & Sciences and Medical Faculties, the Business and Law Schools voting almost solidly against the resolutions which . . . replaced the rather uninspiring and rigid administration formula. Sterling delicately, Lyman and Whittaker angrily, protested that the action was a repudiation of the administration, which annoyed people and will seriously hurt Lyman's chances to become President of this university. Of the history faculty, Potter, Smith, and Lederer voted No, the rest of us Yes, except for those like Vucinich who carefully stayed away.

After the meeting the sit-ins cleaned and cleared the building. Today, at a meeting in White Plaza, the Students for a Democratic Society (SDS) leaders indicated clearly that they will act again when an occasion presents itself and that their ultimate targets are the university charter, the hierarchical principle, the system of tenure, etc. This was always clear, although it seems to daunt some people who voted Yes yesterday, who feel outraged at some of the careful sneers directed at them by [name omitted] at today's meeting. But the important thing is that we have prevented another Columbia situation by yesterday's vote and taken away the SDS's following, who will not support radical demands of the kind mentioned today—unless another administration mistake gives an opportunity for uniting the students again. We can't predict what will happen as a result of our Yes vote yesterday; but I am sure that the result of a No vote was predictable.

In any case the rest of the term should be quiet. . . .

Friday, 10 May 1968. Palo Alto.

. . . In the evening to Ivo Lederer's where I found [name omitted] of Yale and Walter Sokel. Talked about the Student Revolt as everyone does these days. It's like being back in Berlin. . . .

Thursday, 23 May 1968. Palo Alto.

Lunch in honor of James Reston, who is speaking here tonight. In discussion of student affairs, I rather shocked my host, Freddy Glover and others like Bob Walker by arguing that so far the Movement has helped this university and that, to this extent, the SDS deserves credit. Freddy made it clear to me afterwards that I needed to be educated and said he would send me some materials that would start the process. . . .

Tuesday, 4 June 1968. Palo Alto.
Election day. Tonight, after claiming victory over McCarthy in the Democratic presidential primary, Senator Robert F. Kennedy was shot and seriously wounded by a young man in his 20s…

Wednesday, 5 June 1968. Palo Alto.
A depressing day. Kennedy holding on to life barely after a three-hour operation to remove fragments of the bullet from his brain. Condition "extremely critical." The assassin is a young Jordanian born in Jerusalem and in this country since 1957. Apparently hates Jews and may have been inflamed by recent Kennedy statements about necessity of our doing something for Israel… Hard to do business as usual but held my classes even so. Good seminar on Günter Grass… In last days no other serious work. No energy for anything but doodling (whippling) on green paper…

Thursday, 6 June 1968. Palo Alto.
Phyl woke me with the news that Kennedy had died during the night. So to class—the final session of the diplomatic course. . . .

Saturday, 29 June 1968. Palo Alto.
The term ended successfully as far as courses were concerned. The final papers in the diplomatic course were better than I expected them to be, and some of them (one, especially, by a transplant from Princeton called [name omitted], who will do honors work with me, so excellent that I passed it and the course plan on to Dean Sears to show him what we're up to these days). The Craig-Sokel seminar, at a student's request, had an extra session, during exam week, to go into some of the theoretical questions passed over in our consideration of the novels… Much time spent on my *Doktoranden* [doctoral candidates], rushing to finish up their dissertations… Even more time spent in AAUP [American Association of University Professors] meetings, which eventuated in the committee [on Governing the University] listed below in an article about two weeks ago in the *Palo Alto Times*.[107] This group has met four times since then and promises to go on meeting twice a week all summer. Although they are presently proceeding on an agenda which I drew up, out of sheer desperation over the inconsequence of the first discussions, I do not think I have the patience to go to all, or even most, of the projected meetings. . . .

The two weeks that have passed since have been devoted, as much as

---

[107] Craig pasted the undated article, "Stanford professors name study committee," from the *Palo Alto Times* into his diary here.

possible, to Heinrich von Kleist and I am trying to finish my New Orleans paper on him before the end of the month, which is just about here. . . .

Sunday, 7 July 1968. Palo Alto.
. . . [After a family trip to San Francisco] Home by 4 and off to my office to get my mail and to take a look at Wally Sterling's office, burned out, apparently by political activists, early Friday morning…

Since then reading back issues of the *Journal of Modern History*, to catch up with what has been going on in the world of scholarship in the past two years. Not a hell of a lot, apparently. . . .

Thursday, 23 July 1968. Palo Alto.
Finished review of Kennan's *From Prague after Munich* for the *Virginia Quarterly Review*…[108] Saw Carl Spaeth about the possibility of a grant for 1969–70 to supplement sabbatical. Looks good… Yesterday another meeting of the American Association of University Professors committee on governance of university—this time with some students to give us their views, which were odd. One little girl said in effect that she couldn't respect *any* faculty member who didn't feel as she did about public issues (by which she apparently meant Vietnam, but may have meant Huey Newton, legalized abortion, and Heavens knows what else as well). A bearded chap seemed to feel that Stanford could not be a respectable university unless it closed its Business School; and there was a lot of fuzzy talk about the distraction of faculty energies towards the professional associations, rather than the university. Not very helpful.

Friday, 26 July 1968. Palo Alto.
Letter from Peter Paret with some good criticisms of my Kleist piece, which I have already written once but which needs more work.

In an article by A. William Salomone in the current *American Historical Review*, found the following passage from a letter of George Ticknor[109] written from Rome in Feb. 1837 to his friend, Richard Dana:

> The odd principles that gave life and power to society are worn out; you feel on all sides a principle of decay at work, ill-counteracted by an apparatus of government very complicated, and very weary and annoying. The wheels are multiplied, but the motion is diminished,

---

[108] Gordon A. Craig, "Dispatches from Czechoslovakia," *Virginia Quarterly Review* 44:4 (Autumn 1968): 664–65.

[109] George Ticknor (1791–1891) was an American Hispanist and professor of belles-lettres at Harvard.

> the friction increased; and the machinery begins to grow shackling at the moment when the springs are losing their power, and when nothing but firmness can make it hold out. Indeed, almost everywhere, when you come in contact with the upper classes of society...you find weakness, inefficient presumption, and great moral degradation; and when you come to those who are the real managers of the world, you find them anxious about the future, temporizing, and alternately using an ill-timed spirit of concession or an ill-timed severity. The middling class, on the other hand, is growing rich and intelligent, and the lower class, with very imperfect and impractical knowledge, is growing discontented and jealous.

Tickner was talking about Europe, but some aspects of his description fit our own case in 1968. I'm tired of hearing people say our society is sick, but I wish the healthy elements would get a bit better organized.

Reading Rathenau's *Tagebücher* [Diaries] which I must review for the *Political Science Quarterly*. . . .[110]

Saturday, 10 August 1968. Asilomar.

Slept late, and breakfasted in our room. A lot of reading; the second volume of Bertrand Russell's memoirs; Jünger's *Strahlungen* [*A German Officer in Occupied Paris*] (filled with interesting details about the resistance in Paris and showing how the dreamlike atmosphere of *Marmorklippen* [*On the Marble Cliffs*] was Jünger's customary state by 1952, caught in a world of *Lemuren* [lemurs] and Mauretanian ideologues); and the first book of Pliny's letters, in which I found an excellent motto which could be hung in our dining room: "*Potes apparatius coenare apud multos, nusquam hilarius simplicius incautius.*" [You can have a very elaborate meal with lots of people. Nothing is more convivial, simpler, easier.]

To get back to Jünger, there are some fine *aperçus* on literature, much interesting matter on dreams, and not a little usable material on the [Carl-Heinrich von] Stülpnagel-[Hans] Speidel group.[111] Jünger was more a part of the resistance than I had known, although his activities seem to have been pretty well restricted to keeping an account of the conflict between the army and the party and preparing a paper on how to attain peace (which he seems to have destroyed). His reflections on Nazism are always cast in

---

[110] For Craig's review of Walter Rathenau's *Tagebuch, 1907–1922*, see *Political Science Quarterly* 86:1 (March 1971): 148–49.

[111] Stülpnagel and Speidel were German officers in occupied France who were involved with the July 20th resistance plot to assassinate Hitler.

the general, rather than the particular form. Of Hitler (Kniebolo, as he calls him, and once the Head Forester) he says that his career reflects the truth of what a theologian told a friend of his, namely that "*Das Böse erscheint zunächst als Luzifer, um sich dann in Diabolos zu verwandeln und als Satanas zu endigen.*" [Evil first appears as Lucifer, then turns into the Devil and ends up as Satan.] . . .

Tuesday, 13 August 1968. Palo Alto.
Seventh anniversary of the building of the Wall…

Since our return I have been reading the second volume of Jünger's *Strahlungen* (the Paris diaries for 1943 and 1944). More details about the Paris center of the resistance, and a lot of interesting stuff about dreams, which fascinate Jünger. The striking note throughout is the pronounced anti-democratic tone, the constant lament for the old *Ritterschaft* [knighthood] now overtaken by the *Pöbel* [rabble]. I had not realized that [Ernst] Niekisch was the acknowledged leader of the circle to which Jünger belonged in 1929. Much about N, who disappeared into the *KZ* [concentration camps] in 1934. . . .[112]

Wednesday, 14 August 1968. Palo Alto.
Finished Jünger last night. Odd man. Aside from expressing a sense of shock over Stülpnagel's fate after 20 July 44 (and that is almost formal in tone), his only remark about the failure of the conspiracy is that he had always disbelieved in the efficacy of political assassination and had made this clear in the figure Sunmyra in *Die Marmorklippen*…

Reading the second volume of Bertrand Russell's autobiography with great enjoyment despite my reservations about the late antics of the old boy. Filled with perceptive or amusing remarks. Thus, from a letter to his brother from prison in July 1918: "He [Mirabeau on his death bed] illustrates the thesis…that all unusual energy is inspired by an unusual degree of vanity. There is just one other motive: love of power. Philip II of Spain and Sidney Webb of Grosvenor Road are not remarkable for vanity." Or, talking about his nearly fatal illness in China in 1920/21: "I was told that the Chinese said they would bury me by the Western Lake and build a shrine to my memory. I have some slight regret that this did not happen, as I might have become a god, which would have been very *chic* for an atheist."

---

[112] Niekisch was arrested in 1937 and remained in captivity until 1945. For Craig's most extensive treatment of the long-lived First World War memoirist and idiosyncratic right-wing intellectual Ernst Jünger (1895–1998), see his essay "Insouciance," *London Review of Books* (17 July 1997): 18–19.

Later: Finished the Russell and began Helmut Böhme's source book *Die Reichsgründung* [*The Foundation of the German Empire*], which (with his larger volume *Deutschlands Weg zur Großmacht* [Germany's Path to Great Power Status]) is attracting, it seems to me, more attention than it deserves. Both books say what has been well known for a long time: namely, that German history has been too Prussian and too Bismarck-oriented, and that social history has been overlooked. But [Otto] Pflanze has written an article to suggest that this is as important a piece of revisionism as Fischer's book. Odd... The source book has some nice things in it, including a letter of Burckhardt written at the end of 1872 and commenting on the "*siegerdeutsch*" [Victorious German] character of German history writing. But, writes B., he stopped reading German historians after Gervinus anyway. . . .

Monday, 19 August 1968. Palo Alto.
It was announced today that the new president of Stanford will be Kenneth Pitzer, a chemist and for the last seven years or so, president of Rice University. . . .[113].

Tuesday, 20 August 1968. Palo Alto.
Student flak against the Pitzer appointment. The student president and the editor of the *Stanford Daily* have decided that, because they were not consulted, he is an "unknown entity." No mention of his record as a chemist or anything else. . . .

Later: The news arrived, just as Rep. Phil Burton of California thought he was going to put the boot to Secretary Rusk before the Democratic Platform Committee, that the Soviet Union, Poland, and East Germany had sent troops into Czechoslovakia. All the doves caught with egg on their faces. They will rally and say that this happened only because of our Vietnam involvement. Something in that, of course. But what becomes of all the talk about how fear of communism is foolish and how the Cold War, if not an illusion, is a thing of the past... Galbraith sounded a bit disarticulated on TV tonight. I can hardly wait to hear McCarthy and McGovern...

Thursday, 22 August 1968. Air Force Academy, Colorado.
Got to Denver at 5:30 yesterday evening where I was met by a staff car and an escort officer. . . . Much talk on the way to the base about the situation

---

[113] Kenneth Pitzer (1914–1997), a distinguished scientist known for his work on the thermodynamic properties of molecules, was the sixth president of Stanford University, serving from 1969 to 1971. Frustrated by the student protests of that turbulent era, he resigned after a tenure of nineteen months.

in Czechoslovakia. I had been awakened early this morning by Stanford's PRO people wanting my opinion about effects of the crisis on the German situation. My answer was that I figured that Ulbricht had played a big part in the Russian switch-over and that we had better bite our thumbs in the hope that this will not bring another Berlin shove of some kind. The latest issue of *Spiegel*, which I read on the plane, says that the Berliners are remembering '48 and '58 and are scared of '68, and that [West Berlin] Mayor [Klaus] Schütz is telling Kiesinger to call off projected meetings in Berlin of the Bundestag and its committees to avoid needless provocation of the Russians. . . .

Friday, 23 August 1968. Denver.
. . . In between business spending my time listening to TV news from Prague and Chicago. General strike and some shooting in the former; a cry from the Texas delegation in Chicago that, if the Platform Committee or Rules Committee abolishes the unit rule, it will nominate LBJ…[114] Grayson Kirk has resigned as President of Columbia University…

A hard thing to predict is the way in which youth in this country will react to the Czech coup. Some, hopefully, will see in it proof that the Cold War is not dead, that Communists are ruthless, and that the fight for freedom in Vietnam is not phony. Many, however, will probably use the Russian attack as another stick to beat their own government, taking their lead from Senator McCarthy, who said plainly the other day that the U.S. had no business protesting the Russian action, because we had disqualified ourselves by our actions in Cuba, Santo Domingo, and Vietnam. If the latter becomes the prevalent view I am afraid of the future. . . .

Monday, 26 August 1968. Palo Alto.
. . . The Democratic Convention got underway tonight. It promises to be more interesting than the Republican one. A pity that the Yippies etc. have made Chicago look so much like Prague…

Tuesday, 27 August 1968. Sacramento.
. . . Spent the evening listening to the credential fights at the Convention, but went to bed before the debate on the Vietnam plank began, there being

---

[114] The unit rule, which had been practiced up until this time by the Democratic Party, required that the votes of individual state delegations at National Conventions be cast as a unit. At the 1968 Democratic National Convention, delegates voted to do away with the unit rule, over the vocal objections of Texan and other southern state delegations, which had used the rule as a means to marginalize Democratic legates in favor of racial integration.

no prospect of a vote before the small hours of the morning... In Czechoslovakia, the much heralded victory of Swoboda and Dubĉek has turned out to be a capitulation; and the population is reacting with protest and violence. The Russians, having left for the moment, are back in the heart of Prague and Bratislava, and there is shooting...

Thursday, 29 August 1968. Sacramento.
...In the evening listened to the broadcast of the Democratic Convention, satisfied enough with the nomination of Hubert Humphrey but appalled by the violence in the streets. After all the talk of the long hot summer, it materialized only here at this awkward point in the history of the democratic process...

Friday, 30 August 1968. Clear Lake.
Left Sacramento about ten in the morning yesterday. Very hot. Drove west across the mountains to Clear Lake, where we had reserved a suite at the Stillwood Resort, just north of Lakeport. Had a quiet afternoon, a drink on the lake front, a swim, and, in the evening, the Democratic Convention again. Muskie of Maine was nominated for the vice-presidency, a good choice. Both acceptance speeches excellent. Among the deplorable aspect of last night's convention, it is difficult to decide which was worse: the planned demonstration in honor of Mayor Daly; the indignation of the chairman of the Wisconsin delegation, who decided to walk from the hotel to the convention hall as a protest against the police measures against the demonstrators and who invited others to join him, including a lot of clergymen, when he was stopped by the police for leading a march; the amateurness of the vice-president of the Wisconsin delegation and Al Lowenstein of the New York delegation, who nominated Julian Bond for the vice-presidency and worked up a great show of indignation because they were not allowed to have any seconding speeches—all apparently in complete ignorance of the fact that Bond was too young to qualify for such nomination; the sentimentality of the Florida delegate on the previous night who kept talking about what the police were doing downtown to "the children," many of whom were thirty years old; the childishness of the chairman of the New Hampshire delegation who got into trouble with the police when he stuck a Dartmouth College identification card, rather than his delegate's badge, into the admission machine (in some obscure demonstration of outraged principle), and, in the ensuing fracas, bit a police officer; the self-righteousness of twenty members of the Wisconsin delegation who, throughout last evening's proceedings, sat in their places

reading books or (according to their own report) praying; or the bad grace of Eugene McCarthy, who didn't come to last night's proceedings at all. God save the Republic from such as these. . . .

Friday, 6 September 1968. Palo Alto.
A week largely devoted to meetings of the American Association of University Professors Committee, which makes dangerous progress slowly and absorbs two or three hours a day. . . .Wrote Simon and Schuster that I must give up idea of Dulles book and sent back advance. . . .

Monday, 9 September 1968. Palo Alto.
Spent from 1:30 to 7:30 in Owen House beating out final American Association of University Professors report. . . .

Tuesday, 10 September 1968. Palo Alto.
Three-hour meeting with Bob Glaser, the acting president, and Ken Pitzer, the new one, going over our report. No substantial objections. At 12 went to club and, working as we ate, finished the report by 2. It will now be processed and sent to the membership. . . .

Wednesday, 18 September 1968. Palo Alto.
To Washington on the 10:20 plane on Monday evening. Slept a little, had breakfast at the Roger Smith, and slept till 1 p.m. when I dressed and went to the State Dept. for the meeting of the Social Science Advisory Board to the Arms Control and Disarmament Agency. Phil Mosely, Phil Davison, Bill Capron, Abe Bergson (visiting professor at Stanford this year, who came in on an earlier plane), and Morrie Janowitz on hand. Interesting briefing by [William Chapman] Foster, happy because the Nuclear Proliferation Treaty got out of the Senate Foreign Relations Committee earlier in the day. He was reasonably confident that if it came to a vote, the Senate would advise and consent to ratify; but he feared that a filibuster on the [Abe] Fortas appointment as chief justice might intervene and make a vote impossible before the recess. This would surely make for trouble with West Germany, Italy, and India who would all drag their feet… We also talked about the Soviet action in Czechoslovakia which has caused this threat to the treaty. I asked Foster whether the Soviets were not aware of the consequences for the treaty of their action, and he said that, as far as he could see, there was a complete disarticulation between the political and military aspects of the action. He says that no political preparations had been made beforehand; the troops simply banged in and then were uncertain as to what came next. No one even knew—or seemed to know—where the TV and radio stations were… At the end of the day's session, we

were invited to cocktails at Archie Alexander's place in Georgetown in honor of our former chairman Erwin Griswold (now Solicitor General of the United States) and Mr. Foster. . . .

Friday, 20 September 1968. Palo Alto.
Afternoon meeting of the American Association of University Professors. More niggling criticisms, more flinching away from police issue, some sweeping demands that we take a firm stand against the U.S. gov't on the draft, Vietnam, etc.

Wednesday, 25 September 1968. Palo Alto.
First day of classes. Lecture on basic tendencies in German history and opening session of my colloquium on intellectuals and politics since 1914. . . .

Wednesday, 9 October 1968. Palo Alto.
Lecture and seminar. In the evening—with Jan Triska, Gay Almond, Wayne Vucinich, Philip Rhinelander, and Bertram Wolfe—spoke about situation in Czechoslovakia. Large audience (in excess of 200) and all speeches good (Wolfe's, however, a bit long). Afterwards, with Wayne, to Anatole Mazour's for a beer.

Friday, 11 October 1968. Palo Alto.
. . . Earlier at lunch in the Red Cottage talked about the period 1798–1815 with Herb Mann and Peter Paret. Peter likes the Kleist revision, which I shall now send off to *Central European History*...[115] Today learned that my Forster essay will appear in the March number of the *Journal of Modern History*. This morning oral examination of a young man named [name omitted] who did very well, indeed. Exam chaired by Leo Weinstein of the French department whom I offended unintentionally by saying that positivism was the dullest of all philosophical movements for the student. He has been working on [Hippolyte] Taine for years...

At the McLean dinner last evening Sworakowski was willing to bet me $100.00 that the Russians would take Albania within fifteen months. . . .

Tuesday, 22 October 1968. Palo Alto.
. . . The Müller piece is beginning to take shape. I got an idea in the Court House pub on Friday that may pan out—comparing what the historian thought [of] his heroes with what the heroes thought of the historian... A

---

[115] See Gordon A. Craig, "German Intellectuals and Politics, 1789–1815: The Case of Heinrich von Kleist," *Central European History* 2 (March 1969), 3–21.

lot of letters, recommending young men for jobs, and a lot of recommendation forms... Tomorrow I lecture on the Battle of Königgrätz, with maps. It will reinforce the Prussian officer image, I'm afraid... Letter from Blum. He is as atrabilious about the young faculty and the New Left as I am. . . .

Thursday, 24 October 1968. Palo Alto.
A chance to bring Peter Paret into the department missed because of administrative difficulties and opposition on the part of certain dept. members to the Reserve Officers' Training Corps (for which he would give courses) and, in addition, priority difficulties—it being important here, as everywhere, to get a *black* historian to teach Afro-American history. Too bad. We could have had the strongest department in Central European history in the country. He will now go to the University of Pennsylvania. . . .

Thursday, 31 October 1968. Palo Alto.
Another department meeting, this time voting to let university pay for an Afro-American historian from Coe money (a possibility that Howie Brooks dropped in my ear last night and which I passed on). This means that it would not affect our priorities. Department then voted to go for Paret plus an asst. professor in medieval history (a deal Gavin Langmuir jumped at after I had suggested as an alternative a senior medievalist and an asst. professor for diplomatic history. Gavin wants no medievalist who will outrank him). We may get Peter after all.

Friday, 1 November 1968. Palo Alto.
A suggestion from the Dean's Office that money may be forthcoming for our objectives... In the afternoon, a meeting of the subcommittee of the Liaison Committee. Inconclusive. . . .

Wednesday, 6 November 1968. Palo Alto.
Sat up last night until 4 watching the cliff-hanger, went to bed with the issue in doubt, and rose at 7 just in time to hear, first California and then Illinois given to Nixon, enough to put him over in the Electoral College. We are at least spared what we might have had, an election settled in the House of Representatives. That would have been disastrous, but—even so—four years of Nixon—and Agnew! And all because of a lot of s.o.b.s who, to indulge their sense of self-righteousness, sat out the election. I'll never be able to take Robert McAfee Brown seriously again, after reading a letter of his in the *Stanford Daily* which, in my view, advocated a cop-out. That is perhaps not the only reason Humphrey lost, but it is not a negligible one... To my office and then to lecture hall to speak extemporaneously about

Bismarck's post-1870 diplomacy. . . .

Sunday, 10 November 1968. Palo Alto.
Just before we left for the airport, George told me he was empowered to make a hard offer to Peter Paret, and I talked with Peter who is very happy. . . .

Sunday, 24 November 1968. Palo Alto.
A busy week, the last one of my lectures in 19th century German history and complicated by a dinner and seminar in comparative literature given by a chap named [Geoffrey] Hartman from Yale, who is being looked over, and even more so by a blitz I am conducting in the Dean's Office to hurry up the Appointments and Promotions Committee's action on Peter Paret's appointment. The latter part of the week—while Phyl was in the east—was given over to Wayne Vucinich's conference on "Nationalism and Communism in Eastern Europe." I opened this on Sunday evening by chairing the first session which was addressed by Hugh Seton-Watson. A lot of nice people on hand—including Mike Petrovich of Wisconsin, Emanuel Turczynski of Munich, and William E. Griffith of M.I.T.—and some good parties. . . .

Today—rather this evening—I spoke at Trinity Episcopal Church in Menlo Park on the student movement. Good audience…

De Gaulle has refused to devalue the franc, one in the eye for the speculators. Question is whether he can get away with it. . . .

Thursday, 12 December 1968. Palo Alto.
Lunch with [names omitted] to discuss possible congress on world youth movements… In the afternoon and evening read the final exercises of my colloquium. The theme: a 1968 *Magic Mountain*; the results lugubrious (alienation, Vietnam, drugs, race relations, etc.) but in at least four cases ingenious. A good enough average… James Reston has written an interesting piece in the *Times* in which he talks about M.I.T.'s failure to take Walt Rostow back as a denial of academic freedom. Judging by the spurious arguments put up by *our* economists when the possibility of Walt was raised, he is right. Hardly an example to encourage national service. . . .

Saturday, 28 December 1968. New York.
Called at 7. Room service running 45 minutes behind. Drank ginger ale and read the papers by Robert Kann and [name omitted] on dissolution of Austria-Hungary and reshaping of Central Europe in 1918/19. At 9:15 started for conference room. Elevators so crowded barely made it in time. Piotr Wandycz, the commentator, had some trouble and was late. Started

session without him, but saw with relief that he was with us within five minutes. Session a good one, despite Robert Kann's heavy Austrian manner and [name omitted]'s imitation of an inhabitant of the *Zauberberg* [*Magic Mountain*] in the penultimate stage. Audience coughed and sneezed every time he did. What the wags are calling "Mayor Daley's Revenge" seems to be claiming dozens of victims, and I expected the stretcher bearers to arrive at any moment. Even so, session went along and the floor discussion was lively. . . .

Sunday, 29 December 1968. New York.
Up early. Drank a coke and worked over my paper on Johannes von Müller. At 11 to Doug Unfug's room for a meeting of editorial board of *Central European History*—Pat Hale, [Otakar] Odlozilik, [Theodore] Hamerow, Kann, and I only ones on hand, both Holborn and B. Schmitt in a bad way—the former having suffered a stroke, the latter an amputation and emphysema at the same time… At 12:30 to the Grand Ballroom for the luncheon of the Modern European Section. Only about 200 on hand—most disappointing. Perhaps my subject the reason, perhaps the price of lunch (I had to pay $6 to hear myself), perhaps flu and absenteeism. After business meeting and a rather silly introduction by Lynn Case, and while the dishes were still rattling, I gave them Johannes von Müller. Good reception and much complimented after… To bar with Lew Hertzman to discuss some business and then to my room to rest… At 5 to the Grand Ballroom again, this time for the Stanford Smoker which I had arranged. A good turnout . . . after which we came back to the Princeton and Yale Smokers. The former was dull, but at the latter I found Wolfgang Mommsen and Ernst Nolte and had a good talk with them. . . .

Monday, 30 December 1968. New York.
Up at 6:30 and down the elevators at 7 and by cab to Westside Air Terminal, the driver delightedly telling me on the way that another Brink's truck had been hijacked in Boston to the tune of half a million dollars. Left my bags and walked across town to 42nd and 6th where I had a large breakfast at the 42nd St. Cafeteria, one of my long-time New York favorites. Walked up to 53rd in the chance that the Museum of Modern Art might open at 9. No dice. Back down 5th, admiring the Christmas Decorations and the girls. Very cold. Admired the wearers of mini-skirts. Went to [the Hotel] New Yorker and heard four queer papers in a session on Psychology on History

chaired by Stuart Hughes. Fellow named Binion[116] drove me up into the trees. Thence to tag end of session on relations between Commander-in-Chief and Chief of the General Staff (Wilson-Pershing / FDR-Marshall) where I said hello to Forrest Pogue and Jay Luvaas and talked with Trumbull Higgins, who gave me a copy of his latest book. Then to Statler-Hilton for luncheon meeting of *American Historical Review* Board—my last, since I am being replaced by Peter Gay. Had a good talk with Bob Palmer who—when I expressed disappointment that so few Princeton types were here—said bitterly that Princetonians never go *anywhere*, being the most self-centered and provincial types in the world and adding that he will not be there next year. Ann Arbor, I guess. . . .

[1969]

Sunday, 5 January 1969. Palo Alto.
Spent the day organizing for the new year—tying up three years of *Der Spiegel* and *Harpers* and making a small index of likely references for my text book, cleaning out books that belong elsewhere, and putting clippings into folders, and writing thank you notes. This does not really prepare me for the new year, but it helps me move. . . .

Tuesday, 7 January 1969. Palo Alto.
In the morning gave the first of my lectures on Germany after 1914. . . . In the afternoon and evening planned my graduate seminar on Aspects of the Intellectual History of Austria and the German States, 1815–1848. It will center on Goethe, Friedrich Schlegel, Eichendorff, Rahel, Hegel, Clausewitz, Büchner, Börne, Heine, Nestroy, and Grillparzer. Looks interesting. . . .

Thursday, 9 January 1969. Palo Alto.
Met with Mathias of CIA today and agreed to serve as consultant to Board of National Estimates. . . .

Thursday, 23 January 1969. Palo Alto.
Meeting with Carl Spaeth to talk about possibility of setting up a Central European Studies Center—a brainchild that emerged from a meeting at Lew Spitz's last night. . . .

Monday, 17 February 1969. Palo Alto.
Meeting after my morning lecture in the undergraduate library (UGLY) to

---

[116] Rudolph Binion (1927–2011), an intellectual and cultural historian and a pioneer in the field of psychohistory, taught at Brandeis University for nearly half a century.

consider the report on International Relations written (badly) by Lederer and Mancall.[117] Nothing will come of it, and I am heading a new committee to go over the whole damned business again… In the afternoon, a meeting of the Humanities and Sciences Assembly to consider the sections of the Stanford Study on Education which deal with freshman requirements. I talked on the history requirement, and there was a debate in which a young psychologist, arguing for *no* requirements, spoke brilliantly, and the senior people spoke with no inspiration and much repetition. . . .

Wednesday, 19 February 1969. Palo Alto.
Very good seminar meeting on Ludwig Börne.[118] The students all charged up by the *Briefe aus Paris* [Letters from Paris]. Börne strikes me as an unpleasant type, but the letters are fascinating, not least because of what he says about theater and opera in Paris in 1830–31. . . .

Thursday, 20 February 1969. Palo Alto.
At noon a luncheon with Joshua Lederberg's[119] group which exists in order to have breakfasts with Congressman McCloskey. Interesting discussion of anti-ballistic missile problem, Presidio sentences on soldiers accused of mutiny, etc.[120] This discourse of reason interrupted by eruption into the Club of the Black Student Union, shouting "We want Pitzer!" Bourgeois audience sat frozen while President came out and told the invaders that he would negotiate in a climate of reason. Invaders retired after an announcement by some undefined person that president would meet them at 2 p.m.… At 2 went to President's Office. Largish crowd. No president. Black leadership (very SS-ish) marched off. Crowd followed and (this I did not see) decided to satisfy its frustrations by invading the bookstore, which

---

[117] Mark Mancall (1933–2020), a scholar of Chinese, Central Asian, and Southeast Asian history, joined the Stanford faculty in 1965. His many contributions to undergraduate education at Stanford included his founding of the vibrant, residence-based Structured Liberal Education program (SLE), and a re–envisioning of the Overseas Studies Program.

[118] Ludwig Börne (1786–1837) was a German-Jewish journalist and editor whose satirical *Briefe aus Paris* (1834) drew attention to political oppression and social injustice.

[119] Joshua Lederberg (1925–2008), a recipient of the Nobel Prize in Medicine, was a molecular biologist.

[120] Craig is referring here to the treaty negotiations between the United States and the Soviet Union on anti-ballistic missiles, and a series of disciplinary problems, including sit-down protests by soldiers opposed to the Vietnam War, in October 1968.

a small group did, causing $5,000 of damage… In the evening, dinner with Phyl at the Club, our guests being my classmate Gordon Smith and his wife and daughter. Afterwards, a meeting at home of our Central European Studies Group. Very contentious. . . .

Thursday, 27 February 1969. Palo Alto.
. . . Dinner with the Germanists in honor of Hans Mayer[121] who lectured afterwards on Oskar Matzerath (the subject of my final Hist 129 lecture this morning) and Felix Krull. Drinks afterward and a discussion in which I chivvied him about Hermann Broch, of whom he has a poor opinion. A fine critic from whose writings I have learned much, and an amusing man.

Friday, 28 February 1969. Palo Alto.
Met with Walter Lohnes to iron out differences of opinion in Central European Studies Group and devised what strikes me as a pretty good document. . . .

Thursday, 13 March 1969. Palo Alto.
W. J. Mommsen of Düsseldorf in town… Lunch with him and Wheelers and [name omitted]… At 4:15 he gave a not extraordinary lecture. Europeans are always an odd bunch in this respect: they always repeat commonplaces as if they were something Moses brought down from Mt. Sinai… In the evening dinner with Mommsens and Lohnes… Then, after Phyl went home, a half an hour at Vucinich's, where there was a party for the East European graduate students, and where I spent most of my time agitating against the Anti-Ballistic Missile [Treaty]. . . .

Sunday, 6 April 1969. Palo Alto.
A week full of ups and downs. On *Saturday*, on reaching home, I had a call from Davie Napier, asking me to deliver the eulogy at the Eisenhower Memorial Service to be held on Monday. This took more time than I had to give to it and, when I got down to it, it was hard going. At 5 a.m. *Monday* morning, after a hard night's work, I had made little progress. Four hours sleep helped and at 1 p.m. the speech was finished and at 4 I marched in full regalia into the chapel and gave it…

On *Tuesday* evening, Amandalee Knoles called and said that Dilys Potter had shot herself. She and George had gone up after David had called George and had coped with coroners and sheriff's deputies and the like. I drove up at 9 and found David and Cathy alone, composed but obviously

---

[121] Hans Mayer (1907–2001) was a prolific and innovative German literary scholar, best known for *Aussenseiter* [*Outsiders*] (Frankfurt: Suhrkamp Verlag, 1975).

in a state of shock. I didn't stay long. . . .

Thursday, 10 April 1969. Palo Alto.
. . . At the University, I have been pursuing my three concerns: the undergraduate diplomatic course, which promises (despite the confusion of the young when confronted with such a radical change of format) to go well; my graduate seminar in diplomacy; and my graduate colloquium on the age of imperialism. I have also written two reviews and attended a long department meeting. Meanwhile, the Students for a Democratic Society and supporting types are sitting in the Applied Electronics Laboratory in an attempt to force the Trustees to go further than they have in withdrawing Stanford from "war research." This is a *déjà vu*, and I am more interested in the ongoing controversy involving the Fitzgerald Baking Company which, in absorbing Foster's English Muffins, has started to issue them sliced, to the horror of purists who believe they must be opened with fork and fingers! . . . Today did a tremendous amount of mail, accepted my appointment as Intermittent Consultant to the CIA. . . .

Thursday, 17 April 1969. Palo Alto.
Timmy's birthday party. After it was over, a call from Ray Bacchetti in the President's Office asking me to go down at 9 p.m. for a special meeting in connection with the sit-in. Idea was that we should go into the Applied Electronics Laboratory in faculty teams after President Pitzer had closed the building, in order to get the names of those who refused to leave. But Pitzer changed his mind and decided to hold off until the morning, when a special meeting of the Academic Council will be held...

Friday, 18 April 1969. Palo Alto.
Before Academic Council met this morning, the sit-inners decided to come out for a week. The President had simultaneously closed the Applied Electronics Laboratory for the same period. The Council passed two resolutions approving the President's policy and then—after some Neanderthal types sought to close off the meeting by adjournment—passed a resolution proposed by Josh Lederberg calling for an earnest dialogue with all members of the community in the hope of finding a solution to our concerns, now that order has been restored... Lunch in the Portola Valley, then a visit to the mass meeting of the students in Frost, which approved the sit-in... We shall have more trouble... In the evening to the city by myself. . . .

Tuesday, 29 April 1969. Palo Alto.

This morning a long session with John Gardner,[122] along with a representative group of our old AAUP [American Association of University Professors] committee. Subject: re-structuring the Board of Trustees… The campus heating up again on the Stanford Research Institute issue and the left trying to use the threat of another sit-in to spook the trustees into holding their hearings in Frost Amphitheater—as John Gardner said publicly at noon today, the silliest idea imaginable.

Wednesday, 30 April 1969. Palo Alto.
A call from Ray Bachetti of the Provost's Office saying that it looked as if there would be another sit-in and asking me to stand by in case the only way to identify those violating the rules on campus disorders would be by sending faculty in. The Trustees' hearings were, however, not disturbed and there has apparently been no sit-in… This afternoon a good session of my imperialism colloquium, and a wearying department meeting with graduate students who are trying to reform requirements so as to relieve their anxieties. . . .

Thursday, 1 May 1969. Palo Alto.
Yesterday's assumption was wrong. I woke this morning to learn that the left wing of the April 3 Movement had gone into Encina Hall at 1 a.m. this morning.[123] Dick Lyman, with the President's assent, called in Santa Clara deputies at 6 a.m. and they cleared the building. No violence, no arrests; but suspension of all students who can be identified. Prevalent feeling on the campus is anti-sit-in; and it appears that the April 3 movement is badly shaken… Academic Council meeting this afternoon, in which the President reported on the situation, and Dick Lyman made a fine speech. . . .

Tuesday, 6 May 1969. Palo Alto.
A meeting of the department's Student-Faculty Liaison Committee, a group that has proved its usefulness. . . .

Friday, 9 May 1969. Palo Alto.
Lunch with [name omitted], who wanted to discuss possibility of Rudi

---

[122] John W. Gardner (1912–2002), a distinguished Stanford alumnus and member of the Board of Trustees from 1968 to 1982, was Secretary of Health, Education, and Welfare under President Johnson and the founder of Common Cause, a civic organization dedicated to campaign finance reform.

[123] The movement at Stanford against the Vietnam War became known as the April 3 movement after it held an organizational community meeting in Dinkelspiel Auditorium on April 3, 1969. It subsequently organized the sit–ins at the Applied Electronics Laboratory and Encina Hall.

Dutschke being allowed to enroll at Stanford to work for a Ph.D. in history. Pointed out some difficulties…

Sunday, 11 May 1969. Palo Alto.
. . . Home at 6 and to the Dodds for a meeting of the Discussion Group. At dinner Paul Hanna[124] very insistent that this will be the bloodiest week in Stanford's history. There could be trouble—the Students for a Democratic Society have announced a boycott of classes—but I doubt that it will get to the point of violence expected by Paul. John talked about the shape of things to come in 2000 AD. Depressing thought… My articles on Kleist and Forster are now out, and Müller will be out in the *American Historical Review* in June. Now I'm working on an article for Walther Hofer's symposium on *Europe und Deutsche Einheit* [Europe and German Unity]…[125]

Monday, 12 May 1969. Palo Alto.
The students are boycotting classes—or at least the April 3 Movement is—to show the Trustees how concerned we all are about the Stanford Research Institute issue. I met my morning class and had fair attendance, and my seminar from which only one man was absent. . . .

Tuesday, 13 May 1969. Palo Alto.
Second day of the boycott, which has not been very successful… In the evening, learned that the Trustees have decided to end Stanford's connection with the Stanford Research Institute (SRI). This flies in the face of the demand of the April 3 Movement, who want Stanford to retain SRI and to transform it. . . .[126]

Monday, 19 May 1969. Palo Alto.
The April 3 Movement attempted this morning to occupy an SRI building in the Industrial Park, in order to stop work on counter-insurgency there. I was awakened by the sound of a helicopter overhead (KGO on the job)

---

[124] Paul Hanna (1902–1988), a Professor of Education at Stanford, lived on the campus in a house designed by Frank Lloyd Wright.

[125] Gordon A. Craig, "Transatlantischen Perspektiven," in *Europa und die Einheit Deutschlands: Eine Bilanz nach 100 Jahren*, ed. Walther Hofer (Köln: Verlag Wissenschaft und Politik).

[126] The Stanford Research Institute was a non-profit scientific research institute established by Stanford in 1946. Specializing in computer and information technology, robotics, and other fields, military and government agencies were frequent clients. As Craig reports, the University decided to end its association with SRI due to ongoing student protests against SRI over concern that it was part of the military-industrial complex during the Vietnam War.

and listened to its reports as I shaved and dressed.[127] The police were, in the end, too smart for them and, although it took time, removed their barricades and drove them off, not without some window-smashing… Usual classes…

Tuesday, 20 May 1969. Palo Alto.

Another attempt by the Movement. This time a complete fiasco, reflected in the discouraged mien of the members whom I bicycled past on the way to work… The gas is running out of the movement here. In Berkeley, however, the fight for the "People's Park" has escalated and gripped the whole campus; there is daily fighting between police and students; the government over the weekend sent in the National Guard which has been a bit too liberal with gas, spread in some cases by chopper; and one young man has died as a result of a buckshot charge fired by an Alameda County Deputy Sheriff. All as ugly as can be and bound to have some of the effects which the death of Benno Ohnesorg had in Berlin. . . .

Wednesday, 28 May 1969. Palo Alto.

Lunch with a Czech scholar named [Antonin] Snejdarek, Wayne [Vucinich], and an unmarried Yugoslav economist who reproached Snejdarek because the Czechs didn't fight in August. Said Yugoslavs would have helped by invading Bulgaria and that Americans couldn't then have stayed out. Very bloody-minded. Snejdarek very Czech… In the evening a meeting of our seminar on international relations. Talked about political gaming. Very interesting.

Saturday, 14 June 1969. Palo Alto.

Marched in procession at Pitzer's inauguration. No Students for a Democratic Society disturbance. Excellent speech by John Gardner, poor one by Pitzer… In the afternoon Donald Kennedy[128] and I gave speeches to Class of '69 at their Class Day, Kennedy very lively but a bit too egotistical. . . .

Sunday, 22 June 1969. Palo Alto.

. . . Bad news in today's *Times.* [Craig pasted the obituary of Hajo Holborn

---

[127] KGO is the local ABC television affiliate.

[128] Donald Kennedy (1931–2020), a neurobiologist and environmental scientist, was the eighth president of Stanford University (1980–1992). He was a founder of Stanford's interdisciplinary Program in Human Biology, the Haas Center for Public Service, and the Stanford Humanities Center. He received the Lloyd W. Dinkelspiel Award for Outstanding Service to Undergraduate Education in 1976.

into his diary.][129]

Monday, 30 June 1969. Palo Alto.
A farewell lunch for [name omitted], my former *Assistent* in Berlin, who has been teaching here this year. He tells me that the Friedrich Meinecke Institut has been firebombed in retaliation for the dismissal of the tutors by the Acting Director. Thus does stupidity invite mindless violence. The Free University is very close to collapse. . . .

Tuesday, 8 July 1969. Palo Alto.
Before going to bed last night read [Heinrich von] Treitschke's essay on [Ludwig] Uhland, very useful when I get around to writing on the poet. Today his essay on Byron which, along with the Lessing one, could be included in an edition of the essays. Under the influence of this, read *Childe Harold's Pilgrimage* which has some passages that can be used in my text revision. . . .

Saturday, 12 July 1969. Palo Alto.
Dinner at [name omitted]. Smoked pot for the first time. Didn't have any perceptible effect, except to make more lively a discussion of British poet laureates. . . .

Sunday, 20 July 1969. Palo Alto.
MOONDAY. Our astronauts landed on the moon today. We returned from the city and in the evening saw the walk...

Twenty-five years ago today Hitler was blown up—but, unfortunately, not high enough. . . .

Sunday, 27 July 1969. Palo Alto.
. . . I have been reading furiously for the revision of my text—Solzhenitsyn, Dickens, Fleming's *Arts and Ideas*, Brion's *Art of the Romantic Era*, Conquest's *The Great Terror*, Reyna's *Concise History of Ballet*, Hobsbawm's *The Age of Revolution*, Bill Langer's *Political and Social Upheaval, 1832–1852*, Byron's *Childe Harold's Pilgrimage*. Also listening to Berlioz and making interminable lists of reminders to myself. I'll get down to the dog work this week, although I have a review to write and some dissertation chapters to go over and a long overdue manuscript for Norman Cantor. And my long neglected correspondence, such as it is...

A characteristic note, separating us from the Russians: while Collins was navigating around the moon he was asked by Houston Control Center if

---

129 "Hajo Holborn, 67, a Yale Professor," *New York Times* (21 June 1969): 27.

there was any news he wanted brought up to date on. He asked what had been happening to the Dow Jones Average. . . .

Thursday, 28 August 1969. Palo Alto.
A busy month has passed since my last entry [in which Craig recorded the unexpected death of his mother on July 31st]. . . . [After a trip back to Peterborough in Canada for the funeral] I settled down to a liquorless existence filled with work, which has gone very well, despite distractions like correspondence, watering, marketing and cooking, Ph.D. essays, calls from the office, and running the washing machine. . . . And I managed to revise the first 23 chapters of my text and will get to the 24th tonight. It goes best after midnight with Berlioz "Romeo and Juliet" or Beethoven sonatas or the last piano concertos of Mozart played very loudly on the music box. . . .

[After a visit to the Air Force Academy in Colorado Springs on the 24th, Craig flew to San Diego for a conference session on "Modern German History and Psychoanalysis."] Took a cab to San Diego State College and bumped into a lot of types like Charlie Delzell and Earl Pomeroy. Found the room assigned me had been changed to a larger one. Filled that one and had to move to a still larger one. Finally got show on the road. [Richard M.] Hunt paper most unoriginal and without a hint of a new idea. [R. G. L.] Waite's filled with improbable data about impossible Hitlerian neuroses and dark hints about sex practices too scabrous for our ears (I can't take Waite seriously anymore. Pity. He once had talent). [Name omitted] was very good both in the presentation and the discussion and [Arnold A.] Rogow was excellent. The audience obviously interested. Lots of questions. Lots of good comments afterwards. . . .

This evening another long call from Francis Loewenheim in Houston about his long-protracted feud against Harvard University Press, the National Archives, the American Historical Association's secretary, Paul Ward, and the past present and future presidents of the AHA Julian Boyd, Vann Woodward, and Bob Palmer. To say nothing of Lou Morton, Arthur Link, and Dick Challener. His crusade has cost him $5000 so far and, if he goes on this way, will cost him that again. He is expecting the newspapers to take up the case when they see our letter to the *Times* and the feeble and disingenuous answer of the Archivist...[130]

---

[130] Loewenheim's accusations against the archives and organizations listed in Craig's entry are commonly known as "the Roosevelt Library Case." Francis Loewenheim claimed that he was inappropriately denied access to correspondence

My review of the Holborn volume was in last Sunday's *Times*. . . .[131]

Sunday, 1 September 1969. Palo Alto.
Quiet day. In the evening, [name omitted] called to say that, after my departure from San Diego, I had been elected Vice President of the Pacific Coast Branch of the American Historical Association, which means that I will succeed Earl Pomeroy as President. This will amuse [names omitted] who claim that they have been campaigning for me in the AHA Sweepstakes, working through Tom McGann, who is a member of the Nominating Committee. I can think of at least half a dozen people more qualified than I to be president of the AHA (Gordon Wright, David Potter, Arthur Schlesinger, Jr., Peter Gay—the list is extensible), but I guess I needn't feel embarrassed about getting the presidency of the Pacific branch. . . .

Wednesday, 10 September 1969. Palo Alto.
As I was waiting in the Club today for Phyl to come for lunch, George Knoles told me that I had been appointed the first J. E. Wallace Sterling Professor of Humanities. Gordon Wright has also been given a new chair in French history. . . .

Friday, 12 September 1969. Palo Alto.
. . . *The Palo Alto Times* has the story of my appointment in an item that is as usual filled with small but irritating inaccuracies and omissions. More striking, as I said to Jerry in a letter this evening, is the evidence it gives of the continued inferiority complex felt by some Westerners: it is clear for the story that its writer takes it for granted that to write books is much less important than to write reviews in the *New York Times*.

Tuesday, 16 September 1969. Palo Alto.
Up betimes and off to see Lorenz Eitner to discuss possible illustrations

---

between the American ambassador to Germany, William E. Dodd, and President Franklin Roosevelt because a member of the library staff was using those documents for his own book project and did not want to be "scooped." Loewenheim also attacked Harvard University Press as the prospective publisher of the Dodd-Roosevelt papers and the American Historical Association for inadequately defending him. Loewenhim's letter, signed by Craig and nineteen other historians, appeared in the *New York Times Book Review* of 7 September 1969. See Richard Polenberg, review of "The Roosevelt Library Case: A Review Article," by Francis L. Loewenheim, *American Archivist* 34:3 (1971): 277–84.

131 Gordon A. Craig, review of *A History of Modern Germany, Vol. III: 1840–1945* by Hajo Holborn, *New York Times Book Review* (24 August 1969): 3, 34.

for my text. As usual, he was full of useful suggestions and showed me some splendid things—a painting by Caillebotte, for instance, called "Place de l'Europe on a Rainy Day" (1877) which I want to use, and some lovely Biedermeier things, especially by Moritz von Schwind. Gradually what seemed to be a difficult problem is getting solved, and I shall end up with more illustrations than my publisher will allow me to use. We'll see what Agnes [Peterson, of the Hoover Institution] has to offer me tomorrow… Last night I finished the cultural section for Chapter 29 managing to work in everything from the *nouveau roman* [New Novel] and the *nouvelle vague* [French New Wave cinema] to Evelyn Lear and the Beatles and today I found in Monday's *New York Times* a comment by Sean O'Casey on Ionesco's *Rhinoceros*, which I can use in a footnote. Originally I had no footnotes in the book; now I have taken to using them for anecdotes which would clot up the text. . . .

Thursday, 18 September 1969. Palo Alto.
Yesterday morning to the Hoover Institution where Agnes Peterson had collected some stuff for me—some wonderful posters from the period 1917–22, the Soviet heroic age, some useable portraits and photographs of Lenin, a very good drawing of Trotsky which I will use and—best of all---some hitherto unpublished German photographs of the signing of the Nazi-Soviet pact. I am getting all of these photographed so that I can show them to Snyder, the Holt man, when he gets here next month. . . .

. . . [The following day] back to Stanford to meet a nice German from the Yale Law School who is preparing a report for the Ministry of All-German affairs on research interest in East Germany in the United States. He was very interesting on the policy of the *Grosse Koalition* [Great Coalition]—down-playing reunification, dismantling the Hallstein Doctrine, stressing *Nachbarschaft* [neighborhood] and the necessity of preventing Central Europe from becoming another Middle East.[132] We also exchanged the usual melancholy reflections on the current state of German universities. . . .

Later: The other night, in a kind of *Ruhepause* [rest period], I went through some of the early volumes of this journal, including the ones written at Oxford. They led me to recall a remark of Harold Macmillan, after he became chancellor of the University, to the effect that those who

132 Germany's "Great Coalition" was a government coalition between the right-wing Christian Democratic Union and the left-wing Social Democratic Party of Germany.

had not known Oxford before 1940 were like those who, as Talleyrand said, had never known the *douceur de la vie* [sweetness of life] before the French Revolution. Talking of the beauty, charm and grace that he remembered, MacMillan said Oxford "has given us more than we can ever hope to repay." Much in that. (Here a short pause, while we all recite Belloc's "God be with you, Balliol men!")

Friday, 19 September 1969. Palo Alto.
The [*San Francisco*] *Chronicle* this morning reported that a major revision of the composition of the Stanford Board of Trustees will be made at the end of the year. In the main, it follows the recommendations of our American Association of University Professors Committee of last summer which I drafted, although there are some features obviously inspired by John Gardner and, in some respects, it goes further than we dared. . . .

Wednesday, 24 September 1969. Palo Alto.
The first half of chapter 29 now up to date—that is to say, British, French, Italian, and German politics (to say nothing of Spain and Scandinavia) have been up-dated to yesterday. But, of course, the Germans have an election on Sunday and then someone will die, and, from now until publication day, I shall be making changes...

I received the official notification of my appointment as Sterling Professor from the President's Office today—with my first name misspelled on both the envelope and in the letter itself! . . .

Tuesday, 7 October 1969. Palo Alto.
. . . Reached p. 275 in my typing chore... Carl Spaeth has made Peter Paret my successor as chairman of the International Relations committee. A good choice but I suspect Carl of ulterior motives, and I think Ivo Lederer is being shafted. Not that he hasn't been asking for it. . . .

Wednesday, 15 October 1969. Palo Alto.
Finished typing the bibliography for the text... Today is M-Day, the day of the Vietnam moratorium. All the newspapers seem to agree that it is all very noble and impressive. All I think of is that we have now started the slide back into a native-kind of isolationism and that the cost of this, in South East Asia and in Europe, will be very heavy, indeed. Meanwhile, with Apollinaire's Tatars in *Alcools*, I can only say to my colleagues who are engaging in this emotional binge: "*Nous n'irons pas à tes sabbats*" [We shall

not attend your sabbaths].[133] . . .

Wednesday, 22 October 1969. Palo Alto.

. . . In connection with my entry above of 15 October, the article below ["Topics: From Bombing Halt to Unilateral Withdrawal," *The New York Times*, October 18, 1969] by Gene Rostow is interesting. I suppose we should all have been prepared for a slide back towards isolationism, but I don't believe that it would have taken so great a hold on so many people if it had not been for Vietnam. The desire to get out has become so great that people won't listen to arguments about cost and consequences. And as Gene says, the cry "Let's negotiate!" has changed in many cases to "Let's get out now!" without those who have shifted their view realizing that they have done so. . . .

Monday, 3 November 1969. Palo Alto.

Last night and all of today, worked hard revising the transcript of Norman Cantor's interview of me concerning tendencies in modern diplomacy. Dreadful to see what nonsense you talk into a tape recorder after it has been transcribed and returned to you…

Sunday, 9 November 1969. Palo Alto.

Last Tuesday left for Philadelphia on the 9 a.m. plane, and worked right across the country on the bloody manuscript for Norman Cantor. . . . Wednesday rose at 9 and got another hour's work in on the Cantor piece, finishing it off, although not as well as I would have wished. . . .[134]

On Thursday rose early and took my bags to the Roger Smith where I had breakfast and then went on to the State Department for a meeting of the Social Science Advisory Board to the Arms Control and Disarmament Agency. Met [name omitted], now in Archibald Alexander's spot at the head of E Division and Gerald Smith in Bill Foster's job as head of the agency. Smith gave us an interesting briefing on the approach to the Strategic Arms Limitation Treaty Talks in Helsinki. Says Russians seem to mean business, but their approach is so different from ours that no very comprehensive agreement can be expected. Also, the speed with which they are turning out nuclear subs throws some doubt on their intentions… Had a good talk with

---

[133] The poem by Guillaume Apollinaire referenced here was based on the "Reply of the Zaporozhian Cossacks to Sultan Mehmed IV of the Ottoman Empire," a historical event depicted in a famous painting by the Russian artist Ilya Repin.

[134] Gordon A. Craig, "Twentieth-Century Diplomacy and International Relations," in *Perspectives on the European Past: Conversations with Historians*, vol.II, ed. Norman F. Cantor (New York: Macmillan, 1971), 305–38.

Phil Mosely, who is encouraging me to visit Moscow when I am abroad. (East Berlin, Warsaw, Moscow, Kiev, Prague, East Berlin.) Good idea... Walked from State to 15th, passing the place where I worked during the war and thinking of the luncheons during which Carmichael used to spin out his erotic theories and the boring afternoons in Research and Publications where I used to sit and doodle at my desk in desperation before I shifted to Joe Green's Special Division and became a drafting officer. . . .

Sunday, 16 November 1969. Palo Alto.
. . . The November Moratorium has passed with a minimum of violence, but what will December bring? Certainly greater attempts to radicalize the movement...

The Strategic Arms Limitation Treaty talks begin tomorrow. . . .

Sunday, 7 December 1969. Palo Alto.
Pearl Harbor Day. It is being celebrated by 300,000 young Americans still trying to get back from Altamont Race Track where the Rolling Stones gave a free rock concert yesterday which caused a 20-mile traffic jam and four deaths, one a murder, two victims of a hit-and-run driver and a suicide because of LSD. How to account for these mass binges of the young? They are like medieval frenzies, or gang-sprees like the Children's Crusade. Because of alienation, the urge for comfort from rubbing against others, like the Japanese students who link arms and reel forward by the hundreds with closed eyes droning monosyllabic chants. . . .

Monday, 8 December 1969. Palo Alto.
I have suggested that the way of solving the problem of the introductory course of our new international relations program is to bring Phil Crowl from Nebraska to give it, and I have talked it over with Phil and got him interested. Today Peter Paret and I sold the idea to Alex George and Dick Brody (while agreeing with their proposal to bring a guy named Nowell from Santa Barbara to give the gaming course), and then Peter jockeyed Carl Spaeth into a corner and persuaded him to promise to pick up the bill ($22,000). If Crowl and Nowell actually accept now, we're in the business, and four years of fiddling around will have produced results despite Spaeth's reluctance to make commitments and his fertility in devising administrative diversions and obstacles. And—I should add—despite the lack of positive contributions by any of the members of the many committees I have had to sit on except the historians. . . .

Tuesday, 9 December 1969. Palo Alto.
Lunch at home with Ivo Lederer, an act of diplomacy to keep him happy

about the decisions Peter and I have been taking without consulting him. He is perfectly in accord with what we've been doing and, in any case, is too deeply involved in his plans to persuade the university to bring Leo Labedz and his journal *Survey* to Stanford. The odds on his pulling this off are very long, since the university is experiencing a set of financial jim-jams. . . .

Thursday, 11 December 1969. Palo Alto.
Once one starts to read about Heine, one turns to the works, and then it is Katy bar the door. Heine is a contagion, a disease that recurs and must periodically be let to run its course. Instead of doing my proper work, I have been finishing [Manfred] Windfuhr and reading things like the letters on the French theater (filled with marvelous stuff on Berlioz, Meyerbeer, Liszt, and Spontini), *From the Memoirs of Herr von Schnabelewopski* (with the Flying Dutchman chapter which influenced Wagner), the [*Über Ludwig Börne*] book (which Thomas Mann admired so highly) and some of the late prose, like *Geständnisse* [*Confessions*] and *Gedanken und Einfälle* [Thoughts and Ideas]. The last should be checked on a later occasion for the brief sallies against Johannes von Müller as an unread and unreadable classic and Gervinus as one who accomplished at great length and in a boring way what Heine had done with economy and spirit (The *Literaturgeschichte* [*Literary History*]) are eminently useable.

As is true of Dickens, Heine's early sketches are almost as good as anything that he wrote later—the little piece on the exasperating mass success of the *Jungfernkranz* [Chaplet] song from *Freischütz* [*The Marksman*], for instance, which is in the *Briefe aus Berlin* [*Letters from Berlin*] of March 1822.[135]

I am thinking of using Delacroix's *Liberty Leading the People* on the cover of the new edition of my text. It is interesting to read Heine's description of it (*Französische Maler*) and his *Cri de Coeur* (applicable also to the Days of May of 1969): "*Heilige Julitage von Paris! ihr werdet ewig Zeugnis geben von dem Uradel der Menschen, der nie ganz zerstört werden kann. Wer euch erlebt hat, der jammert nicht mehr auf den alten Gräbern, sondern freudig glaubt er jetzt an die Auferstehung der Völker. Heilige Julitage! wie schön war die Sonne und wie groß war das Volk von Paris! Die Götter im Himmel, die dem großen Kampfe zusahen, jauchzten vor Bewunderung, und sie wären gerne aufgestanden von ihren goldenen Stühlen und wären gerne zur Erde herabgestiegen, um Bürger zu werden von Paris!*" ["Sacred and memorable days of July! Ye shall unto all times be a witness of mankind's

---

[135] *Der Freischütz* is a romantic opera composed by Carl Maria von Weber (1786–1826).

innate nobility, which can never be entirely destroyed. He who has lived to see you will never more join in sad lamenting o'er the buried hopes of the past, but will joyfully believe in the resurrection of the nations. Holy days of July! How brightly shone the sun, and how grand was the populace of Paris! The gods above looked down on the glorious combat, and the heavens re-echoed with their admiring shouts. Gladly would the immortals have left their golden thrones, to descend on earth and become citizens of Paris."][136]

The contemporaneity of Heine is amazing. His remarks about Young Germany in *Cervantes* can be applied to both the New Left and the Negro intellectuals of our day.

"*Der Lorbeer eines großen Dichters war unsern Republikanern ebenso verhaßt, wie die Purpur eines großen Königs. Auch die geistigen Unterschiede der Menschen wollten sie vertilgen, und indem sie alle Gedanken, die auf dem Territorium des Staates entsprossen, als bürgerliches Gemeingut betrachteten, blieb ihnen nichts mehr übrig, als auch die Gleichheit des Stils zu dekretieren. Und in der Tat, ein guter Stil wurde als etwas Aristokratisches verschrien, und vielfach hörten wir die Behauptung: Der echte Demokrat schreibt wie das Volk, herzlich, schlicht und schlecht.*" ["Our republicans hated the laurels of a great poet even as they hated the purple of a great king. They sought to level the intellectual inequalities of mankind, and in as much as they regarded all ideas that had been produced on the soil of the state as general property, nothing remained to be done but to decree an equality of style also. In sooth, a good style was decried as something aristocratic, and we heard manifold assertions: 'A true democrat must write in the style of the people—sincere, natural, crude.'"][137]

Windfuhr's analysis of *Atta Troll* and *Deutschland: ein Wintermärchen* [*Germany: A Winter's Tale*] is good, and perhaps I should take the latter as my jumping off place for my German history—playing on the failure of the Germans to develop according to the hope expressed in the *History of Religion and Philosophy*.

Windfuhr is interesting also on Heine as comparative sociologist, although he is wrong in believing that Heine was the first to use the theater as a data bank for this. Wilhelm von Humboldt preceded him, and it might be interesting to compare his conclusions about French and German character with Heine's. The *Letters on the French Theater*, where the latter are to be found, are filled with fascinating passages, not the least of which is

---

136 See Heinrich Heine, *Prose Miscellanies from Heinrich Heine*, translated by S. L. Fleishman (Philadelphia: J. B. Lippincott & Company, 1876), 68–69.

137 See Heinrich Heine and Havelock Ellis, *The Prose Writings of Heinrich Heine* (London: Walter Scott, 1887).

the one in the fourth letter in which he discusses sentimentality as a specifically German trait and says it is a product of materialism. This idea, to which he comes back at the beginning of *Geständnisse* [*Confessions*], is one that I must think about...

Must read *Elementargeister* [*Elemental Spirits*]. . . .

My latest thought on Richard Nixon is that he is all syrup and no pancake, but I dislike hearing speeches like Hilliard's threatening his death and view with contempt those liberal tail-waggers who find excuses for the Hilliard outburst. . . .

Friday, 12 December 1969. Palo Alto.
. . . Read Heine's *Elementargeister* [*Elemental Spirits*] and found no reference in it to the legend of the Willis nor any claim in Heine's letter of 7 Feb. 1842, in which he writes of Carlotta Grisi's dancing in *Giselle*, that he had influenced the composition of Adam's ballet. (As Windfuhr claims. A better case can be made for his influencing Wagner, for *Elementargeister* ends with a discussion of the Tannhäuser Legend.) The letter in question is to be found in *Lutezia*, a collection of Heine's letters from Paris in the 40s which has much to say about Louis Philippe (whom H. dubbed "The Napoleon of Peace" after the settling of the 1840 crisis) and about Thiers and Guizot and George Sand and Liszt.[138] Found some usable stuff for my text.

Surprising to see how much Heine cooled off in revolutionary ardor in the 1840s. He became a firm supporter of Louis Philippe whose fall he later deplored because it brought communism and enforced equality of economy and culture closer... Heine very funny on the complete failure of the French to understand a Fräulein Lowe who sang Beethoven's "Adelaide" to them—(when I was in P.S. 23 in Jersey City a large German lady sang it to me and my Italian and Polish schoolmates, and we didn't understand it either)—and on Donizetti, whose *Don Pasquale* had its premiere in the spring of 1843 and of whom H. wrote "*. . . sein Talent ist groß, aber noch größer ist seine Fruchtbarkeit, worin er nur den Kaninchen nachsteht.*" [His talent is great, but even greater is his fecundity, in which he is second only to rabbits.] ... In 1843 an opera "The Flying Dutchman" by Dietz failed. Heine seems to have regarded the plot idea his own and to have resented the way in which the French text screwed it up. . . .

---

[138] The 1840 Crisis is more commonly known as the Rhine Crisis of 1840. In order to deflect attention from a recent diplomatic defeat in the Near East, the French foreign minister, Adolphe Thiers, made claims upon German territory on the west bank of the Rhine River. Ultimately, Thiers lost the support of his king, Louis Philippe, who wished to avoid conflict.

6

The Seventies: Stanford and Berlin, 1970–1980

Thursday, 1 January 1970, 1:15 a.m. Stanford.
. . . Looking back on the 60s, we have nothing to complain of and much to be thankful for. At the beginning of the decade, we moved to California, and that is something none of us has regretted. I should be happier if I had done more work than I have done and were further advanced on a major work than I am. But, I have not been idle and, God willing, the big book will come. And other things, closer things, are more important than books. . . .

Thursday, 8 January 1970. Stanford.
. . . T. S. Eliot's description of the way the world ends may turn out to be perfectly accurate. In 1885, August Bebel wrote (to [Friedrich] Engels): "*Ich lege mich jeden Tag mit den Gedanken schlafen, daß das letzte Stündlein der bürgerlichen Gesellschaft in Bälde schlägt.*" [I lie down to sleep every day with the thought that the last hour of bourgeois society will come soon]. He was probably just about 100 years off and definitely mistaken with respect to the forces that will bring collapse, which will not be war and revolution but the high birth rate and the exhaustion of food supplies—although, to be sure, these will probably touch off violence in many forms. . . .

Tuesday, 21 January 1970. Stanford.
During my trip I read Günter Graß's new novel *Örtlich betäubt* [Local Anaesthetic], a weak effort after his earlier ones but interesting. A pity he didn't see fit to say more about Berlin in a book dealing with the student movement of 1967, but one can't have everything. I have now been reading the reviews, which I had kept. Interesting to note the tone of outrage against their great man who has let them down by writing what they call an "*epigonenhaft*" [unoriginal] novel, to say nothing of Marcel Reich-Ranicki's gloomy conclusion that perhaps this is not Graß's fault but a sign of general malaise, "*ein Symptom . . . ein Alarmsignal, das uns der Zustand der zeitgenössischen*

Literatur bewußt macht" [a symptom . . . an alarm signal that makes us aware of the state of contemporary literature].

I am sending Graß a copy of my essay on Georg Forster, since his anti-hero [Eberhard] Starusch is working on him. . . .

Friday, 30 January 1970. Stanford.

Basil Liddell Hart died yesterday. I never knew him very well, but our acquaintance spanned 25 years. I met him first in Princeton at lunch with Ed Earle and listened impressed as he fought over Civil War battles with his host. Later I was his host when he returned as a guest lecturer, and still later I visited him in England and had dinner with Kathleen and him and Mrs. Chester Wilmot, whose husband was killed in a crash of one of those luckless Comets—a dinner possible only after Basil had cleaned up sheaves of notes and manuscripts and dozens of pipes that had crept out of his study and taken over the dining room. I saw him last in Davis (during a trip cut short by illness), when Kathleen and he gave me a very good lunch which was so completely un-Californian as to be comic—including Yorkshire pudding and stewed prunes with clotted cream, plus French wines—and during which he talked about his marvelous waistcoats and warned me that Americans cleaned their suits too often. He was a good historian and also contributed greatly to the gaiety of nations...

This morning talked with Larry Ryan, Assoc. Dean of Humanities, about the Dawson case—explaining my own position in case Phil's agitated supporters try to make too much of my vote for him. The Appointments & Promotions committee's vote against him was unanimous, so only an act of God can save him now. On the balance, blocking his promotion will be good for the department, particularly since our associate professors are already weak enough without an addition to their numbers. Also talked with Larry about Walter Sokel, who has been weeping on my shoulder again because Harvard has made him another offer and so has Ohio State, and, although he doesn't want to accept either offer, he wants to be made much of and praised and have guns fired at Fort Mason. Larry wants me to quiet him down.

Tuesday, 3 February 1970. Stanford.

Finished taking notes on [Helmut] Böhme [*Deutschlands Weg zur Großmacht* (Germany's Path to Great Power Status)] with a sense of relief. It is doubtless a very useful reminder of the importance of economic factors, but I am of a mind with Schiller, who once said: "In the end we are idealists, and would be ashamed that it could be said of us that things formed us, and not that we formed things." (Come to think of it, Schiller may be articulating a German weakness, a tendency to take refuge in will when reality becomes too pressing. But that is another matter.)

Reading [Heinrich von] Treitschke with pleasure. It will be fun to do an edition of his literary stuff for Krieger… I learn from him that Cotta the publisher first "introduced the unheard-of luxury of a sofa into the unpretentious town of the Muses (Tübingen).". . .

Monday, 23 February 1970. Stanford.
. . . I stayed behind and read Townsend Hoopes's *The Limits of Intervention*, an account of the Lyndon B. Johnson Vietnam policy which is highly critical of Walt Rostow and most laudatory of Clark Clifford's role in putting an end to the escalation. A good book which makes me ashamed of my own failure to see sooner than I did how mistaken our policy was. It's no comfort to say that I was in good company. The truth of the matter is that those of us who opposed isolationism in the 30s and were (with reason) cold warriors in the 50s were insensitive to the changes of the 60s and held to old ways too uncritically. We made a policy in South East Asia that was disastrous and may have revived the isolationism we once fought. That—apart from certain temperamental idiosyncrasies and a tendency to become drunk with his own eloquence—was essentially what was wrong with Walt.

Hoopes writes that, on the night that LBJ made the speech in which he announced the partial bombing halt and his own withdrawal from the presidential race, Clark Clifford, who had been invited to the White House, was handed an advance copy of the last two paragraphs and disclosed their contents to his wife and Elspeth Rostow. As he did so, a photographer snapped a picture. Clifford said later: "The ladies look as though they had just been hit by a wet towel." I can well imagine. Elspeth . . . must have seen in a flash that there was the end of glory. . . .[1]

Saturday, 28 February 1970. Stanford.
The beginning of the big book is lurking like a big formless beast somewhere close by, and I think I'm actually going to be able to coax it out of the bushes. Finished Höfele's *Geist und Gesellschaft der Bismarckzeit* [Spirit

---

[1] Elspeth Rostow (1917–2007), wife of Craig's longtime friend Walt Rostow, was among the founders of the discipline of American Studies, a veteran of the wartime OSS, and, from 1977 to 1983, Dean of the LBJ School of Public Affairs at the University of Texas at Austin.

and Society in the Bismarck Era],[2] which is going to be useful. One thing for sure: the new book will be more a *Kulturgeschichte* [cultural history] than a politics of the Prussian army, and I shall try to deal with the style of the period I cover…

I wish someone would do something to improve the style of our own. *The Stanford Daily* reported the other day that in a debate in the Student Senate, the president of the student body, [name omitted], Rhodes Scholar-elect, was asked by another senator to explain a remark he had just made and answered, "I was trying to say that what *you* just said was a crock of shit." It would be difficult to decide which is more appalling: the language used or the fact that he could find no other way of explaining his meaning… We seem to live these days in the midst of a concerted attack by the young upon our greatest treasure, the English language, which they denature by profanity or mindless exaggerations or violate by attempts to democratize it by means of bad grammar. A long manifesto in the *Daily* last week was written in a bad imitation of ghetto jargon; the writer, who was obviously white, systematically omitted verb parts and committed other crimes in the hope, apparently, that he would sound Third World-ish, sincere, and nobly revolutionary. What he actually sounded like, was Stepin Fetchit… Tonight I listened on TV to the Chicago Seven, who have been released on bond, speaking to their admirers about the outrages they have had to suffer in jail—(they've had their hair cut)—and, leaving aside the fact that they appear to be emotionally disturbed, their style of discourse is about as elegant as what I used to hear in the playground of P.S. No. 23 in Jersey City. Not the least ruinous effect of the Vietnam war is the fact that it has made these illiterate mouthings seem respectable and invited the young to imitate them…

Meanwhile, the mob at the University of California, Santa Barbara have burned up a Bank of America branch and otherwise comported themselves like savages (as the mob in Berkeley did last week). The result of this will be to give the Reagans and Raffertys and Agnews more support for the savage policies *they* are capable of. In the end, a lot of reasonable types are going to be caught in the middle, unless they're lucky…

The blow-up in Laos and the escalation of Arab terrorism in the Middle East are not calculated to make a helpful contribution to the general situation, or to dissuade Americans from doing what comes naturally.

When in danger,

---

[2] Karl Heinrich Höfele, *Geist und Gesellschaft der Bismarckzeit (1870–1890)* (Göttingen: Musterschmidt Verlag, 1967).

When in doubt,
Run in circles!
Scream and shout!

Thursday, 5 March 1970. Stanford.
In the current issue of the *Princeton Alumni Weekly*, the appended article about Howie Davis,[3] who was one of our little group in the class of 1935. It is interesting that our class has no statesmen among its members and no one of whom I can think right now who became a successful politician. Most of my classmates became businessmen, and some of them very successful ones, who, after they were established, turned to good works. The intellectuals in the class turned to the church, like John Coburn (now a bishop), John Thompson, and Dave Pyle, or education, like Charlie Shain and Archie Lewis and John Edie and Howie and me—to say nothing of Tom Elliott, although he would prefer to do nothing but paint. There were also some unconventional types like Bill Schiede, who had lots of money and, early on, decided to spend his major energies running the Bach Choir, and Jac Weller, who combined real estate with being a weapons expert and a private historian. But the prevailing note, in a class that has not been undistinguished, is business. The contrast with my Oxford class is sharp. It also had its share of academics, but it produced diplomats and government advisors too, although some would say, I guess, that, in encouraging Walt Rostow to go into government, it blotted its copybook. . . .

Friday, 6 March 1970. Stanford.
A disturbing article in *Die Zeit* about the activities of Rotzök[4] at the Free University, which has now prompted the resignation of Helmut Arndt, the director of the *Institut für Konzentrationsforschung* [Institute for Merger & Acquisition Research], by effecting a takeover by means of the powers given the junior faculty by the new University Law, and by ideologizing the program in the direction of Marxism… Soon we will have attempts of the same kind here, and they will succeed if our liberal colleagues don't wake up to the fact that [the] threat to the university is real, since these monkeys are not fooling. It is amazing that otherwise intelligent men can convince themselves that the Society for a Democratic Society people don't really mean it, when they say that they intend to destroy the university as a center of objective truth and—worse—how many of them, concerned about the weaknesses in the university, believe that they can correct them in

[3] Howie Davis was a professor of art history at Columbia.

[4] This stands for "Rote Zelle Ökonomie" (Red Cell Economics).

collaboration with the wreckers... In a paper sent out by the Committee for a Rational Alternative, Oscar Handlin reproves a liberal type from the Massachusetts Institute of Technology for objecting to any criticism of the New Left by asking him whether he ever had to pass through a mob of students armed with axes or was forced to stand guard all night in a great library to repel a possible attack upon it.[5] Handlin had both experiences, and more of us may, if the people like his correspondent don't wake up. . . .

Thursday, 19 March 1970. Stanford.

. . . Willi Brandt is in East Berlin for talks and has received a tremendous reception in the streets. Recognition of the German Democratic Republic, and something more, may be in the works.

Wednesday, 1 April 1970. Stanford.

. . . Three hundred hooligans went on a window-breaking spree on campus last night—as a protest against the faculty vote on the Reserve Officers' Training Corps. I wish we could return to summary expulsions... As in the days of Christian Gauss at Princeton...[6]

Thursday, 2 April 1970. Stanford.

. . . As a follow-up of Tuesday's vandalism, a girl, masked and gowned, poured red paint over President Pitzer as he and his wife were dining with students in Grove Center last evening. An outrageous business! Following Peter Paret's example, I wrote Pitzer a letter this evening. . . .

Saturday, 4 April 1970. Stanford.

A deplorable report from the University News Service on the attempts made yesterday by demonstrators against the ROTC to disrupt the meeting of the Academic Council. It shows that the Council, having forced sitters-in to vacate the hall, then turned right around and invited them to send three representatives in to make statements! The demonstrators refused, showing more dignity than my colleagues, who allowed themselves to be spooked by a group which, at top strength, according to the News Service,

---

[5] Oscar Handlin (1915–2015) was a distinguished historian of American immigration history at Harvard for over fifty years.

[6] Christian Gauss (1878–1951), one of Woodrow Wilson's original corps of preceptors in 1905, became chairman of the Department of Modern Languages and then Dean of the College at Princeton University from 1925 until his retirement in 1946. A central figure at the university for more than forty years, he influenced and corresponded frequently with F. Scott Fitzgerald and Edmund Wilson.

amounted to "about 200, including quite a few high-school-age and younger children." It was widely known that the Council meeting would be accompanied by exercises in guerilla theater. This may account for the fact that only 80 faculty members(!) were present when the meeting started and only 175 when it was allowed to begin its business, which, as far as I can gather, consisted of passing votes of confidence in Pitzer and Lyman. When will it dawn upon my colleagues that it is *their* authority and dignity and the cause of reason itself which is under attack and that they had better start defending them before it is too late?

Tuesday, 7 April 1970. Stanford.
. . . The anti-ROTC forces, with the aid of some high school hoodlums, broke about 60 windows on campus last night and briefly occupied the ROTC building today. . . .

Thursday, 23 April 1970. Berlin.
The Opera is in Tokyo at the moment and, in its absence, the *Tagesspiegel* is asking some interesting questions about its future... Also in the news: the attempt to form a Great Coalition in Austria has failed, and Kreisky is going to try going it alone; the Poles are saying that Brandt can get nowhere unless he first recognizes the Oder-Neisse Line; and, here in Berlin, the radical students are attempting to prevent the establishment of an independent *Wissenschaftszentrum* [Science Center] (like the Max-Planck-Institut) for the study of management and development problems (presumably because it would be free of their ideological control), while the red cell in the *Wiso Fakultät* [The Faculty of Economic and Social Sciences] is threatening reprisals if two tutors are dismissed because they refused to work with the students on the themes set for them by the professors. . . .

. . . Later: Went to Zehlendorf to the Historische Commission where I found old Herzfeld *wach und munter* [awake and alert]. "We have received our first attack," he said as soon as we had exchanged greetings, and he handed me a fly sheet issued in the Friedrich Meinecke Institut which explained the attack on the press conference the other day when the director of the proposed *Wissenschaftszentrum* was howled down, and which then turned its guns on the independent Historische Commission. . . . Most of our talk was about the radicals and what they have done to the university, and he told me that he is associated with [Georg Nicolaus] Knauer's "Notgemeinschaft für eine Freie Universität" [Emergency Society for a

Free University].[7] He is also against [Hans-Ulrich] Wehler's[8] being appointed *Direktor* of the *Kennedy Institut* here on the grounds that no one who is a follower of William A. Williams should be teaching American history, which I think is a good point.[9] After Wehler said last night that Palmerston's Far Eastern policy was determined by fear of Chartism, I felt I had to tell him [he] was talking nonsense and did so. But perhaps he talks nonsense on other subjects. . . .

Saturday, 25 April 1970. Berlin.

To the Brewster Morrises for lunch. A newspaper affair: Boelcke of the *Tagesspiegel*, Bernd Conrad of the Berlin bureau of *Die Zeit*, Don Cook of Paris office of *Los Angeles Times,* and Marquis Childs of the *Washington Post* with his new wife, my old friend Jane McBaine. Pleasant and interesting group. Found ourselves talking, however, about university troubles, and Brewster shocked me by saying that the Armed Forces Network had announced that two buildings at Stanford had been fire-bombed last night…

Sunday, 26 April 1970. Berlin.

. . . The Chinese have put up a whopping satellite, their first. That will give the Russians a turn!… No more news about Stanford…

The state of this university is illustrated by the fact that although it is hard to keep people here (another professor submitted his resignation yesterday), a psychologist in Darmstadt who has received a call from the Free University has just received a letter from Red Cell Psychology and another signed by 14 tutors, assistants, and at least one *Wissenschaftlicher Rat* [Scientific Council], telling him that his presence in Berlin is undesirable because he has shown in his published works no political or social

---

[7] Georg Nicolaus Knauer (1926–2018), a German-American Vergilian philologist, was a professor in the Classics Department of the University of Pennsylvania. He taught at the Freie Universität Berlin from 1954 to 1974. Knauer and other faculty members at the Free University formed the *Notgemeinschaft für eine Freie Universität* to advocate for academic freedom at German universities and to oppose the more radical demands of the student movement.

[8] Hans-Ulrich Wehler (1931–2014) was a trailblazing left-wing German historian who promoted the study of sociocultural factors in history using the methods of the social sciences. His primary scholarly work was a five-volume history of German society from the eighteenth to the twentieth centuries, *Deutsche Gesellschaftsgeschichte* (Munich: C. H. Beck, 1987–2008).

[9] Craig is referring here to William Appleman Williams (1921–1990), a revisionist historian and fierce critic of American foreign policy.

engagement and no apparent interest in the subjects which these two groups believe to be the only legitimate ones for psychological research—things like family structure, social indoctrination, and the like... On the national front, the Christian Social Union is trying to find a handle on anything that will serve to beat the Social Democratic Party for their policy in Poland (which *Die Zeit* finds logical and promising) and is furious about the gov't's declaration that 8 May (the day of the Nazi surrender) will be celebrated this year, but not 17 June. The opposition attacks have prompted my former Princeton student Horst Ehmke,[10] SPD-Minister im Kanzleramt [the Chancellery], to fire back. . . .

Tuesday, 28 April 1970. Berlin.
. . . [Marquis] Childs was an interesting man.[11] Hates Lyndon B. Johnson. Says that when he came here as Vice President, he asked [Willi] Brandt at the end of his tour of the city, "What's to buy here?" Brandt told him about the *Kngl. Porzellan Manufaktur* [Royal Porcelain-Manufactory], and LBJ wanted to go there at once. Brandt explained that it was closed to which LBJ's rejoinder was: "What kind of mayor are you if you can't open up a store for the Vice President of the United States?" With considerable difficulty, Brandt got the place open, and LBJ toured it, finally stopping before a dinner service that must have cost $4000. "I want that!" he said and went his way, making no attempt, however, then or later, to pay for what he had demanded... Jane was full of stories of how completely Walt Rostow has sold out to LBJ, being now a complete (and very well paid) sycophant. A tragic business. Gene Rostow was able to go back to academic life virtually unscathed. Walt's reputation is, I fear, gone forever... I told Childs of a conversation with Jerry Blum during my Princeton stay in which Jerry said that his greatest fear is that the violence in the universities, etc. will encourage the rise of an ugly wave of anti-Semitism in the States. Childs said he couldn't agree more and that it is already being expressed in letters to newspapers, which, in general, are already more menacing than during the McCarthy era... Childs is doing, or is going to do, a book on Dulles. I told him of my former plan to do the same and promised to send him a Xerox copy of my piece on Dulles, which I have now arranged to have

---

[10] Horst Ehmke (1927–2017) was a German lawyer, law professor, and politician of the Social Democratic Party (SPD).

[11] Marquis Childs (1903–1990) was a journalist, syndicated columnist, and novelist. His political commentary earned him a place on President Richard Nixon's "Enemies List."

done. . . .

Thursday, 30 April 1970. Berlin.
American troops engaged in Cambodia and Soviet jets flying over their rocket bases in Egypt. Not good. . . .

Friday, 1 May 1970. Berlin.
Woke this morning to find snow on the ground and, although it soon melted, it is a bleak day. I had intended to go to the New *Nationalgalerie* with [Hermann] Rupieper, but it is closed.[12] Decided, therefore, to stay here until evening, when I must go out for supper, and work on Fischer's massively repetitive *Krieg der Illusionen* [*War of Illusions*]... Wrote Phyl and brooded over the invasion that is not an invasion in Cambodia which—whatever else it does—will inflame every campus from Berkeley to Berlin. There has already been a protest meeting at Stanford attended by 3000 people. . . .

Saturday, 2 May 1970. Berlin.
. . . I have been reading Eichendorff in the U-Bahn and today finished his marvelous essay "Halle und Heidelberg," a good corrective when one is feeling atrabilious about youth.[13] Not that there aren't good causes for criticism of the young. The six o'clock armed forces news yesterday announced that Nixon's Cambodia speech had touched off a rock-throwing melée in Stanford, in which several people, including the astronaut [Walter] Schirra's son (trying to calm the crowd) were injured. . . .

Sunday, 3 May 1970. Berlin.
. . . Lunch at Herzfeld's with Bill Bark's son, who has finished his doctorate here. We both talked sadly of recent events in Stanford, trading items of horror—viz. the burning of ten studies at the Ford Center with the notes and manuscripts of their inhabitants, representing years of hard work. A completely pointless crime, representing resentment or mindlessness...

Wednesday, 6 May 1970. Berlin.
The events at Stanford, which, according to the reports forwarded to me

---

[12] Hermann-Josef Rupieper (1942–2004), after receiving his Ph.D. under Gordon Craig's direction at Stanford in 1974, became a leading German historian in the field of international relations and a professor of contemporary history at the University of Halle.

[13] Joseph von Eichendorff (1788–1857) was a Prussian civil servant and a major literary figure of the Romantic era whose poetry was frequently set to music. See Joseph Eichendorff, *Eichendorff über die Romantik*, ed. Anton Mayer (München: R. Oldenbourg, 1925).

by [name omitted] culminated on 23 April with a new sit-in (which was broken up by a police raid in which, among others, Mrs. Hal Kahn was arrested), the breaking of $40,000 worth of glass in response, the throwing of Molotov cocktails into the building housing the Free Campus Movement, and the (possibly unconnected) burning of ten studies at the Ford Center (with the destruction of the life work of M. N. Srinivas of New Delhi, among others)—all this I say has been put completely in the shade by the killing of four students by National Guardsmen during disorders at Kent State University two nights ago.

This affair will give a spurious retroactive justification to all the acts of unreason on the students' side. It is deplorable that these students should have been killed. It is almost equally deplorable that a student observer, talking of events prior to the shooting, could say that it was "almost comic to see how a stone thrown by one of the demonstrators bounced off the helmet of a Guardsman and how he turned and glared through the glass in his gas-mask at the crowd." And what is one to make of the sitters-in at the Old Union, who cheered the news of the fire-bombing of the Free Campus Movement, but then, when they were raided, accused the university of betrayal and responded by a glass-breaking spree? I see that my colleague Mancall has described the raid (upon which the police apparently insisted) as "outrageous." How is one going to talk with Mancall, or with Kahn,[14] about the future of the university? What collegial ties are possible with these corrupters of the young?

Mr. Nixon's Cambodia invasion may well go down in history as the event which triggered the unrestrained plunge of the American University into chaos and self-destruction. Until then, we were, just barely, holding back the forces of barbarism. It's not going to be easy to reform our lines...

Here we have had the firebombing of the America House, which, I dare say, was to have been expected. Since violence breeds violence, and conflagrations fascinate fire-bugs, there has also been a wave of fires (like the . . . fire last week in *Rathaus Schöneberg* [Schoeneberg City Hall]), the motivation for which seems obscure. . . .

Meanwhile, the destruction of the universities goes on apace in Berlin. Students in the introductory *Übung* [tutorial] in Old English at the Free

---

14 Harold L. "Hal" Kahn (1930–2019), a specialist in 17th- and 18th-century Chinese history, mentored students at Stanford for more than forty years. During the 1970s, he was one of the Stanford faculty's most vehement critics of the Vietnam War.

University have had to ask . . . for protection against further disturbances of their work by "*Rote Zelle Anglistik*" [Red Cell English Studies][15] which has taken the position that there is no justification for an *Übung* in historical linguistics, since the discipline is a product of the 18th and 19th centuries, since it supported fascism in Germany, and since it makes no contribution to the solution of the Vietnam problem... Meanwhile, the Technical University, operating under the Berlin University Law, has, like its sister university, elected an *Assistent* as president. This will almost certainly be followed by new resignations among the senior staff...

The news on the other fronts is no happier. Nixon's move into Cambodia may have been prompted in part by the Soviet policy in Egypt, where the Soviets seem to have pulled off what they could not work in Cuba. If so, it may have an adverse effect upon the Strategic Arms Limitation Treaty talks, to say nothing of those in Paris and those which we would all like to see started in Geneva to redo the work of 1954. . . .

Sunday, 10 May 1970. Berlin.
. . . According to today's papers, demonstrations by the *Außerparlamentarische Opposition* [Extra-Parliamentary Opposition] yesterday in the Hardenbergstraße and Ernst Reuter Platz caused injuries to 250 policemen; three people were wounded by shots fired wildly by a plainclothesman trying to protect himself from a group trying to kick him to death; two police horses had to be shot, one because both its front legs were broken when a demonstrator hit them with an iron bar, the other because of catapult wounds; and almost a million Deutsche Marks of damages were done to banks, the IBM building at Ernst Reuter Platz, and other buildings. The Amerika Haus, firebombed last week, was saved. All of this as a protest against the Cambodia invasion. Less violent disturbances in London, where, nevertheless, one female demonstrator said over the radio (I heard her) that the American embassy would have to be burned down, since this imperialistic power could not be allowed to have representation in London...

Monday, 11 May 1970. Berlin.
. . . Worked all afternoon and got well into the first chapter of my book. Encouraged, I went off to the Opera House to hear *Das Rheingold*. . . . Walked

---

15 In the late 1960s and early 1970s, the Socialist German Student League and the Extra-Parliamentary Opposition began to splinter and an assortment of radical left-wing groups were formed in the West German university departments, including various "Red Cells."

down, afterwards, to the Ernst Reuter Platz and looked at the damage. Frightful. In the IBM building, windows broken as high up as the fourth floor, and *all* of the show windows on the street, as well as those in the Deutsche Bank on the opposite corner, were smashed... At home the big demonstration in Washington apparently went off quietly, but at the University of Colorado the oldest building on campus was burned down. We have raised a generation of fire-bugs. . . .

Whitsunday, 17 May 1970. Berlin.
. . . Friday, dinner at the Horst Hartwiches, who have a nice place on Schmidt-Ott Straße, around the corner from the Botanical Gardens. The G. N. Knauers were on hand (the last time I saw them they were translating the address of welcome to JFK on the occasion of his visit to Berlin). He is now the leader of the *Notgemeinschaft für eine Freie Universität* [Emergency Society for a Free University] Berlin and believes the Communists have already captured the university. He has no regard for anyone I mentioned: everyone is either weak or a scoundrel. I learned some interesting things, among them that Harry Press is now professor of journalism and actually gave a job to Ulrike Meinhof, who the day before yesterday helped an *Außerparlamentarische Opposition* member named Baader, in jail for setting fire to a warehouse in Frankfurt, escape.[16] Baader had been allowed, under scanty guard, to go to the Sociological Institute of the Free University to look up some stuff for his doctoral dissertation. She [Meinhof] was waiting for him and, as they were using the catalogue room, two accomplices broke in and started to shoot out the place, and they all lammed out leaving three people wounded, one of them, a 62-year-old caretaker, so badly that his life is in danger. Crimes of this kind are very rare in Germany, and this is the first political case in which arms have been used with intent to kill. . . . In any event, Press had given [Meinhof] this job, despite the fact that, when she had separated from her husband, the editor of the journal *Konkret*, she and some of her friends from a Berlin commune in which she was living, had a "go-in" in her husband's house and destroyed his pictures and furniture and defecated in his bed. This is a true story. Others that I heard from Knauer I found hard to believe, and, on the whole, it was a depressing evening, with all the talk on the same subject. . . .

---

[16] Ulrike Meinhof (1934–1976) and Andreas Baader (1943–1977) were founding members of the Red Army Faction, a radical left-wing terrorist group that engaged in bombings, robberies, and other attacks against the West German government and capitalist institutions. Both Meinhof and Baader died by suicide in somewhat mysterious circumstances while serving time in prison.

My Eisenhower review was in the *NY Times* last Sunday and has been reprinted this weekend in the Paris *Tribune*.[17] Also my article on Weimar intellectuals has been singled out for mention in an article by Carl Schorske in *The New York Review of Books*, in which I am set up as a conservative straw man for Carl to pull down. He doesn't quite say so, but his description of my article, which is inexact and without any quotations, makes the point.[18] I shall lie in wait for an opportunity to reply...

Monday, 18 May 1970. Berlin.
Schorske's article is intended to defend the non-party intellectuals against the charge that they helped kill the Weimar Republic. His paragraphs on me begin: "Significantly, the scholar who opened this inquest (i.e., the examination of the intellectuals) was Gordon A. Craig etc." The exact meaning of the adverb is never made clear. *Na ja*! [Well yeah!]. . . .

Saturday, 23 May 1970. Berlin.
. . . Yesterday morning I went to the Kennedy Institute and managed to find the copy of the *New York Review of Books* that has the second half of [Carl] Schorske's piece on Weimar intellectuals.[19] An interesting piece but one in which he shows the innocence that Henry Turner complains of in a letter he sent me after reading the first part of Schorske's article and an excessive desire to prove that he, as an American intellectual, is not making the mistakes the Weimar intellectuals did (if, indeed they made mistakes, and he is a bit ambivalent on this point). In the second part, he discusses Peter Gay's book on the subject and accuses him, first, of not reading his literary sources carefully enough (Gay will be clever enough to see that Carl really means that he doesn't understand Rilke and Hofmannsthal as well as Carl) and, second, of having values that are those of "America's older generation liberals, appreciative of aesthetic culture but suspicious of the world of instinct with which it is connected." I guess Carl would put me in the same boat... I have to review George Mosse's *Germans and Jews* which has a chapter on Weimar intellectuals. It will be interesting to find where he stands, although I think I can guess. . . .

Monday, 1 June 1970, Berlin.

---

[17] Gordon A. Craig, "The Papers of Dwight David Eisenhower," *New York Times Book Review* (10 May 1970): 1, 26.

[18] Gordon A. Craig, "Engagement and Neutrality in Weimar Germany," *Journal of Contemporary History* 2: 2 (April 1967): 49–63.

[19] Carl E. Schorske, "Weimar and the Intellectuals: II," *New York Review of Books* (May 21, 1970): 20–24.

Worked all day. In the evening to the Hartwiches again, this time for a discussion with [Otto] von Simson of Art, Horst Sanmann of Economics, Fischer, Dean of the *Wiso* [Economic and Social Sciences] faculty, Bernd Rüthers of Law, and a couple of others. All agreed that the "movement" in the universities here is passing ever more into the hands of the Marxist-Leninists, that the "Rote Zellen" [Red Cells] are in close touch with the *Kommunistische Partei Deutschlands* [German Communist Party], and that they probably have contacts with people in the East. All agreed that the universities—the Free University, Technical University, and mostly the *Pädogogische Hochschule* [teacher-training colleges]—are "*untermauert*" [fortified] to an extent that new appointments are only possible if the candidates are Marxists. All agreed that the schools are "*untermauert*" also, by people like [name omitted], and that this extends even to the Kennedy School, where one now sees pictures of Mao and Che next to those of JFK. The American teachers are worse in some cases than the Germans. Item: Taubes[20] at the Free University, who couldn't make a career at home and now does it here in politics and is married to Margarethe von Brentano,[21] a vice president of the FU who [is] all but a declared Communist. General criticism of Brandt's *Ostpolitik* [Eastern policy], feeling that he is over-intent on a success and will pay dangerously for it. Meanwhile, the sentiment grows in the left wing of his party that perhaps Germany should think of the Yugoslav solution to its problems. Most interesting is the general agreement that the most encouraging thing here recently was the Allied cold shoulder to Pres. [Alexander] Wittkowsky's (Technical University) demand that the route of the Allied Forces parade be changed. Several people said that the Allies should take a stronger, even ultimative position *vis-à-vis* the city gov't here or the federal gov't in Bonn... Interesting and depressing evening. . . .

Wednesday, 3 June 1970. Berlin.

. . . In the evening to the Brewster Morris's. . . . I gave Brewster the gist of Monday's discussion. He was most interested, saying that his people are

[20] Jacob Taubes (1923–1987) was a charismatic and controversial figure in the field of Jewish Studies, attracted to transgressive and apocalyptic themes in the Jewish mystical tradition.

[21] Margherita von Brentano di Tremezzo (1922–1995), who had received her doctorate in philosophy under the supervision of Martin Heidegger in 1948, was the first woman to hold the office of Vice President at Freie Universität Berlin, from 1970 to 1972. From 1971, she held a professorship at Freie Universität Berlin Institute of Philosophy before being appointed Professor Emerita in 1987.

aware that meetings are being held between *Rote Zelle* [Red Cell] leaders and people in the East, but that he cannot keep on top of such things because his staff has been cut 30%, Washington—reassured about the threat from the right—apparently believing that Berlin is secure. He strongly urged me to see the man on the German desk in the State Department, James Sutterlin, and is writing to tell him to give me some time. . . .

Saturday, 6 June 1970. Berlin.
On board Lufthansa 408 to NYC. Hard work all week and finally finished the second chapter yesterday. It looks all right and what this means is that I have finished 30,000 words in the last month, which is not bad. . . .

Wednesday, 17 June 1970. New Hampshire.
Finished proofs of first 13 chapters of the new edition[22] and mailed them back to New York… With Phyl to Sharm… Otherwise, a quiet day…

The *Freie Demokratische Partei* [Free Democratic Party] did badly in the state elections the other day, and it looks bad for the *Sozialdemokratische Partei Deutschlands* [Social Democratic Party of Germany] in the months ahead. Too many people are afraid of Brandt's *Ostpolitik*, I guess—afraid of the things I told Huizinga and Sutterlin about… The *Los Angeles Times* has reversed itself on the Vietnam war and is now calling for complete withdrawal. The *Washington Star* has come out with a strong attack on Nixon's policy of stoking the fires of the right in the country—remaining silent while Agnew arouses suspicion of the young and the free press, accepting a hard hat from construction workers after their kind had beaten up college kids, etc. . . .

Friday, 19 June 1970. New Hampshire.
Finished and mailed proofs of chapters 14 to 21… Despite all the polls and the newspaper articles (including a feature piece in the *N.Y. Times Magazine* last Sunday called "All's Well with the World of Harold Wilson" by Anthony Lewis), the Conservatives have won a whopping victory in the British elections, and another classmate of mine, Teddy Heath, will become P.M. (while yet another, Denis Healey, will cease being Secretary of Defense—a pity, for he was good at it). Economic fears and, I guess, the racism brought into the campaign by Enoch Powell probably effected this result. When I wrote the first draft of my revised text last summer I predicted it, and now I shall merely have to add to but not change, the

---

22 Harcourt published the third edition of Craig's textbook, *Europe Since 1815*, in June 1971.

proofs of my chapter 29. But why are newspapermen and pollsters so egregiously wrong all the time? Surely because they are always too close to events and because they make no adjustments for what happened yesterday and the day before. . . .

Tuesday, 30 June 1970. Berlin.
. . . The situation in the universities has not improved in the three weeks of my absence. In Heidelberg the Dept. of Law has closed because one of its faculty had acid poured over his back by a student, apparently in retaliation for a box on the ears which he gave to a woman student who had called him a *Dreckschwein* [filthy pig]. The *Sozialistischer Deutscher Studentenbund* [Socialist German Student League] has been banned in Heidelberg, but have apparently won in elections to governing bodies. Since only 40% of the student body voted, there as here, the extreme radicals have increased their hold over the student representation. Tonight, in Heidelberg, there are 5000 people in the streets in a demonstration of solidarity with the SDS. At the Free University and Technical University similar demonstrations have been called for tonight, with what kind of response I do not know. At dinner tonight [name omitted] told me he has been expecting a call from Berlin but that, in all likelihood, it will be blocked by the students and assistants because he is considered a conservative. In Munich, the vacancy left by Bußmann's departure can't be filled because the students want Wehler and the professors don't and a complete stalemate has been reached. If this sort of thing goes on, we will soon reach a stage where permanent vacancies will result from all resignations and deaths. And there will be lots more resignations. Another law professor has left the Free University—to go to Bielefeld! And yet the FU president . . . says that all is well, except in the eyes of those who believe in the "*ewige Gestrige*" [eternal yesterday]. In a statement couched in a kind of Nazi style, he has now directly attacked the "*Notgemeinschaft für eine Freie Universität*" [Emergency Society for a Free University]. (Walter Kelly in an interesting article in *Die Zeit*, "*Leichenrede auf eine Fakultät*" [Funeral speech at a faculty], says that one need only substitute the word "Jews" for "Professors" in student newspapers these days to find oneself reading the purest *Kreisleiterprosa* [Nazi District Leader prose].) . . .

Thursday, 2 July 1970. Berlin.
. . . The big news today, sent on by Lew Spitz, is that Ken Pitzer has resigned as president of Stanford. His resignation letter is very odd, blaming everything on Cambodia. His press, however, is mixed, with no little

emphasis on criticism of his weakness during the May troubles, much of it from Southern California, and the loss of money by offending donors by his concessions to the left.

Soviet-Chinese boundary talks in Peking have broken down, which may help bring some cooperation between the U.S. and the Soviet Union in the Middle East. Nasser is in Moscow, but is apparently having a hard time. . . .

Mittwoch, 8. Juli 1970. Berlin.

. . . Everything is politicized. The Berlin Film Festival has just broken down because of a dispute over a German film *O.K.* about the rape of a Vietnam girl by four American soldiers, played not against a Vietnamese background but a Bavarian one. The jury, quite properly, asked the selection committee (which had barred an American documentary film about the Soviet action in Czechoslovakia in 1968) whether it had considered the preamble of the festival's constitution (which talks about promoting international understanding) when it selected *O.K.* for prize competition. This was blown up by the producer and the press into a suppression of free speech. Result: breakdown of festival, with no prizes awarded but—*aber natürlich* [naturally]—an invitation from San Francisco to the producer of *O.K.*, asking him to show his film at the festival there… *Unerfreulich*! [None-too-pleasant!]. . . .

Monday, 27 July 1970. Vienna.

. . . To the hotel to change and off to Sacher's to meet Andreas Psomas of the Ministry of Education in Cyprus, a former student of mine at Stanford, who, for reasons I can't understand, was refused the right to work for a Ph.D. in the Stanford International Development Education Center despite a record of straight As. . . .

While drinking a glass of sherry with Psomas I noticed a tall man with a cane and a heavy limp and a florid face come into the bar and, after a second, recognized him as Axel von dem Bussche, who once sought to blow Hitler up. I knew him years ago in Ed Earle's seminar on German rearmament, and he was instrumental in getting me an *Auswärtiges Amt* [German Foreign Office] invitation for a month's visit to Germany in 1958. I introduced myself and we arranged to meet tomorrow.

Alarmist news from Christian Democratic Union sources about the concessions Brandt is ready to make in Moscow in regard to Berlin. Grim warnings from Palestine guerillas about what they will do if the U.S. plan is accepted. . . .

Thursday, 30 July 1970. Budapest.

I was never able to determine what Bussche was doing, although he seems now to live in Switzerland and have something to do with the World Bank and similar organizations. He was amusing on the Austrians' *gringo* complex *vis-à-vis* the Germans, was caustic about Brandt's *Ostpolitik* [Eastern policy], and said that the only people practicing diplomacy in the classical manner and doing so with conspicuous success were the Russians—a thought worth bearing in mind. He urged me to visit him in Switzerland, and said that one of his neighbors was Golo Mann,[23] who was finishing a book on Wallenstein. . . .

Saturday, 1 August 1970. Belgrade.

The clippings over ["Disillusionment in Havana," *International Herald Tribune*, July 28, 1970] represent in my mind the biggest story of last week, although this might be disputed in view of everything else that is going on—the Germans in Moscow, the hassle over the U.S. plan for the Middle East, which is splitting both the Arab world and the Israeli government, the horrors of Charles Manson's trial for the murder of Sharon Tate, and the smog and electricity crisis in New York City. But the extent of Castro's failure and his candor in admitting it are staggering. It (the latter) reminds one of Stanley Baldwin's confession about his miscalculation of German military power and Nasser's assumption of responsibility for failure in 1967. In both of those cases, the enormity of the failure was so palpable that it paradoxically aroused sympathy, and even admiration, for the culprit; and that will probably be true in this instance too. Nor is there much hope of radical youth grasping what the *NY Times* calls "the real moral" of the story. Castroism is more an idea than a system, and Fidel, incompetent as he is, will remain a hero, just like that muddled and painfully inept guerilla Che Guevara. . . .

Monday, 10 August 1970. Rome.

. . . There is a cease fire in the Near East, although it does not cover Lebanon and there is fighting between the guerillas and the Israelis on the borders there. There is also a treaty between Bonn and Moscow (Brandt goes to Moscow for the ceremony of signing this week) and it apparently does *not* include anything resembling recognition of the German Democratic Republic. According to a story in the *Sunday Times*, the Russians

---

[23] Golo Mann (1909–1994), son of the novelist Thomas Mann, published his biography of the Bohemian military commander Albrecht von Wallenstein (1583–1634) in 1971.

have admitted privately that the treaty is necessary to provide them with scientific assistance and prevent their falling further behind the U.S. in this respect. . . .

Wednesday, 18 August 1970. Stanford.
We have been home for a full week, and I am beginning to feel that home is normal. . . . On Thursday, I began to get things in order by returning to my office most of the things [name omitted] took out at the height of the troubles in May when arson was a very real threat. . . .

Monday, 7 September 1970. Labor Day. Stanford.
Norman Stone[24] of Caius College, Cambridge, to lunch. Shop talk about Russian army and economic production in WWI. A Glaswegian, very intelligent and energetic and with strong money sense. In love with Stanford, he says. Would like to stay. Who wouldn't? . . .

Monday, 14 September 1970. Stanford.
On Friday started checking quotations in Treitschke's essays on Byron and Milton, since Annemarie Holborn, who may translate them, consulted "expert advice" and was told they would be very difficult to track down. I have found 22 of the Milton ones and 12 of the Byron, and the problem is, as far as I am concerned, solved. I have also learned that Treitschke was often sloppy and sometimes dishonest with quotations—citing them from memory, adding to them, putting one of the Tempter's speeches in *Paradise Regained* into Jesus's mouth, etc. All in all, I have good sport with this, have re-read much of Milton, and have discovered the charm of Byron's letters. . . .

Yesterday Phil Crowl arrived to stay for a week with us, before he moves into his apartment, and we sat up and talked about the state of the world. He has been serving on an advisory board to the Marine Corps and feels that the boys in green are feeling so unjustly pushed by the academic mind that they are beginning to feel themselves an oppressed minority. Here we have the beginning of a military mind, to say nothing of an American version of the "stab-in-the-back" theory…

Thursday, 17 September 1970. Stanford.
. . . Over the weekend [Jacob] Jack Viner died, a remarkable man from whom I learned a great deal, including humility. I can remember once, in a

---

24 Norman Stone (1941–2018), a prolific historian of modern Europe, taught at Oxford and Cambridge and at Bilkent University in Turkey, and served as an adviser to Margaret Thatcher.

seminar at the Institute when I attacked his expressed views with fire and authority, and he sat before me, crushed and discomfited. A week later, he said, almost timidly, "Last week I expressed certain opinions here that were attacked so devastatingly and persuasively by Gordon Craig that I wondered where I could ever have found such insubstantial notions. So I checked my files and found that they were all in an article by Gordon Craig."

He was a lovely man and a wise one, and I clung to him as a fellow spoiler. He loved climbing over the fences into other people's disciplines and was always delighted, maliciously, when the specialists were annoyed. I have lived to see why he was amused and how insubstantial the claims of proprietorship by the "experts" often are.

All in all, a gay soul who leaves a world not overly supplied with such. . . .

Monday, 21 September 1970. Stanford.
. . . In the evening to Lew Spitz's to meet with the conservatives (Potter, Wright, Fehrenbacher, Lederer, Paret, etc.) to discuss situation in the university and the department. Not a very pleasant occasion—smelling of a cabal. But I guess the times call for this sort of thing. I still maintain that we must retain our contact with our students and (given the irrationality of our associate professors) with the younger men, and that this, in the long run, will be the most effective tactic against the illusionists, the loonies, the resentful, and the revolutionaries.

Monday, 28 September 1970. Stanford.
. . . During the day Nasser died, re-opening the whole barrel of snakes in the Middle East, for there is every chance that the agreement just patched together between Hussein of Jordan and the Palestinian guerillas will now break down. The Soviets must be biting their thumbs, for Nasser was their man, in a sense, and without him they may not be able to control all the wild men. Although it should be added, perhaps, that the Syrians, who lost 100 tanks in their drive into Jordan, may not be anxious to get into action again soon. Their experience may make the Soviets clamp down on any Egyptian plan to cross the Suez. After all, it's their equipment that is being chewed up.

Wednesday, 30 September 1970. Stanford.
. . . Lunch with Phil Crowl (very cock-a-hoop because he drew 341 students to the introductory International Relations course which our committee planned and which I named "How Nations Deal With Each Other"). He's

taking a hard line (or what he calls a "hard-hatted-intellectuals" line) and I hope doesn't overdo it... My grad colloquium on the period 1850–1890 has drawn 21 people, so I'll have to teach it in two sections. Had first session with them all today, and I must say that it is good to be teaching again. . . .

Friday, 9 October 1970. Stanford.
At 10 meeting of Committee on International Relations, which is flourishing. . . . The course "How Nations Deal with Each Other" now has over 400 students and will, because it is a success, have to be staffed for next year, and we should build upon it by funding new courses. (I have decided to take a section of 40 in Phil's "Nations" course, thus persuading him to do the same and increasing its umph.)... Lunch with the Department Right in Portola Valley where Carl Degler[25] called to my attention the story in yesterday's *N.Y. Times* that the U.S. and Israel were prepared to take coordinated action to support Jordan if the Syrian tank attack had been more successful. The story in the *Times* is detailed enough to be convincing and to justify Nixon's boast that we played a part in the backdown. It is to be hoped that the Soviets learned something from this.

Tuesday, 19 October 1970. Stanford.
. . . Call from Don Winbigler[26] who informed me, to my horror, that [name omitted] had resigned from the University Senate and that I, as first alternate (no one had even *told* me I was an alternate)—will now have to serve. That shoots my Thursday afternoons, and, if we have troubles on campus this year, much more besides. . . .

Wednesday, 20 October 1970. Stanford.
An excellent session this morning with a dozen students in Phil Crowl's course—on the dropping of the bomb and the beginning of the Cold War. Phil himself is delighted with Stanford students. He says they are friendly

---

25 Carl Degler (1921–2014), an American historian, joined Stanford's Department of History in 1968 and retired as Emeritus Professor in 1990. He received the 1972 Pulitzer Prize for History for *Neither Black nor White: Slavery and Race Relations in Brazil and the United States* (Madison: University of Wisconsin Press, 1971) and was elected President of the American Historical Association in 1986.

26 H. Donald Winbigler (1909–2000) joined the Stanford faculty as an assistant professor of speech and drama in 1940, receiving a full professorship in 1949, but spent most of his career in administrative positions, including a long tenure as Dean of Students from 1950 to 1967. As academic secretary to the University from 1967 to 1974, he helped to develop the charter that became the constitution for the Faculty Senate.

and as intelligent as the students in Princeton when he taught there in the 40s and says that he wishes he had a few of them in Nebraska... In the afternoon, a good meeting of the second section of my colloquium (Mazzini and Cavour)... In a conversation with George Knoles, I found that the members of our department who are Senators are Potter, Wright, and I—a very conservative trio. Dawson, who was seeking to make a career of being a senator, was not re-elected, which must have surprised some of his ardent supporters in Pitzer's office. . . .

Thursday, 21 October 1970. Stanford.
Worked at home all day. In the evening to the Law School for a meeting of Herb Packer's committee on Faculty Discipline. Interesting but inconclusive. Several members . . . are opposed to faculty members doing anything to call attention to the irresponsibility of other faculty members, arguing that this is the responsibility of the Administration. Majority feel that we can't do anything about the radical zealots but that we might, by defining a few rules, make some of the younger dopes understand what their job is all about. . . .

Tuesday, 10 November 1970. Stanford.
It has just been announced that Charles de Gaulle is dead. The last of the giants of whom Sulzberger wrote. Or almost. Tito is still alive. The President is flying to France for the funeral services...

Busy with correspondence. It is dreadful how much of my time goes to writing letters about professional things, when I might be getting some work done! What with Pacific Coast Branch business and that of the Central European Section of American Historical Association (of which I am vice chairman) and letters from all points asking for my opinion of So-and-So, who is up for promotion (and of whom I have never heard), and requests from students asking for recommendations or something else, all my time is eaten up. . . .

Thursday, 19 November 1970. Stanford.
A heavy day of meetings. . . .

In the afternoon a meeting of the University Faculty Senate. Hours of logic-chopping on questions like: wouldn't it be less offensive to call any "emergency force" raised to work during campus disorders a "building surveillance team." Afterwards, Dick Lyman said he was waiting to hear my maiden speech. I answered evasively that I had to learn the waters in which I would have to swim. "There are great depths here," he said. "I wouldn't have put it quite that way," I answered. "Why," he retorted. "There are depths of shallowness here that have never been plumbed!"

In the evening to the Law School for a meeting of the Commission on Faculty Self-Discipline. . . . Making some progress. We'd better. The Senate is waiting for our report and the President keeps saying publicly that he hopes it will be hard-hitting.

Wednesday, 25 November 1970. Stanford.
. . . The bombing of North Vietnam has started the radicals marching again and has led to a rampage which cost $9000 in glass breakage on Monday evening. There is, according to the local press, some faculty participation in these affairs, and that is one more reason for the Herb Packer's Commission's existence. I dare say Herb is hard at work on a first draft of the report and will be trying it on us soon. . . .

Wednesday, 9 December 1970. Stanford.
. . . At 2:15 Colloquium II, very lively; and then, at 4:15, upstairs to lecture to graduate students on how to lecture. I had taken some care with this, going back to my Marine lectures but writing an essentially new lecture on (1) choosing a theme, (2) organizing the lecture that will develop it, (3) composing it, and (4) delivering it. Under point 1, I had a bravura description of Felix Gilbert giving me a theme for a lecture on 18th-century diplomacy ("Passion in the Age of Reason: The Whim of the Prince and the Dream of Law"), and under point 4 I had descriptions of Sontag, Buzzer Hall (the invisible object, and the steam engine), and Thomas Jefferson Wertenbaker (the famous spectacle bit).[27] With this cast of characters, the lecture could hardly fail. Carl Degler said afterwards: "I had no idea you were so *funny* on the platform!" The students seem to have been diverted, and they may have learned something. . . .

[1971]

Monday, 11 January 1971. Stanford.
Lecture this morning in my course, and again, at 1:40, in the arms control course. In evening, with Phyl, to Club for reception for participants in UN Conference being put on by Hoover. Learned that small band of thugs had broken up first session by refusing to allow Henry Cabot Lodge to speak. . . .

---

[27] Craig repeated this lecture on how to give a lecture several times, and eventually consented to a video recording of it by the Center for Teaching and Learning at Stanford.

Tuesday, 19 January 1971. Stanford.
After my lecture this morning, went to Dick Lyman to tell him of my CIA connection. Afterwards, we talked of the Packer Commission Report which he does *not* like and does not think the Trustees will accept unless modified. He says it leaves him with responsibility but diminishes his power to fulfill it. He is in a hard-boiled mood and has brought charges against [name omitted] and 10 students for their part in the disruption of the [Henry Cabot] Lodge meeting. In [name omitted]'s case, he has also by-passed the Interim Board set up by the Senate until such time as the Packer Commission Report was accepted. A fine kettle of fish. Meanwhile, I have been put on the Floor Management Committee to put the Packer Report into legislative form. That will not be an easy job now. . . .

Wednesday, 27 January 1971. Stanford.
. . . Contentious department meeting on role of student representation at department meetings. Bleeding heart Liberals (Degler, Dawson, Langmuir) against intellectual hard-hats (Fehrenbacher, Spitz, Lederer, Vucinich, Craig). . . .

Thursday, 28 January 1971. Stanford.
Discussion in Academic Senate of Packer Commission Report. A not unfavorable reception, despite the fact that the President reported earlier on his handling of the [name omitted] business and received a lot of flack from English department lefties like [Ronald] Rebholz[28] and [John] Felstiner. We received some criticism from the right (Baxter et al.) which I fended off, but on the whole, it was not unfriendly. Even so, the job of the Senate's Floor Management Committee (of which I am chairman), which has the task of whipping this into legislative form, is not going to be easy. . . .

Thursday, 18 February 1971. Stanford.
David Potter died at 6 a.m. this morning.

Friday, 19 February 1971. Stanford.
Senate meeting yesterday afternoon was highlighted by an attack by Linus Pauling upon Dick Lyman for his suspension of [name omitted]. The old ass—for that is really what he is, a man besotted by his self-importance—accused the president of an unheard of breach of academic freedom and

---

[28] Ronald A. Rebholz (1932–2013), a specialist in English Renaissance literature, taught at Stanford from 1961 to 2008, and was a recipient of the Lloyd W. Dinkelspiel Award for Outstanding Service to Undergraduate Education in 1980.

betrayed, as he was speaking, a curious insensitivity to what academic freedom is all about. One senses, as one listens to Pauling and all the English department liberals (Rebholz, et al.) that they have no feeling for the responsibility that goes, or should go, with freedom and that they are always ready to believe the worst of any form of authority, locally or nationally. We went on to debate an English department resolution deploring the recent extension and proximate further extension of the war in South East Asia—a resolution imprecise in language and emotional in tone and with no apparent purpose except to display the virtue of its author. We poked holes in it and forced it to be held back until the next meeting. By then, of course, the situation in S.E. Asia may have worsened and we shall get something more violent in tone. I am opposed to the Senate passing resolutions on national policy, since most Senators are innocents with respect to it; but I see no possibility of preventing this kind of breast-beating. And, I must say, President Nixon does not help us conservative types. He is less than candid about his intentions.

Saturday, 20 February 1971. Stanford.
. . . My Floor Management Committee met with Dick Lyman yesterday, and I was surprised to hear him say that he wanted us to meet with him and the university lawyer and work out a document on faculty self-discipline that would be satisfactory to us and to the administration before taking it to the Senate. This I immediately vetoed, saying that our committee was a Senate committee that would bring in its own report and that, while I welcomed consultation, I had no desire to bring in a report that would be attacked because it had been written in the President's Office. Dick was distinctly unhappy about this, but I was firm and was supported by my committee. I find it odd that he should have thought we could have gone along with him on this. I have no desire to bring in draft legislation that will weaken presidential power substantially in matters of discipline, but his view of what can be done here and ours will be different, and I intend to take ours to the Senate. In the long run, this tactic is more likely to support his position than the one he seems to have in mind. I can, of course, see his position. He has to worry about the Trustees, and his authority over them may be less secure than he wishes and, for that reason, he may not wish a Senate action that goes to the heart of their power, as well as his own...

Sunday, 21 February 1971. Stanford.
. . . Came back to read the *New York Times* and brood over the Laos business. All the *Times* writers (Johnny Ochs [Oakes], Tom Wicker, and

Scotty Reston) seem to have lost all faith in Nixon and appear to see in the future only an ever-expanding war. Their unanimity makes me doubt the validity of my own position, which has been to support the Nixon policy and to take the Cambodian and Laotian invasions as necessary parts of our withdrawal policy. Could be that I am naïve. It is interesting to find that, in *Die Zeit*, Marion Gräfin Dönhoff is taking U.S. withdrawal for granted and is already talking about the future Sino-Japanese rivalry. . . .

This evening got back to my *Deutsche Geschichte* [*Germany, 1866–1945*] and made good progress with last section of the Bismarck foreign policy chapter. I hope to finish it in the next few days, although this will depend a bit on other commitments. I have three new lectures to write before next Tuesday, and I must take two classes for Ivo Lederer, who is ill… The fact is that I really work very hard at teaching, which outsiders seem to regard as a somehow automatic skill like pumping up tires or winding clocks. My session on Hegel, for instance, took nearly two days of preparation, and these new lectures will involve a very heavy expenditure of time. . . .

I was reminded this evening that it is a scant two years since Dilys Potter died. On 31 March 1969 I gave the eulogy for Dwight Eisenhower in the Memorial Church and Dilys and David came. The next day Dilys shot herself, a Tuesday that was; and on Saturday Marty was married and David telephoned her in the morning before the wedding to wish her well. And now he's gone too, and I wish I had seen him more often in his last days. I was very remiss in this, going up the hill only twice, the last time a week before his death, when he was too far gone to talk much… He was a great man, and it is good to know that he finished his book for the American Nation series before he died.[29] And, apparently, his two presidential addresses (Organization of American Historians and American Historical Association) as well. . . .

Sunday, 28 February 1971. Stanford.
Memorial service for David. Large crowd, including Don Treadgold and Tom Clark as representatives of American Historical Association and Society of American Historians respectively. All talks good, even Napier's, and music excellent. Had dreadful time doing my piece, which I finished only 40 minutes before the service. Made some use of *The Pilgrim's Progress*—

[29] David M. Potter's *The Impending Crisis, 1848–1861*, completed by his colleague Don E. Fehrenbacher, received the Pulitzer Prize for History in 1977.

Mr. Valiant-for-Truth, "a true man a long season."[30] Seems to have gone down well enough. Had the feeling that this was the first such service that I had ever attended in which everything said in praise of the deceased was true. The loss of David came to me more powerfully today than when he died, and Carl Degler told me that he felt the same way. . . .

Thursday, 1 April 1971. Stanford.
. . . In the afternoon, a long debate in the Senate about medical appointments, which led to some speeches by [name omitted], Rebholz of English, and a young man in Education complaining about the way in which the promotion system at Stanford over-emphasizes research and discriminates against "brilliant teachers." After listening to this nonsense for a while, I raised my hand and was recognized in due course and made a very hard speech, which I described as "a small Tory caveat" to [name omitted]'s remarks. I said I had been listening to moans about the poor underprivileged brilliant teachers for 32 years but that it had been my experience in that time that there are many fewer of them than one is led to suppose and many of them don't remain brilliant. I added that evaluation of teaching is difficult and always parochial, which is not true of research, which is why research is the most reliable criterion of judgment for promotion. After we adjourned, Hofstadter,[31] the Nobel laureate in physics, congratulated me.

Thursday, 20 May 1971. Stanford.
Last lecture in my German history course—today on cultural tendencies in the Bonn Republic, with particular reference to Günter Grass as the engaged artist. Much use of *The Tin Drum, Dog Years,* and *Locally Anaesthetized*, as well as some of the political speeches. The lectures have gone very well this year. My style, as I get older, seems to combine tight organization and the high literary style with alarming sallies into the unexpected. Very little preaching, although the occasion often rises (it's better to let the customers see the contemporary parallel and draw their own conclusions) and no damned whimsy. And never—a principle I've remained true to for 32 years now—anything off-color. Historians have so many funny stories to tell that I have never found that necessary. I do find myself succumbing to an unfortunately reminiscent vein—the reaction of

---

[30] See Gordon A. Craig, "In Memoriam: David M. Potter," *Pacific Historical Review* 40 (1971): 415–16.

[31] Robert Hofstadter (1915–1990), a recipient of the 1961 Nobel Prize in Physics, taught at Stanford from 1950 to 1985.

my generation at Oxford to Hitler's early triumphs, for example, or how I felt when France fell. The students seem, however, to like this because I am talking about someone their own age and his reaction to dangerous and tragic events. . . .

Friday, 18 June 1971. Stanford.
. . . The government is seeking to prevent the *NY Times* from printing papers on the Vietnam war that were leaked to it. Right on both sides: the public has a right to know but it also has a right to know that most of the papers printed in the *Times* so far are contingency papers. This will not be realized. By and large, the disclosure of papers does not result in large numbers of people reading and understanding them. But once released, papers become dangerous when the government seeks to withdraw them. No more people read them, of course, or even want to read them, but they resent the restriction on their *potential* reading. As long as publication is allowed, the most faithful readers are from the New Left, who proceed with great authority to misinterpret what they have read, often quite innocently. By and large, the documents—all documents—should be open, unless they compromise non-nationals or menace national security. Neither of these things are true, as far as I can see, in this case. . . .

Thursday, 24 June 1971. Chadd's Ford, Pennsylvania.
. . . The papers are full, and have been for over a week, of the government's attempt to block further publication by the *NY Times*, the *Washington Post*, and the *Boston Globe* of papers from a secret Vietnam documentary report produced by the government at Secretary McNamara's order. Everyone is on a John Peter Zenger kick, and, while I started out on the newspaper side, I have [been] progressively less so as I have listened to the pontifications of James Reston *et al.* Even more troubling is the way in which the press is presenting documents, out of context and with tendentious introductions. This means that contingency papers and first drafts by relatively junior officers are being presented as high policy decisions. This will surely cause misunderstanding and lead to widespread misinterpretation by the smart boys of the New Left school. The report itself must be a curious compilation. At least, one must infer that from the appallingly frank and singularly ill-written letter by its director, Leslie Gelb. His description of the people who worked on it—"uniformly bright and interested, although not always versed in the art of research"—is hardly calculated to inspire confidence in their product. . . .

Friday, 9 July 1971. Cliveden House[32]
We have been here now for ten days and we are getting settled into a very comfortable existence in a lovely setting—the Astor house in which so many extraordinary people did so many extraordinary things—witness the appeasement group of the 30s and, at a later time, John Profumo and Christine Keeler whom that unfortunate man met in the swimming pool in which I swam this afternoon (while Phyl soaked in Lady Astor's bathtub—for we are living in that lovely politician's bedroom and adjoining study, while Charlie has a room to himself across the way). It is pleasant to live among these unobtrusive ghosts—I guess they could hardly be very obtrusive in this group of 80 American students. The students are pleasant, and so are our colleagues. . . .

We came over on the charter flight with the students, leaving New York at 7:30 p.m. on the 29th and arriving in time for breakfast next morning. We had a long weekend to get used to things, which I used to read, for I am teaching British history for the first time since my days at Yale and my first semester at Princeton. It has not been easy, in my first week (now complete) to deal in three lectures with the period 1688–1760, but I have done it and also launched my colloquium on Britain and Europe from 1919 to 1939. Perhaps things will go easier now. . . .

The big issue in the country at the moment is whether Britain will go into the Common Market, and the debate is already heated and, to a foreigner, fascinating. Mr. Heath has laid an effective White Paper before Parliament and the country and backed it with an effective plea for entry. Mr. Wilson is being inscrutable since his front bench is pro-entry and the unions are against. Much talk about suppressed gov't figures, which are probably non-existent. Tonight Wilson's speech in answer to Heath struck me as not very effective, in view of his own past statements in favor of entry. In any case, I agree with Lord George Brown's statement yesterday: "The last time Britain tried to go it alone, Harold got an arrow in his eye."

According to public opinion polls more than half of the country is anti-entry. The polls may be as inaccurate as they were in the last elections. In any case, Heath is not apparently moved by them. Cummings in the *Express* today shows him as Oliver Cromwell pointing to a mace labeled "opinion polls" and saying "Take away that bauble!" . . .

---

[32] Cliveden, an Italianate mansion built in 1666 by the 2nd Duke of Buckingham as a gift to his mistress, housed Stanford's British campus from 1969 to 1983, when the program moved to Oxford.

Saturday, 17 July 1971. Cliveden.
. . . Despite the rallying of the majority of the unions against entrance into the Common Market, the polls indicate some shifting of opinion towards approval of going in. The unions are showing their usual selfishness and stupidity, and it would be a pleasure to see them defeated.

Meanwhile the diplomatic bombshell of the year is the announcement yesterday by President Nixon that Henry Kissinger and Chou En-Lai have agreed on a visit by the President to Peking before May 1972 to regulate relations between the two powers and to discuss matters of common interest. This will spike the guns of the Maoists and the Democrats and those counting on a continuing bear market. . . .

Sunday, 18 July 1971. Cliveden.
. . . Overheard at *The Feathers* [pub] today: An assertive type holding forth to three younger men: "All I say is we've had to beat the Germans twice in the last sixty years and both times the French ratted on us and the Italians ran like hell and I see no reason why we should tie ourselves up with such inferior people."

Tuesday, 24 August 1971. Cliveden.
. . . There seems to be a Four-Power Berlin agreement, guaranteeing access and W. Berlin privileges in E. Berlin, but forbidding future meetings of the Bundestag in Berlin. I haven't seen enough details yet to make sense of it all. . . .

Friday, 24 September 1971. Chester.
. . . A diplomatic sensation that is sure to have widespread repercussions. As a result of information provided by a high-ranking KGB officer, the British have expelled 105 Soviet representatives from this country for espionage and planned sabotage. They have announced also that agents expelled for this sort of activity may not be replaced. This will certainly invite retaliation, but the Russians will suffer more than anyone else. This is a repetition of what happened in 1927, and the Russians have learned nothing since that time about the disadvantages that accrue from basic dishonesty in international relations. Nor do they seem to have learned how to make industrial progress without resorting to the theft of other peoples' technical discoveries, for it is industrial espionage that most of the expelled agents were conducting. What effect this affair will have on plans for a European Security Conference no one can guess at this time. Certainly, however, it will strengthen the hand of the opponents of Willi Brandt's policy. . . .

Sunday, 26 September 1971. Ludlow, Shropshire.
. . . The Russian spy affair is now ballooning in every direction. The *Daily Express* is promoting a search for the British accomplices of the Russians, and others are coming up with revelations, most of which seem contrived; Mrs. Barbara Castle, one of the chief anti-Marketeers in the Labour Party, has advanced the theory that the Conservatives have started the spy story only in order to stampede the country into Europe. The Russians meanwhile, first through Tass but now apparently through more official channels, are claiming that there was no spying at all, and that this is all a dirty Conservative attempt to revive the Cold War. The Russian line is that friendship with them involves—indeed, demands—toleration of espionage (which, in any case, is not official since the Narkomindel [Soviet Foreign Office] does not recognize, and certainly has no control over, what the KGB does). . . .

Mr. Justice [Hugo] Black, who resigned from the Supreme Court ten days ago at the age of 85, is dead in Bethesda Naval Hospital. In 1936, when our group of Rhodes Scholars came to England, he had just been appointed to the court by FDR, and there was a great *brouhaha* because it was discovered that he had once been a member of the Ku Klux Klan. That was the first issue that agitated our group and separated—or helped to separate—the sheep from the goats. He had a long run and a good one, and to the end he was sharp and sensible, as in the Pentagon Papers affair, where I disliked his opinion [defending their publication on the grounds of free speech] but feel that he was, unfortunately, right. . . .

Thursday, 7 October 1971. Cliveden.
I noticed yesterday in Blackwell's that W. H. Auden has published his commonplace book. The art of keeping a commonplace book, aside from publishing it, has always puzzled me. How does one choose what goes into it, so that a deadly sameness does not characterize its pages? When one is taken by some piece of printed wisdom, does he write it down immediately, or wait a week to see if it is still impressive? Are there rules about how many entries per author are allowed? I once started a commonplace book, and at the end of the first week had six quotations from Marcus Aurelius and eight from Bernard Shaw's *Back to Methuselah*. I discontinued it after that.

Sunday, 10 October 1971. Cliveden.
. . . At home, Senator Muskie has ruffled all the dovecotes by announcing, as a regretful fact, that no one can be elected president with a black running mate and by telling New York liberals that it is time that they re-assessed

the meaning of liberalism. . . .

The visit of Emperor Hirohito to Europe has occasioned all sorts of rumpus. I have heard of no American objections to the President's flight to Alaska to greet him as he passed by, but in London there were minor objections and demonstrations, and Lord Mountbatten refused to attend any public ceremony with the Emperor; and in The Hague the demonstrations have been stormier, with burning Japanese flags thrown at his car and shouts of "Murderer!" and the like… Abbie Hoffman has cut his hair, saying long hair has become an affectation of the children of the rich, and has said there may be some hope in the ballot-box after all. Paret thinks that this is a significant sign of changing times. . . .

Friday, 22 October 1971. Cliveden.
. . . Meanwhile, Willi Brandt has been given the Nobel Peace Prize, a fine choice. *The Guardian* had a good feature piece on the choice yesterday . . . and today's press is filled with stories about the excitement generated in Germany by the choice. The last German laureate was Carl von Ossietsky. . . .[33]

Friday, 29 October 1971. Venice.
. . . China is in the UN and Britain is in the Common Market! The world is changing tremendously around us! . . .

Thursday, 16 December 1971. Cliveden.
. . . As the trip, and this volume, comes to an end, I find myself a bit melancholy, glad to be going home but sorry to be leaving England. It is time for me to be getting back to serious work. Aside from fifty lectures and an enormous correspondence, I have written nothing here except my Gervinus piece[34] (of which I am not proud) and my obituary piece for the *Proceedings of the American Philosophical Society* on [Sir Llewellyn] Woodward.[35] The latter did have one sentence with which I am pleased: "There was, perhaps, more of Schlosser than of Ranke in his approach to history, but

---

[33] Carl von Ossietsky (1889–1938), journalist, pacifist, and editor of the left-leaning magazine *Die Weltbühne*, received the Nobel Peace Prize in 1935 for a series of articles that exposed Germany's clandestine rearmament during the 1920s. After years of mistreatment and torture in various Nazi camps, he died of tuberculosis in 1938.

[34] Gordon A. Craig, "Georg Gottfried Gervinus: The Historian as Activist," *Pacific Historical Review* 41 (1972): 1–13.

[35] "Sir Lewellyn Woodward (1890–1971)," *American Philosophical Society Yearbook 1971* (Philadelphia: American Philosophical Society, 1972), 200–202.

he was a better historian than the former, as he was a livelier one than the latter." . . .

[1972]

Wednesday, 5 January 1972. Stanford.

. . . Thinking back on England, I decided to reread my diaries for 1936–1938. Most interesting for emotional comparisons, and for other things, like the account of the tour of the Balliol Players, in which no mention of Teddy Heath occurs, although he was on hand for two weeks. Travel and amusement was, of course, in sub-groups, and there were no group bashes except the performances themselves... Aside from this, I am appalled by the emphasis on booze in the 1936–37 volumes and can only conclude that it is exaggerated, otherwise how did all that work, so faithfully recorded, get done? Much mention of scotch, but of course we drank that only on the ceremonial Thursday pub crawls in the spring of 1937 and at the big parties, and then only at the fag-end of them. Our tipple was, as now, bitter; and, although one entry says I drank seven pints before noon one day, that is clearly a misprint or a flat lie. (Probably seven half-pints)... Once Phyl enters the picture, everything changes tone and becomes very Scott and Zelda. We are always dining at Leoni's *Quo Vadis* in Dean Street or looking for friends in *The Plough* or finding them at Bertorelli's. All this accompanied by stupendous bouts of work in the Public Record Office and the British Museum. What fun it all was. Too bad that

> ...we'll go no more a-roving
> So late into the night,
> Though the heart be still as loving,
> And the moon be still as bright. . . .[36]

Friday, 7 January 1972. Stanford.

. . . Learned that of all Ph.D.s turned out by the department between 1955 and 1971, 13 were trained by Bailey, 21 by me (in ten years!), and 18 by George. Only 14 by Gordon Wright, but then only one each by Dawson and Lederer. Years ago, at an AHA meeting, I overheard Freddy Arzt, then emeritus, boasting that he had produced 30 Ph.D.s. I have already passed that number, if I add in my Princeton chaps. . . .

Friday, 4 February 1972. Stanford.

Al Hastorf asked me today to become chairman of the department for at

---

[36] Craig is quoting from Lord Byron's "So We'll Go No More a Roving."

least the next two years. A job I do not want and one that will slow my real work even more, but one that I can hardly turn down, if only because there is, quite literally, no one available except me who can be trusted with the job. . . . I have the gravest of doubts, but perhaps that is a healthier attitude than the mood of feckless enthusiasm with which Jerry Blum entered upon his chairmanship. Phyllis seems to feel that I should take the job, arguing that, since I am always grousing about interruptions in my work, I might as well have something real to complain about and that all things considered, I am the best available candidate and would suffer under any other. Sensible advice. . . .

Wednesday, 9 February 1972. Stanford.
On Monday afternoon I told Al Hastorf that, against my better judgment, I would serve as chairman for two years. Posed some conditions which he accepted... Since then much work. . . .

Thursday, 30 March 1972. Stanford.
Brought the Faculty Self-Discipline Statement in to the Senate. We didn't get very far, but far enough to destroy Ron Rebholz, who was foolish enough to attack it straight on as shameful without really having studied it closely enough to understand it. Rhetorical questions which he thought would show our ignorance were laughed down by his audience, and Bill Cohen, speaking for the committee, finally made mincemeat of him. He was, for the first time in my experience in the Senate, reduced to silence. Nor did Mark Mancall, that great mind, fare much better. In general, the longer the discussion lasted (and we never got beyond Roman I today) the stronger the report appeared and the more respectful the comments from the floor. It's going to be a long road, but we may win through. . . .

Friday, 21 April 1972. Stanford.
Yesterday in the Senate, we made some progress with the Self-Discipline Code. On the other hand, the President made it clear that he had changed his mind about our reduction of presidential powers (or that the Trustees had changed it for him). He proposed a not unreasonable amendment to our document. I answered by saying that my thinking had not changed and that, although I would, of course, study the President's proposal, I thought the line we had taken was the correct one. I admitted that I could no longer speak for a united committee, and this was true enough. . . . On other aspects of the statement, we had surprisingly little opposition, and a straw vote indicated by a large margin that the Senate would go along with our exclusion of personal misconduct as a basis for discipline. The President

was not very happy about this, but we presented a united front and were apparently persuasive…

Afterwards, to a large party at the Richard Staars in honor of George Kennan, here to do a couple of days' research…

This morning at 7:45 picked George up and took him home for a hearty breakfast. We did not talk about our moustaches, which we have acquired since our last meeting, but about his plan to write a new study on the origins of the Franco-Russian alliance of 1894… Took him back to campus which seemed reasonably normal despite the fact that this is the day of the anti-war strike. . . .

Tuesday, 2 May 1972. Stanford.

Lectured on Hitler's *Gleichschaltung* [coordination of society]. Later informed that the senior class has elected me as one of its favorite lecturers and that I must speak on Class Day. The third time this has happened. . . .

I feel an urge to write coming over me, and think I might get the Treitschke done.[37] Have written Krieger to ask if the publishers really want it, everyone being on the shorts these days…

J. Edgar Hoover died in his sleep last night. . . .

Monday, 8 May 1972. Stanford.

President Nixon announced this evening that, since the North Vietnamese respond to peace overtures with new attacks, we are going to mine Haiphong harbor and interdict rail supply to Hanoi. If, on the other hand, they see the light, agree to a cease fire and release our prisoners, we shall withdraw all our forces within four months of the agreement. A curious amalgam of threat and promise, stick and carrot, the force of which was not enhanced by Mr. Nixon's constant references to American honor. The only predictable result will be new violence on the campuses, which, I guess would be tolerable if the new(?) stance facilitated the attainment of a settlement. In this regard, much, I suppose, will depend on the attitude taken by the Russians. Most of our pundits seem to believe that Nixon has destroyed the Moscow summit, Europeans hold that the Russians want it too much for that to be true. I rather incline to the latter view. I think Mr. Nixon will go to Moscow. . . .

---

[37] Craig's abbreviated edition of Heinrich Treitschke, *History of Germany in the Nineteenth Century*, trans. Eden and Cedar Paul (Chicago: University of Chicago Press, 1975) appeared in a series entitled "Classic European Historians," edited by Leonard Krieger.

Wednesday, 10 May 1972. Stanford.

Lots of trashing last night. Bob Brown and Paul Seaver[38] and others are trying to control this by directing protest into more constructive channels and having the university go to the community and attempt to educate it. They are asking for Senate approval of a re-scheduling of classes for a day to get this started, and I have promised to introduce their resolution tomorrow. . . .

Finished Bracher's *German Dictatorship*, a good book. Now reading Hillgruber's big study of Hitler's strategy in 1940–44. I hope I can keep this up in the weeks ahead, for it restores my confidence in my ability to write my big book. I pray for a quiet and productive summer. . . .

Friday, 12 May 1972. Stanford.

. . . I went directly . . . to the Senate, where—after some dull business about grades—we resolved into Committee of the Whole House and, at long last, got through our discussion of the Faculty Self-Discipline Code, which we will now bring before the Senate in an amended form next Thursday. When we dissolved the Committee and began acting again as the Senate, I introduced the resolution [to approve rescheduling classes for a day]. . . . This touched off a long debate in which members as usual took refuge in amendments to the language. This was resolved by sharp speeches by Donald Kennedy and me, and the resolution passed. . . .

Monday, 15 May 1972. Stanford.

Today George Wallace was shot while campaigning in a supermarket in Maryland. He is still alive and is expected to recover, although there is danger of paralysis. What kind of a country have we become when this sort of thing happens—not only happens but is becoming normal! . . .

Our German department has distinguished itself by taking a quarter-page advertisement in *The Daily* to call for the impeachment of Richard Nixon. Not much worse than Anthony Lewis's article in the *N.Y. Times*, calling upon "those holding office in Washington…to consider resigning from this Administration." All this will look pretty silly if the Moscow summit really comes off and has positive results. In any case, I can't understand why Lewis has started his column by reproducing e.e. cummings's poem "Buffalo Bill's defunct." . . .

---

[38] Paul Seaver (1932–2020), a leading scholar of Puritanism and the social history of early modern London, began his career at Stanford in 1964. He was a recipient of the Lloyd W. Dinkelspiel Award for Outstanding Service to Undergraduate Education in 1987.

Friday, 19 May 1972. Stanford.
Yesterday we finally got the approval of the Senate for the Faculty Self-Discipline Code. The debate was surprisingly tame and mercifully short. . . .

Monday, 29 May 1972. Stanford.
Big things happening in the world. Mr. Nixon has been to Moscow and has got an arms freeze and an agreement re anti-ballistic missiles and the start of a new trade deal and a surprisingly cordial popular reception in Leningrad. The Duke of Windsor has died. Humphrey and McGovern have had their first TV debate, and the former vice president's experiments with the French language have led me to name my car Hubert, the Fiat Accompli. There has been another senseless shooting at an election meeting (one of Senator George's) and people have been killed. . . .

Tuesday, 8 August 1972. Stanford.
Hard at work, at long last, finishing chapter 6, and I'm hopeful that when it is done I shall be able to push on. I'm always happier when I'm working at writing and generally nervous when I am not…

Aside from that, not a great deal has been going on. George Knoles has finished briefing me for my job as chairman. My piece in the *Times* [on Henry Kissinger][39] has brought me a job offer from the Fletcher School, two offers—or rather invitations—to write books, another request for an article on Kissinger for a new encyclopedia of notable Americans, to be published by Harper & Row, a letter from Bob Palmer, congratulations from a type standing about in Mac's Smoke Shop, who turned out to be a former student of mine at Princeton, and today, from Harvard, an invitation to join a McGovern task force on Europe. Since the ticket has been strengthened by [Sargent] Shriver's acceptance [to be nominated as candidate for vice-president after the resignation of Thomas Eagleton], I might just do it. . . .

Wednesday, 9 August 1972. Stanford.
Finished chapter 6 of my German history, writing 4000 words on literary and artistic movements from 1871 to 1914 and emphasizing the lack of political commitment. A lot of fun, dealing with Wedekind, Sternheim, Heinrich Mann, and the early Expressionists. I told Phyl that, if anything happens to me, this section should be put together with my other pieces on intellectuals and politics and my two pieces on history, and an attempt

---

[39] Gordon A. Craig, "Just Who Does He Think He Is?," *New York Times* (28 July 1972): 29.

should be made to get all this published. The result might be a pretty good book. . . .

Tuesday, 22 August 1972. Stanford.
. . . Had a call in the evening from Joe Stevens who is passing through on business. He said that "everybody" in Princeton had seen my article in the *NY Times*. An exaggeration. I don't quite understand why the piece has aroused such interest and praise (Harrison Salisbury of the *Times* wrote me a note praising it, and David Rosenhan stopped at my table this noon and told me how marvelous it was). There is nothing original in it; in large part I was plagiarizing something I wrote in 1961, with a contemporary twist; and, when I had sent it in to New York, I was not at all sure they would print it. The plain fact is that it is *not* a good essay, and has not a trace of the distinction that informs my *Daedalus* article,[40] for instance. But then, for most people, a piece in the *NY Times*—!

Since last Tuesday I have written 8000 words. About *their* quality I have as yet no judgment, but the chapter is shaping up…

Mr. Nixon was nominated for the presidency this evening. In the attendant ceremonies, too much Sammy Davis, Jr. and much too much about the distressingly antiseptic Youth for Nixon gang. . . .

Friday, 8 September 1972. Stanford.
Back from another trip to the east, this time to the Army War College at Carlisle Barracks, Pa., where I had not been, by my calculation, for 13 years. . . .

To Washington on Thursday. Arriving at National Airport, I checked my bags and took a cab to the Library of Congress, reading meanwhile the first circumstantial press accounts of the appalling business in Munich, in which it is now clear that all of the kidnapped Israeli [athletes] have lost their lives. The Germans, I think, did the right thing in opting for a shoot-out, but it is a pity they didn't have more shooters.

Arriving at the Annex I hunted down Blum's study but he wasn't there, so I called it a bad gamble and caught a cab to the old State Department building where I used to work and did some walking, during which I found a bookstore and bought Solzhenitsyn's new novel, *August 1914*. At 12 I was at the Metropolitan Club and, somewhat later, was at lunch with General Al Gruenther (late Supreme Commander of NATO) and Eugene Becker, Asst. Sec. of Defense (Army). The point of this exercise was to get me

---

[40] Gordon A. Craig, "Political History," *Daedalus* 100:2 (Spring 1971): 313–24.

interested in doing a history of NATO, which is, of course, an exciting prospect. I explained my commitments, but promised to do a "feasibility study" for them. . . .

Monday, 11 September 1972. Stanford.
. . . In the mail, a letter from Knauer of the *Notgemeinschaft* [Emergency Society] in Berlin. He is even more pessimistic than I expected and, if he is correct, I shall probably never teach in Berlin again, since I shall be *emeritiert* [emeritus] before things improve. Let us hope that the projected tie with the Berlin Historical Commission comes to something, for that at least would provide the means for my getting to Berlin for a time. I don't like to think of the Berlin phase of my life as being definitely past. . . .

Tuesday, 12 September 1972. Stanford.
. . . I have been re-reading Knauer's letter. He is really waiting for the waters to rise, and he may be right. It is difficult, however, to see a connection between the state of the Free University and the kidnapping of the Israeli athletes in Munich... Knauer's reference to our common work on the address of welcome to JFK has made me look up my diary for June 1963, when I went up to Berlin from Bellagio and Vienna and came by chance upon the Knauers frowning over the problem of translation in Hartwich's office. *Schon lange her!* [A long time ago!] That diary has some interesting stuff in it, particularly in the pages on the Vienna visit and Henry Kissinger's comments on the Kennedys. . . .

Thursday, 21 September 1972. Stanford.
The end of summer. As if to symbolize the change of season, there was a meeting this morning in the President's Board Room of establishment figures interested in seeing that the Faculty Self-Discipline Code, which has been challenged by the Faculty Political Action Group (Charles Drekmeier,[41] for God's sake, and Avram Goldstein[42] and the like) gets by the Academic Council Meeting next Friday without crippling amendment. On hand, Halsey Royden, the new President of the Senate, Don Winbigler, the permanent secretary, Bill Clebsch, who is considered to be the parliamentarian *par excellence*, [name omitted], the lawyers (Cohen, Brest,

---

[41] Charles Drekmeier (1927–2020), a political scientist and social theorist, co-founded the Stanford Committee on Peace in Vietnam in 1965.

[42] Avram Goldstein (1919–2012), a professor of pharmacology at the Stanford University School of Medicine, was one of the principal architects of the school's emergence as a major center of medical research during the 1950s and 1960s.

Packer, etc., Packer talking too much as usual), etc. Many wise tactical maneuvers planned, most of which will probably go astray, as I think Jerry Lieberman suspects, as I do. Even so, if the [Code] fails after all the work that has gone into it, I shall be surprised and confirmed in my belief in the idiocy of most academics...

At 12 lunch with Peter Duignan and Wayne Vucinich (just back from Yugoslavia) to talk about means to improve relations between the History Department and the Hoover Institution to our mutual advantage. An important matter that should be worked on... In the afternoon, a talk with an interesting student from Munich who wants to work on American reactions to National Socialism. . . .

Monday, 25 September 1972. Stanford.
Inaugurated my chairmanship formally yesterday with a large party for the History faculty, plus the Hoover and the Center. A hundred people enjoying themselves, and the house looking beautiful. Food good, too. . . .

Saturday, 30 September 1972. Stanford.
Rose late yesterday but got to the office in time to do my stint of departmental business... In the afternoon the Academic Council's review of the Faculty Self-Discipline Code which was roundly attacked by the Left (Kahn, Dawson, DeLeau, *et al.*) and the Young, who seem to be genuinely afraid that it hides a plan to fire them on pretexts of professional misconduct in order to lower the budget) and the Muddled, of whom there are many. Aside from the Old Team (Royden, Brest, and Craig, who were adequate, and Kennedy, who was ineffective, and some floor managers who were not wholly on the ball), the Code had few public defenders. There is a curious disinclination to stick one's neck out and be tagged as an organization man. We couldn't get the Code passed on the floor but before sending it on to a mail ballot, we beat down all amendments (except one calling for deletion of the word "Self" from the title) and deflated a few smarty-pants... So off to the city, not totally discouraged but disgusted over the number of Wigglers and Lacedaemonians in our profession. . . .

Tuesday, 17 October 1972. Washington.
. . . Reading the *NY Times* yesterday I was impressed by the violence that has crept into the columns on the op-ed page. Wicker, Shannon, *et al.* used words like "obscene" and "fatuous" as a matter of course now when talking of Nixon and his aides. Despite the obliquities of the administration (the Watergate affair stinks more highly every day) I prefer the calmer tone and magisterial attitude of the *Washington Post*, which yesterday took Nixon's

campaign manager, Clark MacGregor, to pieces in a devastating manner. The *Times*, in contrast, sounds shrill and its photographic digs at Nixon (Quangtri: this was once a city) are becoming a bit obvious. . . .

Henry Kissinger is off to Saigon, and there is a general feeling, expressed, for example, in Scotty Reston's column this morning, that significant progress must have been made in his talks with the North Viets in Paris and that an interim peace settlement is not beyond the realm of possibility. . . .

Tuesday, 7 November 1972. Stanford.
Election day. I had a meeting at noon to discuss the future of [name omitted] and a seminar meeting at 2:15, so that I never got around to voting until 6 p.m. By that time the issue was beyond doubt and, by the time I went to bed, Nixon had swept every state except Massachusetts and the District of Columbia (although Minnesota was still in doubt). He even won in New York City for the first time since Coolidge.* [Craig later added the following note: *Not true. In the end, McGovern took the city by the narrow margin of 51.6.] All of which goes to show that intellectuals are simply not in touch with the thinking of the American people, who showed a nice discrimination in their voting, giving the Democrats control of Congress, passing the good and rejecting the bad referendum propositions, and deciding that McGovern was simply not big enough for the job. . . .

Wednesday, 8 November 1972. Stanford.
An important department meeting. I gave the brethren some of the facts of life, discoursing for ten minutes on the ramifications of the billet system to which they listened in sober silence. Then Seaver and I spread the new freshman plan before them, which they approved; and I warned them of a general re-structuring of the undergraduate program. . . .

Tuesday, 16 November 1972. Stanford.
. . . So home, to help Phyl get her car to the Toyota Garage and then, after dinner, to do some reading, which, however, took the wrong direction, for, after going through two issues of *The Economist*, I found myself reading Martin Gilbert's volume on Winston Churchill 1914–1916 on the pretext that I should check out Zeppelin raid material for one of my honors students. Which I found: e.g. Jacky Fisher so panicky about the Admiralty being blown up that he wanted the gov't to tell the Germans that, if any bombs were dropped on London, reprisals would be taken by shooting German prisoners-of-war. But I went on too long on other matters, discovering among other things that Lloyd George, arguing against

concentration on the western front in January 1915, told the War Council that "as far back as 1879 the Russians, under one of the best generals they ever had [Mikhail Skobelev] had been held up by the Turks at Plevna" and that since then the "power of the defensive" had enormously increased, and finding myself in danger of getting involved again in the contorted Dardanelles question. The Fisher plan for an attack across the North Sea upon the Germans via Borkum and Schleswig-Holstein is interesting, although demented. Churchill, who supported it, as Margot Asquith said, had "a noisy mind." He was not given to reflection. Thinking to him was only a brief prelude, indeed, an incitation, to action. The action taken was often ill-considered, and, in result, disappointing, if not disastrous. But what saved him was a dauntless spirit and a willingness to squander his own reputation if only the action went on. He was a combative spirit at a time when spirit was needed more than reflection. The Chamberlains were the reflective men. Winston bet on the impossible and won. . . .

Sunday, 19 November 1972. Stanford.
. . . It turns out now that the Social Democratic Party of Germany and the Free Democratic Party have had a real triumph and that Brandt now has a majority of 48 seats. The *Ostpolitik* has, in short, been endorsed by the electorate and can be pushed further. There is going to be lots to think about in the months ahead. . . .

Monday, 20 November 1972. Stanford.
. . . Another election turned out favorably today. Don Winbigler called to say that the Faculty Discipline Code had passed by a vote of 442 to 349 (56% to 44%) in a heavy ballot, some 72% of the eligibles casting votes. This is gratifying and much better than I had expected. KZSU called tonight and characteristically asked (1) whether I was surprised by the size of the No vote and (2) did I expect any immediate use to be made of the Code... There will be a lot of angry young men when the news appears tomorrow morning, including that type in Communications who kept writing to warn against heedless action on such a badly thought-out code. This was hardly persuasive to those who had followed the Code through the long two years that we worked on it. Nor were the publications of the Faculty Political Action Group. At the cost of appearing vindictive, I must admit that it is a pleasure to beat the Drekmeiers and Dawsons and [names omitted] and Goldsteins, and to do so without having become shrill and abusive (although, to be sure, Don Kennedy did become excessively emotional in the Academic Council debate). And it is pleasant to see the fat boy's tactics

of making their flesh creep fail so conspicuously. . . .

Tuesday, 28 November 1972. Stanford.
Thought for the day, prompted by the current obsession with sex: Americans talk about sex in the same way that Germans talk about democracy. They talk so much about it that they haven't got the time to learn how to practice it. . . .

[1973]

Friday, 23 February 1973. Stanford.
Section meeting at 9 and, as usual since I began to teach sections of undergraduates again, I came away with a sense of exhilaration. Teaching undergraduates is the greatest joy in the world, provided you are in complete control (which some of my colleagues forget) and provided you keep the students in a state of intellectual stretch or apprehension. In this Friday section I have a couple of students who are extraordinary in their ability to analyze and summarize. It's a joy to chivvy them. . . .

Thursday, 26 April 1973. Stanford.
The Watergate scandal is assuming ever wider dimensions. A sickening business which threatens to destroy the effectiveness of Kissinger's appeal to our European partners for a new Atlantic Charter. . . .

Monday, 30 April 1973. Stanford.
. . . Today Kleindienst, Haldemann, and Ehrlichman left office, and the President made a pitiful and shameful speech on television explaining his high regard for his office. I cannot help feeling that this will deepen isolationism and weaken Nixon's authority abroad, and I have said so in an article I wrote today for the [*Stanford*] *Daily* on Kissinger's Waldorf Astoria address of last week. . . .

Tuesday, 8 May 1973. Stanford.
Two ridiculous attacks on the History Department in the *Daily*, so ridiculous that one felt confident. Nevertheless, spent the day mending positions, i.e., writing a long letter to [name omitted], justifying Fehrenbacher's search for the best person in American colonial history. The search left much to be desired, but [name omitted] now knows that I will retire if its result is not accepted. . . .

Thursday, 10 May 1973. Stanford.
. . . The Watergate business more and more disgusting and increasingly troubling. I had a letter from Willard Matthias of the Agency the other day,

saying that things in Washington are, in his words, "so fucked up" that he is cancelling the June meeting of the consultants. It looks as if that pleasant club in the piney woods may be permanently disbanded. If that were all, one need not worry, but I fear that the intelligence community will suffer in many other and more serious ways. Indeed, government is being paralyzed at every level. I saw Sid Drell at the open house tonight, and he said that all of our friends have been swept out of the Arms Control and Disarmament Agency and, while Nixon plays his game of musical chairs with his diminishing group of available "honest men" ([William] Ruckelshaus to the FBI, [Elliot] Richardson from Defense to Justice, [James] Schlesinger from CIA to Defense, [Alexander] Haig to the White House, etc.) nothing is being done throughout the government, and no one knows what will happen next. (Today [John] Mitchell and [Maurice] Stans were indicted and face criminal charges.) Meanwhile, what will become of the brave new initiative in European affairs? Anthony Lewis said quite properly in the *N.Y. Times* today: "Heads of governments are not usually finicky about the morals of other powers. Leonid Brezhnev and Georges Pompidou have not lived only with saints. But when they deal with an American president, they want to know that he speaks with authority, that he can bring Congress along on a trade agreement or a security treaty." They will have their doubts now. . . .

Sunday, 17 June 1973. Stanford.
The 82nd annual commencement at Stanford, held this time in the morning, a welcome change. The address was by John Usher Monro, who left Harvard to go to run freshman admissions at Miles College in Birmingham. His theme: Watergate and the work and death of Martin Luther King. I approved of everything he said, but thought he came on a bit strong. Dick Lyman, in some well chosen remarks about the moral crisis of our time, was, to me, more persuasive…

I received the Lloyd W. Dinkelspiel Award for Outstanding Service to Undergraduate Education, which much pleased me, handed the attached cheque* (*4,000.00!) to Phyl who had come to see the award with Charlie, Debbie, Timmy, and Lee, and went off to present diplomas to the history graduates, a long, hot but pleasant business. . . .

Monday, 18 June 1973. Stanford.
Now that I am winding up the academic part of my first year as chairman, I feel that it has, on the whole, been successful. . . . On the more positive side, I made the first real step toward appointing women in the department

(one assistant professor, one teaching fellow, and two visiting professors) and conceived and persuaded the department to accept a new freshman history sequence. In addition, I ran the International Relations program for six months and presided over the search for and choice of [name omitted] as new chairman—director—(It was essentially for this and the new freshman course, I suppose, that I got the Dinkelspiel Award.)—and did my stint on other university committees…

Most of this would not have been possible without the solid support of Al Hastorf, the Dean.[43] He brought me in to get the department off dead center and turn it around, and I think that it has happened. The subversive element has been gravely weakened (I *may* have got rid of Dawson), and there is a better feeling in the department and among the graduate students. . . .

Thursday, 21 June 1973. Stanford.

. . . We came back to our empty house . . . and went about our business. . . .

Which included a problem. Colonel Allen Griffin, the prospective donor of the chair on War and Diplomacy, has been annoyed by the tone of the commencement speeches and has written Dick Lyman a wrathy letter and a calmer one to me, which is nevertheless disturbing, since he appears to wish to make me his guarantor, to see that his money is not used to give a chair to—as he says in his letter—"one of the kooks with whom Stanford is so plentifully endowed." This is not my line of country and I am uncomfortable finding myself in this kind of situation. I shall have to consult Dick, who will be dismayed when he comes back tomorrow and finds the Colonel's blast. . . .

Wednesday, 1 August 1973. Stanford.

The chapter on domestic policy is in bed, typed and with all the notes checked, and I must get down now to the chapter on foreign policy from 1890 to 1914. Today, however, I have spent reading and correcting two chapters of Herman Rupieper's dissertation on the Cuno cabinet. Very good stuff on German industry's trying to duck the responsibility for reparations and Poincaré trying, by going into the Ruhr, to stick them with it. All my views of the Ruhr invasion will have to be modified in light of

---

[43] Albert H. Hastorf (1921–2011), a professor of psychology and one of the founding directors of Stanford's Interdisciplinary Program in Human Biology, joined the Stanford faculty in 1961 and retired in 1990. He served as dean of the School of Humanities and Sciences from 1970 to 1974, and as provost from 1980 to 1984.

what Hermann has dug up. And certainly my book will benefit. My *Doktoranden* are supporting me in fine fashion. . . .

In checking footnotes for my last chapter, I came again upon Alfred Kerr's *Caprichos: Strophen des Nebenstroms* [Stanzas of the Tributary] (1926).[44] Aside from the political verse, which I have used, there are some charming poems about Berlin, written, I gather, in 1910 but still true enough to the Berlin I knew 50 years later to make me sentimental. . . .

It is a pity that I cannot share the feeling I get from lines like this with anyone. Leaving aside the fact that Berlin is a private life of mine into which no one has penetrated, except, briefly, the members of the Magrebinian Society,[45] I regret that I have no friends any longer, at least outside of Berlin, with whom I can talk about people like Kerr, or indeed, German literature in general. I dare say that there are such people around and about, but I never meet them anymore, and the young these days seem to have no memories, not having learned the lesson that you must remember everything, including things that never happened to you, and singers and songs you never actually heard, and dishes one can no longer order, and dances that are no longer danced, because life is short, and we should expand it by adding vicarious to actual experience. . . .

Thursday, 23 August 1973. Stanford.

. . . Still writing my 1000 words a day and nearing the end of this chapter…

Secretary of State [William] Rogers has resigned, and Henry Kissinger has been nominated for the job. Press reaction very good. One newspaperman asked Henry if he wanted to be called Mr. Secretary or Dr. Secretary. He answered. "I don't want to stand on protocol. As long as you call me Excellency, that will be okay."

Tuesday, 29 August 1973. Stanford.

Finished my chapter. Now, after some odds and ends (proofs and a review for the *American Historical Review*) I must get down to the next…

Meanwhile, the political situation in Germany is troubled. [Hans] Motz the other night was in a catastrophic mood and was asking [name omitted] whether he would really invest in the Federal Republic any more, now that

---

44 Alfred Kerr (1887–1948) was a prominent German (and Jewish) theater critic whose books were among those burned by the Nazis when they came to power in 1933.

45 This is a reference to a group of Craig's friends in Berlin who were amused and inspired by Gregor von Rezzori's *Tales of Maghrebinia*, trans. Catherine Hutter (New York: Harcourt, Brace & World, 1962).

it was ripe for conquest by the Communists, with the aid of the Social Democratic Party of Germany and Willy Brandt's *Ostpolitik*. I haven't got to the point of believing that, but I must say that some of the dire prognostications of my friends in the Berlin *Notgemeinschaft* [Emergency Society] seem to be coming true. The left wing of the SPD is much stronger and the middle much flabbier than I thought, and the *Frankfurter Allgemeine Zeitung* is beginning to be concerned, as the article of 10 August indicates... Left wing of the Free Democratic Party is acting up, too. . . .

Tuesday, 25 September 1973. Stanford.
Rockefeller Foundation has shown some interest in giving money to Princeton, Johns Hopkins, and Stanford to promote the humanities, and today we had a meeting to discuss what proposals we might make. . . . I've been through all this before. In Princeton, Jack Viner and I shot down a bad Humanities Program proposal two years running. It was finally licked into shape. I can't see anything much coming out of this group. . . .

Wednesday, 10 October 1973. Stanford.
Our vice-president Spiro Agnew has resigned, after pleading *nolo contendere* [no contest] to charges of income tax evasion. He is, in short, a crook, for whom no excuse can be made. It is shameful that we have been governed by people of this kind—(Agnew was taking kick-backs as late as last August, four years after becoming vice-president) and I wish Dick Nixon would appoint Barry Goldwater as Vice-President and then resign himself.

The war is not going well for Israel whose enemies increase daily and whose losses, in men and equipment, have been heavy. The Soviet Union is not only supplying the Arab belligerents but openly calling upon other Arab states to join in the war, as the Iraqi have already done. We should begin to get tough with Moscow, as we can do. I should imagine that all of this is going to complicate the security talks, and that nothing much can be expected from the Mutual and Balanced Force Reductions conference that is due to open in Vienna on the 30th of this month. . . .

Saturday, 20 October 1973. Stanford.
. . . Nixon has fired his special investigator for Watergate affairs and the asst. Attorney General Ruckelshaus who wouldn't go along, and Attorney General Richardson has resigned, and I now am in favor of impeachment and I have called Sid Drell to ask whether some of us *Honoratioren* oughtn't to do something about this...

Monday, 22 October 1973. Stanford.
A weekend of minor failures. The opera was lousy. . . . Second, [Reinhard]

Bendix became ill, and couldn't get to our planned lunch. Third, the fishing was bad. . . . Meanwhile, the mess in Washington continues. Sid Drell called back last night and said that things were so confusing that it would be best for us to hold back, telegrams from professors being, in any case, of little weight these days, our credibility having been destroyed by liberal professors during the Vietnam business.

The news this morning is that both the Egyptians and the Israelis have accepted a cease fire. I have seen no comment and can only hazard the conjecture that the Egyptians felt that their politically advantageous military position was eroding, that the Israeli losses were reaching the point of insupportability, and that joint Soviet-American pressure was too much for the principal belligerents. On balance, it looks like a Soviet-Arab victory although more limited than they had expected. . . .

Thursday, 25 October 1973. Stanford.
National alert caused by Soviet moves in the Middle East. The Egyptians east of the Suez are now encircled, and the Soviets would like to bail them out. Henry Kissinger very firm. Unfortunately, a good many Americans suspect Nixon of manufacturing crises to get off the hook at home. "A crisis a day keeps impeachment away." . . .

Thursday, 6 December 1973. Stanford.
Phyllis last night suggested that it might be a good idea for me to give up the chairmanship in June. Since I only contracted for two years, I could do that and go on leave until January, when I could take over the job of running our new Berlin center. An attractive prospect. But—ah! the "buts" in life. Unless Charlie graduated half a year early, it wouldn't make much sense, for I couldn't be away when he got out of high school or was sweating his way through college applications. And, for that matter, can I retire as chairman at a time when no one is clearly *profiliert* [profiled] as a successor? I have a lot of things going and would like to see them finished before I step down, and I would like to be sure that my successor would not reverse things or drop them. And who will be my successor? . . . And what of the International Relations program and the Foreign Campus Committee, which is now getting up steam?

Phyl, who urged me to become chairman, now sees how destructive of time the job has become and what it does to anyone who takes it. Destructive and seductive. One gets interested in seeing one's ideas actualized and in putting the bastards down. And, after all, we really are turning the university's undergraduate education around, and the improbable Mancall-Craig collaboration is an important force in the process. . . .

[In mid-December 1973, Craig traveled to West Berlin for a series of meetings related to the establishment of a local Stanford Study Center in partnership with the Free University.[46]]

Tuesday, 18 December 1973. Stanford.
After checking in at the Schweizhof [in Berlin], I turned around and went back to the "Rostlaube" [Rust Heap], where the Friedrich Meinecke Institute (FMI) is now located. This time I went through the right door and avoided the throngs of young members of the KSV [Communist Student Union] in *Germanistik* [German Philology] who practice placard-making in all the corridors. I found [Ilja] Mieck who took me through the library (very impressive) and then to a *bunter Abend* [Evening of music and entertainment] of the history department, where I met [names omitted] . . . Very pleasant, and almost the first time I have felt at home—indeed welcome—in the FMI. Lots of interest expressed in my coming back… At 8:30 by car to Rüdesheimer Platz to [Reinhard] Rürup's home for a pleasant party, with food, with a new group, including Ernst Schulin of the Technical University (who will soon, however, be leaving Berlin to go to Frankfurt) and Robert Gottwald of the Kennedy Institute who is going to court to save his job there, all *Assistenten* [Assistant Professors] being threatened with non-renewal of their jobs, for reasons he did not make clear. For a while, watched the latest episode in the TV series on "25 Jahre FU" [25 Years Free University], this one dealing with the stormy period after 1967 and starring such types as Margherita von Brentano, [name omitted], and Rudi Dutschke (who sounded very much like A. Hitler).

Up early on Friday and with Hermann to the *Bundeshaus* [Federal Parliament Building], where we met [Henryk] Skrzypczak and had a talk with *Ministerialdirektor* [Assistant Secretary of State] [Hermann] Kreutzer who assured us in the name of his minister (Egon Bahr) that our program is welcomed and who had some interesting suggestions to make about housing… So to the *Deutsche Institut für Urbanistik* [German Institute for Urban Affairs] where we looked in vain for a Dr. Haus whom Herzfeld wanted me to meet. . . .

So off with Hermann to the new Berliner Museum in Kreuzberg, stopping on the way to buy flowers for his wife and a bottle of scotch for his party. The Museum a revelation, beautifully laid out with artful displays

[46] Stanford in Berlin was established in 1975.

of home furnishings of different periods, a good theater display with programs etc. from the days of Devrient[47] to that of Tilla Durieux,[48] and portraits of Berlin *Prominenzen* [notables] from earliest times, and some marvelous paintings showing bits of Berlin that one can no longer see. Among all this, I found—with an unpleasant shock of recognition—the Lenbach portrait of Mommsen which used to hang in his grandson's room in Princeton and later in the Faculty Lounge and which I saw for the last time in the Senate Room of the Free University in 1958, the day before I heard the news that Ted had just killed himself in Cornell.

Unusual for a museum, this one has an excellent *Kneipe Berliner Art* [Berlin-style pub], with good food and drink and music. Unfortunately, it was jammed, and Hermann says that this is always true. . . .

Some special memories this time. The eerie sensation of flying over Germany and looking down on towns and villages in the early morning and seeing absolutely no traffic, since the energy crisis has brought a Sunday *Autoverbot* [ban on private cars]. The pleasure of sitting in the Schultheiss restaurant *an der Gedächtniskirche* [by the Memorial Church] alone in the early evening, with a Bismarck and a Pilsen, looking out through the windows and up the Kurfürstendamm in the direction of Halensee, the street with the dark falling and light coming on looking not much different than it does in a painting of the late 20s by Lesser Ury, which I bought in the Berlin Museum, noting that at the table next to mine there was an old dame dressed like the schoolmistress in *Mädchen in Uniform*[49] and two tables further on a handsome couple in advanced 70s style, cardigans and jeans and cocky hats in bright greens and yellows and maroons, and all around typical Berliners of middle age, the women undistinguished in dress and the men looking as if they were wearing borrowed neckties, Chaplin's *Goldrausch* [*The Gold Rush*] playing at the *Gloria* across the street, and the crowd streaming by, late shoppers for Christmas and now and then a young man carrying a placard which, an hour before, he had carried in a demonstration in the Tauentzienstraße ("*Hände weg von KSV!*" [Hands off the Communist Student Union!]) A wonderful evening. . . .

---

47 Ludwig Devrient (1784–1832) was a German actor noted for his playing in the works of Shakespeare and Schiller.

48 Tilla Durieux (1880–1971) was an Austrian theater and film actress of the first decades of the 20th century.

49 A pioneering 1931 German film with an all-female cast and a plot revolving around the passionate love of a fourteen-year-old girl for her teacher.

[1974]

Wednesday, 2 January 1974. Stanford.
Two sessions with the dean, the first about money, the second (at the Club) dealing with a replacement for Wayne, with Fred Bowser (who has been passed by the Provost's Office) and with my chairmanship—namely, with its prolongation. I agreed to stay another year. . . .

Thursday, 21 February 1974. Stanford.
Meeting of Committee on Foreign Study Programs on forthcoming publication... Other things going on. Saw the dean today and told him I had told our black candidate that we would not change the terms I offered him on 14 February. He wants too many guarantees, and I decided that the time had come to stop. I have left the door open, but I think we have lost him... We will lose the Chicano too, if the Americanists have their way. They have decided that he's not good enough and that Chicano history is, in any case, a passing fad. *Sancta simplicitas* [the times]! I told Fred Bowser he'd better tell them that we have a university responsibility in this matter. Having made the dean unhappy with our stand on the black candidate, it would be unwise to make the provost unhappy here. Besides it's time we improved the department's image in the black, chicano, and female communities. . . .

Monday, 1 April 1974. Stanford.
Lunch with Pat Thompson[50] and the instructors in History III. Encouraged them to draw up a new teaching plan for the whole year of History I–III, with films etc. so that I could go out and try to raise money for it. It is clear that films will play an increasingly prominent part in our teaching program and that we shall have to find the money to buy them—or rent them if the university won't set up a film center of some kind. . . .

Thursday, 4 April 1974. Stanford.
Long day. Lecture at 10. Meeting of Committee on Foreign Studies at 11, to discuss future role of Leo Labedz in our foreign program. At 12, meeting of Committee on Foreign Campuses. Nothing of great consequence, although we used up a lot of time. Busy work for an hour, and then to the Senate, where we had the beginning of a discussion of the new Academic

[50] Pat Thompson was the usual way in which people refereed to the British historian A. F. Thompson (1920–2009), the influential Senior Tutor at Wadham College, Oxford, where he also served as Tutor for Graduates and Sub-Warden. He had several stints as a visiting professor at Stanford.

Freedom document, which is intended to complement the Faculty Discipline Code. [Name omitted] and some friends used this occasion to bring forward a series of amendments clearly intended to transform this code in such a way as to de-gut the Discipline Code, supporting them with the same arguments he used in the curious debate of May 1971. . . . All the old business about how campus judicial procedures are elitist and tools for supporting the establishment and how all cases of discipline or infringements of freedom should be tried before civil courts. *Trahison des clercs* [betrayal of the intellectuals], and potentially destructive of the university. . . .[51]

Tuesday, 23 April 1974. Stanford.
Back from a satisfying trip to the east. It is always a thrill to go to meetings of the American Philosophical Society because of the traditions of the society and its location and the distinction of its members. After all, how many organizations are there in which the president can say, at the annual dinner, anything like: "I now ask you to drink to the memory of our founder Benjamin Franklin, whose spirit is always with us"? . . .

Wednesday, 1 May 1974. Stanford.
May Day, and I didn't realize it until now (7 p.m.). There should be some local equivalent of the Oxford greeting to the day, with the choristers in Magdalen Tower and the punts on the river and love in the ascendancy as the sap rises… As for me, I woke to a call from Mark Mancall, saying that [name omitted] had decided to take a job with UNESCO for at least the next two years. That means we have no director for our projected Berlin Study Center and will have to scramble if we hope to open it in January 1975… Went on to lecture on Heinrich Brüning and to perform other chores. . . .

Phyl picked me up at 3, and we did some shopping and picked up my jacket at Stankovic who has been having trouble making it fit me. Home and decided to have a swim but had to postpone it to take calls from Gerry Lieberman[52] and Dick Lyman to ask me to run for the chairmanship of the Senate—as the conservative establishment candidate, obviously. The job is important, and I shall say yes. Whether I can be elected will depend on the

---

[51] The phrase *trahison des clercs,* borrowed from a famous 1927 book by the French novelist and philosopher Julien Benda, refers to political interventions by intellectuals that compromise their integrity.

[52] Gerald J. Lieberman (1925–1999), former Stanford provost and a pioneer in the fields of statistics and operations research.

complexion of the new Senate, which will be elected this month… Phyllis dubious, not about my chances at the polls, but about the advisability of my taking on new responsibilities. I'm dubious myself and wonder whether I am trying to escape more important things, like scholarship. But keeping a great university running smoothly is important, too… In any case, the rads may beat me. . . .

Sunday, 5 May 1974. Stanford.
. . . The Nixon tapes have made Hearst decide that the man must be impeached. This shows how the revelation of shabbiness and moral emptiness affects even those who have taken desperate comfort from his indisputable talents in foreign affairs. We really must get rid of the man…

Tuesday, 7 May 1974. Stanford.
. . . Willy Brandt has resigned. . . .[53]

Friday, 10 May 1974. Stanford.
I was elected chairman of the seventh Senate yesterday. . . .[54]

Wednesday, 15 May 1974. Stanford.
. . . I imagine that I shall have to write a final lecture on Willy Brandt. Few things in politics have stirred as much interest and concern as his dismissal, at least for the last two years. There are not many heroes in the world these days, but he is one of them, and a lot of young people are worried about what his resignation will mean. He seems to have become fed up with the infighting that has been going on in his party, and the spy affair, in which my former Princeton student Horst Ehmke seems to have played an unfortunate role, seems to have completed his disgust.[55] A great man. I hope that his role in European politics is not at an end… A lot of people are pointing fingers at Wehner and at Honecker as the real authors of his fall; and, of course, this is not entirely far-fetched…

---

[53] At the time, Craig was preoccupied with the hiring of the historian of medieval Japan, Jeffrey P. Mass, by the Stanford History Department, so he did not immediately comment on Brandt's resignation.

[54] A brief overview of Craig's chairmanship of the seventh Stanford Senate (1974–75) can be found in Peter Stansky et al., *The Stanford Senate of the Academic Council: Reflections on Fifty Years of Faculty Governance, 1968–2018* (Stanford: Office of the Academic Secretary, 2018), 27–29.

[55] Willy Brandt resigned from the German Chancellorship after it was revealed that one of his closest advisors, Günter Guillaume, was an East German spy who had been passing high-level intelligence to the government in East Berlin. Horst Ehmke held various ministerial-level positions in Brandt's government.

Meanwhile, Mr. Nixon persisted in letting it be known that he will not resign and that impeachment will fail. . . .

Tuesday, 9 July 1974. Stanford.
The Treitschke (selection of contents from the Paul translation and an introduction of about 6000 words plus notes) done! I finished typing it last night at midnight and it's being mailed off to Lennie Krieger today. Of course, it is possible that Chicago has terminated the series by now, but at least I have now paid back the advance. This would make a hell of a good book though. I have, by judicious fitting, managed to get all the highlights of the seven volumes of the English edition into the 376 pages allotted me, and I am pleased with my introduction. I think I give the old boy a kind of rough justice—rougher perhaps than the treatment accorded him by my *Doktorvater** (*R. J. Sontag in *Germany and England*). I hope the book gets printed, if only to round out my writings on Treitschke—which consist of a paper written for Buzzer Hall forty years ago when I was a sophomore in Princeton. He gave me only a 2, the old rascal...

Treitschke has absorbed all my time for the last ten days. Three of them were spent in the city alone, trying to find, and finally finding, the hook for the introduction. . . .

Sunday, Bastille Day 1974. Stanford.
. . . Spent the last three days reading Eckart Kehr's essays and choosing the ones for my edition of them for the University of California Press. Now I must write my introduction. . . .

Tuesday, 16 July 1974. Stanford.
. . . The advance freshman registration for History I is only 349. I think this means that we can count on a 240 total, and that we will not exceed 300 in any of the courses. Here we see the impact of pre-med studies. If, as a chap who seemed to know what he was talking about told me at the Wassermans ten days ago, the man who gets a medical degree can count on an income of a quarter of a million dollars in the next ten years, course selection in college will reflect this. The effects on liberal education promise to be ruinous, as I have said in my forthcoming *Daedalus* article. . . .[56]

Thursday, 18 July 1974. Stanford.
Yesterday, with a university car and driver, went to Monterey (or rather to Pebble Beach) with Phyl and the Parets, to beard Colonel Alan Griffin in

---

56 Gordon A. Craig, "Green Stamp or Structured Undergraduate Education?," *Daedalus* 103:4 (Fall 1974): 143–50.

his lair and to attempt to move him closer to a decision to give us that chair (which, when we get it, will go to Paret). We did not, of course, mention the real subject of our visit, but confined ourselves to a description of what we were doing in military studies and then, when the Colonel kept harking back to the Reserve Officers' Training Corps (ROTC) issue, to an explanation of the political difficulties and possibilities in this matter. The Colonel feels that it is lack of leadership on Lyman's part and un-American behavior on the part of the majority of the faculty that prevents the return of ROTC to Stanford. We refused to accept this and begged him by the bowels of Christ to consider that he might be mistaken. We were handicapped in our efforts by the fact that the advice of the General Secretary's Office, to attempt to impress the Colonel by telling him that Admiral [Elmo] Zumwalt will probably spend 1975–76 in Stanford, working with our Arms Control people, completely misfired. Griffin *hates* Zumwalt. (When I discovered this, I almost collapsed in helpless laughter and felt like saying, "The hell with it, Colonel. Let's have a drink!") . . .

Saturday, 20 July 1974. Stanford.
. . . Today is the 30th anniversary of the *attentat* [assassination attempt] against Hitler and the fifth of our landing on the moon. Meanwhile, the mess in Cyprus, touched off by the deposition of Makarios by the Greek-officered National Guard, has caused the Turks to invade the island. Where this will lead no one can say, although I would, as I told Phyl, bet on the fall of the Greek government.

Thursday, 25 July 1974. Arlington, VA.
[Craig had traveled to Washington D.C. for a meeting of the Commandant of the Marine Corps Advisory Committee. After the briefing finished, Craig received a phone call.] . . . Nancy had some good news. Lennie Krieger has written to say that he is delighted with the Treitschke and that, although the series was discontinued two years ago, he exacted a pledge from the press to publish the Treitschke when it came along. Consequently, he foresees no difficulties.

Read in the first Vietnam monograph (draft), covering the years 1954–64. Good stuff on Vietnam Marine Corps and fascinating stuff on how we got sucked in deeper and deeper. Found that Don Weller commanded the 3rd Div. in 1961 and was scheduled to be commanding general in Laos, an assignment that was aborted by the Geneva agreement on Laos. He was then appointed Chief of Staff of the forces sent into Thailand. . . .

Tuesday, 6 August 1974. Sault Ste Marie.

[Craig was on a family holiday in Canada.] . . . Mr. Nixon's fortunes have hit a new low with his release of new tapes that show that he was participating in the Watergate cover-up very soon after the break-in, and nine months earlier than he has admitted up till now. Some of his strongest supporters are now switching (Wiggins, Sandman) and urging him to resign. Nixon met with the Vice President and the Cabinet today, and I was expecting an announcement that he had resigned. No such luck! He is determined to tough it out, and we shall have to put up with the ordeal of a House debate and a Senate trial. . . .

Thursday, 8 August 1974. Calgary, Alberta.
. . . We thought we might go to the movies tonight, but we have a long drive tomorrow. And in any case this is a night in which one must stay glued to TV, for Richard Nixon will announce his resignation, and we shall not, *Deo volente* [God willing], see the like again. One might feel sorry for the man if he had not invited his own destruction. The workings of Hubris and Nemesis have never been demonstrated more tellingly. We shall be among the millions to listen to his last speech as President at 9 p.m. Eastern Daylight Time. The Republic will be the better for his going, for we shall be able to start the mending process that is needed if we are to solve the formidable problems that face us…

Later: Nixon has announced his decision to resign in a speech in which he gave no reason for doing so except that he no longer had the congressional support to keep him in office. He gave no intimation of any feeling of culpability, and spent most of his time dwelling upon his triumphs in foreign policy and upon his own courage as a fighter. He used a long and embarrassing quotation from Theodore Roosevelt about the feelings of gladiators to embellish his remarks about his own combativeness. . . .

Well, in any case, as of noon tomorrow, we shall have a new president. It is a pity that it is only Gerald Ford, who will not be another Harry Truman, whatever his admirers may think, but is rather an honest Harding. As I. F. Stone said today, we really need a man of the stature of FDR, but there aren't any FDRs around these days. We must hope that Ford will recognize his own limitations and choose the best men for advisors. It would be good to think that he would start by firing [Treasury Secretary William E.] Simon and [Director of the Office of Management and Budget] Roy Ash, but I don't think he has the guts for that.

The speech was so clever and the TV people so awful, that we shall probably have a wave of sentimental support for Nixon. In the last two days, 10,000 callers to the White House urged him not to resign, and there are doubtless many more thousands who will feel that he was hounded out of office by the *NY Times*, the *Washington Post*, and all of those liberals and Jews who, as Nixon said on one of those tapes that were released the other day, are connected with the arts. But that won't change the fact that Tricky Dick is done for. The attempt that he made to impose a fascist regime on the country was defeated by the republican tradition and we have an abundant reason for satisfaction. . . .

Friday, 9 August 1974. Jasper.
. . . We headed West following the Bow River's course towards its source. . . . Somewhere in this stretch (before we got to Banff, I guess) we stopped by a lake side and listened to Gerald Ford take the oath of office and give a rather effective speech in which he mentioned Nixon only to ask prayers for him. Aside from that, the emphasis was on honesty, and the tone in general was infinitely more ingratiating than that gladiator stuff that Richard laid on us last night. It is reassuring to note that we have moved from the Nixon to the Ford Administration without anything catastrophic happening.

Shutting off the radio before the commentators began to give bizarre interpretations of what he had said in plain English, we went on our way. . . .

Monday, 9 September 1974. Stanford.
Have agreed to teach one more course than I am required to do, because the graduate students need it: a colloquium on the Weimar period. . . . Wrote Max Knight of UCal Press about the Kehr edition and suggested, among other things, that it be called *Economic Policy: Essays on German History by Eckart Kehr.*[57]

Wednesday, 25 September 1974. Stanford.
First day of classes. History I has 447 people enrolled for sections! A triumph for the History 1, 2, 3 concept and an answer to all those across the country who keep saying that History is dying and who make this a self-fulfilling prophecy by never trying anything new and daring. . . .

Thursday, 26 September 1974. Stanford.
. . . First meeting of the Senate with me in chair. A couple of procedural slips. Nothing serious…

Have started, as an experiment, to index my diary, starting at its

---

[57] The University of California Press published this translation of the essays of the pioneering German Marxist historian Eckart Kehr (1902–1933) under the title *Economic Interest, Militarism, and Foreign Policy: Essays on German History* in 1977.

beginning. It will take years, but has its interest and perhaps its usefulness, although I'm not clear about the latter. . . .

Sunday, 6 October 1974. Stanford.
Today I finished indexing the first four volumes of my diary, covering the summer of 1935 and the period from December 1936 to the summer of 1939. In carrying out this amusing but indubitably trivial exercise, I am proving once more that

> . . . at even-tide
> When level beams should show most truth,
> Man, failing, takes unfailing pride
> In memories of his frolic youth.[58]

There follows a gap of two years, surely the most lamentable, although by no means the longest, of the gaps in my record. It is a pity to have nothing about the first two years of our marriage, our apartments (we grew out of the first one) at Sherman Place and Chapel Street, our cocker Winnie (named after Winnie Davin), our first ventures at party-giving (which featured a horrid drink which had a lot of grenadine in it and made Louise Averill ill when she visited us);* (*The "Kidneybean," whom I met in Munich in 1935 and whom I visited at Wellesley in 1936, when I took her to see the Red Sox play, along with Alan, Sky Crane, Red Snyder, and Red's girl, Mae Spencer.) the fine evenings when we would dine richly at Childs, go to a two-feature movie (usually with Warner Oland as Charlie Chan in one and all too often with Ronald Colman in the other); my mother's visits and the many arrivals of friends, including, on one occasion, Lucile and Leah Vogel and the romantically sinister McCulloch, who did not live up to his advance billing (this was the last time I saw Lee, although I wrote to her at least once a year until her death); and our first unsuccessful attempts to start a family, which were worrying, but only temporarily.

It is too bad also that I have no record of my first impressions of Silliman College of which I was the first History Fellow with a magnificent office; and of my worries when pitchforked into teaching situations which I had not expected (lectures in British history for Lewis Curtis, for instance, and an undergraduate colloquium on English liberalism); of the sound advice given me about teaching by Ted Mommsen, that superb teacher who used his mornings with me in the long-vanished College Toastie to instruct

---

[58] This is another reference to Rudyard Kipling's "To the Companions."

me in the art of discussion—leading and drafting examinations; and of my introduction to university politics by the way of learning that it was not wise for the young to attach themselves to senior professors disliked by the majority of their peers (as my good friend to be, Hajo Holborn, was).

Finally, I wish I had some kind of a record of how the coming of the European war in September 1939 affected us. I know that it affected my career, for Yale got into a financial funk and the History Department fired all its non-Yale instructors, relenting in the case of Ted & me,* but letting Gilbert Tucker, Douglas Adair, and Henry Guerlac go on to brilliant careers elsewhere. (*Only temporarily. Ted was let go a year later and taught during the war years at Groton School, removing to Princeton in the late 40s. Nor did Yale show any disposition to keep me when Sontag offered me a job at Princeton in the early spring of 1944.) This gave a feeling of insecurity to our life in New Haven as did, of course, the sound assumption that we made about the inevitability of American involvement in the war. In contrast to friends like Frank Baumer, I was an ardent interventionist, a fact that caused some social awkwardness at parties, for Yale was a center of America First sentiment. In this movement, Dick Bissell (later one of the prime movers in the Bay of Pigs mess) played a prominent role, as did Augie Heckscher, against whom I spoke in a public debate. The year 1940–41 was full of controversy and doubt. But Phyl and I had time to produce babies—she, Susan; I, my Princeton dissertation—and to have some fun with friends—Ted, the Baumers, the Adairs, the Ralph Gabriels, the Mendenhalls. The Oxford years were golden ones, but these no less so in a different way (in both cases the shadow of war added an edge to existence), and it is regrettable that we have only a few photographs and a play I wrote for a History Department party as records. . . .

Monday, 14 October 1974. Stanford.

The financial crisis has caught up with us. Two sessions with the Dean today. All searches halted; replacements for people on sabbaticals in doubt. Gloom prevails. . . . The atmosphere is not improved by the fact that last night a girl was murdered in the Memorial Church after being assaulted. . . .

Tuesday, 22 October 1974. Stanford.

Excellent session of undergraduate colloquium, although reports on the Berlin airlift showed an undue amount of irony. This generation is afraid to be enthusiastic or to admire heroism for fear of being let down by the heroes or of finding their enthusiasm misplaced. Understandable. But surely it is ludicrous even to intimate that Ernst Reuter was unkind to the

Russians.[59]

After the colloquium, off to a meeting with Bill Clebsch, Dirk Waleska, and Lewis Spitz, called by Halsey Royden[60] who is worried by projected cuts in the budget of the School of Humanities and Sciences. What worries me is that the people wielding the meat-axe may have no tolerable philosophy of education. At least, that is what we have to find out and to do so I am, at Halsey's suggestion, planting a couple of questions to be asked in the Senate. . . .

Friday, 25 October 1974. Stanford.
Have been working on the gaps in my *Tagebuch*. With the aid of my pocket diaries, I have now written memoirs for the missing years 1946–1954 and 1954–1958. When I have done the same for 1958–1962, the record will be complete from 1936 to the present, with two volumes of occasional verse for the period 1932–1938 and a diary for the summer of 1935. If anyone should ask me why I indulge in this labor, I would have to answer: "*Es macht mir Spaß!*" [It pleases me!]—or, in Bismarck's words, "*Car tel est mon plaisir.*" [Because this is my pleasure.] . . .

Wednesday, 6 November 1974. Stanford.
Department lunch… A lot of thinking about how to cut the dept. budget, which will be a necessity. Word that the natives are getting restless. Lorenz Eitner and his merry men in Art flabbergasted by the projected 17% cut. Their reaction time is a little slow… Meeting with Bob Ward, Paret, and Büsch on question of applying for support to German foundations. Bob very cool and handled Peter well.

All our financial problems may pale in face of greater troubles. The pundits are beginning to worry about another war in the Middle East. It may well be that Fulbright's formula is the only one that will work: namely, to force the Israelis to satisfy Palestinian claims and, at the same time, to give Israel a public guarantee of its independence and territorial integrity. There is a growing note of defeatism in the articles of Scotty Reston. This worries me. . . .

Thursday, 14 November 1974. Stanford.
. . . Yesterday's speech by Yasser Arafat in the UN Assembly is the lowest

---

59 Ernst Reuter (1889–1953) was the mayor of West Berlin from 1948 to 1953, during the first phase of the Cold War.

60 Halsey Royden (1928–1993), a mathematician, served as Dean of Stanford's School of Humanities and Sciences from 1973 to 1981.

point in the troubled history of that organization*, and it is doubtful whether it can survive many incidents like it. (*except, perhaps, U Thant's egregious performance in 1967). The spectacle of this fanatic, actually with a revolver under his gown, bullyragging an organization that was dedicated to the cause of peace is sickening. . . .

Monday, 18 November 1974. Stanford.
A meeting with Bill Miller about the Buckley Law, which would open all our confidential personnel files to students and parents of students who asked for them. We shall have to remove all confidential materials from the files before they are released, thus obeying the letter but not the intent of the law and hoping that Congress will see what it has done and amend the law.

A meeting . . . on the financial situation. We must make projections of what the consequences of a 6%, a 12% and a 17% cut in our operating budget over a period of three years would be; and we did that in rough form today. To cut 17% would involve, among other things, no replacement for Johnson, only an assistant professor for Wright—(both retire in June 1977)—and a choice between losing two assistant professors or five teaching fellows. A sad look-out! We might be able to avoid this by doing something different with our summer school, by doing more on the foreign campuses and getting credit for it, and by expanding our M.A. program in order to get more money. All these will have to be looked at hard. I have decided to talk money to the Department at Wednesday's regular department meeting in order to allay fears and correct rumors. . . .

A letter from Blum, saying that Dick Challener, who is chairman of the department [at Princeton], is having trouble. The department has apparently got to make up its mind to drop some assistant professors (the department has only three tenure slots for the next four years), and Dick has no firm opinions and is giving no leadership. And, Jerry adds, "our department is filled with schnooks who bleed and who are incapable of making up their minds."

These things are difficult and will become more so as the recession (depression?) deepens. My eloquent letter to department chairmen around the country about our fellows program and the talents of our teaching fellows whom we must let go in accordance with the terms of their contract, has received a surprising amount of sympathetic response, most of which, however, is coupled with the intelligence that the writers are in no position to make *any* appointments in the foreseeable future.

I wonder what advantage might be gained by restoring the rank of instructor and going over to a system of more hiring, greater turnover, slower promotion rate? . . .

Saturday, 30 November 1974. Stanford.
. . . I saw Mark Mancall yesterday. He has come back from five days in Berlin absolutely sold on the city and on the possibilities of a success for our program there. He is so pleased with the work that Hermann Rupieper has been doing that he is nominating him as Associate Director. He has made contact with Hartwich, the city authorities, Günter Grass, the people at the Meinecke Institut, and any number of other people, and everything seems to be laid on for the opening of our Center—without any possibility of meddling interventions by people like Büsch and Mrs. Fischer. . . .

Sunday, 15 December 1974. Stanford.
The best American stroke of statecraft in ages was John A. Scali's speech to the UN Assembly on 6 December, making certain grim predictions about its future if its present behavior is continued. The Arab nations are still suffering shock and outrage, but the warning may do some good. The Arafat meeting, the rulings of the President of the Assembly, an incompetent Algerian, limiting Israel's right to answer charges against her in debate, and the decision of UNESCO's General Assembly to exclude Israel from some of the organization's work are shameful, and there is no doubt that—in Scali's words—"many Americans are questioning their belief in the United Nations."...

Walter Lippmann is dead, and the papers are filled with deserved eulogies. Scotty Reston has recalled the judgment of Clinton Rossiter and James Lare, that Lippmann was perhaps the most important American political thinker of the twentieth century and one of the "essential" men of private station of the last half-century, along with John Dewey, Thorstein Veblen, Frank Lloyd Wright, Charles A. Beard, H. L. Mencken, Robert Frost, Lewis Mumford, Roscoe Pound, and Reinhold Niebuhr. Reston has also, in lieu of a column of his own today, printed excerpts from some of Lippmann's old columns. . . .

I first got to know him in 1952 and 1953 after he had used a quotation from one of my articles in his column. I had dinner with his wife and him in Rome in 1954, and we received degrees together in 1970. He was a pleasant man of balanced judgments.

Friday, 20 December 1974. Stanford.
. . . I want to get some serious work done for a change, and have been thinking that the easiest way to do so, with my schedule, would be to try to

wake up my "Intellectuals and Politics" project, first, by writing a piece on Heine as a political journalist, and then by going on to essays on Caroline von Humboldt and Alexander Varnhagen von Ense. . . .

Monday, 30 December 1974. Stanford.

. . . Read Katherina Mommsen's *Kleists Kampf mit Goethe* [Kleist's Struggle with Goethe], which, while not my kind of book, is skillful, thorough, and interesting. Goethe disliked Kleist because he sensed that he was seriously ill, a neurotic who was prone to the unhealthy passions and the senseless violence that were the worst German traits. Many years later Thomas Mann was to share that dislike for Kleist, for he had lived to see where such passions and violence could lead…

I admire Kleist, although not for *Die Hermannschlacht* [The Battle of Hermann] or *Penthesilea*, which are pretty hard to take. I cannot say that the Mommsen book makes me want to throw myself back into any of his works, but I have no time to do so even if it did. I am too busy with Heine, who, as is usually the case when I turn to him, drives all other writers away and enchants me utterly. He is one of the very few writers in any tongue who can make me laugh aloud, as I did today as I read the sixth of his letters "Über die französische Bühne," [On the French Stage] where he says that Alexandre Dumas's head was like a hotel into which many good ideas came, although they did not stay longer than overnight, and which was often empty…

Tuesday, 31 December 1974. Stanford.

Up early and off to the University to have one of my regular meetings with the Provost.[61] I asked him whether Santa Claus had brought him a few $ millions with which to save the university. He said he couldn't claim that much, but that the fund drive is holding up, and lots of people are still writing Stanford into their wills. As for the economies ahead, he gave a broad hint that the Drama Department may be slated for elimination, as well as the Tours and Bentelsbach campuses abroad—(Cliveden's status is not clear, although it seems safe for the moment, and I suggested something that might make it safer—joint responsibility on the part of History and English for its future operations)—and a good part of [name omitted]'s Office of Undergraduate Studies. The elimination of other departments (Sociology(!), for example) has been discussed but decided against for the

---

[61] William Miller (1925–2017), a founding member of Stanford's Computer Science Department, served as provost from 1971 to 1978.

time being. Elimination of departments does not save money if the tenured professors are simply shifted to other departments, and there is no way of avoiding that unless the Trustees declare an extraordinary emergency and eliminate tenure. I suggested that the time had surely not come for that yet, and Bill agreed. We talked a bit about the Senate, and I told him that I felt that the questions that he would have to answer as the economies were revealed in detail (between now and the end of February, I gather) would have to do with the emergent shape of the university as the belt was tightened and that he would have to justify all actions taken with an educational philosophy that would be acceptable to the majority. This touched off a typical Miller speech, about how most people thought of him as a computing-machine type, whereas he was really a humanist at heart. This is not entirely bogus. Bill seems to believe that it is high time that disciplines like sociology, philosophy, and political science return to their classical forms and to their former pedagogical usefulness, which they lost when they turned to methodology. . . .

1974 was a good year. Any year that ends with all members of the family in good health and spirits, and all of them busy and happy in their busy-ness, *must* be accounted a good year. We have good reason to thank the Lord for His blessings and to pray to Him for the wit and courage that we will need to cope with the problems of the New Year, which will certainly confront us with even more vexing economic perplexities than our present ones and, in all probability, will threaten us with involvement in a new war in the Middle East. . . .

[1975]

Thursday, January 2 1975. Stanford.
. . . In Richard Ollard's new biography of Pepys, I found a quotation from Robert Latham about the origins of the diary. Latham believes it was a by-product of Pepys's "energetic pursuit of happiness. The process of recording had the effect, as he soon found out, of heightening and extending his enjoyment." I have made the same discovery in keeping this record... Ollard's book led me to Pepys himself, and I found myself reflecting on the number of fascinating people one finds in his pages, like the Major Waters mentioned in the entry for 12 January 1661, "a deaf and most amorous melancholy gentleman, who is under a despayr in love." . . .

Saturday, 4 January 1975. Stanford.
Read, and took notes on, the two Heine books of Hans Kaufmann, *HH: Geistige Entwicklung und Künstlerisches Werk* [HH: Intellectual Development

and Artistic Work] and *Politisches Gedicht und klassische Dichtung* [Political Poem and Classical Literature], the second a study of *Deutschland: ein Wintermärchen* [*Germany: A Winter's Tale*]. A Marxist, K is inclined to believe that Heine's meeting Marx in December 1844 caused a significant change of direction on the poet's part and, in fact, radicalized him. I am not convinced, for Heine does not seem to have changed, most of the things that Kaufmann points to having been evident, or at least emergent, in earlier writings. It is surprising that, in the things I have been reading, so little is said about the content of *Französische Zustände* [*French Affairs*] and *Lutézia*, apart from a few well-known ideological passages. No systematic attempt is made to study HH's choice of topic and his method of dealing with it. The war scare of 1840, for example, engaged HH for days and what he says about it is fascinating, as is what he omits. Surely, it deserves more attention from people who write essays on the poet. More needs to be done also by way of comparing HH and Börne as reporters by looking at subjects they both treated. . . .

Tuesday, 14 January 1975. Stanford.
Heavy day. . . . The cold wind of the budget has reached . . . the Dean of Undergraduate Studies, and he has come out in favor of the termination of the Stanford Committee on Independent Research in Education and the phasing out of the Stanford Workshops on Political and Social Issues. The cat is among the pigeons, and the squawking is loud, but this is long overdue. The sins committed in the name of innovative education by untrained and unqualified teachers sponsored by permissive faculty members who don't do the job of supervision that they promise to do represent a slaughter of the innocents. We are giving the best students in the country fraudulent courses on the grounds that they want them, as if that were a valid consideration. No one has really had the guts to insist on an end to this. Now it appears that we may be constrained to do what we should have done for other reasons because of our financial stringency. . . .

Thursday, 20 February 1975. Stanford.
Senate: Largely concerned with minority admissions and hence we had representatives from a minority task force protesting the committee's report. Two of their speeches the high point of the afternoon, aside from Fred Hargadon's performance. I don't know how good a Director of Admissions he is, but he certainly handles himself well in debate. . . .

Wednesday, 5 March 1975. Stanford.
Lectured on Karl Marx with some new material on his attitude as a Jew

toward assimilation; taken from Cuddihy's *The Ordeal of Civility: Freud, Marx, Levi Strauss, and the Jewish Struggle with Modernity* (an interesting but uneven and repetitive book) and on Engels's *Condition of the Working Class*, taken from Steven Marcus's book on Engels (which is very bad). Urged the class to read *Little Dorrit*, which Bernard Shaw said was more seditious than *Das Kapital*. They won't follow that advice, since they never read for pleasure. Too busy grubbing for grades, poor creatures. We really must do something about that. . . .

Tuesday, 11 March 1975. Stanford.
Lectured on international relations from 1871 to 1890. Twice. And a coffee hour with students afterwards... At noon a meeting of the Committee on Foreign Studies... At 2 a session with Grete Heinz, whose translation of the Kehr essay on the German navy in the 90s is very good. It is clear, however, that I shall have to write a lot of footnotes in this edition, not only to explain references to politicians and events, but also to explain what we think Kehr is trying to say, for he often lapses into a kind of shorthand as if talking to himself and he quite often uses words to mean things which they do not ordinarily mean at all. Still I am becoming increasingly enthusiastic about the project and have been thinking of things that I shall want to say when I re-write and expand my introduction. I would like among other things to expand my criticism of the "*England-hass*" [England-hate] essay and also to use his treatment of Stein as an example of how revisionists are driven to attack the *Doktorvater*'s [doctoral advisor's] heroes. I shall have to re-read what Meinecke and Hintze have to say about Stein. . . .

Friday, 2 May 1975. Stanford.
. . . I went on to the office to learn the depressing news that despite all our efforts in History 1, 2, 3, the number of majors in the department has dropped to 161. . . . We have altogether too many courses with *very* small enrollments. All of this means trouble; and I foresee not only further cuts in office staff . . . but also the loss of some of our assistant professors. . . . Apparently Political Science is suffering as badly as we (we have both lost students to the new International Relations major, which, ironically, we collaborated in founding). Economics, on the other hand, is booming, for reasons that are obscure. Depressing.

There is also, apparently, a morale problem in History 3, the fellows feeling that Gordon Wright has depressed them to the status of Teaching Assistants, whereas under Lew and me they felt like collaborators and equals. . . . Things like this always affect teaching adversely and lead to bad notices and further decreases in enrollment.

All things considered, I am beginning to fear that members of the department have been travelling too much and getting too much leave and have been teaching automatically, without new ideas or even much enthusiasm. Now it's beginning to show, and we're being outclassed by the competition. How do I tell my colleagues to pull their socks up? . . .

Monday, 12 May 1975. Stanford.

A busy day marked by the accumulation of small problems. . . . Had a meeting . . . with Wright, Spitz, and Paret on appointment of new Teaching Fellows, in which I sought to head off another of the recurring attempts to preempt the jobs for Stanford graduate students who cannot get jobs, a tendency that Spitz tends to support. My exhortations about remaining true to the idea that inspired the establishment of the course may be without effect when the meeting is held to make the appointments. Spitz is stubborn, and Gordon Wright, for reasons that he has not made clear, seems discontented with the course and said something today about whether it would not be as well for him to return to his old course (i.e., giving History III in its old form, as an independent 20th-century Europe course with a simple TA system under his control). I answered by saying that I sometimes regretted having given up Germany in the 19th Century in order to give History II, but not often and not very intensely because I believed in what we were trying to do with the freshman course. He responded to this with one of his exasperating silences. I shall have to find an occasion to ask him point-blank what is troubling him. Could be he's as tired of my sermons as I am of his studied taciturnity...

I have been asked by Bill McNeill of the *Journal of Modern History* to write a piece in a special issue devoted to A. J. P. Taylor. (Woodward must be turning over in his grave.) I shall say No, tempting as the idea is for it would further delay progress on my two books. . . .

The news from South East Asia demonstrates that the domino theory was not as foolish as a lot of people said it was. What is happening in Cambodia is frightful, and it promises to become more so. . . .

Thursday, 29 May 1975. Stanford.

Last lecture in History 129. I have been using the last few lectures to instruct the young in the dangers of the present situation in Europe (e.g., by using the Czech crisis of 1948 to point to the meaning of what is going on in Portugal). The sad thing is that such instruction comes to wholly untutored minds. My students do not appear to know, except in the vaguest way, what is happening in the outside world. No wonder they lack perspective and get all worked up about a trifling contract with the Iranian government while failing to notice that NATO is going down the drain. With respect to this last possibility, I doubt that it will be prevented by Gerald Ford's rhetorical exercises in Brussels. . . .

As my department chairmanship nears its end, I have been thinking about what has been accomplished in my three years. Since it is clear that no one is going to give me a plaque that lists my triumphs, I shall have to make my own. It is true, of course, that some of my colleagues would regard most of the items on this list as something *less* than triumphs. But I am proud of having, in three years,

1. established History 1, 2, 3 (which now draws enrolments up to 400);
2. added two women, one Black, and one Chicano to the faculty (not counting the women Teaching Fellows);
3. strengthened the Far Eastern Section by getting and filling a new Japanese slot (despite the desperate attempts of the Far Easterners to retreat at the crucial point in the negotiations);
4. secured the strength of the Latin American Section by getting tenure for Fred Bowser;
5. strengthened the American side by forcing through the appointment of [name omitted], despite the efforts of the Women's Caucus;
6. got a promotion and a chair for [name omitted];
7. reduced friction within the department and improved the atmosphere of History Corner . . . ;
8. improved relations with the Hoover Institution, most notably by means of the joint party at the American Historical Association meeting of 1973;
9. got decent raises for the most talented members of the department and extra funds for the brethren when it seemed important . . . ; and
10. shown the flag effectively by my Senate activities and my campus conference speeches.

That's not a bad record. It has not, however, made me a popular chairman, and my departure will be greeted by a fair number of my colleagues and the graduate students with relief and/or satisfaction…

Off to Berlin in the morning. . . .

Sunday, 20 July 1975. Stanford.
It is only as I write the date that I see that today is the 31st anniversary of the *attentat* [assassination attempt] against Hitler. The day is unremarked in the press. One sees why. Hitler and all his works seem as remote from today's problems as Napoleon. This is, of course, an illusion. Things as awful as Hitler may happen to us all again if we don't watch out. But nobody seems to be watching out and, in gloomy moments, one almost agrees with Solzhenitsyn's view that the Third World War has already taken place and that we have lost it...

The week has shot by, as all weeks do when I am working. This week has been filled with Kehr, and I have gone over the whole of Grete Heinz's translation carefully, smoothing it out and sometimes redoing whole pages, and I have written 23 pages of editorial notes. Tomorrow, I shall revise my introduction, which won't take long but will be a bit more critical, as, indeed, some of my notes are. When that is finished I can ship the whole business to the UCal Press... The Treitschke edition is also finished, for my index is being set up and the book then goes to press and will be out in December... Now I must get back to my *Deutsche Geschichte* [*Germany, 1866–1945*].

I have agreed to do an article on the U.S. and the European balance of power[62] for the April issue of *Foreign Affairs* and a piece on U.S. diplomatic style for the *Festschrift* for Theodor Schieder that Hans-Ulrich Wehler is editing.[63] My juices are all flowing. . . .

Tuesday, 22 July 1975. Stanford.
Finished revising my introduction to Kehr. Everything ready for the publisher, bar some re-typing...

Learned today that the History Department will have to move into the Law Annex before the end of the summer. Thus does it appear that I am the destined Moses who will lead the children of Israel . . . into the desert, leaving the role of Joshua to [name omitted]. We shall be in the wilderness three years, but the tents are roomy, especially for the horse holders, and are air-conditioned. Even so, there will be grousing, and I think the best

---

62 Gordon A. Craig, "The United States and the European Balance," *Foreign Affairs* 55:1 (October 1976): 187–98.

63 Gordon A. Craig, "The Democratic Roots of American Diplomatic Style," in *Vom Staat des Ancien Regime zum modernen Parteienstaat: Festschrift für Theodor Schieder*, ed. Helmut Berding et al. (Munich: R. Olderbourg Verlag 1978), 118–28.

thing to do is to expect it and to be reasonably high-handed. Oh dear oh dear! the books, the books, the books! . . .

Monday, 11 August 1975. Stanford.
Am reading Pepys systematically and have once more come upon my favorite 17th century character, Major Waters. . . . I am glad to learn that Pepys did not manage to write up his diary every day, but often got behind, as I do, and did it retroactively, without always indicating that he was doing so. . . .

Saturday, August 30 1975. San Francisco.
The great shivaree [the 14th International Congress of the Historical Sciences] is over, and what follows is the sparest accounts. The salient impressions are (1) that service on the Bureau of the Comité Internationale will be fun but will require me to put my spoken French in order; (2) that historians, by and large, are nice people whether at the beginning of their careers, like a young man named [name omitted] from Brigham Young with whom I had a talk, or eminent like [Karl Dietrich] Erdmann; and (3) that the Russians are bores who sound as if they are being paid by the effrontery of their distortions or the banality of their conclusions. An additional judgment might be made: that the Americans did a magnificent job of entertaining their foreign guests, with symphony and jazz concerts, and trips (including one to Stanford which Wayne stage managed, with good food and a Serbian band and *Singen und Tanzen* [singing and dancing]) and with dinners in private homes, but a less impressive one with the selection of its speakers for the opening and closing sessions. . . .

Monday I spent serving as vice-president of the session on Revolution, with Bob Palmer as president and remarks by Bernard Bailyn, [name omitted], and Eric Hobsbawm, elaborating papers they had written, respectively, on the American and Chinese revolutions and on revolutionary theory, and with comments and criticisms by [Albert] Soboul of France, [Aleksei] Narotchnitsky (USSR), G. Barany of Denver, and [Manfred] Kossok of the German Democratic Republic, the last two very good. I had lunch with Bob and Esther at the Vienna Coffee Shop in the Mark Hopkins and then went back to a long and, on the whole, boring afternoon of "interventions" (some relevant) before the speakers and commentators wound things up. A reference to Czechoslovakia's unhappy historians during an intervention by an earnest Norwegian delegate drove the Russians to furious attacks upon him for unscientific behavior and blindness to the difference between a revolutionary and counter-revolutionary attitude. Bailyn not as interesting as I had hoped he would be. Hobsbawm clearly the star of the day.[64] . . .

On Tuesday, I spent the morning in the WWII session, hearing a dull paper by Forrest Pogue but a brilliant intervention by Arthur Marwick, the Open University chap. Many dull speeches by Russians, who proved over and over that they and they alone had won the war. . . .

Friday, the final session of the conference was held at 10 in the Masonic Temple, with a good speech by Richard Morris, incoming president of the American Historical Association, interesting ones by Erdmann and François. . . .

Had a talk with Dave Pinkney on Thursday. He said that my Heine lecture in Seattle had introduced him to the *Lutezia* articles and that he had found these most provocative. He is working on a book on political thought in France in the 1840s. . . .

Thursday, 23 October 1975. Stanford.

I have, as the gap shows, been working too hard and moving around too much to make regular entries here. . . . On Tuesday I spoke on "The Problem of Continuity in German Foreign Policy" (slanging the Fischer school) to a good audience with a good seminar afterwards; and in the evening we had a pleasant faculty dinner (Simon Fraser/University of British Columbia in the Timber Room of the Hotel, with Dean Sam Shaw as our host.) . . .

Today . . . returned to the Center for Advanced Study in the Behavioral Sciences, where, among familiar faces (four of us were in the "Good-Time-Charlie-Class" of 1956–57), there was an interesting discussion on what most people present called the "crisis" of the social sciences, rising from an acknowledgement that the optimism and high expectations of the 50s have not been justified by results and the pervasive a-historical attitude of the behavioral sciences has hurt them. Interesting for one who was so hard put to defend history in '56–'57 (although I think Bridenbaugh/Krieger/Craig/Stuart Hughes survived pretty well) to hear the behaviorists in a chastened mood. There is no reason, however, for them to throw the baby out with the bath. Their effort has had very positive results, not least of all in teaching historians that theory, used modestly, can sharpen analysis. This is a time for re-appraisal, not for retreat, although, to be sure, they will not

[64] An account of the debates at this session of the conference can be found in Israel Shenker, "Historians Collide on a Slippery Subject: Revolution," *New York Times* (28 August 1975), 34.

suffer from thinking more seriously about what history has to offer them. . . .

[1976]

Friday, 16 January 1976. Berlin.
Second session of seminar, this time on the Tagebücher [diaries] of Harry Kessler for the first months of 1919. The *Künstlernatur* [artistic nature] *par excellence.* As I pointed out, Kessler spent as much time as possible in the theater during these tumultuous weeks—two Wedekind plays, Sternheim's *Tabula rasa,* a Reinhardt production of Tolstoi, the premiere of Kaiser's *Von Morgen bis Mitternacht* [From Morning to Midnight]—and his descriptions of people are influenced by this penchant of his (Emil Eichhorn is a figure from an Offenbach operetta, the Spartacists are Schiller's *Räuber* [*The Robbers*], and Liebknecht a Wedekind figure meeting a Wedekind end. The revolution was a fascinating drama but Kessler kept worrying about what his proper role should be and was never an objective observer, or a very effective one, since he was always putting what he saw into patterns that pleased him dramatically but seem contrived to a reader of different tastes. Even so, something the students in my Berlin course should read.[65] . . .

29 January 1976. Berlin.
Up early and, for once, skipped my twenty minutes with the ropes and pulleys to get a reasonably fast start toward Friedrichsstraße, where I knew the *Grenzkontrolle* [border control] would use up time. It did, but not so much as in the old days of the Cold War, and I was soon on the street and walking to Unter den Linden. I turned up past the university to the *Neue Wache* [New Guardhouse], where they were changing the guard in a modest ceremony before a small and not very curious crowd. The massive stone block that used to stand inside this memorial to the victims of fascism and militarism has been replaced by an ugly glass and plastic compartmented block, inside of which an eternal flame burns with curious effect, flickering uncertainly over the graves of the Unknown Soldier and the Unknown Resistance Fighter. I went on past the *Zeughaus* [armory] and over the *Schloßbrücke* [Palace Bridge], noting once more with sadness, as I passed a spot where I bought a peach from a fruit seller in 1935, that this part of old Berlin is like a face without a nose since the *Schloß* [Berlin Palace] was torn

[65] See Harry Kessler, *Berlin in Lights: The Diaries of Count Harry Kessler (1918–1937)*, ed. Charles Kessler (New York: Grove Press, 2002).

down,[66] and that it is not improved by the clutter of construction work around the *Dom* [Berlin Cathedral] which seems not to have progressed in the last five years.

I went on over to Liebknechtbrücke and up Liebknechtstr. to the *Neue Markt* [New Market] and the *Marienkirche* [St. Mary's Church], which was closed, so that I was baulked again of my desire to see the *Totentanz* [Dance of Death fresco]. In the area to the east, bounded by Klosterstr. and Rathausstraße, where at the base of the *Fernseh und UKW-Turm* [Television Tower] there is a sprawling modern and singularly empty culture center (at least I imagine that is what it is intended to be). I found, at a decent remove, the *Neptunbrunnen* [Neptune Fountain] of Begas, with the wonderful seal, crocodile, and sea-serpents and the handsome naiads, one of whom is, oddly, accompanied by a goat. This unbuttoned creation was in the *Schloßplatz* [Palace Square] from 1891 to 1945, and it was planned to put it in the Gertrandenstraße on the place where the *Petrikirche* [St. Peter's Church] used to be, but it has ended up here, and it helps this otherwise sadly empty area.

I moved on to Alexanderplatz, noting the many new buildings and the heavy traffic, and went to Das gute Buch [The Good Book], looking for an edition of Bettina von Arnim. Alas! nothing has changed here either. Thousands of copies of very few titles. One can find anything he wants provided it was written by Marx, Engels or Lenin, but there is not much else, except novels by hacks like Anna Seghers, and histories of the trade union movement. I retraced my steps and went to an International Book Center by the Liebknecht Brücke. Bottom floor full of Russian books; 1. Etage [First floor], the same things as Das gute Buch. I bought a copy of Engels's *Arbeiterklasse in England* [*The Condition of the Working Class in England*], a Zille sketch book, and Christa Wolff's *Nachdenken über Christa T.* [*The Quest for Christa T.*] Then I walked across the bridge and on through the clutter to Unter den Linden, past the Kronprinzenpalais [Crown Prince's Palace] and the Opera to Bebel Platz, where I admired the [Christian Daniel] Rauch statues of Scharnhorst, Blücher, Yorck, and Gneisenau, looked at the facade of the old Royal Library, understanding why it was nicknamed the Kommode, and looked into the St. Hedwigs-

---

66 The *Berliner Schloß*, the primary residence of the Hohenzollern dynasty, was badly damaged during the Second World War and demolished by the East German government in 1950. From 1976 to 2008, the asbestos-filled East German Palace of the Republic occupied the site, but it too was demolished. Reconstruction of the *Berliner Schloß* was completed in 2020.

Kathedrale, which was empty. . . .

Saturday, 28 February 1976. Munich.

Back after a very satisfactory *Ausflug* [trip] to Munich. We went down by train from *Bahnhof Zoo* [Zoo Station] over Wannsee and Potsdam, to Jena, Ruddstadt, Saalfeld, Probst-zella, Ludwigstadt, Bamberg, Erlangen, Nuremberg, Donenwirth (which I visited with Doctor Priest, Ed Watson, and Aud Wicks in 1935), and Augsburg, and—ten hours after departure—our goal. A comfortable and not uninteresting trip (I now know where Saalfeld, where Prince Louis Ferdinand of Prussia met his death, is in relation to Jena, where the Prussian army was broken in 1806), but, my word! life in East Germany, seen from the train window, is dull and bereft of comfort. Everything in the villages smells of make-do; hardly a shop; not a sign of cheer or escape from labor and care; the only color, an occasional flag on a town hall, or a sign at a railroad crossing saying that socialism makes life beautiful, although everything around it makes the message derisory. Thirty years after the war, the contrast between the appearance of the countryside in the East and that in the West is as startling as it was in the early 50s. . . .

Monday, 17 May 1976. Berlin.

. . . I must say that I find in the government's toleration of open attacks upon the democratic state, as illustrated by [the public mourners of Ulrike Meinhof] and by all of those who ply their trade in the *Germanistik* [German Philology] corridor of the *Rostlaube* [Rust Heap], which is a *Sauhaufen* [dump] of radical propagandists seeking to use the university as a launching pad for revolution, a sign of weakness rather than strength. No one who thinks seriously about the history of the Weimar Republic can help but feel the cold grues as he sees this going on. To say that it is not as bad as it was in 1970 is no argument at all. It is bad enough to be dangerous, and the danger is measurable, for one thing in the vulgar Marxism that beclouds the reasoning processes of German students these days, which is certainly encouraged by the fact that every public room in the university is saturated with it in printed form. It would be a proper defense of democratic liberty to clean out these Augean stables once and for all and to deny those who have created them the privileges of the university. The trouble is that the Nazi experience has so traumatized people in authority that they are afraid to do anything that would invite charges of dictatorial behavior…

In this connection, there is a movement among the student body of Fachbereich 12 (History) to protest against a new study plan that would insist upon attendance lists, examinations on materials assigned, and other normal disciplines, on the grounds that these things are undemocratic. [Name omitted] of the Kennedy Institut tells me that he was accused of authoritarian behavior by a student in his seminar to whom he had directed a question about the reading. To tolerate this interpretation of democracy is to betray the educational mission; to tolerate subversion in the name of freedom is to endanger the basis of the republic. . . .

Friday, 25 July 1976. Oban, Scotland.
. . . We have done little here but read, watch the Olympics on TV, and walk. Today we walked north on the Esplanade, past the good World War I monument (two jocks carrying a wounded comrade) and Dunollie Castle, and on up the road to the beach at Ganavan Sands, where Phyl and I walked in the hills during our last visit. We were not so ambitious this time and merely turned and made our way back. . . .

I find myself increasingly annoyed at what I call Scotchiness—the practice of emphasizing or admiring the wrong things about Scotland. . . . Highland Games are part of Scotchiness. So are excessive tartanry, books about Robert the Bruce, all Scots verse between Burns and MacDiarmid, the haggis, calendars with pieces of heather on them and views of Ben Nevis, phony Glengarry bonnets, gift editions of "Tam O'Shanter's Ride," shephard's crooks manufactured for the tourist trade, pottery replications of the Wallace Monument, songs like "I Lo'e a Lassie," and pipers *en grand monture* playing for pennies at picturesque spots on the highway. Foreigners find all this quaint and fail to see the real Scotland of thrift and hard work and sober intelligence and rough piety. Since tourism is big business, the local inhabitants give the visitors, many of them Scots from overseas, what they want. The result is not gratifying and makes one understand MacDiarmid's rage against Burns idolatry (by people who don't really understand poetry) and phony Scottish culture. Should the Nationalists triumph (which I hope and pray won't happen), the situation will not improve. The people in the SNP are driven either by political ambition or most sordid kind of materialism. They are not interested in culture but in power and oil. Their values are so trivial (perhaps ignoble would be too strong a term) that they could not help but make a hash of things if given their chance. I have a feeling that the Scottish people are basically sensible enough to know that that would be the case; and that the SNP will not be able to sustain its record of growth in the next year. This will depend, of course, on what Labour can do in the months ahead, and how Denis Healey's schemes fare. . . .

Tuesday, 17 August 1976. Oxford.
It's great fun being back in Oxford, for this is the first time I've had the opportunity to prowl about to see what's happened to the town I knew 40 years ago. Yesterday, walking down the Woodstock Road from Maudelay's place, I passed the Horse and Jockey, the Royal Oak, and the Lamb and Flag, at each of which Dan, [name illegible], Garrett, and I used to stop and have one on Thursday evenings as we made our way to the Gardener's Arms. Opposite the Lamb and Flag, the first in the Thursday sequence, there is, I discovered last night, a pub called the Eagle and Child, with sign to prove it. Surely we couldn't have passed such an interesting water hole every week for two years. Unless we disliked the publican, and I can't remember anything of the sort. Ergo, it must be new—that is, founded since 1938. . . .

I began work in the Upper Reading Room of the Bodleian this morning, working on Carl Schmitt and Gottfried Benn and, when I got drowsy, waking myself up by walking around the handsome room or looking out the windows at the stone effigy of Jacobus Rex who presided over the founding of this building. I can't think of a pleasanter way to spend a day. . . .

Wednesday, 1 September 1976. Vienna.
After I completed my last entry, Harms [Kaufmann] and I had a long talk about my plan for a book to be called *The Germans*; and he became quite excited about it; and we ended up by drafting a table of contents, to wit: Prelude: The Retreat from History: The 30 Yrs War and the Birth of *Innerlichkeit* [Inwardness]; /I. The Propensity for Self-Criticism: Germans on Germans; /II. Regionalism; /III. Religion; /IV. Romanticism; /V. *Die Geistigkeit* [Intellectual Life]; /VI. Women and the Family; /VII. On Dying for the Fatherland; /VIII. Obsessions: From Work to War and Vice Versa; /IX. Music: The Suspicious Art; /X. Politics Destroys Character, or *Eine gute Verwaltung ist die beste Regierung* [A good administration is the best government]; /XI. *Deutsche Würde* [German grandeur]: Reflections on Power and the Future.

Harms, who had some good suggestions for reading, wants me to hole up in his new farmhouse near Passow and work on the opus. . . .

Thursday, 30 September 1976. Stanford.
. . . I am reading Pepys again, the fourth volume, which has what must be the most minutely recorded case of flatulence in literary history. I wonder why he wanted to put in this catalogue of farts and stools. Surely its re-reading at a later time would bring little instruction and no pleasure. But

Pepys was convinced that everything that happened to him was interesting and full of wonder, even when it was unpleasant or frustrating (like his encounter on 24 September 1663 with the tantalizing Mrs. Lane, whose willingness to consent to everything "but only the main thing" had disastrous results). (*Put right, however, the following January. See Pepys, *Diary*, V, 17.)

One does not have to read far in Pepys without coming upon something absolutely charming. So, in the entry for 26 December: "Thence to the Coffee-house; and sat long in good discourse with some gentlemen concerning the Roman Empire." . . .

Thursday, 14 October 1976. Stanford.
Reading the page proofs of the Kehr edition. Still lots to correct. This could have been done earlier if they had provided a clean transcript copy for editing. But Kehr was really *such* a lousy writer that one has to go on diddling with the translation in the hope that somehow it will rise above the turgidity of the original. Fat chance! . . .

Wednesday, 1 December 1976. Stanford.
Letter from Köhler in Berlin enclosing a photo of the placard pasted on his door by the Communists attacking him and me as agents of U.S. *imperialismus*. Maybe I can get a job at the Hoover on the strength of it. . . .

Monday, 13 December 1976. Stanford.
Talk with Bob Ward about the problem of replacing [name omitted] as director of the International Relations program. Argued that the new director must be either a historian or a political scientist. Alex Dallin and [name omitted] possibilities. Problem compounded by university's reluctance to fund special programs despite their success and importance in undergraduate education. This makes the appointment of an outsider difficult unless he can be put on a departmental budget, and the right man for the IR job may not fit easily into a department. Stanford should have one of the best IR programs in the country. It won't have as long as the administration won't make a judgment of the importance of that to the university and then spend enough to attain. . . .

Wednesday, 22 December 1976. Stanford.
Writing hard. Problem is how to say something new—that is, something different from what one has said before—about Hitler's foreign policy, a subject on which I have written a good deal. I am trying to solve the problem by going to the documents again and by reading those that have been issued recently, the French ones. But it's not easy.

[1977]

Friday, 21 January 1977. Stanford.
. . . I have been thinking of the "Germans" book, having signed the contract. We shall need chapters on "Originals" and on "Students" (the *Bürgerschreck* [the anti-establishment youth]). And what about popular literature (Hauff, Dalm, May, Courths-Mahler, Marhitt)—"Winnetou and Hitler," perhaps?[67] On Wednesday, in colloquium, we got into the geography of cities and the effect of topography on behavior. Dolf Sternberger calls his book *Panorama: oder Ansichten vom 19 Jahrhundert* [*Panorama of the 19th Century*] (1946) a *Versuch* [attempt] in historical topography. That's worth thinking about. And what about "Das Geld und die Deutschen" [Money and the Germans], making something of Wagner's *Ring*? And "The Wanderers," who try to escape and always come back home, like the typical *Bildungsroman* [coming of age story] protagonist, like [Nikolaus] Lenau and some of Raabe's heroes and Sealsfield? Lots of things to think about and many things to read... Reinhard [Bendix] pointed out the other night that I was leaving out the soldiers. Perhaps a chapter on the military technician and the decline of general intelligence and judgment, using the Halder *Tagebuch* [Diary] which I am reading with fascination. . . .

Sunday, 13 February 1977. Stanford.
... The Berlin Center is gone. Bill Miller broke the news to me on Thursday. I had already told him by private letter that I thought it would be a mistake to leave Berlin; so I didn't indulge in any additional kicking and screaming. This is what is known as "statesman-like behavior." At least that's what Dick Lyman has called it in a note to me. Which caused Phyl to say "Pooh!" or something stronger...

. . . Reading Raabe's *Stopfkuchen* [Stuffcake] and a collection of Franklin P. Adam's (FPA of the old *World*) pieces which I found in a library sale for a dime.[68] The man could write and was an amazing type. I used to love his "Conning Tower" and especially his "Diary of our own Mr. Pepys" and his

---

[67] The proposed title "Winnetou and Hitler" is a reference to a character in Karl May's cowboy stories, which were and are popular in Germany. Winnetou is the Native American hero who appears in several novels.

[68] Wilhelm Raabe's *Stopfkuchen* has been translated into English by Barker Fairley with the title "Tubby Schaumann: A Tale of Murder and the High Seas." See Wilhelm Raabe, *Novels*, ed.Volkmar Sander (New York: Continuum, 1983).

good imitations of Horace.[69] He was, in a real sense, another of my teachers; thanks to that best of all teachers, Bill Dougherty, who introduced him to me—and Heywood Broun, and Ring Lardner, and much else. . . .

Wednesday, 6 April 1977. Stanford.

Lectures: Cavour; Bismarck; Religion. The first two to teach them how to think about international politics and to remind them that men make history (a lesson one young man objected to—but not very strongly—yesterday). I sat up till 4:30 this morning, re-writing the lecture on Religion. To good effect. I ended by quoting "Dover Beach." Not a dry eye in the house.

I have also launched my grad colloquium on "German Themes"—still nibbling away at the edges of the new book. . . .

[Name omitted] is working up the case for Berlin which we will lay before the President and the Provost. I wonder if it would do any good if I pointed out to Dick that he is presiding over two establishments: a complex of training centers (graduate departments and professional schools) and a *Bildungsanstalt* [educational establishment]. The students in the former are lost to education. What good *nous autres* [we others] do in the cause of culture and civilization is done in the latter. It is there that we can have some influence on the people who will run the country, and we should regard that part of the university as the more important. So why are we weakening it by closing Berlin? It makes no sense... It may be too late to reach Dick with that kind of argument. He is pretty remote from the real university these days. If that is true, we have come to a pretty pass. . . .

Sunday, 23 May 1977. Stanford.

We are celebrating the 50th anniversary of Lindy's flight, and this has brought floods of reminiscence with it, like the article by William L. Ryan in the *Chronicle* today about what was going on in 1927. I can remember everything he mentions with great clarity. In 1927 we were living in a third-floor apartment on Van Wagenen St. in Jersey City across the street from Public School No. 23, which my brother Joe and I attended. It was a predominantly Jewish neighborhood made up of large and ugly apartment houses. Times were flush. My father's printer friends, Duck Crooks, Bob Coel, George Forster, all conveniently apart from their wives, were all making good money and using it to take singing lessons from a woman who came over from Brooklyn, named Mme. Hoffman, and to buy stocks on

---

[69] Franklin P. Adams (1881–1960) was a member of the Algonquin Round Table of journalists, critics, playwrights, actors, and wits during the 1920s and 1930s.

margin. My father was spending a good deal of his on booze, but that was cheap enough in those days, and we lived well. There were lots of parties with dancing (one-step and foxtrot mostly) and singing in Van Wagenen Street or elsewhere, for the family had lots of friends, all printers living *la dolce vita* which collapsed soon. I remember some nice men—a red-haired man named Ramsey whose wife was a flapper who took to other men while he took to booze, and another man (Brookie or something) . . . whose wife was ill, and who used to play chess with me. There were excursions to places like Sheepshead Bay (I can still remember the marvelous big shrimps one could buy there) and to Coney Island. And I was in Troop 13, Boy Scouts of America, and there were hikes and things. They were happy enough days, although I had to put up with much from the old man, which embarrassed me more than I guess was necessary. I can't say that my life was blighted in consequence, although it did make me a bit of a loner until I went to high school and started my close friendship with Harold Komoski. When one is a loner, one reads a lot and learns from it. . . .

Monday, 6 June 1977. Stanford.
Last session of my colloquium on "German Themes." Used it to tie up a lot of loose ends by discussing:

1. *Wilhelm Meister* (with some attention to the women and to such occasional themes as Jews, war and 18th-century society, the world of the nobility—with a reference to Eichendorff's fine essay on the nobility and the Revolution—and the problem of a national theater when there was no nation).
2. The *Dichter* [poet] in German history, using *Wilhelm Meister* and Abram's *Natural Supernaturalism* to open out the Romantic view of the poet as prophet, sage, and leader and questioning its influence in German development.
3. *Die Sehnsucht* [Longing] and Music (with some reference to Schopenhauer and Ernst Bloch, and to the theme of death and transfiguration in German music. . . .[70]
4. The evolution of romanticism, . . . and then going on to a discussion of Jünger's *Der Arbeiter* [*The Worker*] and to the attitudes struck by Hauptmann, Carl Schmitt, Heidegger, and Benn in 1933. A full afternoon. . . .

---

[70] "*Die Sehnsucht*" is a poem by Friedrich Schiller that was set to music by Franz Schubert and others.

Tuesday, 21 June 1977. Stanford.
My edition of the Kehr essays is out, and very handsome too! It took a long time to get it through the press, but it's here at last. I shall send one to old Alfred Vagts, the first man to recognize Kehr's merits. . . .

Thursday, 23 June 1977. Stanford.
Dr. Johnson says of the study of law what can be said of any intellectual pursuit, rigorously followed, that it provides "security from those troublesome and wearisome discontents, which are always obtruding themselves upon a mind vacant, unemployed and undetermined." Boredom is nothing but a result of mental laziness. There are so many things to be learned and enjoyed that a man should be ashamed to admit to it. I have been studying the late quartets of Beethoven and those of Hayden with joy and profit and reflecting that there are more than enough of other subjects to keep one busy until it is time to shuffle off this mortal coil.

Thursday, 7 July 1977. Stanford.
The class for the West Pointers paid off. I have to do a piece on diplomatic history for . . . a projected book on the subject.[71] I have decided to do it on "Clausewitz and the Study of Diplomatic History." This could start with a reference to Clausewitz's hope in 1819 of becoming an ambassador and his failure, to which we owe *Vom Kriege* [*On War*]. It is impossible to know what he might have contributed to diplomacy if he had got the post, but there is no doubt the student of diplomacy can gain much from reading his masterpiece, provided that he uses the book seriously as a guide to his study. This will lead to some comments on Clausewitz's view of the utilitarian, pedagogical, and cognitive aspects of the study of war (see Paret)[72] applied to diplomacy, and under the last an application of Clausewitz's views of violence, friction, and genius to diplomacy with historical examples (Godoy, Metternich, Bismarck, Palmerston, Kissinger). Clausewitz's views of the uses of history to broaden understanding of the interplay of these factors should probably precede these historical examples. Something should also be said about Clausewitz's views on purpose and means, and on the two forms of war/diplomacy. Clausewitz's first book, particularly

---

71 Gordon A. Craig, "On the Nature of Diplomatic History: The Relevance of Some Old Books," in *Diplomacy: New Approaches in History, Theory, and Policy*, ed. Paul Gordon Lauren (New York: Free Press, 1979), 22–34.

72 Peter Paret, *Clausewitz and the State: The Man, His Theories, and His Times* (Princeton: Princeton University Press, 1976).

the chapters on friction and "the military genius" would repay careful study, and Paret's book is full of stuff. . . .

Wednesday, 3 August 1977. Oxford.
The man whose room I am living in in Holywell Manor is, as far as I can tell from his books, a philosopher, and one who doesn't believe in wasting his time on light reading, which, apart from *The Oxford Book of English Verse* and Belloc's *Cautionary Tales*, is not represented on his shelves at all. . . . Since I am a bit tired of my steady diet of French, I have had to accommodate my tastes to his and have been reading Davy Hume's *Essays: Moral and Political and Literary.* An engaging man with much good sense, but sometimes one finds that his judgments no longer hold. One would like to believe that (as he says in "The Sceptic") "a serious attention to the sciences and the liberal arts softens and humanizes the temper, and cherishes those fine emotions, in which true virtue and honor consists. It rarely, very rarely happens, that a man of taste and learning is not, at least, an honest man, whatever frailties may attend him. The bent of his mind to speculative studies must mortify in him the passions of interest and ambition, and must, at the same time, give him a greater sensibility of all the decencies and duties of life." That, alas!, applies to few of my colleagues, who are, by university definition, scientists and humanists and who pretend to taste and learning. Some sixty years after Hume wrote those words, Humboldt was complaining about the pettiness of professors. It has increased at an accelerating rate since his day, and so have the passions of interest and ambition, while the learning, if not the taste, has sadly declined. Hume, were he alive today, would be shocked to discover how much academic conversation dwells on money and preferment. . . .

Thursday, 20 October 1977. Stanford.
Disgusted with the report of the Task Force on Western Culture, which seems to want to foist a new model of the old Western Civ course at its worst on all future freshman, and conscious also that such a course would destroy History I, II, III which has proved itself pedagogically, I have been doing some lobbying with influential Senate members. Today I saw Halsey Royden, the Humanities & Sciences Dean, and reminded him of what Western Civ had really been like, urging upon him a multi-track approach that would give students a decent choice. This evening my idea of a tolerable requirement: any three courses from the nine offered by History I, II, III, Humanities 61, 62, 63, and a three-quarter small-group no-lecture course that I call Society and Culture which will focus on societies like

Periclean Athens, 12th-century or 17th-century Europe, and Industrial Britain. Free choice except that at least one course must be before 1300. I'll paper the joint with this tomorrow. . . .

Wednesday, 2 November 1977. Stanford.
Began to read *Le Monde* for the last three months, on Weiler's suggestion, for there have been a number of articles on German affairs. All of them, I find, are interesting although in perverse ways. French intellectuals are an odd bunch and they are, or seem, intent on finding things wrong with Germany that will enable them to assert a superiority that they no longer feel and to avoid having to face up to some unpleasant French realities. . . .

Wednesday, 7 December 1977. Oxford.
Reading the second volume of [name omitted]'s social history of France, which is in the same series as my volume. A wonderfully interesting book to read, but depressing too, since it will give reviewers an excuse for pillorying my effort as traditional and far too intent on elaborating old themes in old ways. I am reminded of Ed Earle saying, "Gordon, I'm just a political historian and that's an important thing to be." I don't find that very comforting. . . .

Monday, 12 December 1977. Oxford.
First 330 pages of proofs have arrived. They look fine and have driven away my . . . depression. I find the book reads well and is filled with unusual information and even some fresh insights. I think. It's hard, at this point, to recognize what is fresh in a manuscript over which I have labored so hard. . . .

Saturday, 24 December 1977. Stanford.
. . . Finished indexing the first fourteen chapters of the book. Must now wait for the rest of the proofs to arrive... Ronald Syme has composed a very elegant Latin dedication to Joe Strayer. . . .[73]

[1978]

Wednesday, 1 February 1978. Stanford.
. . . Read the last chapters of [a book on Henry James], which deals with *The Wings of the Dove*. Guided by them, read in the second half of the book,

---

[73] The dedication reads: "J.R.S. /AMICO OPTIMO / QUI HUNC LIBRUM / CONSILIIS SEMPER SUIS / AUXIT ORNAVIT." [J.R.S./ To my best of friends / Who enhanced this book / With his unfailing wisdom]. See Gordon A. Craig, *Germany, 1866–1945* (New York: Oxford University Press, 1978).

more carefully. I apologize to the shade of Ted Hubler, in whose presence I once slanged James. Come to think of it, I did so in one of those noontime sessions in the Baltimore Dairy Lunch in Princeton in the 40s, where there was always much talk about literature, and I did so in order to elicit a response; but Hubler was a silly man, and he went away in a huff. A more robust defender of James was R. P. Blackmur,[74] and, at his urging I read *The Aspern Papers* and—a story that Dick liked a lot—"The House at Jolly Corner." And "The Figure in the Carpet" and *Daisy Miller.*

The Balt literary seminar was a worthwhile experience.[75] There were really two groups that regularly gathered in that fine establishment. At tea time, those faculty intellectuals who had had some earlier connection with Paul Elmer More's circle, which had also apparently used the Balt in the 20s, gathered there—a small tight group of associate and full professors, the most prominent of whom were the classicists Mike Oates and Frisco Godolphin, a chap in French literature named Borgerhoff, and Donald Stauffer of English. The noontime group (really the 1 p.m. to 2:30 p.m. group) was looser, younger, livelier and had, although this was not clear at the time, more talent. Its members included Elmer Beller and Stow Persons of History; the philosopher David Bowers, my close friend, who died in a stupid railroad accident when I went overseas; the critic R. P. Blackmur, living a peripheral existence in the university but, thanks to Walter Stewart, carried on the books of the Institute for Advanced Study as a junior economist, which brought him a small salary; the poet John Berryman; the composer Roger Sessions, who, because of wartime reduction of curriculum, was teaching history courses to Army Specialized Training Program students, as I was; Jinx Harbison and me; and occasional visitors like Hubler and the art historian Freddy Stollmann, who astonished me one morning in the Balt, as I was poring over the war news in the *Times,* by saying that he never read the newspaper except for the obituary notices.

We went to the Balt because it was cheap and because a few of us, like Jinx and me, had become hooked on the establishment's egg buns and coffee with cream (and the saturnine expression on the counterman Mac's face) when we were undergraduates. But the large booths were conducive

---

[74] R. P. Blackmur (1904–1965), poet and literary critic, began teaching at Princeton in 1940 and became the founding director of the University's prestigious Christian Gauss Seminars in Criticism. See his *Studies in Henry James* (New York: New Directions, 1983).

[75] Craig is referring to meetings of Princeton faculty held at the Baltimore Dairy Lunch ("the Balt") in Princeton in the early to mid-1940s.

to talk (they held eight at a pinch, and one could also add chairs around the outside or even shove up tables), and we rarely had a lunch that lasted less than an hour and a half. There was, of course, some gossip, and some talk of the war, and some shop; but mostly we talked about books. A lot about American authors, I remember, Hawthorne and James and Hart Crane; a good bit about Joyce (Blackmur had never read *Finnegan's Wake,* whereas Aud Wicks and I were at this time going through it with care and enthusiasm, and I rarely keep my enthusiasms to myself); and a very great deal about Balzac and Flaubert. They were splendid sessions, filled with outrageous opinions hotly defended, and from them I learned a great deal, particularly from Bowers and Blackmur.

The luncheon group had an evening extension which met at irregular intervals in the members' homes. I think the idea for this was Blackmur's; he liked to drink in the evening and couldn't afford to do so in his own place. Or maybe it was Bowers's, I was tired of being visited by Blackmur every night. The host supplied the booze, and the talk was allowed to run freely until a theme presented itself, which was then discussed seriously until it was time to break up. The membership was roughly the same as in the noontime group, but there were additions, chief among whom was the German philosopher, Erich Kahler, and, on occasion, the novelist Hermann Broch, who was living in Kahler's house, since he had no job and not much in royalties, for only *The Sleepwalkers* was in translation.

Members of all these groups had a tendency to evaporate. Of the Paul Elmer More group, Oates, Godolphin, and Stauffer all became Marines, and that, thanks to Mike, is what happened to me too in mid-44. (Until March '43, I had been in the Office of Strategic Services and the State Department in Washington). Elmer Beller went off to the Office of War Information and crippled himself in strenuous physical training for overseas service. After the war, the noontime group, or some members of it, used to foregather at the Balt again, but it was never the same. Normalcy brought new preoccupations, and a return to serious scholarly work.

An odd period to look back on. While the war raged on, with good men being killed, we fortunate ones had for a time a period of intense intellectual activity (I was lecturing sometimes six times a week; I was helping edit *Makers of Modern Strategy,* which came out in '43, and writing articles for the *Yale Review* and the *American Historical Review* and reviews for the *Herald*

Tribune, and an essay for a book edited by John Whitton;[76] and I almost finished a play about the History Department called "Death in Dickinson 203, or Who Put the Slug on the Dean?"; in addition to all the talk in the Balt). . . .

Wednesday, 8 February 1978. Stanford.
. . . Read Goebbels's diary for 1945, which he dictated daily.[77] Some astonishing stuff. Goebbels wanted to radicalize the war by getting rid of Goering and Ribbentrop and all the defeatist generals, to give command to people like Schoerner, to use the *Werwolf* organization to murder collaborators, and to fight to the bitter end.[78] His favorite reading was Carlyle's *Frederick* which he kept reading to Hitler in the hope that it would galvanize him to the kind of demonic energy characteristic of him in the *Kampfzeit* [era of the Nazi struggle for power]. But by March the Fuehrer was so lethargic that he would not even speak to the German people. It was clear to him that the jig was up. This did not prevent him from allowing German cities to be bombed to splinters, a process that Goebbels saw not as a retribution but as a sign that the Allies were barbarians. . . .

Saturday, 11 February 1978. Stanford.
34 years after beginning it, I have now finished *The Ambassadors*, finding it both funny and moving. And what an evocation of a period, a class, and, particularly a city! Those marvelous passages in which the reader is made aware of the distant sound, excited and exciting, of the vague voice of Paris! And the perfect realization of his characters—that cold fish Chad who is going to turn out to be a rare son of a bitch, the lovely Mme. de Vionnet, who is going to end up a loser, the awful Pococks and the even more awful, because never seen, Mrs. Newsome, Maria Gostrey, surely one of the most fascinating of James's women, and Strether, finding growing strength and assurance from his happy discovery and partial recovery of the youth he had missed. A great achievement!

Sunday, 2 April 1978. Berlin.
In wee small hours between long sleeps thought of my projected book for

---

[76] Gordon A. Craig, "American Foreign Policy: Retrospect and Prospect," in *The Second Chance: America and the Peace*, ed. John B. Whitton (Princeton: Princeton University Press, 1944).

[77] *Final Entries, 1945: The Diaries of Joseph Goebbels*, ed. Hugh Trevor-Roper (New York: Putnam, 1978).

[78] The *Werwolf* organization refers to a Nazi plan to establish a resistance force that would operate behind enemy lines as the Allies overran Nazi Germany.

Putnam's and concluded that a good organization for same would be:

Introduction: Stereotypes
Chapter I: Perspectives (1870–1945 an aberration? The German question in its various forms.)
Chapter II: The People (regions; *Land und Stadt*; class and status; social stratification)
Chapter III: The Government (leaders, parties, bureaucracy)
Chapter IV: The Churches (authoritarian tendencies and religious underground)
Chapter V: Money (Luther, Goethe, Wagner, Sternheim, Forte; work ethic; bankers and business men; anti-capitalism)
Chapter VI: Women
Chapter VII: Academicians (Professors and students; the university in Germany today)
Chapter VIII: Intellectuals
Chapter IX: Soldiers (on dying for the fatherland)
Chapter X: Problems (foreign and domestic)
Chapter XI: Aspirations (the Blue Flower; romanticism, idealism, and the current moral emptiness) . . .

Monday, 17 April 1978. Berlin.

General Clay is dead, and all the street signs on Clay Allee are draped in black. A great force in this town and much admired for his toughness during the blockade. I heard him speak here in 1962, when he was sent to reassure the Berliners after the Wall, and his reception by the thousands standing in front of the old Reichstag made me proud to be his fellow-countryman. . . .

Thursday, 18 May 1978. Berlin.

A meeting of my colloquium, with reports on the Stalin Note of March 1952 (very good), the European Defense Community (fair), Kurt Schumacher (dreadful). Discussion of re-armament issue revealed not only much ignorance of basic issues but a fundamental lack of comprehension about politics. This naiveté is particularly shocking at a time when the events around them—the [Aldo] Moro murder,[79] the Brezhnev visit, the mud rising in the Congo, the Carter aircraft deal in the Middle East—should be prompting an intense interest in politics. That they don't know

---

[79] Aldo Moro (1916–1978) was a former Italian prime minister who was kidnapped and murdered by the Red Brigades in the spring of 1978.

who the editor of *Der Spiegel* is, is bad enough, but their inability to ask the right questions when confronted with a problem like that of neutralization of Germany is much worse. . . .

Saturday, 24 June 1978. Berlin.
. . . My salary at Stanford for next year is $45,000, which represents my last raise. I started at $2100 at Yale in 1939, went to Princeton at $2500 in 1941, was offered $9000 by Columbia in 1949, and went to Stanford at $20,000 in 1961. I have reached my high point now and can only hope, in retirement, to stay abreast of inflation. . . .

Thursday, 6 July 1978. Berlin.
[James] Boswell at 24 was an awful person.[80] Perhaps later too, but certainly then, and I don't know why his hosts didn't kick him in the arse and send him home. The effrontery of the man is staggering. He found it difficult to believe that Frederick II wouldn't receive him, was furious when he didn't get a dinner invitation from the Elector Palatine, and did not hesitate to ask the Margrave of Baden-Durlach for an order. A self-important, not very courageous whore-chasing coxcomb! His journal is often so vapid as to be comic (his conversation with Rousseau about cats and hens) but has its moments of interest, as when he complained about Frederick II's bombardment of Dresden in 1760: "I hated the barbarous hero. He was under no necessity to bombard Dresden. It was from mere spite that he did it." A footnote at this point says that Carlyle described Frederick's siege of Dresden as "one of the most rapid and most furious...anywhere on record, [filling] Europe with astonishment, expectancy, admiration, horror." In 1945, with far less excuse, Boswell's countrymen were to exceed Frederick in barbarity. . . .

Thursday, 14 July 1978. Berlin.
. . . Most of the group went out to Sternberg near the Sternberger See in the evening. . . . With Wolfgang Mommsen, I talked about Ted. He had never met him, but he told me that Ted's mother was Max Weber's sister and that the depressions that Ted suffered from, and which contributed to his suicide, come from her side of the family. . . .

Wednesday, 2 August 1978. Berlin.
. . . In my French lesson yesterday, after Mme. Werner had corrected letters in French that I had written for dispatch to Biaudet and Berza, we discussed

---

80 See *Boswell on the Grand Tour: Germany and Switzerland, 1764*, ed. Frederick A. Pottle (New York: McGraw-Hill, 1953).

[Jean] Anouilh's *Antigone*, and my teacher was shocked to find me sympathetic to Creon and disrespectful of that blue-stocking Antigone. She wants to read Sartre's *Huis clos* [*No Exit*], for next time, a dreary piece. My taste runs more to things like Pagnol's *Topaze*, which I re-read with pleasure last night, after my walk to Konigin-Luise Str. . . .

Sunday, 20 August 1978. Berlin.
. . . In the Berlin section of *Die Welt* an article on Marga Schoeller, who died on Friday. Her death emphasizes the passing of the age in which Berlin *Buchhandlungen* [bookstores] were more than places where you could buy books, being rather clubs where you spent time when you had nothing else to do, where the staff knew you and sought to satisfy your needs before you expressed them, where there was a genuine interest in all cultural activities in the city, and where one might, now and then, meet representatives of the arts. Marga's shop never quite recovered from its move from the Kurfürstendamm and, although a gulf separates it from Kieperts, at the other end of the Knesebeckstr., that gulf will certainly narrow.[81] My own bookstore, Elwert and Maurer on the Innsbrucker Platz, is not what it once was either, although it is miles better than Blackwells, which has been bureaucratized and computerized and is completely impersonal, and is light years removed from anything we have at home. E und M are not only interested in my Oxford volume but are prepared to help me find a German publisher, if I should need assistance. That sort of thing one does not find in the States. . . .

Thursday, 31 August 1978. Bamberg.
I came back from Rumania starved for news, for after a week there I felt that I had been living on another planet. One sees why people in the satellite states are so bewildered when one talks with them about the West. The commonplaces of our conversation are revelations to them. . . .

This is another world too, a town which, despite the modern shops that line the Lange Str. and the Grüner Markt, is closer to the past than to the present. But *which* past? The middle ages and the age of the baroque commingle in the churches and in the houses of the inner town, while, at the same time, the town is haunted by shades from the romantic age: Hegel, who lived in a house at the corner of Judenstraße and the Pfahlplätzchen and finished the *Phänomenologie des Geistes* [*The Phenomenology of Spirit*] there in 1807–8, as I discovered from a wall plaque as I was poking about in that

---

[81] At the time of publication, the Marga Schoeller Bücherstube is still in business at Knesebeckstraße 33.

quarter; and E. T. A. Hoffmann, who lived for five years in a squeezed little house on the Schiller Platz, where he began to compose his opera "Undine" and wrote many of what later became his *Fantasiestücke in Callots Manier* [*Fantasy Pieces in Callot's Manner*]. It was because I was searching for the house at Eisgruben No. 14, whose doorknob in the shape of an old woman's face inspired Hoffman to write *Der goldene Topf* [*The Golden Pot*], that I blundered into the Hegel house. . . .

Thursday, 28 September 1978. Stanford.
Before I left for Germany, I had begun to read in [Theodor] Mommsen's *Römische Geschichte* [*The History of Rome*], and I have resumed this evening occupation with mounting admiration for a historian whom I had known only for his political activities. I haven't got the time to read the whole work carefully, so, after browsing in the first two volumes, I settled down to the account of Julius Caesar's rise to power and was captivated by the splendid passage in Book V, chapter 7, in which Mommsen talks of our debt to Caesar, who recognized the German tribes as the most formidable enemy of the Roman-Grecian world and, by conducting an offensive defensive campaign against them, secured for the Hellenic-Italian culture the time needed to civilize the West as it had civilized the East. Thus, by preventing Ariovistus from doing what Theodoric later did, he preserved a bridge between the West and the world of Themistocles and Scipio, and his campaigns in the West were analogous in this respect, as well as in the broadening of horizon that came from them, to the discovery of America.

Equally remarkable is the 11th chapter of Book V, "*Die alte Republik und die neue Monarchie*" [The Old Republic and the New Monarchy] with its magnificent description of Rome in the last days of the republic, his reflections on the fateful combination of capitalism and slavery (with a prediction about the harvest of the dragon's teeth sown in the United States), its analysis of the thrust and limitations of Caesar's reforms (with some fine pages on the army), and its assessment of Caesar as a democratic dictator. . . .

Wednesday, 11 October 1978. Stanford.
Lectured to the "How Nations Deal with Each Other" course on the origins of World War I. 450 people!, which demonstrated how our determination to push for an International Relations program has paid off.

Tuesday, 17 October 1978. Stanford.
. . . James Joll has a good review of my book in the *Times Literary*

Supplement.[82] I do wish, however, that people would stop apologizing for the book's "traditional" approach and ask themselves whether it is traditional at all. It would be refreshing to have someone say something about my treatment of Bismarck, or domestic politics after Bismarck, or women, or the Nazi intellectual establishment. Joll came close, but drifted off into fretting about why I haven't said more about Wagner. Next time, James! One mustn't use up all one's ammunition! . . .

Tuesday, 29 November 1978. Berlin.
We stagger from horror to horror these days. While we try to understand the mass suicide/murder in Guyana, where more than 900 bodies have been counted—American men, women, and children who were seduced into going to that godforsaken place by the promise of peace, security, and well-being—the news now comes from San Francisco that Mayor [George] Moscone and City Council member Harvey Milk have been shot and killed by Dan White, who had resigned from the Council in mysterious circumstances and had then decided that he wanted the job back. Moscone had indicated that he did not favor White's reinstatement. There are no details in the paper here about the killing except the information that it took place in the Mayor's office. The rest of the world must be wondering what kind of people we are. . . .

Saturday, 30 December 1978. Stanford.
. . . I got up early on Friday and went downtown on the Muni, asking the conductor, "How much for seniors?" and paying a nickel for the first time. At 9:30 I was interviewed about new tendencies in American historiography by . . . the BBC Third Program. I complained about trendiness, trivialization, and over-specialization, saying that too few people were writing big books (like [R. R.] Palmer's *Democratic Revolution* and [Jerome] Blum's *End of the Old Order in Rural Europe*) and many too few concerning themselves with politics and international affairs; and I said they were not only forgetting that historians are humanists, not scientists, but that their only legitimacy is their tie with the lay public, for whom they are supposed to write, not for each other. A good conservative blast, in fact which pleased me, so I went out into the sun and walked over to Union Square and down Post Street, which I had not done in a long time. . . .

---

[82] James Joll, "From Unity to Dissolution," *Times Literary Supplement* (6 October 1978): 1113.

[1979]

Wednesday, 3 January 1979. Stanford.
. . . My colleagues are eyeing me with a good deal of respect since Felix [Gilbert]'s review [of my *Germany 1866–1945*] in the *New York Review of Books* is out.[83] I hadn't realized that that rag, which I don't like much, inspires so much respect.[84] . . .

Thursday, 15 February 1979. Stanford.
. . . Hans-Ulrich Wehler has sent me a letter of protest which he has sent to the *Frankfurter Allgemeine Zeitung*, claiming that my book has been misrepresented in the review of 27 January and chastising its author for betraying a typical German sensitivity to criticism, as well as what he calls "*ein modischer Eskapismus im Zeichen der Nostalgie-welle*" [a trendy escapism as a sign of the nostalgia wave]. Very feisty letter. [Name omitted] surprised that Wehler should come to my defense, given the difference in our ideological positions. But, when you come right down to it, what exactly is my ideological position? Certainly not one to repel Wehler (who describes me, not very convincingly, as belonging both to the "right middle" and to the "liberal community"). . . .

Friday, 23 February 1979. Stanford.
. . . The mail brought from that nice man Buchanan, who came to see me in Berlin, a tape of a BBC talk by Fritz Stern (to be published in *Encounter*) which is really a lengthy review of my book. Said lots of nice things but criticized me for not dealing with the sub-stratum of German life or with the demonic in German character. Valid enough except that he might have pointed out that no one has done this (least of all Hajo Holborn whose third volume he mentioned favorably). As usual I am criticized for staying on the political level; but, at least, Fritz praised the skill with which this was done. And the character sketches. And the style. Everyone seems to agree on the last, which shows, I guess, that Jean Glassford and Bill Dougherty and Hazlitt and P. G. Wodehouse and The Learned Fowler and lots of poetry and keeping this journal have paid off. The article in *Encounter* will be longer than the one in *The New York Review*, and that will help sell

[83] Felix Gilbert, "The German Leviathan," *New York Review of Books* (25 January 1979):17–21.

[84] After his retirement, Craig would write more than seventy review-essays for *The New York Review of Books*. For a selection of these, see Gordon A. Craig, *Politics and Culture in Modern Germany: Essays from the New York Review of Books* (Palo Alto: SPOSS, 2000).

books.[85] . . .

Saturday, 24 February 1979. Stanford.

. . . Read Nietzsche, *Die Geburt der Tragödie* [*The Birth of Tragedy*]. Written before his criticism in *Unzeitgemäße Betrachtungen* [*Untimely Meditations*], of the German mistake of confusing power with culture and his warning that this could lead to barbarism. But was not the call, in *Die Geburt der Tragödie,* to return to the Dionysian spirit that would restore terror and awe and pity and the myth one that risked encouraging barbarism in a people given to excess? Might they not revel in the *Hexentrank* [witch's potion] and the excesses he deplores in his second chapter and give no heed to the admonitions of Apollo when he sought to urge them to moderation? Nietzsche hated the "theoretical man" as much as he did the Christian moralist, largely because they were such bores and the life they approved of was so flat. But both Christianity and the *Aufklärung* [Enlightenment] were, after all, civilizing agencies intended to put down the barbarians and, indeed, barbarity; and that was not a bad objective. Nietzsche wanted to lift all the lids they had put down and pull all their corks out of bottles with the idea of releasing natural and revivifying energies. But what might be released is what Fritz Stern calls the demonic strains in German character... But this may be all eyewash. I don't like arguments based on national character. German history made Germans greedy and impulsive, and their troubles rose from that. They were probably no more demonic than any other people. . . .

Wednesday, 16 May 1979. Stanford.

. . . In the evening, dinner at the Michael Sullivans (he is Kathleen Liddell Hart's brother) prior to a lecture by Owen Lattimore, whom I had to introduce since it was billed as this year's William Bennet Munro Lecture. I hadn't seen Lattimore since 1957 when I was giving my Johns Hopkins lectures and had dinner with him at Fred Lane's house. Shortly, thereafter, he had his trouble with the McCarthy crowd, and this led to his moving to the University of Leeds in 1963. He is now 79 years, but he has amazing vitality, and his lecture tonight, "A Cycle of Cathay: A Historian's Involvement...in Asia," was lively and at times funny. He began with a good story of an agent from the Hoover Institution going to Mexico to try to get Trotsky's papers. Trotsky wanted to know who Hoover was and was reminded of his Relief Mission in Russia. Then he asked: "What is the name

---

[85] Fritz Stern, "Can One Explain the 'Demonic'?," *Encounter* (June 1979): 57–60.

of this institution?" "The Hoover Institution for War, Revolution and Peace." Trotsky thought for a moment and then said, "That bastard! Got them in the right order, too!"

Wednesday, 6 June 1979. Stanford.
Our retirement party last night, a misnomer, since neither of us is actually going to hang up his skates. But it is a departmental custom to honor its *emeriti*, when they become so; and this time . . . they did themselves proud. Cocktails and dinner for about 150 at the Club—the department and university colleagues, the Discussion Group, Phyl's associates, some former graduate students, some undergraduates, and such old friends as the Brewster Morrises, the Gerald Feldmans, and [name omitted]. . . . Speeches by Dick Lyman, Jerry (the swimming story and the pearls), Joe Strayer, [name omitted] (about my graduate teaching). . . . A great bash. . . .

Monday, 25 June 1979. Stanford.
Reading Thomas Mann's essays, in which I find that Goethe "held on principle that a writer should talk to no one about what he purposed to write; this because the confidant would quite likely not grasp his idea, and would be prone to discourage it." . . . My experience with Blum… The essays are interesting, especially "Goethe and Tolstoy," written in 1922 with Mann resigned to the victory of fascism and the downfall of bourgeois culture just as Russian communism marked Tolstoy's victory over Peter and the return to Asia… "Sufferings and Greatness of Richard Wagner" has much in it that puzzles me and a good deal that is overblown. It was delivered at the University of Munich in February 1933, which may explain its exaggerations. Its section on Wagner's nationalism, with the point that he presented a caricature of Germans to foreigners, I shall use in my book. . . .

Wednesday, 26 September 1979. West Berlin.
We arrived here from Leipzig this morning, and I recovered my diary, which I had mailed in Hamburg to myself at the Park Hotel Zellermayer in West Berlin. Now I must attempt to describe the last ten days…

We remained in Hamburg until the morning of the 20th. On the 18th, in the morning, we had a tour of the city by bus, which hit all the high spots and despite the rain, showed us what a lovely city Hamburg is, particularly for people with money enough to enable them to live on the shores of the Outer Alster. We lunched in the Ratskeller, a handsome place, and I then did my mailing. In the evening, with Phoebe Gagliani and the Morrises, I had dinner with Graf Baudissin,[86] the army reformer of the 50s and now active in the peace movement, and his wife, a sculptress, who now works with refugees. The Fritz Fischers were also on hand, he much reduced (he was very ill two years ago), but she as hearty and merry as I remember her as being in 1958. I spent most of the evening talking with her and Baudissin, who was filled with interesting stories about [General Hans von] Seeckt and the 1926 crisis and Seeckt's funeral, which he had to run as regimental adjutant. . . . His war was in Africa, and he was captured early and imprisoned in England. Thus, he remained alive and was able to exercise a good influence on the new post-1950 German army. I asked him if he was satisfied with the way the army had developed since the 50s and with the implementation of his idea of *Innere Führung* [leadership development and civic education]. He answered that, on the whole, he was. . . .

Wednesday's weather was a *Scheißwetter* [lousy], but I disregarded this and, the day being a free one for the group, took the S-train to Anmühle, where I changed for Friedrichsruh. It was my first visit to Bismarck's home, and I approached it with a proper *pietas* (Bismarck has, after all, served me well). I went through the museum, wondering at the elaborateness of the *Ehrenbürgerbrief* [honorary citizenship letters], all bound in engraved cases set with ivory and silver; and, there being no other visitors to speak of, sat for a moment at the old man's desk. I went on to the chapel where the family tombs are—Bismarck's and Johanna's, Herbert's and his wife's, and that of the Otto von Bismarck who died in 1975. On Bismarck's are engraved the words: "*Ein treuer deutscher Diener Kaiser Wilhelms I*" [A loyal German servant of Kaiser Wilhelm I]; on Johanna's "*Gott ist die Liebe und wer im der Liebe bleibt, der bliebt im Gott und Gott im ihm*" [God is love, and whoever remains in love remains in God, and God in him].

I walked up the hill into the Sachsenwald, past the great stag holding the snarling dogs at bay (erected in 1895) and strolled among Bismarck's trees, finally slipping on the wet clay soil and coming a real purler, bruising my left hip. Something to help me remember Friedrichsruh. . . .

On Sunday, the 23rd, with rain still coming down, we went on to Dresden. For some of the group, who had seen the Dresden exhibition in San Francisco earlier this year, this was the high point of the trip, an

---

[86] Wolf Graf von Baudissin (1907–1993) was not only a key figure in the founding of the Federal Republic of Germany's *Bundeswehr* during the 1950s but also the founding director for the Institut für Friedensforschung und Sicherheitspolitik [Institute for Peace Research and Security Policy] at the University of Hamburg during the 1970s.

impression that was sustained when we were taken through the Green Vault by the Director and through the Old Masters in the Zwinger by a very competent guide. But to me Dresden was a horror, a spooky place, a town of the dead. The combination of the still war-ravaged buildings of Augustus the Strong's time and the awful new constructions (which in 10 years time will be falling to pieces) is simply bloody. It just doesn't work, and to look out the window of an Interhotel upon the artificial streets around it . . . is to have an eerie feeling that one is looking at the future—or what will be the future unless we're damned careful. . . .

Tuesday, 13 November 1979. Stanford.
. . . No break in the impasse in Tehran, where Iranian students have held our embassy with 62 hostages for ten days. Little that the government can do at this point but hope that the UN or friendly powers will persuade Khomeini to be reasonable, but he seems such a loony that that is a forlorn hope. The accumulated record of weakness in our foreign policy (the Cuban debacle etc.) has, I am afraid, contributed to this. We must hope that it will bring people to their senses, and teach us that, while working for SALT and other agreements of that kind, we must be aware of the realities of power and avoid the appearance of weakness. Right now, however, we don't have many options. . . .

Monday, 19 November 1979. Stanford.
[Name omitted] of Putnam feels that my organization of *The Germans* book would make it unlikely to sell and that he will be writing me to say that he cannot go along with it. This is bad news, although I guess I always thought this reaction possible. I can fall back to the older organization, but it is unsettling.

Friday, 30 November 1979. Stanford.
A pleasant lunch with Gordon Wright to talk about Emeritus Council business. But, oh! the fuss by people who were charmed to see the Two Gordons colloquing together! . . .

[1980]

Friday, 15 February 1980. Berlin.
When I first came to Berlin in 1962, I discovered two books of mine (German editions) in a vitrine on the Kürfurstendamm and was accosted in Marga Schöllers [bookstore] by a type who wanted to talk about military stuff. I felt like a famous man. Nothing like that has happened since, but there are signs now of what Otto Büsch calls a Gordon Craig *Welle* [wave].

There has been a long review in the *Frankfurter Allgemeine Zeitung* by [name omitted] of the two volumes of the European history, [Karl Dietrich] Bracher has reviewed the second volume in *Die Welt*, and there have been reviews of both it and *Germany* in the *Tagesspiegel.* Now Beck is insistent that I show up at the Frankfurter *Messe* [trade fair] in October and Meurer wants a *Leseabend* [reading] in his bookstore here. . . .

Saturday, 16 February 1980. Berlin.
Spent the morning on the rooms to be devoted to Enlightened Despotism and the army in peace and war, listening to the presentations of the staff. I objected to the army in war stuff, complaining about tendentiousness—too much on the horrors and victims of war, not enough on *why* Prussia won its wars—and suggesting more on strategy and battle plans by means of lead soldiers rather than charts. Bracher, [name omitted], Sperlich agreed. . . . Schlenke talked me into doing a piece on "Women in Prussian History from Queen Louise to Rosa Luxemburg" for one of the many publications that will come out during the *Ausstellung* [exhibition],[87] and [Rudolf] von Thadden wants me to do a symposium with him and Sebastian Haffner after the *Messe* [trade fair] in October. . . .

Sunday, 24 February 1980. Stanford.
. . . While all this was going on, I received a call from a fellow . . . representing the American Historical Association Nominating Committee, asking me whether I would allow my name to be put in nomination for the presidency. I said yes, although I dislike the new method of putting up two strong candidates to kill each other off (at least, to kill one of them off, for the defeated candidate, who may be a better historian than the elected presidents of the last five years and the prospective candidates for the next five, never gets the chance to run again). Gatewood wouldn't tell me the name of the historian I'm to be paired with. I don't think the Committee would have the bad taste to run me against my collaborator Felix Gilbert, who deserves the presidency, and I can't think of any likely women candidates. My guess is that my opponent will be Bill McNeill of Chicago, who should beat me handily, although no one can predict how the

---

[87] In 1977, the Berlin Senate authorized an exhibition on Prussia. Craig was invited to become a member of an international group of consultants, tasked with developing plans for the exhibition, which opened at the Kunstgewerbemuseum in West Berlin in 1981 with the title, "Preußen: Versuch einer Bilanz" [Prussia: An Attempt to Strike a Balance].

hinterland will react to that pairing. I've got lots of time to think up other possible opponents since the ballot won't be ready until the fall. There will, of course, be a leak. Not from this end, however. *Mein Name ist Hase, und ich weiß von nichts* [My name is Hase, and I don't know anything].[88] . . .

Monday, 17 March 1980. Stanford.
Note the gap. Where the last two weeks has gone I don't know in any detail. What has been going on, of course, is the end-of-quarter rush and an equal rush to make progress with my Texas paper. History [2] finished well I thought, although the exams will really tell. Remembering Buzzer Hall's famous (but to me very muddled) lecture on Garibaldi, I finished the course with a lecture on Garibaldi and the Fall of the Roman Republic, taking as my theme not the Triumph of Heroism and Love (Buzzer's line leaning heavily on G. M. Trevelyan) but rather the End of the Heroic. I used [Arthur] Clough's poem "Amours de Voyage," a curious production... It seems to be the custom now to give professors standing ovations after their last lecture. At least, I received one. Awkward. Caught up in erasing a badly drawn map of Rome from the blackboard one doesn't know how to respond...

Interesting, the change in the times. In the Craig-George course, the students get all gussied up when they have to give their oral reports, the girls wearing silk stockings and high heels and the young men sometimes wearing ties. The style of the 60s is long gone, in dress and in politics, although there is an occasional reverberation to remind us of those times and the damage they caused. . . .

Wrote Blum today to tell him that I am running for the American Historical Association presidency against (as I learned from a note from David Pinkney) his colleague Lawrence Stone. This I find rather comic, the Committee apparently having decided to pit the traditional kind of history (whatever that may be I seem to have to represent it) against *la nouvelle vague* [the new wave]. Lawrence has written to suggest that we jointly refuse to make customary campaign statements, but I am against stuffy attitudes.

Sunday, 31 August 1980. Stanford.
The Polish dock workers, who have been striking, appear to have forced the government to concede that there should be free trade unions. A lot

[88] This is a reference to a student at Heidelberg University, Victor von Hase, who, in 1854, lent his identification papers to another student who needed to flee to France. When university officials came to interrogate Hase, he responded with the line quoted by Craig.

will depend upon what effect that victory will have upon the country as a whole. It is hard to see how things can simply stop at this point. Yet, if they go further, how can they stop at Poland's borders? And, if they don't, how long will it be before the DDR and the Soviets intervene? . . .

[In October 1980, Craig traveled to Germany for an extended book tour and a series of press and television interviews.]

Saturday, 18 October 1980. Berlin.
. . . One begins to feel one's age on these trips. One is constantly thinking in another language or trying to speak or write it properly. There is very little free time, because it is always necessary to do some preparation for the innumerable fixtures. And one must smile all the time. I told [name omitted] last night that I reminded myself of President Doumergue of France who was a great smiler but was discovered one day by a friend in what appeared to be a state of abysmal melancholy. "Doumergue!" the friend said, "What's wrong?" "Nothing," the President answered, "I'm just resting."

Then one must be pleasant while autographing books. There is a lot of this. I get the people to write down their names and then I write my inscription, complimenting them on their fountain pens or, if they happen to be women and young, telling them stories. Sometimes they do the storytelling, as the girl last night who told me of her experiences in Mobile, Ala., where, she said, people were entirely ignorant of Germany. And, I dare say, of much else. But even pleasantries are fatiguing, and I was so tired last night that I begged off when Hartwich tried to take me home with him and let [names omitted] go alone... Before I parted with the Köhlers, [name omitted] told me with much amusement that Herr Ullmann, one of the most radical of the students in our Hitler seminar, had been present. . . .

Still later: Not for the first time did I find myself today irritated by Stanford's bland assumption that everything it does in Berlin should be supported by the Berliners and that the Berliners should stump up for all of the German-related activities in Stanford as well. This was the burden of the luncheon speech of the plump type who was running the show today. Rather spitefully, I argued in my talk that the time had come for more effort on Stanford's part to make the Villa a real center that would give more back to Berlin than have been giving. The plump type said unctuously that he couldn't agree more, but he didn't really mean it. . . .

Wednesday, 5 November 1980. Stanford.
Yesterday was election day in a double sense. At 8:30 in the morning David

Pinkney called from Seattle to say that I had been elected as Bernard Bailyn's successor as President of the American Historical Association; by 6:30 in the evening, it was clear that Ronald Reagan had been elected President of the United States by a landslide.

Pinkney asked me to keep the news secret until I was informed officially by Mack Thompson; but there was no secret about the Reagan results. . . . Altogether a rout.

We had been asked to go to the Almonds to watch election returns, and we did, at 7:30, finding Gay in a state of shock and Dorothea[89] not much better. Gay kept accusing Phyl and me of having cast votes for Reagan by voting for Anderson[90] until Phyl became nettled and ticked him off; and he kept accusing me of gloating because I refused to fall into his funeral mood. He would hear no criticism of Carter, even on foreign policy, and was willing to believe the worst of Reagan. . . .

Friday, 7 November 1980. Stanford.
Mack Thompson called. I got 2400 of 3700 votes. . . . I am myself happy and hope I will do some good, for the job is not the sinecure it was in the old days, and the profession has real problems. I am happy and proud also because I have for a brief time become "Top Banana in the historical Dodge," as I wrote to Julian Boyd when he was elected and because I, thanks to 2400 votes, enter the company of Langer and Holborn and Bridenbaugh and Julian and Joe Strayer and Bob Palmer and David Potter and Gordon Wright, all of whom held the job. . . .

Saturday, 22 November 1980. Stanford.
. . . I went up to the city last night and saw "Tristan and Isolde," which fits in with my recent preoccupation with Wagner. I have been reading the Gregor Dellin biography and writing about "Parsifal" in my book, and I must soon do a piece for *The New Republic* on Cosima's *Tagebuch* [*Cosima Wagner's Diaries*].[91] It is a marvelous opera, although one wonders why King Mark must sing about his feelings about being betrayed for all of fifteen

---

[89] Dorothea Almond (1914–2000) collaborated with Phyllis Craig during the late 1960s and early 1970s in a successful campaign to provide affordable quality child care on the Stanford campus.

[90] John B. Anderson (1922–2017) was a liberal Republican member of the House of Representatives who ran an independent campaign for the presidency in 1980, receiving 6.6% of the popular vote.

[91] Gordon A. Craig, "A Marriage Made in Valhalla," *The New Republic* (7 February 1981): 34–36.

minutes. I read the text again, act by act in the restroom where I usually sit between acts, and having done so I read what is said in the program about the plot. This convinces me that the greater part of the audience must have no idea of what is really going on up there. One could not understand what language [name omitted] and [Spas] Wenkoff were singing in any case. I wonder how much of the plot Wagner's audiences, who would have heard better German, would have understood? It is my theory that they didn't really follow what Wagner was up to but had only a general idea and filled in their own details. In this way they were not offended by the socialism of the Ring or alarmed by the Schopenhauerian demand for renunciation in "Parsifal."

American opera-goers in Germany are, of course, completely mystified, because they can't buy programs in English. The first time I heard the *Ring*, in Munich in 1935, I used to give detailed descriptions of the plot, act by act, to my fellow American students at the University of Munich summer course, a group that included Gretchen Ridder, who was so beautiful and so statuesque that I was completely intimidated by her and dared make no approaches (although her remarks in class were always pretty dumb, whereas I was a Princeton man and hence an intellectual). She listened to my briefings though, which were probably accurate (I always did my homework and still do) but excessive, for I was in love with Wagner and still tend, when I'm not careful, to think that he's the guy who writes the real operas, while everyone else writes something else. . . .

Today I finished my chapter on Romantics. My ninth since 1 June, which is pretty good considering the fact that I have been away for four weeks in that period. I figure that I am a week behind schedule at this point. I had, unfortunately, to tell my agent, in asking her to make an appointment with Peter Israel of Putnam's for 8 December, how much I had written, and now she and Israel are all excited and wanting to see the manuscript and talking about copy-editing and type-setting and Book-of-the-Month Club and much other nonsense. They have no idea of what problems lie ahead and probably don't care what's in the book anyway. They will play it as a pendant to my last book and rely on advertising and my reputation to sell a lot of books. But my reputation depends on the quality of my books, and I won't know how good this one is until I've written the last chapter. All I know at this point is that no one has quite written a book about Germany in this way before and that there is a lot of interesting stuff in it. But is it any good?

Thursday, 27 November 1980. Stanford.

Thanksgiving Day. Just the two of us, but who needs any more? We did some chores, and picked oranges off the tree. . . .

In *The American Scholar*, read a good article on New York by Aristides. Story about an out-of-towner who, after two days in town, said to a native, "Excuse me, sir, could you tell me where the Empire State Building is, or would you prefer that I go screw myself?" Also, a quotation from Theodore Dreiser's *The Genius* about a young man's feelings on first encountering the city:

> The lower part of the island was filled with cold commercialism which frightened him. The upper half, which concerned only women and show—a voluptuous sybaritism—caused him envy.

I was younger than that young man when I first saw New York and used to prowl about its streets and walk from 33rd St. to the Metropolitan Museum on Sundays. But I also felt that envy. But not very oppressively. I was tremendously impressed by the classy dames in the neighborhood of the Plaza. Beauty and wealth had a heady effect and inspired the daydreams that filled my mind in those days. Strengthened my ambition too, I dare say, and may even have influenced my taste.

The article on New York strengthened my decision to write a chapter on Berlin—perhaps on Berlin and Berliners—in my book. The course I gave in our center there will help, and this *Tagebuch* [diary] is stuffed with material, including poems about Berlin—and the Airlift and 17 June and the Wall will all fit. . . .

7

Coda: Chequers, 1990

Friday, 16 February 1990. Stanford.
Yesterday, a call from the British embassy saying that Mrs. Thatcher was planning a meeting on Germany and wanted me and William Shirer to attend. Could I give them some dates on which I could come to London? I did so, without much faith that anything would come of this. . . .

Thursday, 22 February. Stanford.
. . . The Chequers[1] affair is confirmed, by the way, for 24 March. . . .

Friday, 23 March 1990. Hyde Park Hotel, London.
Left San Francisco yesterday at 5:20 by British Airways, going to London via Vancouver. Thanks to the Prime Minister, I travelled Club Class, which was better than Lufthansa's First Class, which I once travelled when the bill was picked up by the Morgan Bank. Wonderful food… We arrived at Heathrow at about 1:30 this afternoon, and I took a cab to this old-fashioned but marvelously comfortable hotel. I called Phyl, who had just seen Susan off, and then—Fritz Stern having arrived—had a light dinner with him downstairs and went to bed and—after some work on questions drawn up by the Prime Minister's private secretary—to sleep…

24 March 1990. Hyde Park Hotel, London.
An extraordinary day. My expectation had been that we would not see much

---

[1] For other accounts of the Chequers meeting, see Charles Powell, "What the PM Learnt About the Germans," in *When the Wall Came Down: Reactions to German Unification*, edited by Harold James and Marla Stone (New York / London: Routledge, 1992), 233–39; Timothy Garton Ash, "The Chequers Affair," *History of the Present: Essays, Sketches, and Dispatches from Europe in the 1990s* (New York: Random House, 1999), 42–46; and Fritz Stern, *Five Germanys I Have Known* (New York: Farrar, Straus and Giroux, 2006), 467–69.

of the Prime Minister, who might have lunch with us, but would then hand us over to aides or boffins from the Foreign Office. No such thing! A car took Fritz and me from our hotel to Chequers, and Mrs. Thatcher was waiting for us when we arrived, with a library copy of Fritz's *Gold and Iron* and a well annotated and underlined copy of *The Germans* in her hands, upon which she complimented us and then led us briskly into a study and got down to work. The others were her private secretary, Charles Powell, and her Foreign Secretary, Douglas Hurd, and Hugh Trevor Roper (The Lord Dacre of Glaston), Norman Stone of Oxford, Timothy Garton Ash, and George Urban (who used to be head of Radio Free Europe), nine in all, counting the Prime Minister. Once we were seated, she asked me to start, which I did by addressing the first point on Powell's list, and then the discussion started and didn't stop, except for lunch and tea, for five hours.

I was surprised by what a good-looking woman Mrs. Thatcher is and how well-turned out she was (in a light grey blue suit with piping) but even more by her energy, and combativeness, and debating skill. The last was most prominent, because she really did not seem to be intent on learning anything from us but really to learn new points of view and to sharpen her arguments in the case of those which conflict with her own. She had done her homework; she had marshaled all of the examples from experience that supported her prejudices; and she obviously enjoyed fighting for her case against "experts" who doubted its validity. Her case is that the Germans are not to be trusted; that Kohl is intent on bullying the European Community into supporting German interests and has pretty well cowed everyone but the Dutch (whom she praised) and the Brits into glum acquiescence; that he and all the Germans are intent on emasculating NATO; that there is every reason to expect a return to the bad old days; that already . . . the *Bundespräsident* [Federal President] (a "sly and smooth one") is talking about "our mission" in the East; that a reunited Germany has to be contained and that we must insist on her membership in NATO and American presence in Germany with nuclear power, and this should have been nailed down before the rush to unification had got under way and may now be too late, given the state of German opinion. All of this met with objection and counter-argument, which she often turned to her own advantage by seizing up debating points and exploiting them. She was, in fact, quite shameless, and I was pleased to note that her secretary was highly amused at her most outrageous sallies. It was amusing to me to see her skill in baulking Tim Garton Ash's worried "If I may say so, Prime Minister..." and George Urban's efforts to divert her attention to the Soviet problem—or rather the problem of Gorbachev's continued tenure. Hanging over our meeting was the problem of Lithuania, and periodically the PM asked her secretary if there was any news. She made no bones of the fact that she had the same opinion of Lithuania that Neville Chamberlain had of Czechoslovakia—that she felt their independence effort might topple Gorbachev with resultant trouble for all of us, and that she feared that George Bush might complicate things by trying to appease the Lithuanian lobby...

A formidable lady! At lunch, where I was her tablemate, she talked about the watering down of education, about her bedside reading (a life of the gospel writer Mark by a former Archbishop of York) and, at my urging, former conservative Prime Ministers (Baldwin she thought not engaged enough; Disraeli, however, admirable in his attempt to define conservatism and create a party that would defend his definition).

The course of the discussion is roughly defined in Powell's letter. . . . As I have said, I am sure that the participants learned a good deal more than the Prime Minister, but she thoroughly enjoyed herself, and at the end of it all, after sending Hurd off to see his children, insisted that everyone stayed for a drink with her in the hall in front of the fireplace and made sure that all the whiskeys (except hers) were doubles...

Chequers is a comfortable house and the grounds green and full of daffodils...

I had a good talk with Fritz [Stern] on the way back to London, which was good for we rarely have time to cut up tacks, although he and I, in the eyes of Europeans, are the best American historians of Germany, and hence are always invited to the same affairs. We seemed this time to find a common chord...

Sunday, 25 March 1990. Hyde Park Hotel, London.

. . . The papers today are full of talk about a grass-roots revolt against Mrs. Thatcher in consequence of the 23-point lead that the polls say Labour now holds over the Tories, a sudden spurt caused, I dare say, by the poll tax idea and the pessimistic economic forecasts that helped cause the loss of a by-election in Mid-Staffordshire. There is already talk of her being succeeded by Michael Hesseltine. I suspect nothing will come of this or the grass-roots revolt. Mrs. Thatcher has more resolution than any of her rivals or followers.

Needless to say, she said nothing about her domestic problems yesterday, but she didn't strike me as being very worried about anything either. She seemed absolutely crammed to the top-knot with energy and health, infinitely more so than her Foreign Secretary, who looked a bit grey and tired, and also a good deal livelier than my old friend Norman Stone, who now holds Woodward's chair of Modern History, who has clearly been eating, smoking, and working too hard and is a flabby shadow of what he was at Leeds Castle two years ago, and who—like Rosemary—is off to a health farm to drink carrot juice and do Swedish exercises... Hurd didn't say a lot yesterday, but when Mrs. Thatcher was at her most outrageous he sometimes intervened and corrected or toned down her comments. Only on NATO did he speak at length, underlining his leader's insisting that Germany must stay in NATO and the USA in Germany, *with* nuclear weapons. He and Mrs. Thatcher have clearly not given up on modernizing the Lance missiles, and both think the Social Democratic Party of Germany is bent on emasculating NATO...

I did not have much chance to talk with Urban, but I was very pleased when he told me that he had been reading my works for years and that his favorite was *Königgrätz*... I was considerably surprised when Dacre, rather abruptly, told me that he much enjoyed my pieces in the *New York Review of Books*... How vain authors are! We think well of anyone who speaks well of what we do. . . .

Friday, 6 April 1990. Stanford.
The reason why Kohl was so much on Mrs. Thatcher's mind on 24 March was that she must have been interviewed a couple of days before by a *Spiegel* crew. That interview appeared on 26 March and made it clear that she was concerned with the rush of Germany towards unification and its tendency to be increasingly unmindful of the right of other nations to have a voice in what kind of a new Germany emerges from the present confusion. The *Spiegel* interviewer kept trying to force her to admit that she was annoyed that Kohl went to Moscow, Washington, and Paris to explain his policy but didn't bother to include London in his itinerary. She simply said that Kohl knew her views. She had never been afraid to express them. "I say often what others feel and think but are afraid to say." She insisted that there were treaties to be signed before the Germans were allowed to go their way, and she said that she had heard Kohl say: "No, I'll guarantee nothing, I don't recognize the present boundaries of Poland." *Spiegel* felt that her suspicion of a united Germany was deep and instinctive and accompanied the interview with a *Daily Mail* cartoon. [The cartoon depicts Margaret Thatcher and her husband outside her home at night, with Thatcher searching the yard with a flashlight, illuminating piled sandbags and the entrance to a bunker. The caption reads: "Maggie, darling, are you a little pessimistic about German

reunification?"]

Looking back on the Chequers meeting, I am intrigued by one of the questions on the Private Secretary's list, which we never got around to discussing. It reads: "To what extent do we need to take account of the growing influence of people of Germanic origin in the United States, as a factor affecting American policy towards Europe?" The answer is not at all, since the history of the last 300 years shows that the Germans in America were intent from the beginning on assimilation and never formed a lobby of any kind. But the question certainly reveals a feeling that the U.S. is turning away from the "special relationship" with Britain to a new preferred relationship with Germany. . . .

Appendix

Speech to the University Fellows, Sixth Annual Reunion [Branner Hall, Stanford University, 25 May 1979][1]

I am honored to have been asked to speak to you this evening, although I was at first a bit unclear as to what my precise role in this gathering was supposed to be. I have now, however, studied the documents, as a historian should, and entered into telephonic communication with the best living source of information on this matter, Pat Devaney, and have concluded that I am to be a kind of Polonius to your Laertes, without, however, being allowed the freedom of discourse that that old gasbag arrogated to himself. Pat said that I should reminisce a bit, say something about education, and keep it light. She didn't say anything about arrases, or what might happen to me behind them if I strayed, but I can tell a hawk from a handsaw. So I shall reminisce, but only in order to give you my impressions of how Stanford education has changed in the last 18 years. And I shall try to be light, the appropriate mode for one who is about to be *emeritiert.*

The proper way to leave a room
Is not to plunge it into gloom
Just make a joke before you go
And then escape before they know.[2] . . .

We liked just about everything we found here. The climate, of course, which promised a perpetual aestival jocundity, with never a chilblain nor a driveway filled with snow. The cheerful inconsequence of the lapidary

---

[1] The full text of this valedictory speech can be found in Stanford's internal publication for faculty and staff: "Gordon Craig Reviews His Past Academic Life for Fellows at Reunion," *Campus Report* 11:40 (11 July 1979): 4–5.

[2] See Gelett Burgess, *The Burgess Nonsense Book: Being a Complete Collection of the Humorous Masterpieces of Gelett Burgess* (New York: Frederick A. Stokes Company, 1901), 69.

inscriptions on the exterior of university buildings, which promised a new freedom from over-precise categories and even from logic.

"Progress and Civilization!," proclaimed the mosaics on the front of the Stanford Museum. "Archeology! Sculpture! Cyprus!" We found this charming. It reminded me of the time when Napoleon Bonaparte became curious about the philosophy of Kant and commanded an aide to boil down his system to a few quarto pages. After this was done and he had read the result, the Emperor said, "All this has no practical value, and the world derives little profit from people like Kant, Cagliostro, Swedenborg, and Philadelphia."

Gustatory pleasures

I was particularly pleased by the gustatory pleasures that appeared to be associated with teaching in my new university. In those days, one repaired after class to the Old Union and stood in line before a window through which were dispensed cups of coffee and those alarming but satisfying California doughnuts, twice the size of the eastern sort and covered with glazed sugars and pink and chocolate icing and liberally sprinkled with nuts. (The doughnuts that [name omitted] has employed in order to keep the Western Culture Committee content amid their labors are a sadly degenerate form of the ones to which I became addicted in 1961).

It was while standing *en queue* one morning that I espied two of my students a little ahead of me, a handsome bronzed young man and woman, and I saw that he was handing her a copy of Hermann Hesse's novel *Journey to the East*, which I had assigned in my course on 20th-century German history. I inched forward in order to hear the expressions of gratified intellectual curiosity that I was sure would be exchanged; but all he said was "Why do you think he assigned us this?" and all that handsome young woman said was "Beats me."

There were, in those first years, other moments of mutual incomprehension between my students and me, and sometimes after a lecture, I found myself thinking of a remark made by Sir Walter Raleigh, the Raleigh who taught English literature at Glasgow and Oxford at the beginning of the century. He once said, "I rather think that when I come nearest to pleasing myself my class regard me as a kind of monster. . . . I might just as well be set to feed hedgehogs with cheesecakes." I imagine that we have all felt that way one time or another.

It was pleasant for me to discover that it happened to me much less frequently in Stanford than it had at Princeton, which was in those days still a male preserve and where students, until kicked a few times, affected a "*je suis blasé de ce genre de lecture*" attitude in preceptorials, and generally tried to stifle any kind of intellectual curiosity or enthusiasm. (It was of this kind of student, although at Harvard, that Prof. Adam Ulam is reported to have said, "I'd flunk the bastards, if only I knew their names.") Of intellectual eagerness and zest there was no dearth among Stanford students; and it was, from the beginning, exciting to teach them.

Negative features

To balance these positive features of the system I was entering, there were some negative ones. Faced with the incursion of eastern carpetbaggers like David Potter, Al Guerard, Al Hastorf, and others, who had been attracted by the gold that Wally Sterling had discovered, Stanford occasionally reacted as the Boers in the Transvaal had reacted to the *uitlanders* in the 1890s with suspicion and with a jealous resentment of any implied criticism or any questioning of accepted tradition or methods. . . .

The kind of sensitivity . . . was apt to surface whenever any of the new boys suggested changes in course structure or teaching methods. Such changes were badly needed in my own department, where there was an inordinate dependence upon lecture courses, and virtually nothing in the way of small group teaching. . . .

Innovation discouraged

Innovation was discouraged also by a high degree of departmental parochialism. I had been used in Princeton to a considerable amount of collaboration in both teaching and research with the departments of economics and political science, and much of my time had been spent with students in the School of Public and International Affairs. I quickly discovered that no such collaboration existed at Stanford, at least between history and the other social sciences; nor was there an international relations program.

Moreover, attempts to set up joint programs, even when funds became available for them (Carl Spaeth managed to get a large Ford Grant in the '60s), always ran into formidable obstacles. A long period of lean years had accustomed the Stanford faculty to live like troglodytes. When a large piece of meat was thrown between them they darted out in order to seize as big a portion as possible and then scuttled back into their departmental caves.

Suggestions that communal banquets might have better results fell on deaf ears or were violently repudiated. When some of us began, in the early

'60s, to draft plans for using part of the Ford money for an interdepartmental program in international relations, we were shelled heavily from several directions and most heavily from the departments that stood to gain most from such a program: our first two plans were shot down in flames; and it took more than four years to make any appreciable progress.

Well, all of that is, as the Germans say, *schon lange her* [a long time ago]. Eighteen years have passed since Phyllis and I came to Stanford, and much has changed, most of it for the better.

Physical surroundings

There has been a dramatic and continuing change in the physical appearance of the campus, and only the most ungenerous of critics would deny that this has had its positive effects upon the academic and teaching program. It is, of course, possible to place an importance upon buildings that is counter-productive and defeats the purpose of education.

You may remember that passage in Boswell's life of Dr. Johnson in which the author confronts Johnson with the question, "if, Sir, you were shut up in a castle, and a newborn child with you, what would you do?"

Johnson seeks to evade this by saying weakly, "Why, Sir, I should not much like my company," but Boswell, intent on finding out something about the old man's educational philosophy, persists. "But would you take the trouble of rearing it?" he asks.

"Why, yes, Sir, I would," Johnson answers, "but I must have my conveniences. If I had no garden, I would make a shed on the roof, and take it there for fresh air. I should feed it and wash it much, and with warm water to please it, not with cold water to give it pain."

But, Boswell asks, "Would you teach this child that I have furnished you with, anything?"

"No, I should not be apt to teach it."

"Would you not have a pleasure in teaching it?" "No, Sir," Johnson replies firmly, "I should not have a pleasure in teaching it."

In short, Johnson is not interested in education at all. All he wants to do is to build a gymnasium on the roof, with a heated pool, and some machines for dispensing junk food; and many educational institutions have been guided by the same prejudice.

This has not been true here, and the university's building program has on the whole enhanced the effectiveness of the teaching program.

I sometimes think that the shape of a room and the furniture that is in it have almost as much influence upon the educational process as the teacher's style. I was never convinced by that stuff about education being a log with Mark Hopkins at one end and a student at the other; and, in a world in which we are learning the techniques of multi-media teaching, logs will certainly not do; we need facilities like Annenberg Auditorium, an almost ideal lecture hall. The variety of spatial arrangements in the new History Corner is going to make it possible for us to experiment with new forms of teaching that would have been quite impossible 18 years ago.

We have come a long way also in breaking down the barriers that existed between departments when I first came here. The flourishing International Relations Program is one evidence of this, and it suffers from little of the departmental resentment that was present in its long period of gestation.

In his talk to the Campus Conference on 19 May, President Lyman listed a number of other joint courses that approach aspects of traditional disciplines in nontraditional and integrative ways and are made possible by interdisciplinary collaboration. I think that it is worth noting that the disappearance of departmental parochialism has been facilitated by two institutions that did not exist when I came to Stanford—the Faculty Club and the Academic Senate.

About the uses of the former in providing situations for interaction and mutual enrichment I need not speak. As for the Senate, it has a tremendous potential as an instrument of innovation and reform and as a watchdog over academic excellence, and it has sometimes fulfilled that potential. Its effectiveness however, like that of Congress, always depends upon the representatives elected by the constituencies, and the quality of the Senate varies from year to year.

Senate dull last year

With apologies to [name omitted], I consider this year's Senate to have been a dull and lifeless one, a gatherum of dead souls hunched upon largely empty benches. I never enter it without thinking of "bare ruin'd choirs where late the sweet birds sang."[3] A proper Senate should have Ron Rebholz in it, and Bernie Roth and [name omitted], and Colin Pittendrigh if we can pipe him in from wherever he is these days. With such stalwarts in place, I have no doubt that attendance would improve, and the weight of the Senate would be felt positively throughout our academic program.

Finally, the traditionalism that I encountered in my first days at Stanford

---

[3] Craig is citing William Shakespeare's "Sonnet 73."

has been replaced by a healthy irreverence for received ideas and an almost Benthamite eagerness to dismantle programs that seem to have outlived their usefulness.

It is true, of course, that after a few years we sometimes replace them with programs not essentially different from the ones dismantled, but there is a cunning of reason in this; and we must take comfort in the fact that we are acting out the process described in Hegel's *Phenomenology of the Spirit*, and that the objectification of each successive reform will carry us upward in a spiral motion until we are at home with ourselves in our otherness and have entered the realm of pure and self-comprehending *Geist* [spirit].

Are we then to say that all is gas and gaiters at Stanford? One would think so if one looks at the latest issue of *The Stanford Observer*, with its banner headlines about "Exciting and Innovative years Ahead" and "Major Curriculum Change." I would put it to you that this is premature.

Five years ago I wrote a piece in *Daedalus*[4] in which I said that American universities, and I did not exclude our own, had in the late 60s "entered the age of the Green Stamp University, in which the student receives the same number of stamps for a course on Bay Area Pollution or Human Sexuality as he does for American History or the Greek Philosophers, sticks them happily in his book, and gets a diploma when it is filled. Whether he has received an education in the course of all this," I added, "is doubtful."

Curricular change

It would be hard to maintain that the situation has improved significantly since I wrote the article. The major curricular change, mentioned by the *Observer*, is the new Western Culture sequence, which will not become a requirement until the year after next, and which is, in any case, not essentially different from the Western Civilization course that was abolished eight years ago.

It is good to have accomplished this much, but it would be better if we were simultaneously doing something to reduce the trendiness and redundancy that have been allowed to affect our departmental course offerings. We are all aware that credit is sometimes given in this university for courses that could not withstand rigorous criticism of their intellectual content; and we also know that the practice of cross-listing and substitution has been carried so far that such courses are sometimes permitted to be

---

[4] "Green Stamp or Structured Undergraduate Education?," *Daedalus* 103:4 (Fall 1974):143–50.

counted toward the satisfaction of the departmental major. This sort of thing should be stopped.

In the old days, there used to be a man in the Widener Library who did nothing but walk the stacks, studying holdings and taking note of things that should be replaced or reshelved and gaps that should be filled. We need an interdepartmental stack-walker, a prowler with authority to make urgent recommendations about courses that should be eliminated and gaps in our curriculum that should be filled.

If he had the strong backing of the appropriate deans, we would be able to strengthen our offerings considerably and even to start moving toward the more structured liberal education that we talk about but still do little to promote.

It would be a good idea also to have some kind of central agency, perhaps under the same department prowler, to correct the absolutely chaotic scheduling system that prevails at present and which seems to be based on principles borrowed from the television industry, so that *Laverne and Shirley* offerings are placed in the same time-slot as courses more central to the purposes of liberal education, as if intent upon stealing their ratings and their auditors. Surely this is something that should be put right; and, with some hard thinking about what it is that we are trying to accomplish, it can be put right.

Unstructured education

Perhaps, while we are doing all this thinking, we can spare a moment to ask ourselves another question, namely, whether the far too unstructured and permissive education that we provide for our undergraduates is doing anything substantial to meet the future needs of the society of which we are a part.

In an age in which the nation is confronting, and will continue to confront, economic, social, and political problems that will test its will and ingenuity and perhaps even the legitimacy of its institutions, an age in which international problems of great delicacy and complexity will affect the lives of every citizen in the land, is it a good thing that so many of our students are permitted to graduate from this university without ever taking a course in American government, or the history of the United States in the 20th century, or modern and contemporary international relations? I doubt it very much.

I think that every university in this country should be giving more courses in international relations than it is presently doing: and it is sad to note that, throughout the country, my own discipline has for the last 10 years been busily training young scholars in social history and intellectual history and regional history and family history and quantitative history and in everything except political and diplomatic history, with the result that there are only about a dozen young historians in the whole country today capable of teaching intelligent courses on post-1945 diplomacy and foreign affairs.

That verges on academic irresponsibility, and it is a sure prescription for fulfilling Woodrow Wilson's gloomy prediction that "We are in danger to lose our identity and become infantile in every generation."

Jacob Burckhardt once said that the university was a "metaphysical necessity." This is a puzzling remark, but one sees what the great historian meant. The university exists, in its undergraduate aspect, not to produce specialists, not to get people into good graduate schools, not to teach them how to make money. Its purpose is to do something to their minds, to teach them how to think, and to teach them what are the things worth thinking about.

The university is here to provide successive generations of academic youth with the knowledge and the ideals that will help the best of them rise above the values of the marketplace and do the world's work ably and conscientiously.

If it is to fulfill that purpose, we—the teachers and administrators of this university—shall have to become more disciplined in our thinking about the purposes of undergraduate education and about effective ways of achieving them. And, at the same time, we must show more imagination in the teaching of those subjects that will prepare students to become useful citizens in a world that is changing so rapidly that it sometimes appears that we are hurtling forward into an age without precedents.

Above all, we must not allow the fascination aroused, or the fatalism induced by this acceleration of change to discourage us from teaching our students to find comfort and counsel in the record of human thought and experience.

If we can accomplish that, we shall have done our duty to those who have come

> to this privileged world
> Within a world, a midway residence
> With all its intervenient imagery.

And they, in return may remember us, not as

> ...old men
> Old humorists...

Not as

> ...grave Elders, men unscoured, grotesque
> in character, tricked out like aged trees
> Which through the lapse of their infirmity
> Give ready place to any random seed
> That chooses to be reared upon their trunks.

But rather as

> ...those with whom
> By frame of Academic discipline
> We were perforce connected, men whose sway
> And known authority of office served
> To set our minds on edge...[5]

[5] The quotations are from Book III of William Wordsworth's "The Prelude, or Growth of a Poet's Mind."

Index

Printed in the USA
CPSIA information can be obtained
at www.ICGtesting.com
LVHW092025131023
760849LV00049B/15/J

9 780930 664350